ART FOR AN

UNDIVIDED EARTH

Jessica L. Horton

ART
FOR AN

Duke University Press
Durham and London | 2017

UNDIVIDED EARTH

The
American
Indian
Movement
Generation

© 2017 Duke University Press
All rights reserved
Designed by Mindy Basinger Hill
Typeset in Adobe Caslon Pro by Copperline

Library of Congress Cataloging-in-Publication Data
Names: Horton, Jessica L., author.
Title: Art for an undivided earth : the American Indian Movement
generation / Jessica L. Horton.
Other titles: Art history publication initiative.
Description: Durham : Duke University Press, 2017. | Series: Art history publication
initiative | Includes bibliographical references and index.
Identifi ers:
LCCN 2016053082 (print)
LCCN 2017000497 (ebook)
ISBN 9780822369547 (hardcover : alk. paper)
ISBN 9780822369813 (pbk. : alk. paper)
ISBN 9780822372790 (ebook)
Subjects: LCSH: Indian art—Europe—History—20th century. | Indian artists—Travel
—Europe—History—20th century. | American Indian Movement—Influence.
Classifi cation: LCC N6538.A4 H678 2017 (print) | LCC N6538.A4 (ebook) |
DDC 704.03/974—dc23
LC record available at https://lccn.loc.gov/2016053082

Cover art: Jimmie Durham, "Attakulakula," 1988. Snakeskin and mixed media, element
from *Mataoka Ale Attakulakula Anel Guledisgo Hnihi (Pocahontas and the Little Carpenter in London)*. Collection of Danielle Fiard, Geneva. Photo by Jessica L. Horton.

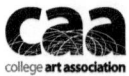

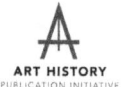

Publication of this book
has been aided by a grant from
the Wyeth Foundation for
American Art Publication Fund
of the College Art Association.

This book is made possible
by a collaborative grant
from the Andrew W. Mellon
Foundation.

FOR GRAM

CONTENTS

ILLUSTRATIONS

Figures

Plates
(following page 128)

ACKNOWLEDGMENTS

This book began when I was a kid helping my dad garden among oak knolls in northern California. There, churned-up earth revealed the long-standing presence of Pomo people whose extraordinary baskets I admired in the nearby Grace Hudson Museum. Equally it started in 2004, when a boulder seated atop a red car in front of the Sydney Opera House, placed by the artist Jimmie Durham, raised questions I was not prepared to answer. There was no turning back after 2006, when I cornered Janet Berlo following her brilliant lecture in San Diego and said, "I want to study with you. Where is the University of Rochester?"

I am enriched and humbled by the intelligence, creativity, humor, and hospitality of Jimmie Durham, James Luna, Kay WalkingStick, and Robert Houle. I additionally thank Durham's partner, the artist Maria Thereza Alves, Durham's assistant Kai Vollmer, Fred Kabotie's daughter Hattie Kabotie Lomayesva, Kabotie's grandson, the artist and musician Ed Kabotie, Walking-Stick's partner, the artist Dirk Bach, and Houle's partner and assistant Paul Gardner, for their support.

A PhD would not have occurred to me without the urging of Teri Sowell, Elizabeth Newsome, Susan Smith, and Norman Bryson at the University of California, San Diego. Mina and Ned Smith at the SANA Art Foundation trusted me to help manage and curate their collection of Native American, African, and Oceanic art. No one has given more to my education and career than Janet Berlo, whom I am honored to call my mentor, collaborator, and friend. To the other brilliant members of my dissertation committee, A. Joan Saab, Rachel Haidu, and Eleana Kim, I owe deep gratitude. Their keen ideas and tireless letters of support helped me to thrive well beyond the University of Rochester. Douglas Crimp, Bob Foster, and other faculty in the Graduate Program in Visual and Cultural Studies were central to my intellectual development. Ivan Minchev's love was crucial and sustaining. Liz Goodfellow, Sam Le, Lucy Mulroney, Shota Ogawa, Alex Marr, Amanda Graham, Alicia Guzman, and other friends made a snowy four years in Rochester socially and cerebrally vibrant. Bill Anthes, Ruth Phillips, Paul Chaat Smith, Kathleen Ash-Milby, Richard William Hill, Jolene Rickard, Mark Watson, Carolyn Kastner, Kate Morris, Nancy Marie Mithlo, Norman Vorano, Alex Marr, Kristine Ronan, and others committed to Native American art history inspired me from start to finish.

Early ideas in this book were shaped during Empires of Vision, a Social Science Research Council (SSRC) Dissertation Proposal Development Fellowship led by Sumathi Ramaswamy and Martin Jay. The international dimensions of this project grew through a Walter Read Hovey Fellowship, a Center for Advanced Study in the Visual Arts (CASVA) Fellowship for Historians of American Art to Travel Abroad, an SSRC International Dissertation Research Fellowship, and a Terra Foundation for American Art Summer Residency in Giverny. I especially thank Veerle Thielemans and Miranda Fontaine for their leadership, Jennifer Roberts for her mentorship, and Anna Plesset and Nenette Luarca-Shoaf for their friendship in Giverny. A CASVA Wyeth Predoctoral Fellowship granted me two years of uninterrupted time to research, write, and finish my dissertation. I spent one of them in Stephanie Frontz's magical house in Santa Fe, enriched by the friendship of Kate Lemay, Maggie Cao, Suzy Newbury, Carolyn Kastner, and Eumie Imm Stroukoff at the Georgia O'Keeffe Museum. I am grateful to Elizabeth Cropper, Peter Lukehart, Lynne Cooke, Stuart Lingo, Estelle Lingo, Yanfei Zhu, Stephen Whiteman, Meredith Gamer, Susanna Berger, and many others for a productive CASVA residency in Washington, DC. Alex Nagel encouraged me to pursue creative forms of scholarship. I continue to learn from the wit and truth-telling of Paul Chaat Smith, who introduced me to Jimmie Durham and advised my postdoctoral fellowship at the National Museum of the American Indian and the Smithsonian American Art Museum. I additionally thank Amelia Goerlitz, Emily Shapiro, Bill Truettner, Joann Moser, Rebecca Trautmann, Elayne Silversmith, Emily Burns, Joe Madura, Katherine Markoski, Amy Torbert, Lynora Williams, Maggie Michael, Dan Steinhilber, Carolyn McGourty, and Sam Le for their support during my time in the capital. I am grateful to Thomas Gaehtgens, Alexa Sekyra, Andrew Perchuk, Sabine Schlosser, Rebecca Mann, and Rebecca Zamora for their hospitality and guidance during my National Endowment for the Humanities–Getty Research Institute postdoctoral fellowship, during which I completed a full draft of the book. Kristin Romberg, Doris Chon, Subhashini Kaligotla, Michelle Craig, Bill Anthes, Kelly Newfield, and Anne Ellegood were great friends and interlocutors in Los Angeles.

Among the many opportunities I had to speak about aspects of this book, a panel convened by Bibi Obler and Ben Tilghman at the College Art Association in 2014 entitled "Objects, Objectives, Objections: The Goals and Limits of the New Materialism in Art History" was especially impactful. I thank executive editor Emily Shapiro and her team for their oversight when I published an early version of chapter 3 in *American Art* in 2015. Equally, I appreciate the work of editor Genevieve Warwick, associate editor Sam Bibby, and others who shaped an essay variant of chapter 5 published in *Art History* in 2016. The feedback of all named and anonymous individuals who read drafts of those essays and this manuscript was invaluable. I am especially grateful to Pat Moran for casting sharp and caring eyes on the entire project in the final hour. The encouragement of my chair, Larry Nees, associate chair, Perry Chapman, faculty mentor, Wendy Bellion, dearest ally, Sarah Wasserman, and other wonderful colleagues at the University of Delaware, helped me to finish during a very busy first year of teaching.

I thank Ken Wissoker, my editor at Duke University Press, for his vision, enthusiasm, and wise counsel. Assistant editors Jade Brooks and Nicole Campbell, along with many others on the publishing team, were kind and helpful at every step of the process. I am extremely grateful for the support this book received from a Mellon Art History Publication Initiative and a College Art Association Wyeth Foundation for American Art Publication Grant.

My mother, Ann Horton, therapist and quilter, inspires with her intelligence, intuition, and joy. My father, Robert Horton, veteran and poet, encourages me to dig—in the dirt and into emotional corners. My brother and dearest friend, Zach Horton, lives the convergence of art and scholarship, heart and intellect. My grandmother, Eula Kahle, shares pie secrets and daily loving emails. I thank Kent, Taylor, Larry, and Erin for offering sweet refuge on sunny beaches and in damp forests. I am sustained throughout this itinerant academic life by my family's love, generosity, and belief in me.

Introduction

In 1988, artist and activist Jimmie Durham (b. 1940) wrote, "I feel fairly sure that I could address the entire world if only I had a place to stand. But you (white Americans) have made everything your turf. In every field, on every issue, the ground has already been covered."[1] He voiced an impasse shared by many indigenous peoples across the Americas in the wake of the American Indian Movement (AIM): colonial nations continued to occupy not only their lands, but the very *ground of their representation*.[2] Modernity, from this perspective, named a process of displacement and dispossession with no end in sight. Durham's haunting essay "The Ground Has Been Covered" appeared in *Artforum* around the time he permanently left the United States and created his first major installation in London. Although he initially responded to settler colonialism with postmodern parody from the margins, Durham's practice abroad doubled back, digging into the past to piece the ground back together.[3] Other artists shaped by AIM, such as Kay WalkingStick (b. 1935), Robert Houle (b. 1947), James Luna (b. 1950), and Edgar Heap of Birds (b. 1954), were likewise challenged to reconfigure the terms of indigenous spatial struggles that reached a deadlock in the final decades of the twentieth century.[4] Consequently they took an unusual approach to accelerating conditions of artistic mobility, setting out to remap the spatial, temporal, and material coordinates of a violently divided earth.

This book is the first to explore lessons from AIM as they were taken up by a generation of artists searching for new places to stand. Upending a frequent assumption that all Native Americans who came to prominence in the 1980s were primarily concerned with identity politics in a national framework, the creative projects I've gathered reposition displaced indigenous people, art, and knowledge at the center of an unfinished story of modernity that rightly concerns the entirety of our shared world. My chapters follow artists across the Atlantic and back in time as they retraced the grooves of Native diplomats, scholars, and performers who reversed the paths of Europeans since the earliest moment of contact. The installations, performances, drawings, and paintings resulting from their journeys creatively occupy European cities as a means of reclaiming ground on both sides. Durham nailed and glued together scraps of stories concerning Algonquian "princess" Pocahontas, who met the king and queen of England in 1616, and Cherokee orator Attakulakula, who negotiated the Treaty of Whitehall in London in 1730 (chapter 1); Luna built a chapel and danced for four days in homage to the Luiseño scholar Pablo Tac, who wrote the first dictionary and history of his people at Mission San Luis Rey de Francia while studying for the priesthood in Rome in 1834 (chapter 2); Heap of Birds erected signposts recalling indigenous travelers with Buffalo Bill Cody's Wild West Shows in Venice in 1890 (chapter 2); WalkingStick drew and painted the entanglement of Aztec codices and Kokopelli with classical and Renaissance artworks in Italy (chapter 4); Houle manufactured a stage for Maungwudaus and other Ojibwa people who performed alongside George Catlin's Indian Gallery in Paris in 1846 (chapter 5). Though varied in their materials and means, each of these projects overturns a familiar narrative of colonization in which mobile agents from an "Old World" discover, divide, and dominate a "New World." Instead of an earth shaped by unilateral occupation, they envision former metropoles long filled with indigenous persons, objects, and meanings. The impasse outlined in "The Ground Has Been Covered" is at once delimited and transformed through their creative retelling of colonial histories from abroad.

These works bolster and broaden AIM-era spatial struggles with historiographical provocations. Collectively they beg the question, how should historians respond when artists encroach on our familiar terrain and expose its limitations? We could subtly police the boundary between creative and scholarly work, praising artistic play while pursuing business as usual. Alternatively, we might welcome mutual influence, inspiration, and collaboration in a shared intellectual space, exploring possibilities for making and writing in tandem. Modeling the latter approach, I have not written a conventional book about contemporary art. Living artists and their artworks are not the sole objects of my study. Instead I have sought to write in dialogue with artists and through the "eyes" of artworks, letting their approaches guide my own detours through the past travels of persons and things. While most chapters unfurl around contemporary projects paired with salient themes, I devote equal room to an extradiegetic unpacking of the histories they invoke. That is to say, I explore adjacent or related objects and stories, complementing and extending the work of living artists in written form. A passage at the center of the book devoted to paintings of Hopi social and ceremonial dances by artist Fred Kabotie (c. 1900–1986) that were displayed in the U.S. Pavilion of the Venice Biennale in 1932 exemplifies this approach (chapter 3). Through an embodied reading of the latent sound and movement of Kabotie's dancers, I demonstrate how the work of contemporary artists can prompt imaginative engagements with past materials that had equally complex lives abroad. History is our shared objective—a ground we work to uncover.

The historical scope of this book explains why I emphasize "modernisms" over "contemporary art" throughout. I aim to encompass and build on indigenous contributions to an ongoing modernity fully shared with Europeans in the wake of 1492. This book is allied with a framework of "global modernisms" or "multiple modernisms" that scholars have lately used to recover objects, histories, and methods that fall outside a Western cultural canon.[5] Literary scholar Susan Stanford Friedman defined an especially ambitious version of this drive: "Examining the spatial politics of the conventional periodization of modernism fosters a move from singularities to pluralities of space and time, from exclusivist formulations of modernity and modernism to ones based in global linkages, and from nominal modes of definition to relational ones."[6] The interdisciplinary move toward modernisms reflects broad awareness that a familiar narrative of modernity centered on the industrial United States and Europe hinders our grasp of the complex interdependencies and profound inequalities that characterize economic and cultural globalization today. The growth of the contemporary art market and proliferation of mega-exhibitions across Asia, Africa, and Latin America have likewise prompted scholars to reflect on the impoverishment of art history, a discipline struggling to branch from its nineteenth-century European roots.[7]

Visiting the Eighteenth Biennale of Sydney and dOCUMENTA (13) in 2012, I too confronted the limits of my American education as I faced demanding artworks from distant locales.[8] Yet those same events contained a subtler lesson that motivates my particular approach to modernisms "in the wake of the global turn."[9] Both exhibited an unprecedented number of works by indigenous artists living inside the borders of English-speaking, settler colonial nations such as the United States, Canada, and Australia. Many of the works demonstrated fluency in colonial cultural forms that shaped indigenous environments since the earliest moments of contact as well as ties to communities long excluded from representing their own histories to others. Some works referenced ancestral arts that were appropriated and romanticized by non-Native artists and critics but have yet to be acknowledged as agents fashioning a shared modernity. Finding themselves in a situation of categorical ambivalence, indigenous artists dwelling inside settler colonial contexts are poorly served by modernisms conceived exclusively in terms of spatial expansion.[10] The works in this book ask us to invest in modernisms' *s* as a methodological and historiographical, rather than merely geographical, challenge.

My use of "modernisms" furthermore moves away from a tendency among scholars to privilege what is new about the current phase of globalization at the expense of continuity with older forms of long-distance entanglement, in particular the European colonization of the Americas. Terry Smith, for one, wrote, "Contemporaneity consists precisely in the acceleration, ubiquity, and constancy of radical disjunctures of perception, of mismatching ways of seeing and valuing the same world, in the actual coincidence of asynchronous temporalities, in the jostling contingency of various cultural and social multiplicities, all thrown together in ways that highlight the fast-growing inequalities within and between them."[11] He argued that globalization after 1989 produced distinct relations of antinomy, which artists around the world are poised to negotiate and transform. In a highly critical account of the same period, T. J. Demos coined the phrase "crisis globalization" to describe an expanded operation of state power that "divides the uninterrupted transmission of goods and capital from the controlled movements of people." The artists, curators, and art tourists who enjoy itinerancy comprise an elite few on this earth, while a majority of displaced humans are "denied legal rights, social protections, and the freedom of movement."[12] I extend the historical scope of these insights by intermixing contemporary artworks with older Native American objects and associated worldviews. WalkingStick's drawings, Durham's installations, and Kabotie's paintings reveal that "radical disjunctures of perception" accompanying "controlled movements" occurred in Rome in the sixteenth century, London in the eighteenth century, and Venice in the twentieth century, as constitutive features of the colonization of the Americas. From this perspective, "crisis globalization" has been incubating for a very long time. Following Walter Mignolo, I trace its material and epistemological roots to the world-shaping events of 1492.[13] Such an expansive view necessarily sacrifices some of the historical detail enabled by traditional periodization. In its place I gain flexibility alongside artists to explore unexpected continuities, echoes, and alliances across time, revitalizing long-standing creative strategies for navigating both painful and privileged forms of mobility to meet contemporary challenges. This book compiles and explores connections between past and present indigenous travelers who have shared and shaped an ongoing modernity. Collectively, these modernisms map alternatives to the ideologies of expansion, progress, and objectification that implicate colonization and globalization alike. The works and words of this book build a picture of a world that is spatially, temporally, and materially interconnected, or what I call an undivided earth.

Space, Time, Material

As I have already hinted, addressing covered ground entails reformulating the terms of spatial politics that fueled AIM and shaped subsequent artistic practices. Native peoples have long participated in—and been outwardly defined by—struggles to maintain or recover relationships to particular places. In a much-quoted passage from his book *God Is Red* (1972), published at the height of AIM activism, Standing Rock Sioux scholar Vine Deloria Jr. asserted, "American Indians hold their lands—places—as having the highest possible meaning, and all their statements are made with this reference point in mind."[14] A conception of indigenous agency rooted in land stolen by colonizers fueled the indigenous nationalisms that culminated in activists' occupation of Alcatraz Island in San Francisco (1969), the Bureau of Indian Affairs in Washington, DC (1972), and Wounded Knee in South Dakota (1973).[15] Although the movement was riven by factionalism and failed to regain much of the territory lost through broken treaties, it radicalized a generation of artists and intellectuals who launched a sustained examination of colonial power relations informed by postmodern and postcolonial theory. Suspicious of succumbing to yet another romantic Indian cliché, many practitioners focused on negative critique, only to find themselves locked in a scenario of unending opposition to authority on the eve of the Columbus Quincentennial. At the same time, accelerating globalization compounded the physical and cultural displacement of indigenous peoples, while foreclosing AIM-generation artists' celebrated positions as subversive "outsiders." Select members of the AIM generation were drawn into a symptomatic explosion of art biennials and residencies around the world, populated by itinerant professionals whose "success is measured by the accumulation of frequent flier miles," to quote a well-known phrase by art historian Miwon Kwon.[16] The implication is that successful artists must traverse the world in order to address it, a paradoxical scenario for Native practitioners who forged their careers protesting violent legacies of dislocation from the margins of modern nations. Does being on the move necessitate moving on?

The works in this book consistently answer no. As artists traveled abroad, they practiced a conceptual shift, away from contested territories and toward entangled histories. But indigenous spatial politics were not relinquished so much as revitalized through this process. The resulting creative projects restore neglected temporal and material dimensions to narrow conceptions of place that have shaped—and, we come to realize, overdetermined—Native representation under conditions of occupation. When severed from a larger complex of indigenous ideas and practices, places and the humans attached to them are rendered particularly susceptible to conquest. As Deloria and others have noted, colonial modernity is filled with images of dynamic, progressive time usurping inert, unchanging place. Mapped along these supposedly universal axes we find Europeans (mobile agents of history) and indigenous peoples (reactionary victims of history), the latter clinging to timeless places until the relentless tide of progress and expansion (colonization, globalization) breaks their grip. Deloria summarized the violent particularity of this understanding: "Western European identity involves the assumption that time proceeds in a linear fashion; further it assumes that at a particular point in the unraveling of this sequence, the peoples of Western Europe became the guardians of the world."[17] Time appears to be the enemy of place.

Native studies scholars have critiqued the parameters of this cosmology, recognizing the degree to which it has corralled indigenous claims to land, identity, and political sovereignty in a divisive framework patterned after colonial nationalisms. As I explore in greater depth in chapter 1, AIM nationalists tended to define Native self-determination within available Western legal-political institutions, including the appropriation of a European notion of sovereignty to support nation-to-nation agreements.[18] In a feminist critique of such efforts, Shari M. Huhndorf described "an inherently limited, contradictory mode of anticolonial resistance" that "implicitly grant[s] authority and legitimacy to [patriarchal] colonial nation-states."[19] Mohawk scholar Taiaiake Alfred elaborated, "It isn't enough just to regain political space; we need to fill it up with indigenous content if it is going to mean anything to our people."[20] Beyond challenging the limitations of Native nationalisms, a number of scholars have heeded Alfred's call to articulate alternative formulations of agency and self-determination. Huhndorf, Jolene Rickard, Robert Warrior, Chad Allen, and others have harnessed the language of "indigenous transnationalism," "global indigeneity," and even "trans-indigenous" to counter the entrenched Eurocentrism of the modern nation-state construct with Native frames of reference.²¹ The strongest accounts invest these terms with anti-essentialist relational values, focusing especially on contemporary literature and arts that transgress the borders of reservations inside the United States and Canada and forge alliances with others around the world. Heeding Alfred's provocation in the realm of contemporary art, Rickard called for an "expressive imaginary of visual [and intellectual] sovereignty" that looks past a U.S. legal interpretation to embody "our philosophical, political, and renewal strategies."²² She foregrounded "an understanding of power in Indigenous cultures" in which "the interconnectedness . . . of all life is sacred and key to human freedom and survival."²³ A similar conviction that Native agency is bolstered by alliances (between persons, things, times, and places) rather than divisions (between races, nations, cultures, and periods) is common to the artistic projects discussed in this book.

Still, recent efforts to alter the terms of indigenous engagement with national and global processes have tended to steer clear of the methodological minefield of history. Reflecting on the trauma of colonization, Chiricahua Apache scholar Nancy Marie Mithlo, curator of numerous contemporary Native art initiatives at the Venice Biennale, wrote, "Our history is dangerous."²⁴ I find that it is equally perilous to reserve agency for the living. The capacity of "global indigeneity," "trans-indigenous," and other spatial concepts and practices to bolster "survivance" (Anishinaabe writer Gerald Vizenor's enigmatic term combining survival and resistance) remains limited so long as they are aimed exclusively at the present and future.²⁵ Divisive concepts of territory and identity may be challenged, but historical teleology is quietly affirmed. Native cultural producers appear as belated arrivals on a global stage, caught in the undertow of transnational capital flows eroding the power of nation-states, while the past remains colonized. In contrast, the artistic practices I examine in this book unearth, in Philip Deloria's terms, "the multiplicity of Native histories, each of which poses political and epistemological challenges to the Western tradition of history-telling itself."²⁶ They integrate creative and culturally inflected conceptions of time, place, and material, producing coordinates that are coeval with, yet irreducible to, the colonial cosmology and attendant nationalisms I have outlined.²⁷ Transnationalism, implying the crossing of national borders, is inadequate to address this crucial temporal dimension, as more than half of the studies in this book point to times before nation-states divided the Americas. Through the restoration of a deep historical dimension, indigenous relationships to earth are rendered assertive (rather than defensive), dynamic (rather than static), and multiple (rather than exclusive). We begin to see how, in the words of Luna, "every place is a Native place"—from the La Jolla Reservation to the canals of Venice.[28]

To space and time I add a third, enabling term: material. As indigenous objects circulated through Europe and other far-flung locales in the wake of 1492, they significantly extended the reach of Native peoples who could not, or chose not to, travel in the flesh. It is most often through an engagement with lively materials that AIM-generation artists summon a relationship to otherwise distant peoples, places, and pasts. Insofar as they tamper with the taxonomic logic governing transatlantic collections, they appear to share what Hal Foster has termed "an archival impulse" with many creative contemporaries, defined by a feverish desire to connect things that were "frightfully disconnected in the first place" in tension with suspicion of longing for the totality that archival systems seem to promise.[29] However, the projects in this book present conceptual challenges to assumptions about materiality shaping this trend. As I use the term, the archive has become "ubiquitous and . . . capacious— encompassing the collection, the inventory, the library, the museum, and even the corpus of our scholarly projects."[30] Artists and scholars alike have critiqued the archive as the "condition of reality for statements" about history, charged with delimiting and classifying the remains of the past, often in the service of an imperial state.[31] In the words of Diana Taylor, the archive "sustains power" because it "works across distance, over time and space . . . [and] succeeds in separating the source of 'knowledge' from the knower."[32] Tending toward objectivity and objectification, the archive appears to present a formidable challenge to the agency of any single human storyteller. Correspondingly, accounts of artistic intervention have tended to bifurcate along a hard line between live subjects and dead (and deadening) materials: on the one hand, a retreat to "flesh" through a repertoire of performance modalities; on the other, tampering with archival "bone" through strategies of deconstruction and/or the creation of "counter-archives."[33]

For artists of the AIM generation, this is deeply familiar terrain. "If there are any people on earth whose lives are more tangled up with museums than we are, God help them," wrote Comanche cultural critic Paul Chaat Smith.[34] As I elaborate in chapter 1, Durham and Luna especially developed a strand of institutional critique in the 1980s, creating parodic installations and performances that registered their deep skepticism toward colonial collections that objectify and dispossess indigenous cultures. Their attitude has roots in AIM, for example, the activists' 1969 proposal for a museum on Alcatraz Island that "will present some of the things the white man has given to the Indians in return for the land and life he took: disease, alcohol, poverty, and cultural decimation (as symbolized by old tin cans, barbed wire, rubber tires, plastic containers, etc.)."[35] Just as activists relinquished pieces of their own histories when they ransacked Bureau of Indian Affairs headquarters in Washington, DC, in 1972, burning documents and destroying Native American objects, postmodern artistic critiques too quickly left the past for dead. Informed by faltering precedents, the projects I describe in this book refuse to accept a foundational divide between the "hard stuff" of history and a fleshly, mutable present. Instead they activate the sociability of select materials, often with recourse to indigenous epistemologies, whether enduring or creatively recovered. When Luna integrated Tac's writing into the tactile surfaces of blankets and baskets, Durham hammered together British colonial documents and refuse from the London streets to construct an eloquent Cherokee orator, or Houle translated a sketch of Ojibwa performers by Eugène Delacroix into a stage set for tableaux vivants, they treated European collections as resonant sites of encounter between the agencies of past and present subjects and objects. In other words, their projects make the transcultural and transmutable dimensions of the archive palpable to visitors, encouraging a mutually enlivening relationship to unfold. What is produced is neither another hardened structure nor a privileging of the live subject, so much as an invitation to engage with the latent performative dimensions of histories not yet stilled.[36]

By drawing on indigenous precepts regarding the agency and sociability of things, AIM-generation artists finally circumvent the deconstructive impulses that dominated cultural theory and practice in the late twentieth century. As I explore in greater detail in chapter 1, the varied discourses of postmodernism and postcolonialism engendered useful critiques of racism and colonialism, but too often celebrated marginality and valorized contemporary subjects at the expense of historical agents. Furthermore, an anthropocentric focus on people and texts overlooked relationships between humans and other-than-human persons central to many indigenous philosophies.[37] At key points in this book, I consider the conflicted relationship between AIM-generation practices and the recently popular, interdisciplinary trend of "new materialisms," in which scholars theorize the vibrancy of matter denied through modern, rationalist divisions of culture and nature, human and nonhuman.[38] When Houle invited visitors to "offer their hands" to paintings of Ojibwa performers who died of smallpox (chapter 5) or when Durham mobilized the latent capacities of stones as sculptors (epilogue), they participated in the continuity or regeneration of very old materialisms, building a picture of European "centers" long filled with indigenous meanings.

Europe

While "Europe" looms large in this project, I hope that the power of the term will dissipate across the pages of this book. I use it to signal both more and less than a geographical boundary and a political territory. In writing about indigenous modernisms, I am wary of a tendency in some postcolonial literature to construct a singular, monolithic Europe as a foil.[39] Countering stereotypes with stereotypes locks Native peoples into a binary, oppositional relationship to Europeans, inadvertently reifying the authority of colonizers over the terms of indigenous representation. A more useful variant is Gilane Tawadros's description of "Europe as an unsettled and fluctuating political, economic, and cultural entity whose past, present, and future can no longer be seen as settled and secure, nestling in the comfort of invented traditions and imagined communities."[40] This is a Europe constituted through colonization, in which Native Americans persist as an unstable "central margin" instead of a mythical outside.[41] It follows that Europe has long been vulnerable to indigenous tampering.

In order to devote as much space as possible to the integral indigenous agents of this relationship, I borrow from existing scholarship on European perceptions of Native Americans, especially Vanita Seth's attention to the differences between Renaissance, Classical, and nineteenth-century modes of representing "Indians."[42] I likewise build on a small literature devoted to indigenous travelers in Europe, especially Norman K. Denzin's experimental *Indians on Display*, Christian Feest's essay collection *Indians and Europe*, Kate Flint's *The Transatlantic Indian*, and Jace Weaver's *The Red Atlantic*.[43] I am indebted to the background and analyses they offer regarding Native Americans who crossed the Atlantic as early as 1009 AD, augmenting the case studies of this book. Allied scholarship notwithstanding, traveling Indians can easily appear as aberrations within a conventional narrative of transatlantic modernity, incommensurate with images of traditional, emplaced, communal Natives usurped by colonizers. Attakulakula was an unusually gifted orator, Maungwudaus an enterprising rebel, Tac an adept linguist, WalkingStick the only Cherokee hired by Cornell University to teach art in Rome, Durham the first artist of Native heritage to garner accolades on the art biennial circuit, and so on. Taken individually, the seemingly exceptional cases of this book may well leave colonial divisions between static indigenes and mobile Europeans intact. Yet, as Philip Deloria noted in his study of turn-of-the-twentieth-century "Indians in Unexpected Places," expectations are rooted in biases as often as facts: "There were and are significant numbers of Indian anomalies, enough that we must rethink familiar categories. . . . Taken together, it seems to me, the cumulative experiences of such anomalous Indians point . . . toward a re-imagining of the contours of modernity itself."[44] What better site to rethink the shape of modernity than through "significant numbers of Indian anomalies" in London, Paris, Venice, and Rome—cities that fostered the colonization of the Americas and the recording of its history?

Once we conceive of a Europe that includes indigenous interdependencies, contemporary artists who travel to former metropoles cannot be considered exiles from the United States and Canada, as some commentators have claimed.[45] Rather, their activities abroad knit relatively young nations, naturalized units of a contemporary geopolitical order, back inside a larger complex of European ideas and practices. Durham succinctly illustrated this gesture when he declared, "Americans are the best Europeans" and "The US is not here, within these specific lands. . . . It has brought Europe to the 'New World,' where it sits a few inches off the savage, dangerous ground."[46] As Native travelers reverse the path of colonizers across the Atlantic, they enact the coeval and contested nature of the ground on either side. By invoking a long view of such activity, the effects of AIM-generation artists' projects are doubled: they at once "provincialize Europe," delimiting the cultural and historical specificity of colonial regimes of knowledge, and make room for hitherto marginalized accounts—the modernisms I unpack throughout this book—to flourish in our present understanding.[47] Both critical and affirmative measures are implied by Durham's formulation "Europe is an Indian project."[48]

The Chapters

Despite growing scholarly interest in contemporary Native American art, no study to date has traced the profound impact of AIM on subsequent aesthetic practices. Chapter 1, "'The Word for World and the Word for History Are the Same': Jimmie Durham, the American Indian Movement, and Spatial Thinking," begins this work by integrating Durham's tenure as the director of the International Indian Treaty Council during AIM in the 1970s with his formative practice in New York City during the 1980s. I lay the ground for remaining chapters by examining the philosophical dimensions of the spatial politics that motivated a generation of activists and artists. Along the way, I dispel any assumption that key figures from the AIM generation have pursued a linear trajectory from identity politics inside the United States to a postidentity condition abroad. Instead, Durham and select peers set out to transform struggles over the definition and ownership of space through artistic practice. From the beginning their efforts to recenter a vast story of modernity on displaced indigenous subjects and knowledge exceeded the "frameworks of identity" that persist in framing our view of much 1980s art today.[49] Commentators soon associated Durham's early assemblages of painted animal bones and automobile parts with the trickster, a mischievous hero appropriated from indigenous cultures to serve the ends of postmodern critique. While promising to rehabilitate painful conditions of marginality, the trickster of late twentieth-century art criticism dangerously resembled the exilic subject of European modernism who transformed loss into "a potent, even enriching motif."[50] She succumbed to a romantic cliché while consigning Native peoples to displacement without end. In the essay quoted at the outset of this book, Durham voiced an impasse for indigenous subjects that extended from lost lands to the very terms of their representation. I conclude the chapter with a discussion of his little-known installation in London in 1988, *Mataoka Ale Attakulakula Anel Guledisgo Hnihi (Pocahontas and the Little Carpenter in London)*, which answers the limitations of the postmodern trickster with an expansive definition of history as world anchored in Cherokee language and carpentry.[51]

Mataoka Ale Attakulakula Anel Guledisgo Hnihi inaugurates the historiographical turn to which I devote the remainder of the book. Chapter 2, "'Now That We Are Christians We Dance for Ceremony': James Luna, Performing Props, and Sacred Space," opens with a suite of three installations and a performance, collectively titled *Emendatio*, exhibited at the Venice Biennale in 2005. In it Luna reconstituted the archive of Pablo Tac (1822–41), a Quechnajuisom (Luiseño) scholar who wrote the first dictionary and history of his people under missionary rule in New Spain, while studying for the priesthood in Rome. At first glance, Tac's mastery of writing abroad suggests his assimilation into a European episteme and corresponding loss of embodied Native knowledge. But when Luna embedded Tac's words among the material culture of a multisensory chapel and danced for four days in a nearby courtyard in Venice, he made palpable the ways in which colonial conversions filled European languages, objects, and spaces with indigenous meanings. Departing from prevailing accounts of an archival impulse in contemporary art, my analysis emphasizes the fluidity of exchanges between human bodies and sensuous materials—what I call "performing props"—that equally populate Luna's performances and installations. *Emendatio* reintegrates a colonial binary of "archive and repertoire" and related Christian dogma separating "spirit and letter" into an expansive framework of undivided earth that preoccupies me for the remaining chapters.[52]

Luna's work culminated a decade of curatorial efforts in the United States and Canada to enhance the visibility of Native artists at the Venice Biennale, the oldest and some say most prestigious art exhibition in the world. *Emendatio*'s emphasis on neglected sacred and sensorial dimensions of modernity transcends the competitive nationalisms linking the mega-exhibition to nineteenth-century colonial world fairs. In chapter 3, "'They Sent Me Way Out in the Foreign Country and Told Me to Forget It': Fred Kabotie, Dance Memories, and the 1932 U.S. Pavilion of the Venice Biennale," I overturn a truism that Native American artists have never exhibited in the nation's proud neoclassical galleries.[53] Archival photographs and letters reveal that the pavilion held indigenous pottery, silverwork, textiles, and gouache paintings, just two years after it was built. But when U.S. organizers determined that the display failed to communicate a nationalist agenda, it was excised from the history of transatlantic modernism. I reclaim this covered ground by looking closely at the exhibited work of Kabotie. Among Pueblo peers, he painted social and ceremonial dances from memory as government-imposed education and widespread bans on ritual practices aimed to transform Native bodies into productive labor for the U.S. economy in the first decades of the twentieth century. Kabotie's early works, as well as the words he repeated about them later in his life, reveal a persistent concern with maintaining Hopi sensibilities amid displacement, thereby allying them with the contemporary artworks discussed throughout this book. I argue that his diagrammatic approach, inspired by recollections of indigenous dance and exposure to European musical notation, enabled the painting to withstand gaps in time as well as space. Recontextualized among the AIM generation's recent work abroad, Kabotie's dancers join *Emendatio* in facilitating embodied connections beyond a framework of colonial nationalism.

Biennials are only the latest staging ground for a modern conception of difference that has long framed encounters between indigenous and European art heritages. The dividing line within art history relates to the development of the discipline alongside racial biology and anthropological definitions of kinship in the nineteenth century. In chapter 4, "'Dance Is the One Activity That I Know of When Virtual Strangers Can Embrace': Kay Walking-

Stick, Creative Kinship, and Art History's Tangled Legs," I argue that Walk-ingStick's artistic practice refuses a logic of difference that lingered in late twentieth-century debates about modernist primitivism, the Indian Arts and Crafts Act of 1990, and the Columbus Quincentennial, by forging affective bonds with white artistic predecessors. Her encounters with worldly Renais-sance collections prompt me to consider similitude as an alternative relational model. For roughly the first century of conquest, Europeans enveloped Native Americans, plants, and animals into a global family of resemblances, rather than positing their essential differences. Indigenous artists likewise bent like-ness to the ends of survival.[54] In copious sketchbooks made during repeated trips to Rome between 1999 and 2012, WalkingStick drew classical fauns and amphorae, scenes of Christ's transfiguration, and Aztec stones, feathers, and codices from Italian collections into sensuous, loving proximity. She then invited figures repurposed from her sketchbooks to dance across the scuffed surfaces of works on paper. The androgynous, racially indeterminate legs of WalkingStick's dancers, entwined in vines borrowed from Etruscan mosaics, claim belonging to a vast history of art, or what I call "creative kinship."

While WalkingStick's fertile, transformational figures enlarge modern-ism's family tree, Houle's mixed-media works revisit the entwined lineages of ethnography and abstraction to tell a survival story. In chapter 5, "'They Advanced to the Portraits of Their Friends and Offered Them Their Hands': Robert Houle, Ojibwa Tableaux Vivants, and Transcultural Materialism," I consider the capacity of paintings to counter objectification, disease, and death that infuse the history of indigenous performers in Europe. Houle's installation, *Paris/Ojibwa*, first exhibited at the Canadian Cultural Center in Paris in 2010, revisits Ojibwa men, women, and children who performed *tab-leaux vivants*, or living pictures, in European cities from 1845 to 1846. As they restaged painted scenes of Native life on view in American artist and busi-nessman George Catlin's traveling Indian Gallery, they were in turn sketched and painted by Catlin, Eugène Delacroix, and others, generating an unset-tling chain of bodies-turned-pictures-turned-bodies-turned-pictures. Houle designed *Paris/Ojibwa* as a stage on which abstracted portraits of Ojibwa performers, based on spare sketches by Delacroix, are poised to perform again. Addressing Bruno Latour's influential text *We Have Never Been Modern*, I consider the relationship between tableaux vivants and his theorization of "quasi-objects" that contaminated modern categories of human and non-human. *Paris/Ojibwa* goes further, inviting us to see how the popular transat-lantic parlor game incorporated Ojibwa understandings of the potential liveliness of images and objects. When wedded to complex indigenous notions of personhood, tableaux vivants reversed Catlin's ethnographic ambitions to preserve "disappearing" cultures: instead of turning living Natives into static images, they made way for the reanimation of pictures. Houle's engagement with the Ojibwa archive prompts us to discard the "new" of the "new materialisms" that have lately compelled scholars across disciplines and broaden the European "we" discussed by Latour. Inviting visitors to participate in an indigenous view of a shared modernity, *Paris/Ojibwa* restores sociability to the archive of nineteenth-century performers and models transcultural materialism in the center of Paris.

I return to Durham's practice in the epilogue, "Traveling with Stones," to consider rocks sprung to life following his relocation to Europe in 1994. A chunk of mineral matter masks the artist's visage, pebbles dent the front of a refrigerator, rocks scatter across the floor of a museum gift store, and massive boulders ground celebrated symbols of modern mobility and progress, the car and the airplane.[55] Often substrate replaces Durham as sculptor, assuming powers to act, narrate, and form alliances with humans. As stones accumulate in the wake of the artist's far-flung travels, they conjure pre- and postcontact piles of rocks that indigenous peoples configured at crossroads in the Americas to protect and orient travelers. Acting as wayfinders for displaced humans across centuries and oceans, Durham's stones point toward a multiplicity of places to stand.

ONE "The Word for World and the Word for History Are the Same"

JIMMIE DURHAM, THE AMERICAN INDIAN MOVEMENT, AND SPATIAL THINKING

Space, Not Identity

In 1990, the Museum of Contemporary Hispanic Art, the New Museum of Contemporary Art, and the Studio Museum of Harlem opened an unprecedented collaborative exhibition. *The Decade Show: Frameworks of Identity in the 1980s* signaled the arrival of previously marginalized black, Chicano, Native American, feminist, queer, and other artists at the center of the New York art world. Many on the exhibition's roster of seventy artists have since become familiar names in contemporary art history: David Hammons, the Guerrilla Girls, Ana Mendieta, Guillermo Gómez-Peña, Lorna Simpson, Fred Wilson, and James Luna. An essay by Jimmie Durham is among fourteen included in the catalogue.[1] As the title of the show hints, institutional validation fixed the terms of the artists' arrival. Curator Sharon F. Patton explained, "The artists analyze their own culture, cultural heritage, and ethnicity to invert the perceived tyranny of an imposed Eurocentric, male identity. . . . Typically, the art engages the viewer in a discussion about who we are, how others define who we are, and how we define ourselves."[2] The varied work of a decade appeared inside and thereafter affirmed "frameworks of identity."[3] While the circulation of postidentity phrases in the 2000s signals identity's fall from grace, especially among a younger generation of art professionals, "postblack," "post-Indian," and even "postfeminism" serve to anchor identity politics all the more firmly in the art of the past.[4] The temporal schema of the "post-" joins forces with *The Decade Show* to stabilize meaning in hindsight.

The Decade Show curators' central argument sits uneasily with Durham's long-standing claim, reiterated to me in an email in 2012: "In the '80s none of us ever discussed our identity, made art about our identity, or used the term. In other words, it was used later, against us."[5] An activist, artist, and writer, Durham resigned as director of the International Indian Treaty Council (IITC) of the American Indian Movement (AIM) in the summer of 1979 and turned seriously to making art in New York City. His "us" reflects the heterogeneity of his artistic community on the Lower East Side, which included Wilson and Hammons, as well as a geographically diffuse network of indigenous artists, especially in the United States and Canada.[6] This chapter is devoted to reassessing Durham's formative role within the latter group, which I call the "AIM generation" to emphasize shared historical and conceptual terrain, rather than a cohesive or contested identity. Throughout the 1980s and early 1990s, Durham exhibited alongside, collaborated with, and wrote about the work of fellow indigenous artists. He profoundly impacted a discourse about Native American art and settler colonialism long after he moved to Mexico in 1987 and to Europe in 1994, at which point he cut his ties to U.S. institutions.[7] Although identity politics undoubtedly shaped many practices of the period, such a framework is inadequate to account for the AIM generation's overlapping political and aesthetic concerns in the wake of organized resistance. Taking Durham's provocation seriously, I dislodge identity from its stable location in recent art history in order to invigorate, rather than remove, the grounds for alliances. In addition to reframing a body of work primarily from the 1980s, this chapter charts continuities between Durham's work in the United States and abroad, against prevailing assumptions that he went into exile.

Specifically, I map the vectors of a spatial politics anchored in lessons from AIM. Material and symbolic struggles on behalf of occupied lands distinguished AIM from African American and other civil rights movements and affected the trajectory of many subsequent artistic practices. Key works by the AIM generation in the 1980s and 1990s addressed the world-shaping legacies of some five centuries of colonization in the Americas, encompassing dominant institutions and practices that designated certain people, places, and things "Indian." I argue that there was far more at play than spatial metaphors such as "centers" and "margins" and "insiders" and "outsiders," frequently invoked in the 1980s to describe the institutionalized segregation of identities. Durham's practice in particular reconnected figurative uses of space to the territorial underpinning of colonization across the Americas and explored the ongoing implications for relationships among *all* humans and the environments on which we depend. His project reflected a form of spatial thinking that recognized, in the words of geographer Doreen Massey, "space as the product of interrelations . . . relations which are necessarily embedded material practices which have to be carried out."[8] Durham's work and words conveyed with unusual clarity the predicament of indigenous peoples displaced by occupation while insisting that colonialism, far from a minority issue, is a problem that concerns the entirety of our shared world.

Still, it is not incidental that Durham's art, along with much creative work of the AIM generation, ceded to the misapprehension of a solipsistic politics of identity. Media images of AIM foreshadowed this slippage, which was repeated in the discourse surrounding the trickster, a sacred miscreant and social critic drawn from indigenous cultural precedents who made regular appearances in AIM-generation art, literature, and criticism. The trickster of the 1980s and 1990s promised to unite elements of Native American philosophy and postmodern theory to emancipatory ends. Yet she inadvertently consigned colonized peoples to displacement without end, a disempowering scenario that was ultimately packaged and celebrated as another romantic identity. In a haunting essay from 1988 entitled "The Ground Has Been Covered," quoted at the outset of this book, Durham described an impasse for indigenous peoples that extended from the loss of their lands to the very terms of their representation in the late twentieth century.[9] His perspective was reinforced by the passage of the Indian Arts and Crafts Act of 1990 (IACA), which resulted in the cancellation of two solo shows of his work on the eve of the Columbus Quincentennial.

I end the chapter with a close reading of *Mataoka Ale Attakulakula Anel Guledisgo Hnihi (Pocahontas and the Little Carpenter in London)*, a large-scale multimedia installation that Durham made in London in 1988, shortly after relocating to Mexico. This little-known artwork negotiates the impasse that befell spatial thinking in the wake of AIM by reopening a historical dimension, wedding the artist's transatlantic journey to those of the Algonquian "princess" Pocahontas in 1616 and the Cherokee delegate Attakulakula in 1730. *Mataoka Ale Attakulakula Anel Guledisgo Hnihi* forms a bridge between Durham's critique of the Americas as "covered ground" and an expansive, affirmative conception of history as world anchored in Cherokee language and carpentry, marking a substantial early contribution to the framework of undivided earth that will preoccupy me for the remainder of this book. The installation prepares us to recognize the recent work of AIM-generation artists abroad not as a linear development toward a postidentity future, but as a reintroduction to modernity's shared ground.

La poursuite du bonheur *and Modernist Exile*

By way of introducing the spatial preoccupations evident in Durham's early activism, writing, and art, I begin with another retrospective. In 2002, in the countryside near his studio in Rome, Durham filmed a parody of a "spaghetti western" (plates 1–12).[10] The short narrative video, *La poursuite du bonheur* (*The Pursuit of Happiness*), introduces viewers via subtitles to Joe Hill, an "American Indian artist, probably of Shoshone or Paiute origin" living somewhere in the western United States. Accompanied by a wordless soundtrack of epic music, the taciturn protagonist (played by Albanian artist Anri Sala) strides across polluted fields and highways, collecting roadkill, discarded plastic, and other detritus. He turns these into collages, which he exhibits at an anonymous gallery for an audience of cowboys, whereupon he pockets a wad of cash, lights his dilapidated trailer on fire, and boards a flight to France. A shot of the airplane disappearing into a blue sky acts as the punch line to a dark thirteen-minute joke: For Joe, "life, liberty, and the pursuit of happiness," the tri-part promise of the U.S. Declaration of Independence, leads inexorably to emigration. Read against *The Decade Show's* preoccupations with identity, *La poursuite du bonheur* shifts our attention toward a complex and shifting spatial politics that concerned Durham before, during, and after AIM.

To begin, Durham cast "an American Indian artist" in the role of exile, a classic modernist trope premised on the conceit of leaving one's identity behind along with one's homeland. The conflation cancels an entrenched colonial binary of static indigenes and mobile Europeans, along with any romance we may have invested in such categories. In Edward Said's classic formulation, "Modern Western culture is in large part the work of exiles, emigres, refugees" who have sought to transform an "unhealable rift forced between a human being and a native place . . . into a potent, even enriching, motif."[11] Caren Kaplan concisely summarized the exile's attributes: "singularity, solitude, estrangement, alienation and aestheticized excisions of location. . . . The 'artist in exile' is never 'at home,' always existentially alone, and shocked by the strain of displacement into significant experimentations and insights."[12] Said found that dislocations wrought by warfare, totalitarian regimes, and other, violent forms of nationalism were so ubiquitous in the twentieth century that exile can no longer serve celebratory notions of humanism. Kaplan gave us reason to doubt that such a wish was ever warranted. The singular, transcendent experience of exile treats attachments to community, place, and shared history as anachronisms. The exilic subject nonetheless imagines he (it is nearly always a "he") can access a surrogate home through his union with non-European lands and peoples, representing the premodern past habitable as a foreign place.[13] Exile and colonialism turn out to be ideological bedfellows. In *La poursuite du bonheur*, we are reminded that a European fantasy of starting fresh in the "New World," a deep colonial subtext shared by the Declaration of Independence and spaghetti westerns, conditions Joe's displacement. His own "native place" is a derelict trailer near a polluted roadway, reflecting the devastating poverty and contamination on many Native American reservations in the twentieth century. Not unlike his modernist predecessors, Joe seeks aesthetic recompense for an experience of loss and fragmentation by collaging roadkill and detritus. Far from redemptive, however, his act merely satisfies his cowboy collectors' romantic stereotypes about Indians in exchange for cold cash. As he reverses the path of countless European exiles from "New World" to "Old," he comes to represent the endgame of colonialism, a figure of indigenous displacement without end.

But *La poursuite du bonheur* also points us toward activist alliances as an alternative to solitary exile. Joe shares his name with the train-hopping poet and musician Joe Hill, who emigrated from Sweden to the United States in 1902. Hill became a renowned activist on behalf of migrant labor rights, only to be convicted of murder on scanty evidence and executed in 1915.[14] *La poursuite du bonheur*'s extradiegetic coda wraps both Joes into a transhistorical and transnational community with others. The credits roll across an outdoor gathering at what looks like a French café—an Italian restaurant supplies the stand-in—where a beret-clad Durham sits talking over espresso with Sala and friends. Here the pretense of a 1960s Sergio Leone western gives way to the reflexivity of another genre of the decade, cinema verité. The coda calls to mind a famous café scene from Victor Morin and Jean Rouch's experimental documentary *Chronique d'un été* (*Chronicle of a Summer*, 1960), in which Morin sits with his cast at Totem, the restaurant of the colonial Musée de l'Homme in Paris.[15] Marceline, a Holocaust survivor; Landry, a student from Côte d'Ivoire; and other leftist intellectuals discuss decolonization in Africa and painful memories of Auschwitz. In my reading, *La poursuite du bonheur*, like *Chronique d'un été*, turns the ethnographic lens upon Paris, revealing distant "others"—a Cherokee, an Albanian—present at the café table. Perhaps they, too, participate in heterogeneous political alliances in place of exilic estrangement.

La poursuite du bonheur's credits finally direct us to 2002, to the scene of retrospection. More than forty years after *Chronique d'un été*, we must consider the possibility that artistic itinerancy, rather than political exigency, conditioned Sala and Durham's collaboration. They could well be sipping espresso during a Parisian layover on the contemporary biennial circuit, where both have been warmly applauded in recent decades. A woman reads the newspaper *Le Monde* at a nearby table, recalling the headlines detailing decolonization struggles in Africa that flashed across the screen introducing *Chronique d'un été*'s café gathering. But today's biennial artists are more likely to be privileged itinerants, buffered from violent inequalities detailed in the news. Echoing Kaplan's critique of exile, T. J. Demos wrote, "Nomadism suggests a contemporary neoprimitivism, one that subscribes to a fantasy of freedom from all attachments, but which cruelly operates in a system that denies that freedom to the very itinerant peoples from whom it borrows its name."[16] Today's mega-exhibitions, featuring exceptional, border-hopping artists, tend to celebrate cultural inclusivity while obscuring the millions for whom globalization means dispossession and dislocation. Holding these vectors together without resolving the tensions between them, *La poursuite du bonheur* maps conceptual interdependencies among modernist exile, colonial displacement, transnational activism, and privileged nomadism. Native Americans come with the territory: coerced, unwitting, or willing participants in multiple forms of mobility that constitute a contested modernity shared with Europeans since 1492.

Lessons from the American Indian Movement

Durham's own trajectory is a lived variant of *La poursuite du bonheur*'s spatial concerns. He was born in Arkansas, related to Wolf Clan Cherokee who headed west before the deadly Trail of Tears in 1838, when the federal government forcibly relocated a majority of remaining Cherokee from their homeland in the southeastern United States to Indian Territory (present-day Oklahoma).[17] Parts of Durham's childhood were spent in Texas, Louisiana, and Oklahoma as his father searched for work. He dropped out of high school at age sixteen, worked for ranchers in New Mexico, and completed four years of service with the U.S. military.[18] Throughout, he joined Native activists in the Southwest, but reports that by the late 1960s he "thought that it was all hopeless."[19] In 1968, the year that AIM was formally established in Minneapolis, Durham followed friends to Geneva. He enrolled in the free École des Beaux-Arts and secured a visa and summer studio space in France.[20] He wrote, "I left for Europe, seriously thinking never to come back. I thought to be an artist in Switzerland, and write poems about love and my nightmares and my sordid past."[21] The attraction of what he called "becoming European" was the promise of a liberating abstraction, away from the poverty and racism experienced by many Native Americans in the United States.

But as news of decolonization struggles in the United States and elsewhere in the Americas reached Geneva, his fantasy of exile was undercut by guilt. Durham wrote, "In a bar in Geneva I met Indians from South America who were doing the same thing. We all accused each other of being empty leeches."[22] His dabbles in modernist painting also became a cause for concern: "How can the world use abstract shapes? Only [Mark] Rothko could be romantic and self-involved enough to carry it off."[23] Heeding a sense of responsibility to the indigenous political situation in the Americas, Durham began organizing international support for AIM in Europe. His apartment was a meeting space for African liberationists and "Indians in exile"; instead of a "Cherokee trying to be European," he became, in his words, "a Third World internationalist."[24] Prompted by AIM events in 1973, Durham returned to the United States. From 1974 to 1979 he ran the movement's New York office as a fundraiser and founding director of the IITC, seeking international allies to support treaty rights granting Native communities autonomy from the U.S. government. He traveled regularly to Geneva, this time as an AIM representative to the United Nations (UN). It is in this context that Durham met his lifelong partner and collaborator, Brazilian-born artist and activist Maria Thereza Alves, who volunteered for the IITC in 1978.

Comprising multiple factions pursuing variously independent and coordinated causes across continents, AIM warrants multiple books to fully explore. Here I focus on key tenets of spatial thinking that shaped the subsequent work of the AIM generation, highlighting essays that Durham wrote during his tenure at IITC. Indigenous leaders emphasized principles of political and cultural sovereignty from the U.S. government, a value shared with activists in Canada and other parts of Latin America who forged alliances during the same period.[25] They asserted the rights of Native peoples to live freely on their ancestral lands, confirmed by treaties that the U.S. government signed in the wake of the Declaration of Independence but repeatedly violated. In particular, activists pushed for the abolishment of the notorious Bureau of Indian Affairs (BIA), the federal agency responsible for implementing policies of Indian removal and assimilation following its establishment in 1824.

Among the most significant legislation, the General Allotment Act of 1887 (also called the Dawes Act) divided communal lands into parcels for private ownership and required that Native Americans with adequate blood quantum register with the federal government to receive a plot, while making a significant surplus available to white settlement.[26] The BIA also suppressed religious ceremonies and enforced acculturation of youths in boarding schools through the 1920s, as I discuss in greater depth in chapter 3.[27] Another spate of policies that aimed to terminate U.S. treaty obligations prompted a mass relocation of Native peoples from reservations to cities from the 1940s to the 1960s. The period known as Indian Termination fomented a new wave of activism and the creation of indigenous political organizations, setting the stage for the pan-Indian politics of AIM.[28] Despite activists' unifying rhetoric, the uneven effects of colonial policies ensured that AIM was split among factions struggling to protect or recover their traditional lands, alleviate poverty on unproductive reservations assigned to their ancestors, or address the alienation of displaced "urban Indians" who had no hope of reclaiming lost territory. As we shall see, these differences compromised the movement's collective ambitions.

Three spectacular occupations at key U.S. sites formed the public front of the movement. Robert Allen Warrior and Paul Chaat Smith stated at the outset of their formative account of AIM, "If it is recalled at all, it is as a series of photojournalistic images of Indians with bandannas and rifles courtesy of television reports from the presatellite age."[29] In 1969, a mixed group of Native Americans, many of whom arrived in the Bay Area as a result of federal relocation policies in the 1950s, launched an occupation of Alcatraz that lasted for a year and a half. The self-named "Indians of All Tribes" compared the sparse island, which featured the barracks of a former U.S. prison, to the dire conditions on Indian reservations, while playing host to movie stars, rock musicians, and journalists. In 1972, activists organized the "Trail of Broken Treaties," pointedly referencing the Trail of Tears on their march to Washington, DC, to demand the replacement of the paternalistic BIA with a new era of policies respecting Native peoples' right to self-determination. When the Nixon administration refused to meet with the protestors, the event escalated into an impromptu seizure of the BIA headquarters and a weekend of ransacking, destroying historical archives and Native American art while contributing to media stereotypes of savage, militant Natives.[30] Today AIM is best remembered for activists' armed takeover of the town of Wounded Knee on the Pine Ridge Indian Reservation in South Dakota in 1973, site of the infamous massacre of Sioux men, women, and children by U.S. cavalry in 1890.

Images of "Indians with bandannas and rifles" aired on national television almost nightly during the two-month siege. Instead of activists' hoped-for federal renegotiation of a violated 1868 Sioux Treaty, 1974 brought the trials of leaders Russell Means, Dennis Banks, and others. After, the national media fell largely silent, although the IITC and other branches of the movement remained active throughout the 1970s and into the present.[31]

Standing Rock Sioux activist and legal scholar Vine Deloria Jr. (1933–2005) published several influential treatises at the height of AIM that give shape to pan-Indian politics and philosophies of the period. A classic text in Native studies that I already discussed briefly in the introduction, *God Is Red: A Native View of Religion* (1972) presents a sustained argument for sacred lands as permanent fixtures in the worldviews of American Indians. Indigenous people engage in what Deloria called spatial thinking, anchored in specific places either continuously inhabited or collectively remembered. More than an empty container for human activities, space refers to complex, reciprocal relationships between humans and other-than-human entities, including the land itself as a life-shaping force. Political and spiritual power are derived "directly from the world around [people], from their relationships with other forms of life. Context is therefore all-important for both practice and the understanding of reality."[32] The purpose of ceremonies is to maintain or restore balance to these relations, patterning indigenous social life according to cyclical changes in the environment. In contrast, Deloria argued, the European episteme is driven by autonomous temporal concerns. Colonial societies grant primacy to progress, envisioning history as the teleological conquest of empty space by humans advancing through stages of civilization: "Time proceeds in a linear fashion. . . . At a particular point in the unraveling of this sequence, the peoples of Western Europe become the guardians of the world."[33] Rather than recognizing indigenes as coeval inhabitants of a shared earth, this cosmology construes Natives of the "New World" as primitives locked in an earlier stage of a single, dominant narrative of history. For Deloria, an essential conflict "between thinking in temporal and spatial terms" provides the philosophical underpinnings of decolonization. Hence, beneath the many protests of AIM lay "the important issue of restoring the old ways and raising the question of people and their right to a homeland; for Indians this meant a return to the ceremonial uses of lands."[34] He charged Native Americans with defending places against progress and spatial thinking against temporal triumph.

Durham's initial treatment of the philosophical dimensions of AIM complemented some aspects of Deloria's better-known argument but differed subtly in regard to conceptualizing time. His most thorough account appears in an essay titled "American Indian Culture: Traditionalism and Spiritualism in a Revolutionary Struggle," written in 1974 in an effort to garner support for the movement from liberal white Americans. Durham claimed that Western capitalist nation-states are "divided in non-connecting squares. Each represents an area of human activity or knowledge." The result of such modular specialization is the alienation of the individual from a holistic view of the relationship between parts. Durham contrasted this "square" episteme with the circular shape of indigenous societies, each "an integrated whole, and non-alienating" in which "knowledge was comprehensible to, and in the hands of, the people."[35] American Indian spiritualism recognizes no division of culture, religion, economics, history, or politics, instead basing human thought and action on the recognition that "sustenance and creation come from the earth."[36] While acknowledging the distortions of indigenous worldviews under nearly five centuries of occupation, Durham argued that surviving, adaptive forms of Native spiritualism could act as a force of "liberation" from an imposed colonial order. Importantly, however, he did not draw the same binary, competitive relationship between spatial and temporal thinking that structures Deloria's analysis. By positing a firm dividing line between cosmologies, Deloria may have inadvertently reinforced colonial representations of Native peoples as static reactionaries, clinging to place and past as history sweeps forward. By contrast, Durham emphasized that notions of time are embedded in indigenous conceptions of space. He argued that an integrated, ecological view of human society is inherently dynamic and responsive to change: "When new things come into our circle it expands. When new things come into Western society another square is added."[37] Durham envisioned an epistemology flexible enough to encompass, rather than merely oppose, colonial relations. His essay bolsters spatial thinking with a temporal dimension that ensures the openness, even worldliness, of the circle.[38]

Though cautiously optimistic as of 1974, Durham's account of indigenous spiritualism switches uneasily between past and present tenses, foreshadowing his resignation from AIM in 1979 in disillusionment and articulation of covered ground in 1988, quoted at the outset of this book.[39] He later declared the essay a mistake, bemoaning, "The FBI [Federal Bureau of Investigation] took it, doctored it, and distributed it to all the Tribal Councils to prove that AIM was 'infiltrated by communists.'"[40] His description of an expansive circle without a fixed outer limit is furthermore at odds with the legal-political definition of sovereignty that he and other AIM leaders simultaneously deployed to strategic ends. The goal of the IITC throughout the 1970s was, in his words, to "get the United Nations, and countries of the world, on our side on issues of treaty rights and sovereignty so that we can begin to negotiate with the US on a more equal basis. We want the United Nations to take official action against US colonization and treaty-breaking."[41] In turn, the organization pledged assistance to "all other sovereign people who seek their own independence."[42] This appeal to the UN borrowed the rhetoric of sovereignty from the nation-states that comprised its membership and in many ways subscribed to the "square" modularity that Durham identified as the source of colonial alienation. His writings from the early 1970s expose a paradox at the core of AIM-era nationalisms: A widely shared view that "the interconnectedness . . . of all life is sacred and key to human freedom and survival" was articulated in and through a concomitant politics of separation (one that, I will show, slides all too easily into divisive battles over identity).[43] Protecting indigenous values during AIM entailed simultaneously appropriating the colonial national model and deploying it against oppressor states.

The efforts of the IITC culminated in a delegation of Native leaders from the United States, Canada, and Latin American countries who made a case before the UN subcommittee on Racism and Decolonization in Geneva in 1977 for the recognition of indigenous communities as nations among nations. The bid formally failed, in part because the United States was a primary building block of the UN, although it planted the seeds for the nonbinding Declaration on the Rights of Indigenous Peoples that was formally adopted by the UN General Assembly in 2007.[44] Subsequently, Taiaiake Alfred, Shari M. Huhndorf, Jolene Rickard, Warrior, and others critiqued indigenous nationalism as "an inherently limited, contradictory mode of anticolonial resistance" that "simultaneously reinforces and contests colonial national power and boundaries," including divisive notions of property and identity at odds with the dynamic circle of relationships described by Durham.[45] The activities of the IITC abroad nonetheless highlight a broader AIM that unfolded through hemispheric and transnational alliances, which received almost no press coverage in the United States and remains poorly studied to this day.[46]

A staged press photograph of the Wounded Knee occupation dramatizes the degree to which spatial thinking succumbed to colonial modularity that ultimately divided the leadership of AIM (fig. 1.1). Two activists perch atop makeshift barracks erected to protect the occupied area, their backs to one another, guns raised, keeping watch. Behind them looms the Sacred Heart Catholic Church, a legacy of nineteenth-century missionaries among the

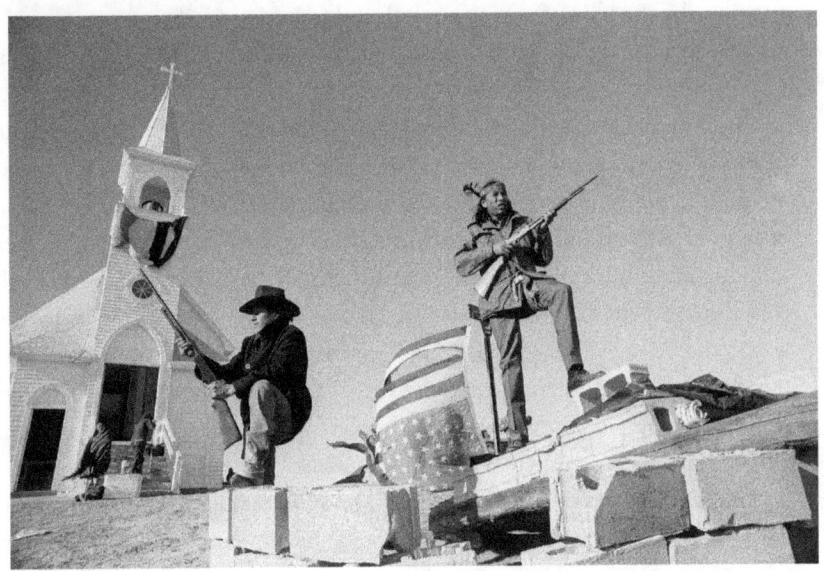

1.1 Members of the American Indian Movement and local Oglala Sioux stand guard outside the Sacred Heart Catholic Church. March 3, 1973. © Bettmann / Corbis.

Sioux. To the right, a torn American flag hangs upside-down, a potent symbol of resistance to U.S. power that nonetheless keeps nationalism in sight as a dominant force shaping the terms of opposition. Monumentalized against an expanse of sky by the low camera angle, the figures' facing backs and contrasting garb—notably a black cowboy hat and a bandanna with feather—create a binary effect, playing to long-standing colonial stereotypes recycled in the media surrounding AIM. The highly staged image calls to mind the cowboys and Indians of the western film genre, as well as the "before and after" of white assimilation staged in George Catlin's infamous *Wi-jún-jon before and after His Trip to Washington, D.C.* (1837–39). Symbolic objects—flag, cross, gun, headwear—appear as overlapping elements flattening the picture plane and blocking our view of Sioux land stretching into the distance. Place, the source of all "sustenance and creation," is transformed into a collage of signs defining the movement's public image.[47]

The photograph foreshadows the factionalism that eventually tore AIM apart. On resigning, Durham circulated a review of the movement's successes and failures. Like Smith, Warrior, and others, he described a fundamental split between "traditionalists," who remained spiritually connected to their land and cultures, and the young, urban militants, who were driven off the reservations by the twin effects of poverty and federal assimilation measures, "in many ways alienated from their roots." He traced a second fracture to the federal government's post–World War I practice of setting up a "'puppet' group of elites" on reservations, including some individuals "so alienated that they [did] not know their own hearts."[48] Federal manipulation of media images, use of anticommunist propaganda, and the infiltration of AIM by FBI agents posing as activists intensified existing ideological differences among these spatially and politically divided groups. Ultimately, factionalism eroded the communal values that AIM leaders sought to cohere. However proudly they waved the banner of "Red Power" and enumerated local triumphs, the movement waned amid infighting and distrust.[49] The U.S. media readily seized on Indian stereotypes at the expense of political complexity, further reducing AIM and its protagonists to a snapshot in black-and-white.

The writings of Anishinaabe (Ojibwa) novelist and critic Gerald Vizenor, who worked as a journalist in Minneapolis during AIM, are especially useful for assessing the role that images played as agents as well as illustrations of the movement's breakdown. In an essay first published in *American Indian Quarterly* in 1974, he argued that militant male leaders adopted colonial stereotypes in order to claim the authority to speak for all Native Americans: "The poses of tribal radicals seem to mimic the romantic pictorial images in old photographs taken by Edward Curtis for a white audience. The radicals never seem to smile, an incautious throwback to the stoical tribal visage of slower camera shutters and film speeds. The new radicals frown, even grimace at cameras, and claim the atrocities endured by all tribal cultures in first person pronouns."[50] Later, Vizenor referred to a long record of colonial images that anchor Native Americans in the past as "simulations." Postmodern theory, especially Jean Baudrillard's theorizations of the culture of late capitalism, gave him a new language to account for the representational pitfalls of AIM. He described the capacity of images circulating without referents to compel Native identification: "That invention becomes the real, so that you have to be suspicious of your own memory, your own experience; you have to suspend them because the power of the simulation has taken control of everything real."[51] Simulated Indians instigate cultural amnesia. The AIM press photograph helps us to visualize this process, as colonial symbols and identities crowd out dynamic interactions between humans and environments. While Durham's critique of AIM's leadership initially took a more sympathetic tone than Vizenor's (he ran the New York office, while Vizenor ended up on AIM's blacklist), both agreed that by assuming the attributes of simulated Indians,

Native peoples participate in colonial regimes that alienate them from one another and short-circuit the spatial thinking that might otherwise provide a foundation for indigenous alliances.[52] Importantly, their insights recall the marginalization of indigenous women from the largely male, often misogynist leadership of AIM. Feminist critiques by Huhndorf, Devon Abbott Mihesuah, Andrea Smith, and others have exposed how Red Power nationalisms replicated divisive structures of gendered oppression—a key arm of colonization—from Western nation-states.[53] It is an all-too-fitting postscript to AIM that activist fame landed Means a role in *The Last of the Mohicans*, a Hollywood blockbuster released for the Columbus Quincentennial in 1992.[54]

The "poses of tribal radicals" captured by the media were not the only images of Native Americans circulated during AIM. Notably, the dangers of simulation were well rehearsed by faculty and students at the Institute of American Indian Arts, which opened under the auspices of the BIA in 1962. Beginning in 1967, instructor Fritz Scholder (1937–2005) was hailed as the leader of a "new Indian art movement" for his painted pop portraits of Native dancers and warriors that riffed on the conventions of nineteenth-century ethnographic photography. By choosing a garish pop palette for *Monster Indian* (1968), or including a pink ice cream cone in the hand of a buffalo dancer in *Super Indian No. 2* (1971), Scholder aimed to cancel the romantic primitivism that persisted in shaping the dominant terms of Native American representation. He pointedly claimed, "I have painted the Indian real, not red," indicating trust in the capacity of images to counter Indian simulations with truths.[55] Nonetheless, Scholder's *Massacre at Wounded Knee* (1970), presciently painted three years before the AIM occupation of the historic site, delivered the "real" as a frozen corpse (fig. 1.2).[56] The work was based on a photograph of the dead body of Sioux leader Spotted Elk (also known as Chief Big Foot) propped in the snow, circulated in the wake of the 1890 massacre (fig. 1.3). Scholder eliminated the officers, isolated the body, brushed the dirty snow from his lap, swathed him in pink and green like a blooming tulip in springtime, and lifted him from the lower left of the photographic frame to the high right of the canvas. The effect is at least partially honorific, raising the chief out of the debasement to which he is assigned in the photograph. But the figure, still distorted in a pose of death, does not break the horizon line visible at the top edge of the painting to join the heroic poses of AIM activists silhouetted against the sky in 1973. Scholder did not fully resurrect Spotted Elk. The body of the leader is trapped in an impasto field of white splattered with expressionist flecks of red and brown, dirtying the transcendent space of

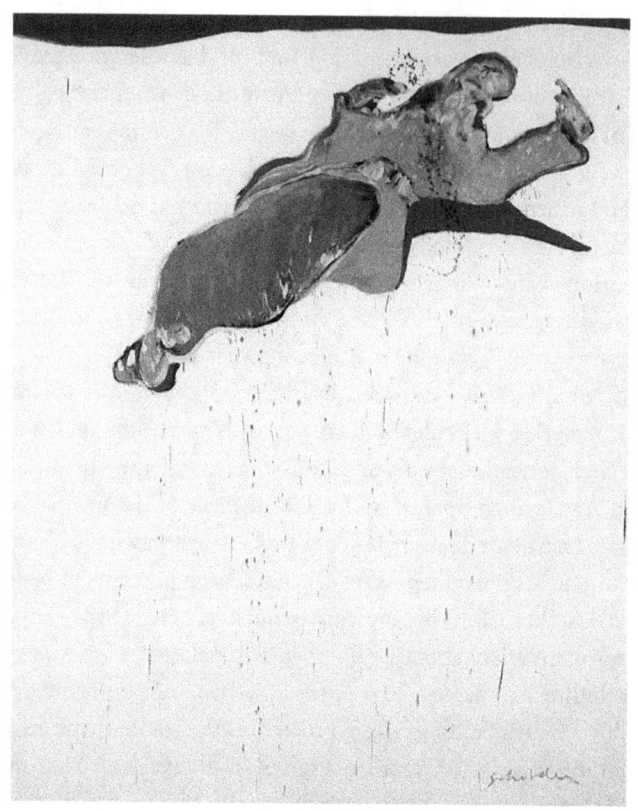

1.2 Fritz Scholder, *Massacre at Wounded Knee*, 1970. 70 × 58 in.
Collection of the Estate of Fritz Scholder.

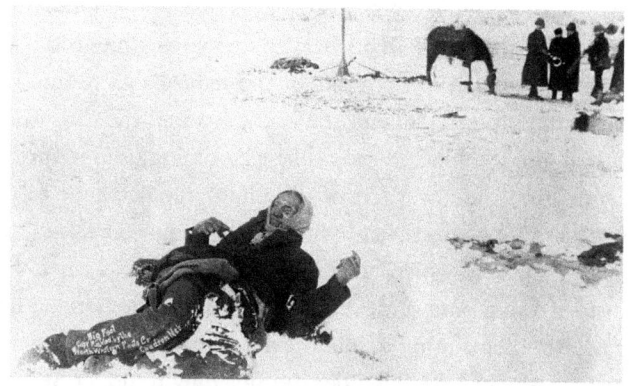

1.3 Spotted Elk (also known as Chief Big Foot), leader of the Sioux,
after the massacre at Wounded Knee, South Dakota, 1890. © Corbis.

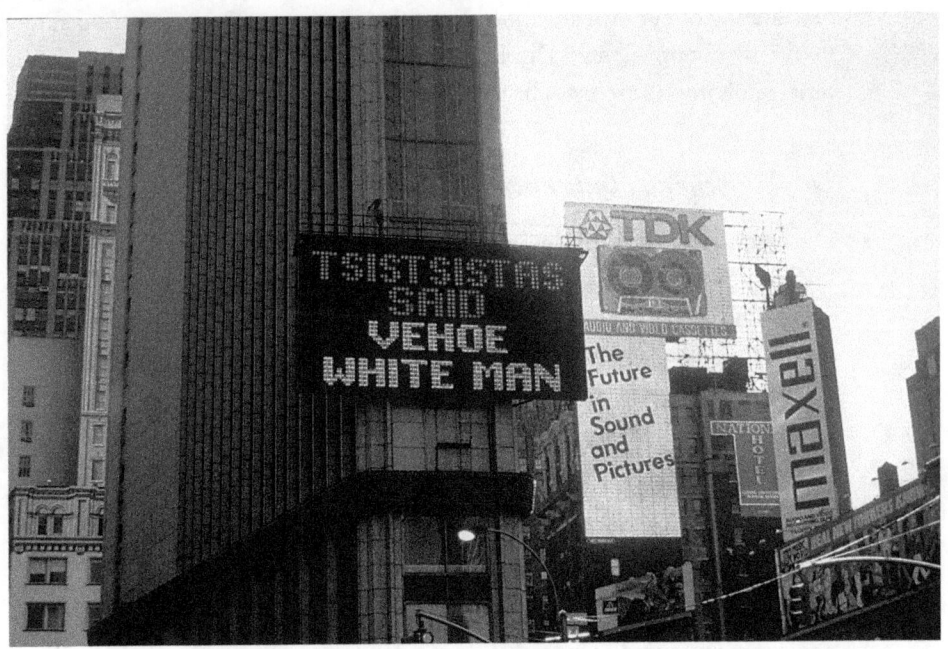

1.4 Hock E Aye Vi Edgar Heap of Birds, *In Our Language*, 1982. Spectacolor billboard, 20 × 40 ft. Times Square, New York. Courtesy of the artist.

the modernist canvas. The Sioux land blocked in the AIM photograph appears here as a colonized space delineating the contours of the dead, foreshadowing Durham's statement in 1988, "The ground has already been covered."[57]

While inheriting Scholder's suspicion of romantic images, Durham and a number of AIM-generation peers remained ambivalent about whether a "real" could be rescued from the "red" to emancipatory ends.[58] Likewise, the dream of reclaiming sovereign space where Native peoples could flourish in full complexity, freed of simulations, was cast into doubt in the wake of AIM. Instead of defending barricades, a generation of artists faced a challenge to translate the faltering politics of AIM into an all-encompassing "center," to create on occupied ground, and to speak through frameworks of non-Native invention. Cheyenne-Arapaho artist Edgar Heap of Birds's *In Our Language*, a flashing billboard in Times Square of New York City in 1982, points in the direction of this struggle (fig. 1.4). Pithy messages mixing Cheyenne with English warned tourists and shoppers, "TSISTSISTAS [Cheyenne] SAID VEHOE [spider] WHITE MAN TRAP YOU."[59] Durham's turn to art making similarly reflected awareness that "to the extent that we do not have a clear political understanding of our own situation and of the enemy's methods, we co-operate in our own oppression."[60] Displacement—conceived, like space, in both material and symbolic terms—became a predominant artistic concern.

Displacement and Institutional Critique

Durham approached the dominance of Indian simulations in both white and Native imaginations as both a means and an effect of the colonization of indigenous lands, evident in his installation *On Loan from the Museum of the American Indian* from 1985 (plate 13). Documentation of this important work is sparse. Among the miscellaneous "Sociofacts" and "Scientifacts" arranged in a display case in Kenkeleba Gallery, a site dedicated to exhibiting nonwhite artists on the Lower East Side, appears a photograph of a bespectacled man in a suit and woman in a red dress, seated in an urban landscape at night, labeled "The Indian's Parents (frontal view)." Among other family snapshots, the respectable, middle-aged couple smiles affably, failing to satisfy audiences' hunger for the signs of difference prominently displayed at the titular ethnographic museum in Upper Manhattan (the forerunner to the Smithsonian National Museum of the American Indian, created in 1990; see chapter 2).[61] A crimson, beaded, feather-bedecked, lacy little number labeled "Pocahontas' Underwear," on the other hand, is pure fetish, hyperbolizing the sexualization of the Algonquian woman at the center of America's founding myth in the form of a bordello souvenir (plate 14). "Types of Arrows" features Durham's playful handiwork: three flint arrowheads attached to wood and other scraps bear the labels "tiny," "wavy," and "short + fat." These and other materials alternately obstruct and humorously overindulge desire for a secure Native subject. If Scholder's canvases promise "real" Indians, Durham's "artifacts" frustrate the search, leading visitors in an endless loop of imperfect information: too little to cohere, too much to trust. Through their failure to coalesce, the materials circumvent the ethnographic promise of fixing Indian identity to cast into relief Western practices of collecting, ordering, and displaying colonized peoples.

These elements of *On Loan from the Museum of the American Indian* allied Durham with artists such as Fred Wilson, Adrian Piper, James Luna, and others in the 1980s who "offered a critical articulation of the history and persistence of race as a form of visual hegemony . . . building room-sized installations and public art projects structured around the twin logics of the artifact and the archive."[62] In an important study of such work, Jennifer González

rejects ethnography and identity as adequate frameworks for such efforts because, rather than aiming to represent members of a particular culture or race,
"the artwork serves as a metadiscursive critique of systems of representation"
that deny speech and agency to those same subjects.[63] An additional fragment
from the miscellany of *On Loan from the Museum of the American Indian* goes
further, embedding racial discourses inside spatial struggles. "Current Trends
in Indian Land Ownership" features a map of the United States repeated
in five successive stages (fig. 1.5).[64] The figures ranged from solid red (1492,
Native Americans occupied all of the land) to a smattering of freckles in an
expanse of white (1978, Indian reservations), recalling the field surrounding
Spotted Elk's body in Scholder's *Massacre at Wounded Knee*. Here Durham
pointedly wed ethnographic parody to the territorial politics underwriting
the long colonial relationship between Natives and whites. The diagram succinctly pictures the European conquest that first divided, then covered the
continent, while foregrounding the tools of modularization (mapping, privat-
ization of property) by which colonization is secured. It provides a "key" to the
other elements of the installation, I argue, resituating the racial codification
of Native Americans within a broader set of displacements that range from
territory, to material culture, to the very terms of indigenous representation.
Through successive loss of their lands, indigenous peoples are rendered vulnerable as "Indians" on occupied ground, their lands divided and mapped,
their histories labeled in museum displays and archives. Durham mocked the
Museum of the American Indian as part of America's field of white, a site
of tangible dispossession that doubled as a fabricator of simulations, the two
reinforcing each other. Prioritizing spatial politics over issues of racial identity
and equality distinguished the philosophical dimensions of AIM from African
American and other civil rights movements and persisted as a component of
subsequent artistic practices. Yet, like the "poses of tribal radicals," it would
waver.

Slightly restated, *On Loan from the Museum of the American Indian* warns
of the dangers of unmooring a "metadiscursive critique of systems of representation" from the spatial underpinnings of decolonization struggles. Recall that Deloria and Durham conceived of space as the product of dynamic
relationships between material and social, human and nonhuman elements.
Their accounts held that specific places were the locus not only of physical
sustenance, but also of political power. This was an important insight in the
1970s, a decade frequently credited with the rise of the so-called spatial turn
in art and cultural studies. Edward Soja, Massey, and others have thoroughly

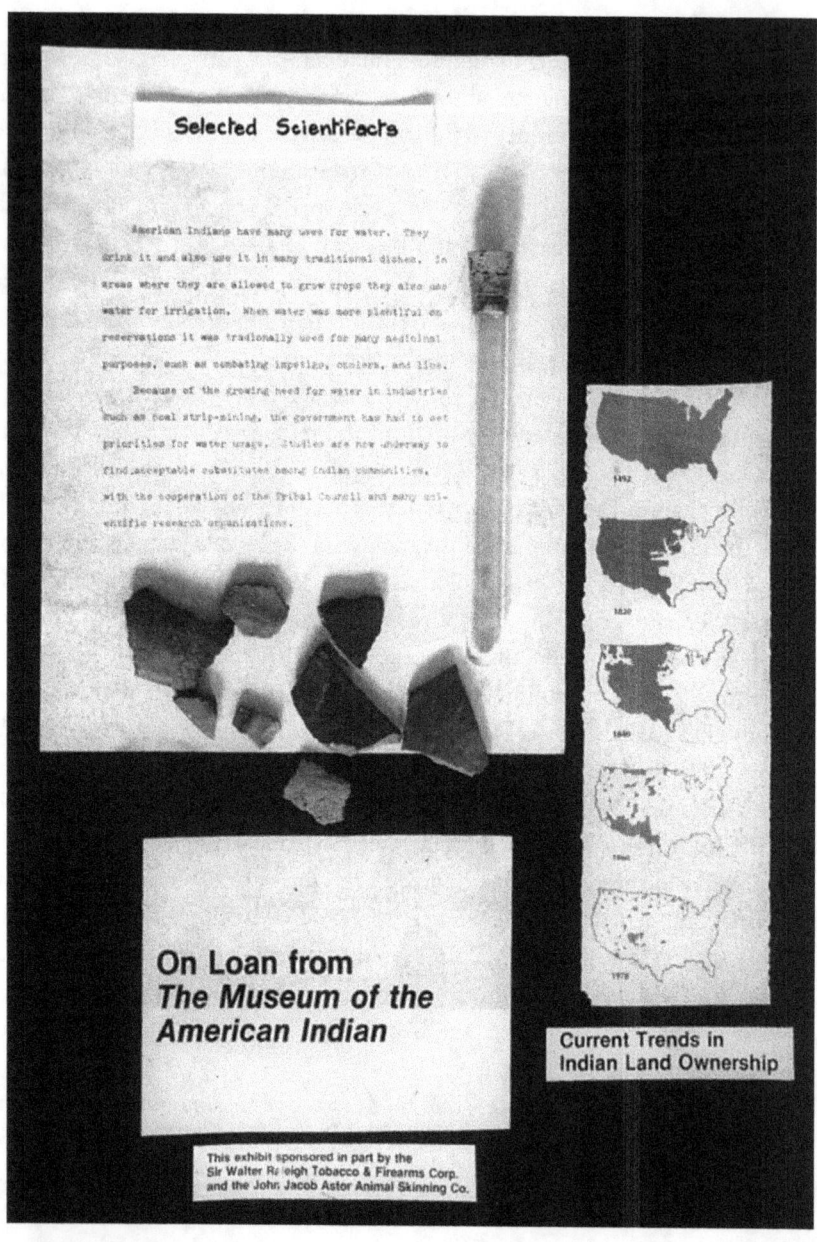

Selected Scientifacts

On Loan from
*The Museum of the
American Indian*

This exhibit sponsored in part by the
Sir Walter Raleigh Tobacco & Firearms Corp.
and the John Jacob Astor Animal Skinning Co.

Current Trends in
Indian Land Ownership

1.5 Jimmie Durham, "Current Trends in Indian Land Ownership," 1985. Element from
On Loan from the Museum of the American Indian, mixed-media installation at Kenkeleba
Gallery in New York. Courtesy of the artist. Photo by Maria Thereza Alves.

critiqued a persistent dualism apparent in period conceptions of space, alternately understood to encompass concrete, material forms to be mapped and analyzed, or mental constructs related to social processes.[65] The former view subscribes to space as inert, objectified, and awaiting conquest, as addressed by Deloria, Durham, and others during AIM and parodied in "Current Trends in Land Ownership." The latter, postmodern approach reduces space to a metaphor for representation, evident in the language of "centers" and "margins," "outsiders" and "insiders" that late twentieth-century commentators used to describe the institutionalized exclusion of artists based on their race, gender, and/or sex.[66] In both cases, through what Massey called "the association between the spatial and the fixation of meaning," space is "deprived of dynamism, and radically counterposed to time."[67] Members of the AIM generation could only accept the division of space into material or metaphor at great cost to the persistence of indigenous values. *On Loan from the Museum of the American Indian* maps a relationship between the arrest of space and the production of Indian simulations, hinting darkly that this colonial process became totalizing in light of AIM's losses. The formula of "Current Trends in Indian Land Ownership" is "white, not real."

Durham's installation finally underscores the crucial yet fundamentally limited role that objects played in the strain of institutional critique he shared with a number of AIM-generation peers. No longer on the nightly news, Native Americans retreated to marketplaces and museums, perhaps their most enduring interface with a wider public since the nineteenth century. There, indigenous stuff followed the grooves of human displacement: severed from ceremonial and everyday contexts, often through unethical and even illegal means, objects ended up fetishized in displays promising authoritative knowledge about "Indians." While I return to ethnographic collecting and colonial archives at greater length in upcoming chapters, here I emphasize that *On Loan from the Museum of the American Indian* foregrounds made-up objects as props for a parody, while relinquishing historical material culture to the prison of Manhattan collections. Implicit in this work is a suggestion that the stuff of the past—and, by extension, its makers—is beyond rescue, vanquished as fetish, specimen, and simulation. Durham left it up to his visitors to decide whether family snapshots, perhaps the only hint of an Indian "real" to appear in the installation, are as mute as their neighbor, "an Indian leg bone." In a related work titled *Artifact Piece* (1987), perhaps the best-known instance of institutional critique by an artist of the AIM generation, Luna took this process to its logical end point, querying the power of institutions to transform

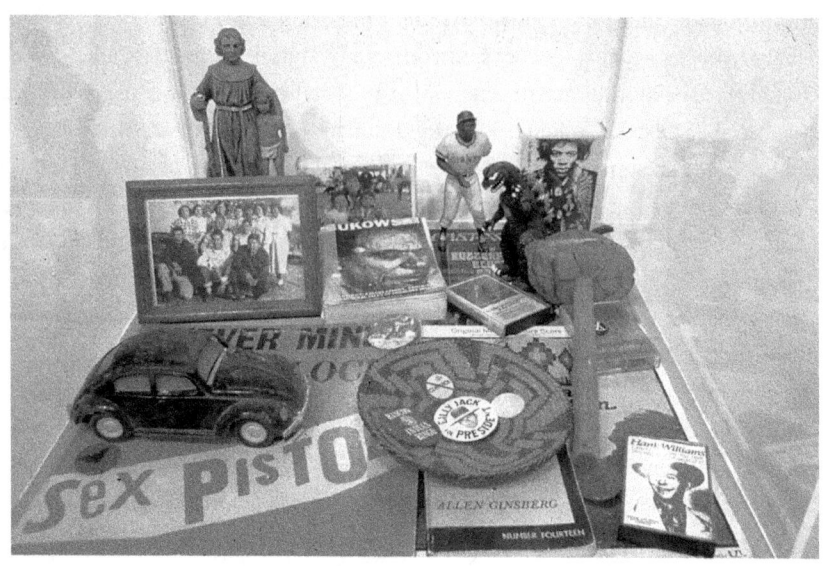

1.6 James Luna, *Artifact Piece*, detail, 1987. Performance and installation at the San Diego Museum of Man. Courtesy of the artist.

living flesh into artifact (plates 15–16). The artist put himself on display in a case at the San Diego Museum of Man for several hours, wearing nothing but a loincloth and submitting his stilled body to the curious gaze of visitors. He affixed labels pointing to unromantic details like scars from drunken brawls, as well as items in surrounding vitrines, such as his high school diploma, divorce papers, music cassette tapes, and comic books (fig. 1.6). *Artifact Piece* poses the question, can a contemporary Native person survive the deadening effects of dioramas, mannequins, and vitrines, the framing devices of the ethnographic museum? Is a living, breathing body objectified as readily as his ancestors' stuff?

González's study of *Artifact Piece* is especially pertinent to this discussion because she employs spatial terms—alternating strategies of *deterritorialization* and *reterritorialization*—to conceptualize the relationship between displaced subjects and objects queried by Durham and Luna. Loosely inspired by the theories of Gilles Deleuze and Félix Guattari, she used deterritorialization to refer to the colonial processes by which Native peoples are physically and psychologically dislocated from their traditional territories and cultures. She pointed to many groups' forced relocation ("reterritorialization") onto reservations in the nineteenth century, visited by tourists and ethnographers in search of authentic "artifacts."[68] (In fact, Luna's ancestors endured displacement earlier due to Spanish missionization, as I explore in chapter 2.) Setting aside the issue of stolen lands, González turned her attention to the materials that ended up in display cases, citing a body of recent scholarship in which the "social history of things is shown to 'situate' human subjects, to contribute to the processes of their subject formation and/or subjection."[69] By framing Native objects as exotic signifiers of difference, marketplaces and museums wield the power to fix subjects and assert truths about them. *Artifact Piece*, she argued, reversed this white-dominated process. When Luna climbed onto a bed of sand and surrounded himself with everyday stuff, he seized an opportunity "to deterritorialize objects from mainstream popular culture, in order to reterritorialize them . . . forming a circuit of relays, a circulation of signs that are parallel to, but distinct from, that mainstream."[70] González's account reflects optimism that artists can intervene in colonial institutions to create new configurations of subjects and objects, thereby recovering alternative histories and meanings.

While I find González's account seductive, I contend that both *Artifact Piece* and *On Loan from the Museum of the American Indian* register profound skepticism toward the possibility, let alone efficacy, of rescuing historical objects or their makers from the field of Indian simulations. Both works speak volumes about the field of white, effectively exposing the mechanisms of colonial displacement and fetishization, but stop short of positing an alternative Indian "real." While Durham relinquished historical collections to the simulations of the Museum of the American Indian, Luna similarly distanced his work from collections of ancestral bones, rattles, and baskets that surrounded his own body and possessions on display in the Museum of Man. Feather panties, rock-and-roll albums, and divorce papers perform the work of deconstruction by marking their difference from nearby indigenous ceremonial and everyday objects, implying that the latter are anachronisms. By relinquishing these nonhuman bearers of history, both artworks hint that past indigenous worlds of material and meaning are beyond reconstruction. They inadvertently affirm the power of white institutions to categorize Native cultures as romantic relics, by suggesting that live subjects can escape the deadening effects of ethnographic display only by resorting to postmodern parody. This attitude was widespread in the 1980s, echoed in Heap of Birds's mantra, "No beads—no trinkets."[71] Too readily accepting the colonial severing of present from past and subjects from objects proved to be detrimental to spatial thinking.

The Postmodern Trickster

In contrast to *On Loan from the Museum of the American Indian* and *Artifact Piece*, Durham's contemporaneous sculptures made from animal skulls join institutional critique to indigenous stories and the materials made meaningful therein. In a bulletin published in 1984, Durham offered an origin tale for this body of work. He described his relationship to Coyote, an important trickster among the Cherokee and other indigenous North American communities: "When I was 13 or so I had to go out into the woods and find my real name. Coyote, who invented death and singing, was the spirit who gave me my name. As is often the case, he also gave me a gift. This is what he gave me as a name gift: that I would always see whatever was dead if it were within my field of vision. For more than thirty years I have seen every dead bird and animal every day wherever I am. So it became necessary to see if that was a usable gift or just a dirty trick that would drive me crazy."[72] Long before he was active in New York galleries, Durham made his gift "usable," for example when he painted a badger skull found in Geneva and enlivened it with a button eye in 1971.[73] In 1982, Durham erected a storefront titled *Manhattan Festival of the Dead* at Kenkeleba Gallery, featuring deer, horse, rodent, human, and other bones crafted with paint, feathers, shells, and beads and mounted on rough-hewn wood bases. The installation mocks the meeting of totemic and tourist forms in reservation trading posts, crowded curio shops, domestic "Indian corners," ethnographic museums, and, finally, an art gallery in New York, where some visitors missed the irony and eagerly paid the asking price of five dollars a head.[74]

Next Durham began to fuse bones, shells, and feathers to spare lumber, car bumpers, and other scraps of the automobile age. The latter can be considered the "dead" stuff of modern capitalism, commodities that have lost their use value and are consigned to obsolescence. The resulting bricolages bridge the modern bifurcation of ethnography and art history by wedding materials coded as "primitive" to cast-off industrial objects revalued in an avant-garde tradition of the readymade stretching from Marcel Duchamp to Robert Rauschenberg. Nailed, glued, and garishly painted with their seams still showing, works such as *Tluhn Datsi* (Cherokee for "panther," 1984) resist consumption as emblems of purified nature or "primitive" peoples more readily than the organic totems of *Manhattan Festival of the Dead* (fig. 1.7). It is notable that Durham made and exhibited many such sculptures in Manhattan around the time of the controversial exhibition *"Primitivism" in 20th*

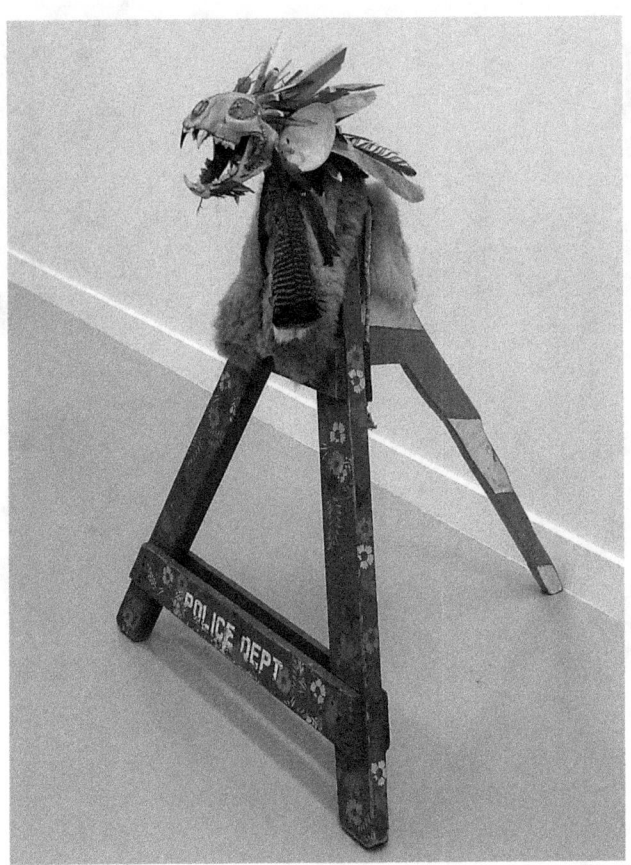

1.7 Jimmie Durham, *Tluhn Datsi*, 1984. Puma skull, feathers, fur, turquoise, acrylic paint, shells, wood, 103 × 91 × 81 cm. First exhibited in *A Matter of Life and Death and Singing*, Alternative Museum, New York. Collection of Mimi Dusselier, Belgium. Photo by Jessica L. Horton.

Century Art: Affinity of the Tribal and the Modern, which took place in 1984 at the Museum of the Modern Art in New York (discussed in chapter 4). By visibly mixing up object categories and values, his works traverse an associated hierarchy of human subjects that long authorized European and American artists to appropriate and otherwise seek "affinities" with the material culture of anonymous Native Americans. Conjuring an unfinished history of modernist exclusion, Durham sought to interrupt the smooth passage of what he perceived as a "very closed, very satisfied and self-congratulatory discourse on Postmodernism."[75]

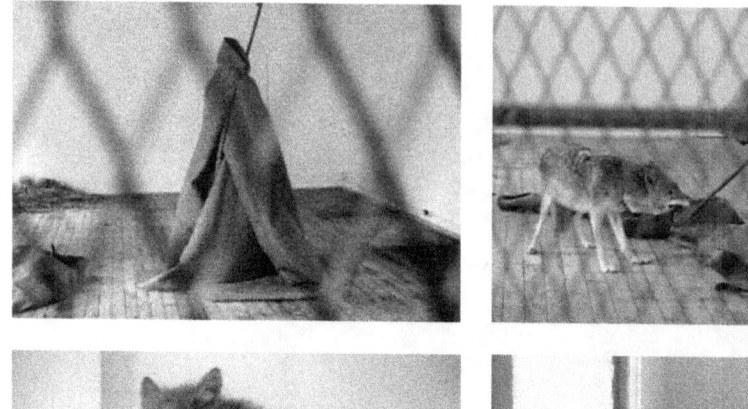

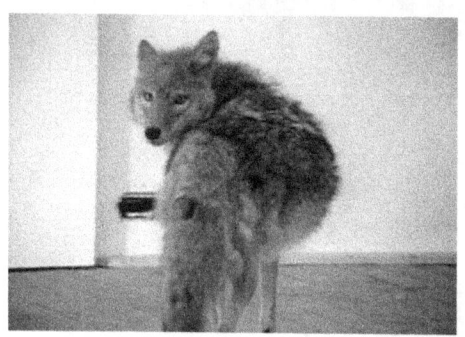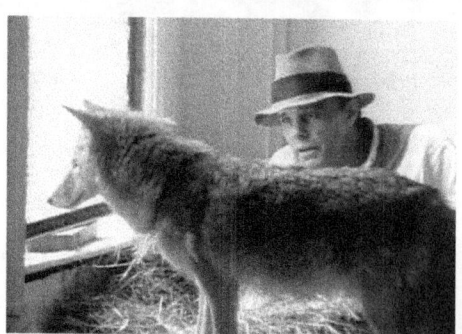

1.8–1.11 Helmut Wietz, stills from documentary of Joseph Beuys's performance *I Like America and America Likes Me*, 1974. 16 mm film (black and white, sound), 37:00. Collection Walker Art Center, Minneapolis. McKnight Acquisition Fund, 2008. Courtesy of the artist.

Not Joseph Beuys' Coyote (1990), among the last works in which Durham directly referenced his name giver, helps us to envision the fate of his "gift" in late twentieth-century art discourse and practices (plate 17). Durham's title points to a famous performance piece, *I Like America and America Likes Me* (1974), during which German artist Joseph Beuys shared a room with a live coyote at the René Block Gallery in New York for eight hours a day over a period of three days (figs. 1.8–1.11). In the wake of the AIM occupation of Wounded Knee, Beuys dressed all in felt and carried a wooden cane to play the role of a shaman, attempting to reckon with the coyote as a representative of "the whole American trauma with the Indian, the Red Man."[76] A maligned murderer of suburban house cats, the coyote symbolizes a once-pure natural world now contained and degraded, as well as Native Americans whose demise Beuys linked to the disappearing land. Luna, who similarly parodied Beuys's performance by sporting a bright striped blanket, moccasins, and a golf club in *Petroglyphs in Motion* (2000), interpreted *I Like America and America Likes Me* as a "statement about a culture that people know more about from the movies than from reality."[77] The logic of the performance rests on a simulation, as indigenes and nature are married in the figure of the coyote and made accessible to the European artist through vaguely mystical means.

Durham's title asserts that the coyote in question is Beuys's construction, pointedly canceling the German artist's authority over indigenous representation. Beginning with negation rather than nominalization, the title further underscores the seemingly impossible condition for the emergence of Durham's work: it can only be defined by what it is not. What are the physical manifestations of this negativity? Photographs of *Not Joseph Beuys' Coyote*, a work now lost, reveal a small painted animal skull with shells for ears fastened on top of a stick with a side-view mirror and an animal horn attached like arms. Durham's characteristic act of rejoining castoff scraps of nature and culture in a painted ensemble granted each component a new purpose in concert, transforming them into the limbs and organs of a single patchwork body. The scrappy, ad hoc appearance of the work contrasts with the heroic nostalgia of *I Like America and America Likes Me*. Peering in the mirror for a glimpse of the receding past, a viewer would encounter her own image, a constellation of projected desires reflected back at her.[78] *Not Joseph Beuys' Coyote* appears to grin and wave, pleased to make a mockery of pathos.

In an important essay from 1992, "The Necessity of Jimmie Durham's Jokes," Richard Shiff argued that humor was an essential strategy for navigating, even rehabilitating, colonial displacement. He casted representation as dangerous fixity, a romantic trap set by a voracious dominant culture for Natives naive enough to stumble into. In turn he prescribed *perpetual mobility* as the only safe option. While Shiff acknowledged that humor is an important component of Native American cultures, he saw Durham's deployment as a "necessary" response to the artist's particular colonial situation: "Durham's comic and ironic elements open up discursive routes of escape from the clichés of character and value that his Euro-American culture—he does not deny that it must in some sense be *his*—imposes upon [him]. The jokes insure that his art avoids all claims to self-mastery as well as any possibility that this particular 'Indian' identity will ever be mastered by the colonizers."[79] With nowhere to go but straight into a trap, Durham's only "escape" lies in parody and puns. No matter how authoritative representations of Indians purport to be, they "always retain a reserve of meaning. Art that jokes exploits that reserve and becomes the natural enemy of categorization, enclosure, and fixity."[80]

Humor is a getaway car for subjects perpetually in danger of entrapment and objectification (or a one-way ticket to France).

Many critics of Durham's work followed in Shiff's vein, conflating the artist with a mischievous culture hero known as the trickster. Obscene, silly, wise, mobile, changeable, and endlessly creative, sacred tricksters cross social boundaries in Native American songs and stories to provoke outrage and delighted laughter. Never mind that human subjects typically assume the role of tricksters in sanctioned ceremonial contexts, often culminating in a call to order.[81] In the late twentieth century, artists and critics appropriated tricksters from Native American and sometimes African contexts to further postmodern critiques of representation. Tricksters appeared to answer a problem widely discussed among postcolonial theorists, namely how subaltern subjects might "speak" in resistance to colonial authorities dominating frameworks of reception.[82] Jean Fisher, a curator and critic who regularly collaborated with Durham on exhibitions in the 1980s, wrote with characteristic flourish, "Talking in tongues, contemporary Trickster is the ventriloquist in the white man's masquerade, opening the colonial discourse to the subversive effects of parody and irony, where the façade of Absolute Truth shatters in the sound of a Babelian laughter."[83] Laura Turney described Durham as "the 'coyote' or 'trickster,' mischievous and cunning—an artist who uses irony to strip away the ornamental packaging that bounds American Indians in, what remains for many, a colonial present."[84] A trickster-like capacity for continual transgression guaranteed his valorization as an indigenous Jacques Derrida—or, in Lucy R. Lippard's memorable terms, a "postmodernist 'savage.'"[85]

Durham's animal skulls do seem to perform Houdini-like acts of escape for which the postmodern trickster was celebrated: the materials vacillate between categories of art and junk, life and death, nature and culture, past and present, seemingly without rest. At the same time, Durham's account of Coyote's gift from 1984 points to an unresolved tension within period conceptions of tricksters. His highly personal story relates how an indigenous culture hero bestowed on the artist the ability to "see whatever was dead" in his environment. The artist in turn recognizes his own responsibility to make this gift "usable," rather than a "dirty trick." In contrast to the negativity of *Not Joseph Beuys' Coyote*'s title, the story raises the possibility that the circle of relations that Durham argued was integral to spatial thinking during AIM might survive ongoing colonial occupation, bolstering the agency of humans and other-than-human persons to mutually enlivening ends. Once reattached to the story and the many other skull works Durham completed in the 1980s,

Not Joseph Beuys' Coyote joins a family of orphans and outcasts—a material collective that points beyond anthropocentric "frameworks of identity" and foreshadows his later animation of stone (discussed in the epilogue). The capacity to grin and wave, to affirm ongoing life and sociability, grants Durham's skull works a tangible, lively presence apart from the work of colonial deconstruction. In contrast, the trickster who moves so effortlessly across the pages of period criticism is a wholly discursive formation. In her, a celebratory modernist trope of exile lingers, repackaged as postmodern critique.[86] The trickster's refusal to be located is furthermore presented as the only viable response to the totalizing power of dominant cultural institutions and simulations. The marginal, subversive other in a colonial formation, she assumes the perpetual burden of undermining, eluding, and critiquing colonial authority. This is a displacement without end.

In hindsight, we can see that the postmodern trickster is not as adaptable as promised. Although Shiff's analysis of humor promises emancipation from the "trap" of imposed identities, critics who championed trickster mobility assigned a new one to Native artists. Curating the work of Métis artist Edward Poitras in the Canadian Pavilion of the Venice Biennale in 1995, for example, Plains Cree and Blackfoot curator Gerald McMaster wrote, "Trickster has lain dormant for five hundred years, but now he has surfaced in many new guises, particularly the guise of artists. . . . Today, these artists can enunciate their identity and alterity in surprising juxtapositions."[87] In 1999, art historian Allan J. Ryan published *The Trickster Shift*, in which he argued for a shared trickster "spirit" uniting two decades of contemporary indigenous art from Canada and the United States.[88] Although Durham's work was pivotal to trickster discourse in the 1980s, it is nowhere to be seen in Ryan's book. Yet this hardly matters, for as trickster came to stand in for the identity of all Native artists, a material remainder—their artwork—was left unincorporated and undertheorized. With the exception of Poitras's *Coyote* (1986), a composite creature made from the bones of seven coyotes, most works by the fifteen artists included in *The Trickster Shift* bear little resemblance to Durham's skull works.[89] A painting by Harry Fonseca, *Wish You Were Here* (c. 1986), features his Maidu trickster alter ego Coyote in a Hawaiian shirt toting a camera during a visit to a Southwest Pueblo, a figural solution to problems of indigenous representation that Durham explicitly rejected (fig. 1.12).[90] Ryan corralled disparate material and conceptual approaches into a single, celebrated identity, not unlike the "Indians with bandannas and rifles" who waved the banner of Red Power on the nightly news two decades earlier. In the after-

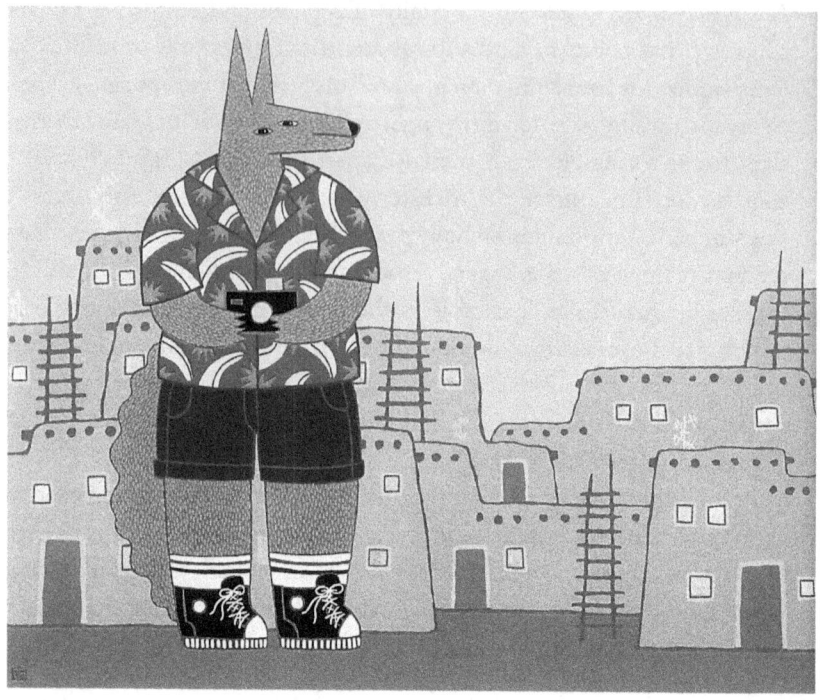

1.12 Harry Fonseca, *Wish You Were Here*, c. 1986. Acrylic on canvas, 61 × 76 cm. Courtesy of the Fonseca estate.

math of AIM, the postmodern trickster bore the projected desires of artists and critics longing for new sites of resistance when they were increasingly hard to find. In an ultimate display of irony, she performed a backflip and landed smack in the middle of another stereotype.

The Columbus Quincentennial and the Indian Arts and Crafts Act

Not all artists of the AIM generation answered shared challenges with strategies of parody and irony. My account of mocking critiques by Durham and Luna is balanced by the persistent investment in abstraction and indigenous aesthetics shared by Kay WalkingStick and Robert Houle, which chart a slightly different course through the 1980s in the final two chapters of this book. Artists of the AIM generation did not share a unified trickster spirit any more than "frameworks of identity." Nonetheless, a committed group of curators and artists worked to create shared exhibition opportunities for a network of Native artists recruited across the United States and Canada, citing a range of political and philosophical justifications much like AIM activists of the previous decade. Although he expressed concern that group shows would indulge white audiences' desire for touristic entertainment, Durham was no stranger to this scene. He regularly exhibited alongside Luna, WalkingStick, and Edgar Heap of Birds and wrote admiring essays about their work, including in the *Decade Show* catalogue. He joined Fisher to cocurate a traveling group show, *"Ni'Go Tluhn a Doh Ka" (We Are Always Turning Around on Purpose)*, in 1986 and *We the People* at Artists Space in New York in 1987.[91] Acknowledging an affective dimension to such endeavors, WalkingStick described a "large extended family" of artists who "love each other and respect each other's work," to which Luna added, "sometime like the ones many of us come from; dysfunctional!"[92] These tenuous alliances were tested by two overlapping events: the Columbus Quincentennial in 1992, which occasioned the voicing of a collective will to resist a monolithic colonial power, and implementation of the IACA, which policed artistic identities according to membership in federally recognized tribes and prompted the airing of deep divisions.

The efforts of the AIM generation to create collective artistic platforms culminated in a series of important publications and exhibitions marking the Quincentennial. While opinions varied widely on whether the artists shared a common culture anchored in indigenous precedents, most commentators seemed to agree on the content of an enemy. Robert Houle's essay in the catalogue for *Land, Spirit, Power: First Nations at the National Gallery of Canada*, a major exhibition in which he cocurated the work of Durham, Luna, WalkingStick, and fifteen others, effectively captures a common proclivity to oppose a colossal colonizer that cohered with particular force around the remembrance of Christopher Columbus in 1992. Houle began with an image of hemispheric diversity: "In 1492, when 'America' was ostensibly 'discovered,' there were untold numbers of indigenous societies, untold numbers of languages and dialects, architecture to rival any, imperial city states with astronomical observatories and solar calendars, a mathematical concept of zero, an extensive knowledge of natural medicine and the healing arts, highly developed oral traditions, and above all, a spiritual comprehension of the universe, a sense of the natural and supernatural, and a profound sense of the sacred." In drawing contemporary artists together some five centuries later, Houle wished to harness the collective force of "local and temporal narratives" to counter indigenous disinheritance by the "master narrative of Christian patriarchal hegemony, Western European ethnocentricity."[93] Notably, the singular and seamless identity in Houle's account is European, not Indian. He suggests that the ultimate purpose of collective indigenous resistance was not cultural unification, but the restoration and maintenance of diversity.

The monolithic colonizer of Houle's account was invoked in countless essays, exhibitions, protests, and performances in 1992. Luna described the poverty and alcoholism on his home turf, the La Jolla Indian Reservation, as the long arm of Columbus to a scholarly audience at the College Art Association, followed by the sarcastic punch line, "Call Me in '93."[94] An illustrated version of his talk was published in an unprecedented issue of *Art Journal* devoted to "Recent Native American Art," coedited by WalkingStick and art historian W. Jackson Rushing.[95] In it McMaster summarized the drive of a major traveling exhibition he curated: "The aboriginal artists and writers in 'INDIGENA' question the process by which European colonists came to dominate the continent's original inhabitants."[96] Elsewhere Salish artist and activist Jaune Quick-to-See Smith introduced her own twelve-venue, multiyear endeavor, *The Submuloc Show/Columbus Wohs*, as a "response to the celebration of the holocaust of the Americas."[97] Durham's contribution to the latter related that "Submuloc, and those who followed him into the 20th century, backed onto the shores of this hemisphere blindly, facing Europe.... He came from a primitive society given to torture and greed" and "shot to kill." Hence the artists in *The Submuloc Show/Columbus Wohs* were "still trying to turn things around."[98] Echoing these sentiments in a series of overtly political works created for *Land, Spirit, Power* and *The Submuloc Show/Columbus Wohs*, WalkingStick explained that she wanted the public "to recognize the truth that Columbus was a murderer and a slave trader, and he was only the first in a long line of murderous adventurers who 'won the west.'"[99]

The mix of colonial dominance, indigenous erasure, and unending resistance shared by these and other accounts helps to explain the melancholic strain in much of the work on display in 1992. Quick-to-See Smith's darkly humorous *Paper Dolls for a Post-Columbian World with Contributions from the U.S. Government* (1991–92) includes an option to dress Barbie and Ken Plenty Horses in "matching smallpox suits for all Indian families after U.S. Gov't sent wagon loads of smallpox infected blankets to keep our families warm."[100] WalkingStick's *The Wizard Speaks, the Cavalry Listens* (1992) meditates on the tangled threads of colonial dispossession and racial violence, indicating the illusory nature of historical "progress" from the perspective of its indigenous victims (fig. 1.13). She painted four copper plates with gray figures sprawled on white snow, abstracted, like Scholder's *Massacre at Wounded Knee* two de-

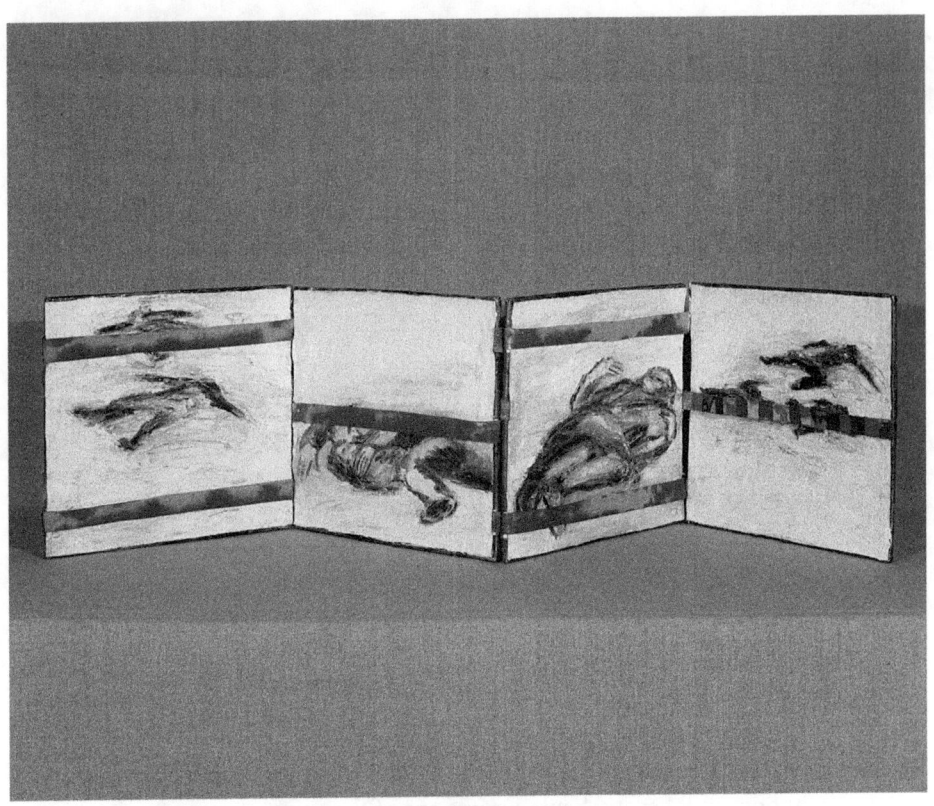

1.13 Kay WalkingStick, *The Wizard Speaks, the Cavalry Listens*, 1992. Copper, oil stick, canvas, fabric belt from Guatemala on wood, 12 × 11 × 2 in. (folded); 12 × 14 × ½ in. (opened flat). Collection of the artist.

cades earlier, from nineteenth-century photographs documenting the dead. On the back appears text from an editorial by L. Frank Baum, author of *The Wonderful Wizard of Oz*, declaring nine days before the massacre, "The Whites, by law of conquest, by justice of civilization, are masters of the American continent, and the best safety of frontier settlements will be secured by the total annihilation of the few remaining Indians."[101] The statement by a beloved American writer exposes the colonial ideologies underpinning maps and massacres alike. Red-stained strips of Guatemalan fabric used to bind copper plates that unfold like a Mesoamerican codex connect the atrocity of Wounded Knee to the longer story of colonization across the Americas. On the five-hundred-year anniversary of Columbus's fateful voyage, the history on view in *The Wizard Speaks, the Cavalry Listens* was defined by Baum's dialectic of European settlement and indigenous elimination. The proud, upright "warriors" who occupied Wounded Knee in 1973 were nowhere to be seen. In their place was a memorial to hemispheric violence, perhaps the only Indian "real" to which artists could agree in the wake of AIM.

Amid the heightened visibility of the Quincentennial, Durham inadvertently landed in the center of an embittered public battle over Native American identity. Planned exhibitions of the artist's work at the American Indian Contemporary Arts gallery in San Francisco and the Center for Contemporary Arts in Santa Fe in 1991 were canceled when he refused to provide paperwork proving his Cherokee bloodline in light of the newly implemented IACA.[102] The "truth in advertising" law requires indigenous artists to certify their tribal heritage in order to label their work "Native American," ostensibly to protect the lucrative Indian art market centered in Santa Fe from the threat of foreign knockoffs. The penalty for violating the act is up to $250,000 in fines or a five-year prison term, or both.[103] Chippewa painter David Bradley and the New Mexico–based Native American Artists Association were instrumental in promoting the legislation and lobbying for the cancellation of exhibitions in violation of the law. They launched a public hunt for "Wannabees, a tribe of the master race" (i.e., whites posing as Native American). Durham, who is not federally registered with the Cherokee Nation and had garnered unprecedented attention from non-Native scholars, critics, and institutions well beyond Santa Fe, was one of the group's targets.[104]

The IACA reiterated colonial definitions of racial identity anchored in nineteenth-century federal Indian policy, supported by some Native individuals while challenged by others as anathema to indigenous systems of value.[105] As WalkingStick clarified in an essay in *Artforum* in 1992, to be a registered member of the Cherokee Nation requires tracing one's bloodline to an ancestor who enlisted with the federal government following the passage of the devastating General Allotment Act. Whether in protest of the violation of treaties, the breakup of communally held lands and associated kinship networks, and the "humiliation" of being "catalogued," or for reasons of economic destitution and displacement, many Cherokee could not or chose not to comply. While WalkingStick's Cherokee grandfather worked as a clerk in an Oklahoma enrollment office in the late nineteenth century, Durham's ancestors headed west prior to the Trail of Tears and did not settle on a federally designated reservation. He is among many self-identified Native people who cannot produce paperwork.[106]

This difference aside, both artists used the IACA as an opportunity to address broader ideologies underpinning the U.S. government's regulation of Indian blood, land, and art. Durham issued an oft-quoted open letter protesting, "Authenticity is a racist concept which functions to keep us enclosed in 'our world' (in our place) for the comfort of a dominant society." He stated, "I am Cherokee, but my work is simply contemporary art [and] not 'Indian art' in any sense. . . . I do not want a Cherokee license to make money selling 'Indian' art or any other art."[107] The law and related attacks were further affirmation of "just how badly [AIM] lost."[108] While Durham insisted that the address of a Cherokee could be as worldly as that of any other artist, the reception of his work in the United States, which reduced indigenous perspectives to battles over assigned colonial identities, rendered such a project illegible.[109] When he moved to Europe in 1994, the artist announced that he would no longer make bricolages from bones. In an interview from 1995, during which Dirk Snauwaert noted that people found such elements charming, he responded, "And of course I don't trust it and I see now I'm going to have to find a way out of that."[110] Critics looked to dead animals as forensic evidence of Durham's Cherokee credentials, a trap that the IACA debates baldly exposed.

It is a final irony that Durham's tenure in Europe and subsequent decision to stop exhibiting in the United States are characterized as "voluntary exile": "He made it over the wall. Jimmie Durham is our Houdini."[111] Such claims echo efforts to redeem displacement as "a potent, even enriching motif," despite Durham's efforts to map transatlantic interdependencies between modernist exile, colonial displacement, and activist alliances.[112] The repurposing of an exilic trope likewise overlooks Durham's increasing engagement with forms of artistic itinerancy in the context of neoliberal globalization and art biennials, themes that I take up in greater detail in subsequent chapters. For now, I posit Durham's emigration and gradual omission of bones as a refusal, not of his Cherokee identity—which was never the subject of his art—but of a strain of critical practice that succumbed to "frameworks of identity" and thereby failed to "address the entire world."[113] As the coda of *La poursuite du bonheur* hints, Durham's tenure abroad is less about escaping into a blue sky than doubling back, in search of new tools to uncover the colonized ground of modernity.

Carpentry, History, and World

Among Durham's first projects in Europe following his move to Cuernavaca, *Mataoka Ale Attakulakula Anel Guledisgo Hnihi (Pocahontas and the Little Carpenter in London)*, a four-part multimedia installation created for Matt's Gallery in London in 1988, charts a course apart from the stuttering trajectory of postmodern trickster.[114] Notably, a carpenter, rather than a coyote, guides us through the vast assembly of elements. Durham merged two distinct indigenous voyages: that of the famous Algonquian woman Mataoka (known as Pocahontas to the British colonists), who accompanied her husband, Englishman John Rolfe, their infant son Thomas, and approximately ten other members of the Powhatan nation to London in 1616, and the little-known Cherokee diplomat Attakulakula, or "The Fixer" (translated by the English as "The Little Carpenter"), who sailed to England with a delegation of six others in 1730. Pocahontas appears in *Mataoka Ale Attakulakula Anel Guledisgo Hnihi* primarily as a simulation, raising doubts that she can be rescued from the "terrible unreality of a false story badly told," as Durham wrote in a pamphlet accompanying the exhibition.[115] Yet the artist's treatment of the legacy of Attakulakula reframes both travel tales inside an affirmative, nonanthropocentric Cherokee understanding of history as world.

Pocahontas has been made to play many roles in the United States: "medicine woman, spy, entrepreneur, diplomat," Indian princess, Christian convert, and Englishman's wife.[116] It is difficult to know which, if any, of her circulating images corresponds to the historical person, daughter of a powerful Algonquian chief who repeatedly mediated relations between the Powhatan Confederacy and the English colony of Jamestown. The information in history books relies on accounts of Jamestown captain John Smith, her husband Rolfe, and other Englishmen. The problem with these sources, Durham explained elsewhere, is that "the colonists arrived with script in hand. They invented the story of Pocahontas, and made it replace her own history, as a way of owning her and her people."[117] Most importantly for my analysis, Pocahontas has been appropriated as a national origin myth to bolster U.S. legitimacy in the face of violent colonization. Ziauddin Sardar summarized, "The earliest iconography of the new continent depicted America as a nubile, available maiden with long, loose tresses. It has been argued that the representation betokens a woman ripe for rape; certainly, the languor of the sexually charged figure of America was intended to suggest she was at the very least ready to be husbanded by Europe."[118] Durham had already mocked this fantasy with the tassels and red feathers of "Pocahontas' Underwear" in *On Loan from the Museum of the American Indian* (see plate 14).

While some scholars hope that a "real" Pocahontas can speak through the "red," *Mataoka Ale Attakulakula Anel Guledisgo Hnihi* confronts us with characteristic skepticism.[119] In a pamphlet accompanying the installation, Durham explained, "When I began researching the lives and myths of Pocahontas and Attakulakula in London I found such a morass of lies and of important truths untold, I realized that there was no way I could present a counter-narrative, even on the most elemental level."[120] The carved wooden face of the figure who stands in for Pocahontas exhibits the gaunt stoicism of a cigar store Indian, a type of wooden sculpture carved in a caricature of a Native American first used to advertise tobacco from the Americas in Britain in the seventeenth century.[121] Her fleshy lips are downturned, her mismatched eyes stare vacantly, and a pair of neon New Age feathers droop from her wig of cornrows (plate 18). A glittery faux-gold medallion around her neck and a spill of fake roses and cigarettes on the gallery floor below lend an air of cheap romance, indicating that Native women's bodies, like tobacco crops, accrued value as commodities in an imperial economy. Beneath the figure's head, the semblance of portraiture gives way to raw construction. Pocahontas's "torso" is composed of scrap lumber resting on a wooden chair. Beneath it a mournful, bodiless black gown falls to the floor. Fisher's sober description of *On Loan from the Museum of the American Indian* as "a portrait of a body dismembered and reassigned to the dead space of the museum" is suited to the pathos of this portion of the installation.[122] Pocahontas even assumed an exchange value within Durham's artistic practice. He later reconstituted her head for a sculpture titled *La Malinche* (1988–91), after the Nahua woman who famously became the lover and interpreter for the Spanish conquistador Hernán Cortés, on view in Antwerp for the exhibition *America's Bride of the Son: 500 Years of Flemish Influence on Latin American Art* in 1992 (plate 19).[123] She shares a condition of negativity with *Not Joseph Beuys' Coyote*: not John Smith's (or Walt Disney's) Pocahontas.[124]

While photographs indicate a life-sized Pocahontas, the painted wood sculpture of a spindly man in colonial garb at her side stands around two feet tall. His orange-mustached mouth gapes open and arms fling wide as if to amplify a miniature voice. Still, he requires a high stool painted in red, white, and blue to approach the shoulders of his companion; his diminutive form assumes powers of signification with the aid of British imperial might. If Pocahontas is substitutable, Durham rendered the colonizers equally so: the figure is *The Two Johns*, that is, Smith and Rolfe at once. The arrival of humor at the scene appears belated, mocking and undermining patriarchal dominance too late to rescue Pocahontas from the burden of colonial fantasy. The unlikely couple occupies one corner of the gallery, the base of their ensemble visible through plywood frames erected as makeshift walls. Visitors could enter their "SHRINE," announced in bold letters at the doorway. Posters made from the colonial image archive are pasted along the interior walls, bearing the simulated faces of Pocahontas. The most famous among them is a painting after an engraving by Dutch artist Simon van de Passe, reproduced in the pamphlet accompanying the exhibition with this caption: "'An unbeeleeving creature, namely Pokahuntas,' was taken to England by John Rolfe and baptized the Lady Rebecca. In 1616, an unknown artist painted this proper portrait of the transformed child of nature."[125] Her pale complexion, confident gaze, and elaborate imperial attire contrast with the downcast abjection of Durham's figure. This is a shrine to an invented romance, a script already written, a circuit of simulations.

Near the entrance to "SHRINE," Durham appointed a "GUARDIAN" in tribute to the young delegate who returned from London to become a savvy leader in the ongoing negotiations between the Cherokee, French, and English in the years leading up to the American Revolution (plate 20). Photographs reveal a masklike red face with golden curlicues and turquoise eyes that suggest the figure's multiple heritages and affiliations. The head is anchored in a base of wood planks and branches that are crudely cinched together with twine. Durham associated the figure with the honorific Cherokee title of Colona or Raven, identifying among Attakulakula's many historical roles one who watched closely for danger. A clipboard dangles from a carved stick arm, bearing a reproduction of the preamble of the 1730 Treaty of Whitehall between Cherokee delegates and the British Ministry of Trade in London. The treaty perilously promised to the Cherokee—in vague terms with many flourishes—the friendship and guardianship of the British Crown and "the privilege of living wherever they please" in return for British title to Cherokee lands and rights to exclusive trade (thereby expelling French and Spanish competitors).[126] From the figure's other arm juts the form of a horned rattlesnake, a surviving element that continues to bear the name "Attakulakula." The serpent appears to be brandished in the place of a weapon, staff, or writing utensil—tools manipulated in Europeans' struggle for control of North America.

Two final sections broaden the conceptual apparatus for the installation by juxtaposing distinct methods of producing knowledge about the past. "HISTORY" is filled with high stacks of unreadable newspapers and enormous, leather-bound volumes crusty with age (fig. 1.14). The objects cover stages in the winnowing process by which history's script is written, through the cropping and deleting of an unwieldy archive of printed facts and ample fictions. Among numerous twentieth-century critiques of the links between writing

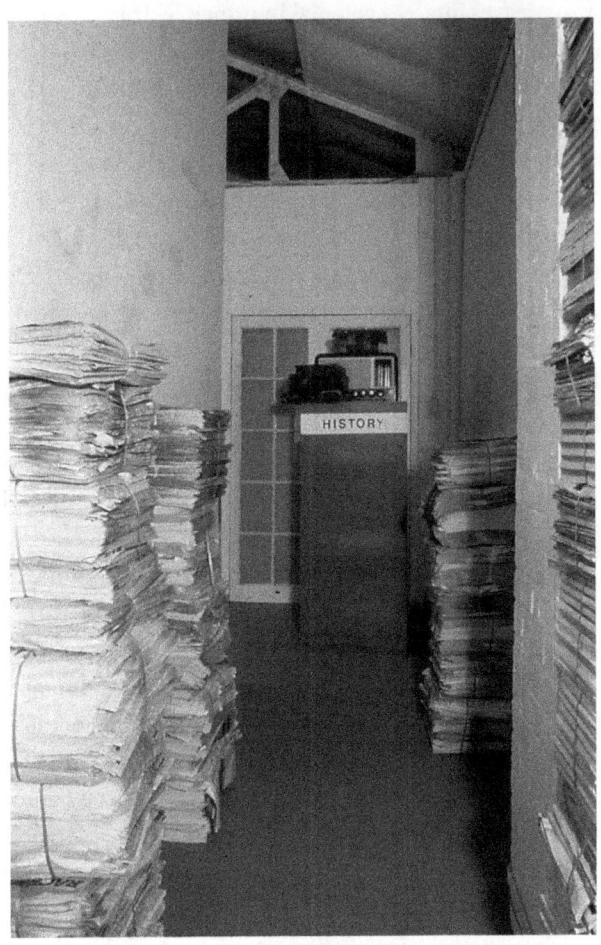

1.14 Jimmie Durham, *Mataoka Ale Attakulakula Anel Guledisgo Hnihi (Pocahontas and the Little Carpenter in London)*, detail, 1988. Mixed-media installation at Matt's Gallery in London. Courtesy of Matt's Gallery and the artist.

and power, that of spatial theorist Michel de Certeau is especially pertinent to *Mataoka Ale Attakulakula Anel Guledisgo Hnihi*: "The power that writing's expansionism leaves intact is colonial in principle. It is extended without being changed. It is tautological, immunized against both any alterity that might transform it and whatever dares to resist it."[127] Durham echoed this view when he insisted that the Pocahontas myth arrived with the colonists, the drama of "New World" love and conversion already rehearsed in Orientalist texts and images. The soundtrack to the installation, an audio play entitled "A Few Words Exchanged at Charleston," recently rediscovered in the Matt's Gallery archive, features his own mocking, subjective voice.[128] Durham introduced the scene based on an event from the transatlantic slave trade: in 1693, a delegation of Cherokee traveled to Charleston, South Carolina, to meet with colonial authorities in order to arrange for the return of two Cherokee men taken captive by British settlers.[129] We learn, "It was the first official meeting between the Cherokees and the Carolinians. The city of Charleston named after a man called Charles is located near the historic James River, named after a man called James . . ." Enter J. Durham, British officer. In a high-pitched, nasal voice, he explains to the Cherokee, "Your brethren were sold into slavery in Jamaica." Confusion and wailing ensue. This section of the soundtrack deconstructs official historical narratives by mocking British authority to name and control the Americas. Yet a shift occurs in the second half, featuring the music of indigenous instruments including a turtle-shell rattle, a drum, and a *khola*, played by rubbing a stick against notches in the shoulder bone of a horse.[130] "A Few Words Exchanged at Charleston" conjures the interconnected geographies of African and Native American slaves as well as the aural and material means by which they mitigated cultural losses associated with captivity and displacement.

The final section of the installation, "EVIDENCE," intermixes texts, images, and objects from European archives with found oddities and playful handwritten notes (fig. 1.15). Designed to break European writing's seal against alterity, "EVIDENCE" features Durham's characteristic tool kit of humor and irony. Yet the constellation of scraps hints at another materialist conception of history that is fully realized in the figure of "Attakulakula." Affixed to the gallery wall are a page of the *Gentleman's Magazine* from 1731, a reproduction of a painting of a muscular Indian and a British officer in a deadly struggle at the edge of a cliff, an illustration of fencing techniques in which one man's sword juts through the center of the other's body, labeled simply "Instructive pictures of sports and games," and a two-column spread listing "uses of iron"

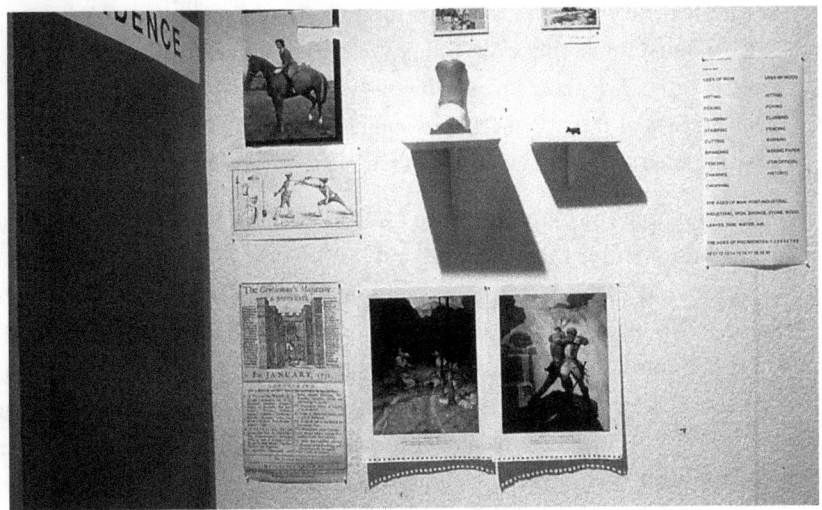

1.15 Jimmie Durham, *Mataoka Ale Attakulakula Anel Guledisgo Hnihi (Pocahontas and the Little Carpenter in London)*, detail, 1988. Mixed-media installation at Matt's Gallery in London. Courtesy of Matt's Gallery and the artist.

and "uses of wood." The latter included "hitting," "burning," and "making paper (for official history)." Some of the assembled scraps survey the nonchalance of colonial military violence lurking in the myth of "New World" lovers' embrace. Others are apparently authored by Durham, such as the absurdist list "The ages of man: post-industrial, industrial, iron, bronze, stone, wood, leaves, fire, water, air." Certainly this miscellany is not evidence that holds up in a European court of law. It is a trial run by the vanquished of history, who find few reliable allies in archives and books. Durham builds his case through the accumulation of scraps and inventions. Every partial testament to violence, every material survivor, every creative act, every tiny triumph of a joke, is made to count.

In a pamphlet accompanying the installation, Durham introduced a Cherokee concept of history as world and a related notion of the historian as a carpenter, moving well beyond a liminal reading of scraps. He wrote,

> I want all of our history. I need every name, every artefact, every effort.
> I need to know the minute specific of our history because I need to
> be part of it. But I am part of it, and could not choose otherwise, the
> way a Jew is part of the Holocaust. In the Cherokee language the

word for the world and the word for history are the same. . . . We, you and I, must remember everything. We must specifically remember those things we never knew. Obviously that process cannot begin with longer lists of facts. . . . Perhaps we must trust confusion more, for a while, and be deeply suspicious of simple stories, simple acts.[131]

The notion that the Cherokee word for history and world *are the same* should not be mistaken for the classical—and unsupportable—anthropological assumption that indigenous societies are timeless, that is, lacking a concept of history.[132] Rather, Durham's definition emphasizes the unbreakable continuity of the present with all that has already happened ("I am part of it, and could not choose otherwise") and with every place and thing ("the world"). Durham does not specify the Cherokee word in the 1988 pamphlet, but a statement from a decade earlier yields clues: "In the language of my people . . . there is a word for land: Eloheh. This same word also means history, culture, and religion. We cannot separate our place on the earth from our lives on the earth. . . . We are taught from childhood that the animals and even the trees and plants that we share a place with are our brothers and sisters."[133] Durham elaborates further in his contribution to *Land, Spirit, Power* in 1992: "Perhaps the best literal translation would be process. We do not traditionally see the earth as a mother but as a process that intimately includes us. . . . Within the concept of Eloheh is the idea that existence, the universe, is like a big council meeting. It is obviously one's duty to be part of it, and that entails listening well and speaking well."[134] Echoing Durham's earlier writings on indigenous spiritualism, *Eloheh* encompasses not only Cherokee ancestral lands in the southeastern United States, but also dynamic, ethical relationships between times, places, humans, and other-than-human persons that are not reducible to division, occupation, and marginalization.

From these various sources we can grasp that Eloheh is large enough to encompass the fictions, outright lies, and selected facts through which Europeans narrated their encounters with Natives, as well as everything that falls outside the borders of that story, including what is not available to the human mind by any direct means ("those things we never knew"). Eloheh is a human name for a non-Eurocentric, nonanthropocentric history of the world that does not depend on our recognition or validation of it, at the same time that we are an integral part of it. It is a conception that avoids privileging what people think they know about the world and mistaking that partial view for the world itself. Furthermore, since Eloheh does not center on humans, writing is not its privileged form. This has implications for those dispossessed in and by European writing. A history that both includes and transcends the limits of books and archives implies, for example, that the once-living woman assigned the name Pocahontas cannot be absented from it, no matter how many simulations pile up in her wake.[135] Rather, knowledge about the past is redistributed among the countless humans and other-than-human persons that comprise the "big council meeting" of the universe. Beyond authorial books and images, every scrap, every stone, "every name, every artefact, every effort," is revalued as a legitimate bearer of history. Durham extended human resources available for telling stories about peoples, pasts, and places well beyond the colonial archive, to the profusion of everything around us. *Mataoka Ale Attakulakula Anel Guledisgo Hnihi* challenges us to hold as much of this in our grasp as possible, without seeking to iron out the resulting confusion.

Durham indicated that there is an ethical dimension to this process of shared storytelling, a responsibility to listen and speak as one among many vocal parts, embodied in the snakelike orator and carpenter, "Attakulakula" (plate 21). He wrote in the pamphlet: "Let the Little Carpenter be your spiritual guide, as he is the guardian of these trashy dime-novel treasures I've laid out. In his language he is known as Attakulakula, but his nick-name was 'The Fixer.'"[136] Unlike the invented script of Pocahontas, Attakulakula's forceful words and deeds were recorded in their moment. We can glean that he earned his nickname, The Fixer or The Little Carpenter, by exercising the skill to "bring together society's disparate elements, disputing factions and potentially profitable trade undertakings," working for more than four decades to negotiate with the colonists on behalf of Cherokee interests. In a transcribed meeting with the governor of South Carolina in Charleston in 1752, Attakulakula demanded reforms of the grossly unfair trade practices inflicted upon his community: "I am the only living Cherokee that went to England. What I now speak the great King should hear. We are brothers to the people of Carolina, and one house covers us all."[137] His words model the undivided world key to Durham's notion of history, a vast meetinghouse for a political council that includes the Cherokee and the British, as well as the land and other life-forms contested in their treaties. "Attakulakula" appropriately appears among the assembled scraps as a composite formed from a rattlesnake skin, with a painted stick for a horn and a tail of colored plastic beads with a bell in place of a rattle.[138]

The remixed organic and manufactured elements call to mind the many other creatures Durham made throughout the 1980s and early 1990s. But instead of a trickster who came to embody fragmentation and displacement, Durham characterized Attakulakula as a carpenter who nails, glues, and hammers scraps of the world back together. Elsewhere, Durham explained, "The word in Cherokee that is used for carpenter means a 'fixer'—someone who joins things together in a clever fashion. The word is also used colloquially to mean a married couple. And also to mean a poet—someone who joins words together."[139] Words and materials are equally elements to be assembled, and even—after one too many acts of postmodern deconstruction—rejoined to each other.[140] Correspondingly, *Mataoka Ale Attakulakula Anel Guledisgo Hnihi* presents language as yet another element embedded in the world, instead of a filter or a barrier to it. Durham subjected the vast miscellany of the installation—archival scraps, battered history books, refuse from the London street, recorded voices, handwritten notes—to acts of suture that restore their latent connections to each other, to us, and to the wider world of which we are a piece. Here a carpenter-fixer-poet-historian acts as our "guide," shuttling us between the seemingly abstract constructions of language and the material activity of gluing and nailing things together. "Listening well and speaking well" involves attending to metonyms, not metaphors. Literary scholar Rob Appleford usefully wrote of Durham's work, "What is important is the fitting join of things, not the self-conscious craft of the joiner. . . . Carpentry is as much about a relationship (between a married couple or between things) as it is about a facility with tools and materials." He went on to argue that Durham is involved in a struggle to "translate this complex Cherokee idea of carpentry into a contemporary art context," resulting in ambivalence.[141] I propose instead that Durham, acting as more than a tentative translator in *Mataoka Ale Attakulakula Anel Guledisgo Hnihi*, decisively resituated *everything*—carpenter and colonizer, book and snakeskin—inside an expansive framework of history as world. We humans are invited to join up with the parts, to speak and listen alongside them, rather than master, decode, or deconstruct them.

Considered within the larger constellation of stories and materials that compose *Mataoka Ale Attakulakula Anel Guledisgo Hnihi*, the figure entitled "Attakulakula" can finally help us to reframe the pathos of Durham's patchwork Pocahontas and the presumed alterity of his many bone works. The skin of the sinuous figure is a metonym for live snakes of the sort that Durham encountered growing up in Arkansas. They appear throughout his poetry as eloquent beings modeling confident speech and action. Durham wrote in 1983, "I want my words to be as eloquent / As the sound of a rattle snake / I want my actions to be as direct / As the strike of a rattlesnake / I want results as conclusive / As the bite of a beautiful red and black coral snake."[142] So, too, does "Attakulakula" recall Cherokee stories about a powerful horned serpent named Uktena. In a version recorded at the turn of the twentieth century, a man transformed into Uktena strives to rescue his people from an angry sun intent on destroying them; he fails to complete the task, but his offspring live on in lonely mountain passes, stories, and perhaps too in the scraps that form Durham's composite creature.[143] The artist's words in the exhibition pamphlet further imply that snakes and humans trace common ancestry. The Cherokee keep "an absolutely true and scientific account of [their] origins" in which Coyote impulsively bit every animal present at a council and re-gurgitated the flesh in the form of humans.[144] A swatch of boa constrictor skin covers Pocahontas's right cheek, indicating that the two figures share kinship with snakes. A material manifestation of Eloheh, or history as world, "Attakulakula" in turn provides us with conceptual tools to reconnect a larger family of patchwork beings Durham made before, during, and after *Mataoka Ale Attakulakula Anel Guledisgo Hnihi*. The project of carpentry aids in the reclamation of materials coded as negative in works such as *On Loan from the Museum of the American Indian* and *Not Joseph Beuys' Coyote* by relating them to each other and to humans inside a house big enough to include them all.

Not long after London, Durham received invitations to participate in an expanding network of art biennials that promised to turn select "margins" into "centers" and "outsiders" into "insiders." An inaugural work in a period of intensive artistic activity abroad, *Mataoka Ale Attakulakula Anel Guledisgo Hnihi* suggests that he did not treat privileged itinerancy as a means to move on from the spatial thinking that motivated his art and activism in the United States. Retracing the past voyages of Pocahontas and Attakulakula to London, the installation foregrounds the city as one node in a long-standing transatlantic network bearing indigenous and European travelers back and forth across the ocean. For artists of the AIM generation, contemporary art nomadism is only the latest iteration of mobility that includes displacements engendered during some five hundred years of colonial occupation. Perhaps exhibiting in London reminded Durham of his failed experiment with mod-ernist exile in Geneva on the eve of AIM two decades before. Rather than embracing estrangement, he engaged with history in an unprecedented man-ner, rejoining scraps and words to forge continuities between times, places, persons, and things. The additional, crucial lesson of *Mataoka Ale Attakulakula*

Anel Guledisgo Hnihi is that the methods by which history is narrated must be retooled. Without new conceptual and material resources—or, better yet, old indigenous ones—the artist and his kin remain trapped by simulations and severed from the past. Refusing the colonial endgame of perpetual displacement, other artists of the AIM generation would follow Durham to piece the ground back together abroad.

TWO

"Now That We Are Christians

We Dance for Ceremony"

JAMES LUNA, PERFORMING PROPS,

AND SACRED SPACE

The *Pocahontas* sailed from San Diego to Mexico City in 1832.[1] On board were two youths, Pablo Tac (1820–41) and Agapito Amamix (1820–37), Quechnajuisom or "people of Quechla" (commonly known today as Luiseño), who would never again see their ancestral lands on the West Coast of North America. Raised Roman Catholic at the Mission San Luis Rey de Francia in Alta California, part of the newly independent nation of Mexico, they were selected by the Franciscan missionary Antonio Peyri to study for the priesthood. In 1834, after beginning their education at a missionary college in Mexico City, they enrolled in the Collegium Urbanum de Propaganda Fide in Rome along with other youths from colonized regions around the world to study Latin, Italian, Spanish, and religion.[2] The following year, Tac produced a Spanish-Quechnajuisom dictionary and the first written history of his people, *Indian Life and Customs at Mission San Luis Rey.* He recorded his recollections of culturally significant activities such as dances and ball games, thereby transforming embodied indigenous knowledge into writing, a form privileged by colonial authorities. The work of the multilingual translator and scholar, preserved today in the library of the Università di Bologna, forms a rare indigenous-authored archive in Europe.

Tac wrote at a moment when missions occupied Native space across the Americas and the Bible was a key tool of colonization. Franciscan missionaries brought with them a religious framework divided according to "spirit and letter": Natives could, like Europeans, transcend mundane, earthly flesh to join Christ and God in heaven ("spirit"), provided that they obeyed the word of God ("letter").[3] Though marginalized from predominantly secular accounts of modernity, the principles of conversion had formative effects on indigenous communities that are everywhere evident today. Artist James Luna's four-part exhibition *Emendatio*, a collateral event of the Venice Biennale sponsored by the Smithsonian National Museum of the American Indian (NMAI) in 2005, revisits Tac's archive to parse entangled processes of spiritual repression and renewal during and after missionization.[4] The suite of three multimedia installations and a performance make palpable the ways in which colonial conversions rendered Catholicism vulnerable to indigenous meanings and European architecture host to diverse experiences of the sacred. "Chapel for Pablo Tac," in particular, transforms Tac's text into sensuous textiles, granting them a new life beyond archival inertia. Throughout, Luna reintegrated spirit and letter inside a framework of material, bodily, and spiritual exchanges that survived missionization and profoundly affected its terms.[5] *Emendatio* builds on Jimmie Durham's interpretation of Pocahontas's and Attakulakula's travels in London through an expansive Cherokee definition of "history as world," modeling essential components of an undivided earth that will preoccupy me in the remainder of this book.

To "read" Tac's legacy in this manner necessitates grappling with the authority and limits of the colonial epistemologies that framed him. In recent postcolonial and performance studies, scholars contrast two systems for organizing and transmitting knowledge: the archive of durable materials (e.g., texts, documents, artworks, buildings, and bones) and the repertoire of embodied practice (e.g., spoken language, religious rituals, dance, and sports). In Diana Taylor's influential account, missionaries arriving in the Americas consolidated power by controlling and extolling literacy. Equally, they devalued and at times violently suppressed indigenous nonverbal practices deemed idolatrous.[6] It would be easy to read Tac's mastery of the form amid displacement as assimilation into a European episteme entailing the loss of embodied indigenous knowledge. But *Emendatio* blends archive and repertoire along with spirit and letter—divisions that derive from a European worldview full of slippages, rendered doubly permeable inside an indigenous framework of undivided earth. Luna's wide array of performance paraphernalia and spiritual accouterments facilitate the migration of qualities normally reserved for human bodies onto the "hard stuff" of the archive. To reflect this process, I call the objects found throughout *Emendatio* "performing props." By drawing out a potential shared by Catholic and indigenous sacred spaces for objects to instantiate other-than-human agencies, Luna resumed the transatlantic material and spiritual relations that lay dormant in Tac's archive and were neglected in the work of the AIM generation. To do so at the Venice Biennale, the oldest and some say most prestigious mega–art exhibition in the world, finally shifts the terms of recent debate about the place of indigenous makers within the globalization of contemporary art. Instead of a next stopover on an itinerant circuit of spectacles, Luna approached the biennale as a historically situated laboratory for rethinking the sacred grounds of modernity.

Materializing Tac's Archive

Luna's treatment of Tac's writing foregrounds the interplay of archive, performance, religious dogma, and everyday spiritual practice needed to unpack multifaceted indigenous conversion experiences. The works shared the grounds and temporary exhibition spaces of the Fondazione Querini Stampalia, a Venetian mansion preserved as a civic library and art museum in 1868, with artist and feminist Kiki Smith's installation *Squatting the Palace*.[7] For the centerpiece of *Emendatio*, an architectural installation called "Chapel for Pablo Tac," Luna erected two temporary sidewalls draped in white cloth painted with bold crosses and diamonds (plate 22). At the front, a plain wooden box forms the foundation of an altar draped with lace and linen cloth. It is fitted with an LCD screen displaying a montage of historical and contemporary images of California missions, indigenous peoples, Venice, and the Venetian Resort and Casino in Las Vegas. Above hangs an enormous striped tapestry of cream, mauve, and blue bearing excerpts from the Tac's oeuvre in simulated handwriting (plate 23). A smaller, matching textile featuring another quote appears on the floor in front of the altar behind a wooden balustrade.[8] Atop the altar and in several vitrines lining the walls, Luna placed objects related to indigenous and Catholic rituals. Rows of salvaged wooden pews invite visitors to take a seat and listen to the video's looped soundtrack of lapping waves, church bells, a Luiseño "Eagle" song, and a cover of Procol Harum's "A Whiter Shade of Pale."[9] Luna also danced using various costumes and props for four days in "Renewal (A Performance for Pablo Tac)" and set digitized historical photographs of Luiseño people in motion in smaller installations called "Spinning Woman" and "Apparitions (Past and Present)." I consider all of these elements but focus at length on "Chapel for Pablo Tac" and "Renewal (A Performance for Pablo Tac)" because they are directly concerned with Tac's legacy.

On the banner hanging above the altar of "Chapel for Pablo Tac," Luna quoted a lengthy section of Tac's *Indian Life and Customs at Mission San Luis Rey* titled "Of the Dance of the Indians" in Tac's original Spanish:

> Each Indian people has its dances, different from other dances. In Europe they dance for joy, for a feast, for any fortunate news. But the Indians of California dance not only for a feast, but also before starting a war, for grief, because they have lost the victory, and in memory of grandparents, aunts and uncles, parents already dead. Now that we are Christians we dance for ceremony. The dance of the Yumas is almost always sad, and thus the song; the same of the Diegueños. But we Luiseños have three principal kinds for men alone, because the women have others, and they can never dance with the men.

On the floor in front, translated from the original Spanish into English, appears a statement that Tac wrote for his mentor, Italian linguist and cardinal Giuseppe Caspar Mezzofanti, upon the completion of his dictionary in Rome: "I could have taught more, but who could teach others what they don't know? What I knew I taught. What I didn't I've left. Better to be quiet than saying lies." Both excerpts alert us to the challenges of transmitting embodied knowledge through language alone. In the former, Tac attempted to explain the cultural significance of communal songs and dances from which he was displaced. Instead of clarifying, his classifications pose the limits of text as a vessel for performance. In the latter, Tac openly acknowledged all that writing leaves behind, asserting that silence is preferable to words that mislead.

Luna stated, "To write, and to be written about, holds high value in the Western world—you become validated . . . you exist. Can we talk?"[10] His pointed selections from Tac's manuscript at first glance support a binary of archive and repertoire, extensively theorized by performance studies scholars. In Taylor's influential definition, "the archive" includes written documents, maps, charts, archaeological objects, bones, and other materials that appear resistant to change. It "sustains power" because it "works across distance, over time and space . . . [and] succeeds in separating the source of 'knowledge' from the knower."[11] Taylor contrasts hardened archival knowledge with the embodied enactment of memory (repertoire): oral culture, gestures, dance, and other activities performed by live subjects, commonly assumed to be ephemeral and nonreproducible.[12] Although she stated that in practice they often work in tandem, Taylor demonstrated that the conceptual splitting and hierarchical valuation of archive over repertoire guided Europeans' struggle to control indigenous peoples during the conquest in the Americas. Colonial officials ordered the archive and the repertoire sequentially in time and space. Representing an advanced stage of civilization, writing would supplant performance as the dominant mode of cultural transmission upon the arrival of European modernity at distant shores. Prior to Tac's manuscript, the Quechnajuisom had no formal system of writing, nor did the structure of their spoken language permit easy translation of foreign doctrines.[13] Colonial authorities regularly argued that absent such a scheme, Natives lacked legitimate religion and history. Documents—land deeds, ledgers, the Bible—were wielded like weapons over communities without access to literacy. At least on paper, missionaries condemned Native rituals and their associated material culture as idolatrous, a threat to the word of God (letter).[14]

This colonial logic fueled not only the early denigration of Native peoples, but also the nostalgia surrounding their contemporary representation.[15] Rebecca Schneider asserted that the archive *produces* loss and at the same time generates a powerful desire for the lost thing or state—an "archive fever," in the words of Jacques Derrida.[16] The sentiment is evident in French theorist Pierre Nora's influential vision of the rise of modern historiography: "The remnants of experience still lived in the warmth of tradition, in the silence of custom, in the repetition of the ancestral, have been displaced under the pressure of a fundamentally historical sensibility. . . . We speak so much of memory because there is so little of it left."[17] Nora posited the crystallization of "sites of memory"—graveyards, museums—as an inevitable response to the disappearance of "real environments of memory"—flesh, ritual. His account helps to explain the preservationist impulse driving modern institutions to collect and order Native American possessions and remains, discussed already in the previous chapter. The concrete traces of the past promise to bolster history against the mutability of flesh, that which "slips away. Flesh can house no memory of bone. Only bone speaks memory of flesh."[18] As Luna investigated at length in his prior performances and installations, Native Americans are regularly subjected to archival fever while very much alive, their stuff and stories systematically collected, preserved, and mourned. The popular "Indian craze" for California indigenous baskets that began in the nineteenth century, explored elsewhere, is emblematic of the disease.[19] Displaced from the "real environments" of his people, Tac's writing was destined for the archive and the material culture of the Quechnajuisom, the ethnographic display case. Criticizing this process only to reverse it, Taylor joined other performance studies scholars in championing embodied arts as a form of resistance to authority. As I indicated in chapter 1, critics applauded Luna in the 1980s on precisely such terms.

Yet Tac wrote of his people using the present tense. Neither Nora's progressive schema, nor archival condemnation, can account for a repertoire of indigenous knowledge coeval and dynamically interacting with archival forms. After drawing a neat contrast between European and Native dance practices, Tac stated, "Now that we are Christians we dance for ceremony." The phrase is ironic, given that the Franciscans did not bring with them a Christian tradition of ritual dance. Instead, missionaries often relied on indigenous performances to translate Christian doctrine, ensuring that Native dances persisted and occasionally flourished under colonization. Father Peyri, head priest at Mission San Luis Rey, was known to be unusually lenient toward dancing, even as he complained of "infirmities, idolatries, and witchcraft."[20] French sea captain Auguste Duhaut-Cilly reported on witnessing a dance at Mission San Luis Rey in 1827 (while Tac was still in residence), "Although they may all be Christians, they retain many of their former beliefs, which the padres, as a matter of policy, pretend not to notice."[21] Tac, who was trained as a ritual assistant at a young age, slyly pointed to a gap between official colonial rhetoric and the impure realm of practice. The scholar's insistence on the present tense combined with his idiosyncratic account of conversion suggest that he approached writing as a complement to, rather than replacement for, embodied practice among the Quechnajuisom. By foregrounding such revelatory passages, Luna implicitly challenged nostalgia for "real environments of memory" deemed lost, *as well as* the tendency in performance studies to valorize embodied practice as inherently resistant to hegemonic writing. First in Tac's manuscript, then in Luna's work, the opposition between archive and repertoire eases.

Lisbeth Haas, the foremost historian of Tac's archive who shared her research with Luna for *Emendatio*, read Tac's manuscript as a limited act of defiance in the context of a "New World" politics of translation. She explained that Tac "used categories of analysis such as 'dance' that offered an indigenous way of understanding Luiseño society . . . [and] leaves traces of Luiseño spiritual practice and thought."[22] Haas acknowledged that the work of Native translators was a double-edged sword: "On the one hand, native scholars formed part of the cast of scribes and translators involved in the creation of empire through the written word. On the other, without a written grammar, indigenous societies remained less able to document their histories and claim their legal rights." Even while accommodating the new authority of documents,

Native scribes bent Spanish words toward indigenous understandings. For example, Tac translated the Quechnajuisom word *cheiis* as "the act of dressing," important to the process of conversion because donning European clothing established Indians' new status as "civilized" Christians, at least on the outside. At the same time, he used the word to refer to the *cheiat*, a headpiece of sacred feathers worn for important Quechnajuisom dances. Here Haas read "along the archival grain" to imagine how indigenous people brought "remembrance of dance ritual into the daily language of the missions."[23] Haas's account vacillated with regard to archival logic; in some places she read the text as assurance that embodied culture survived colonialism; elsewhere, she fell back on what Schneider referred to as the archive's "trace-logic emphasizing loss," commending Tac for "leaving a sign."[24] Luna intervened in Tac's historiography to recast the apparently conflicted relationships between archive and repertoire as one of complex interdependency.

In particular, "Chapel for Pablo Tac" presents writing as one among many nonhierarchical, sensual forms of transmission. Luna's rehousing of the text returns words to the fulsome material forms they invoke. The letters are difficult to discern inside the bold stripes of textiles conjuring blankets and clothing Native women produced with wool from mission-raised sheep throughout southwestern North America.[25] Their capacity to signify diminishes as their sensual, tactile qualities intensify. Translating ink into cursive thread calls attention to the shared physicality, the "handiwork" that connects nineteenth-century writing and weaving. As text is woven into textile, writing is brought qualitatively closer to another activity distanced by the division of archive and repertoire: dance. Reading deeper into Tac's manuscript reveals that he incorporated contingency and change into his descriptions of bodily activity: "They dance in a circle, kicking, and whoever gets tired stays in the middle of the circle and then follows the others."[26] At such moments, text approximates the bodies it describes, exhausting itself in pursuit of elusive forms of movement. Dance in a circle for how long? Kicking who, what, how? Follows the others where? Humans that weave, dance, and write grow weary. The blanket, a product of manual labor, is also a refuge for tired bodies, and in this case, Tac's struggling words.

The manifestation of text in blanket form points to another resonant feature of the manuscript: Tac's passages on dance are as filled with material culture as with human bodies. Haas discussed the extensive "skills of feather, stone, bone, wood, basket and shell work" needed to produce elaborate regalia worn and carried during dances: "Those people, skills, and practices remain outside most . . . histories of the missions, yet are central to Tac's history."[27] Beyond "people, skills, and practices," however, both Luna and Tac turn our attention to the efficacy of material itself. In "First Dance," Tac writes vividly of a coming-of-age ceremony for "a youth of ten or more years," an initiation he may have undergone prior to his departure for Mexico City at age twelve: "When they have learned, then they can perform the dance, but before this they give him something to drink, and then that one is a dancer; he can dance and not stop when the others dance." Tac's vague "something to drink" most likely refers to the ritual ingestion of datura, the sacred plant through which trained Quechnajuisom initiates could enter altered states conducive to spiritual contact. He continued,

> On this occasion the clothing is of feathers of various colors, and the body painted, and the chest is bare, and from the waist to the knees they are covered, the arms without clothing. In the right hand they carry a stick made to take off the sweat. The face is painted. The head is bound with a band of hair woven so as to be able to thrust in the *cheyatom*, our word. This *cheyat* is made of feathers of any bird, and almost always of crow and of sparrow hawk, and in the middle a sharp stick in order to be able to insert it. Thus they are in the house when immediately two men go out, each one carrying two wooden swords and crying out, without saying any word, and after stopping before the place where they dance, they look at the sky for some time. The people are silent, and they turn and then the dancers go out. These two men are called by us *Pajaom*, meaning crimson snakes. In California there are large red snakes. These do not bite but lash out at those who come near them.[28]

Ingested substances, paint, feathered costumes, and wooden swords do more than boast the skills of human makers; they fundamentally alter the bodies of dancers. Metonyms for powerful entities in the environment, the materials temporarily transform performers into extraordinary beings capable of effecting human prosperity.

Notably, "First Dance" is one of two places in the manuscript where Tac provided a supplementary illustration on the opposite page, acknowledging again his limited capacities for description (fig. 2.1). He drew two smiling dancers, both frozen in midstep, wearing feather headdresses and skirts with wooden swords in hand. As the spatial and temporal elements of the dance fell away, Tac focused on details of costuming that aid the transformation of dancers into other-than-human persons. *Cheyats*, weapons, and bodies assume discrete identities in the handwritten text. By contrast, sacred materials and dancers merge through being drawn by the same pen. Vertical marks across the head of the rightmost figure render boundaries between headdress, hair, and facial features indistinct. Parallel lines confuse the boundary between wooden stick and grasping hand. Uneven hatch marks and scallops delineating rows of skirt feathers continue across the surfaces of whole figures. Tac's blending of subjects and substances conveys the bodies' extraordinary status—"*Pajaom*, meaning crimson snakes," he ended by telling us, recalling Durham's imaginative construction of Attakulakula as an eloquent snake. In a vitrine along one side of "Chapel for Pablo Tac," alternating geometrical symbols of snakes and humans are handwoven into the curvature of a coiled basket. Nestled inside is a brightly painted dance rattle (fig. 2.2).

Performing Props

During the 1980s, Luna became known coast-to-coast for works that "abjure categorical purity" in an effort to rescue living Natives from the impasse of colonial simulations.[29] Born of a Mexican American father and a Payómkawichum (Luiseño)/Ipi (Digeño) mother, the artist used his own body and related experiences as a malleable medium. An enrolled member of the Luiseño Band of Mission Indians, he grew up in the mixed Chicano and Native American community of La Colonia Juarez in Orange County while visiting family in the coastal mountains of the La Jolla Indian Reservation in northern San Diego County. He earned a BA in studio art from the University of California, Irvine, in 1976. The only indigenous person in a department focused on minimalist sculpture, painting, and performance art, Luna experimented with abstract designs from southwestern Native basketry and took courses with Dutch artist Bas Jan Ader, feminist artist Eleanor Antin, and others then exploring the body as a flexible artistic form.[30] Parallel to his art education, Luna witnessed AIM events unfolding around the country, including protests that involved what Paul Chaat Smith described as "a self-consciously theatrical sensibility, with a sophisticated understanding of what it would take to convince the international news media to pay attention to political grievances."[31] Luna attended conferences in southern California that hosted prominent Native activists and leaders, danced in powwows, and went to jail for protesting the display of indigenous mummies at the Southwest Museum.[32] Engagements with pan-Indian politics and spiritualism inflected

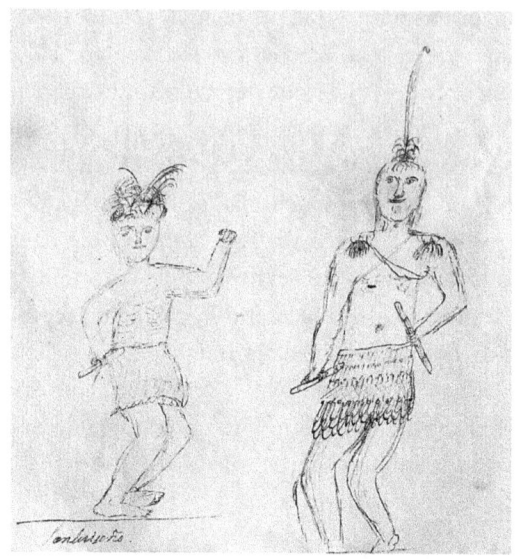

2.1 Pablo Tac, "Lingua californese lavori in prosa," Fondo speciale Giuseppe Mezzofanti, caps. III, fasc. 1, carta 105r.

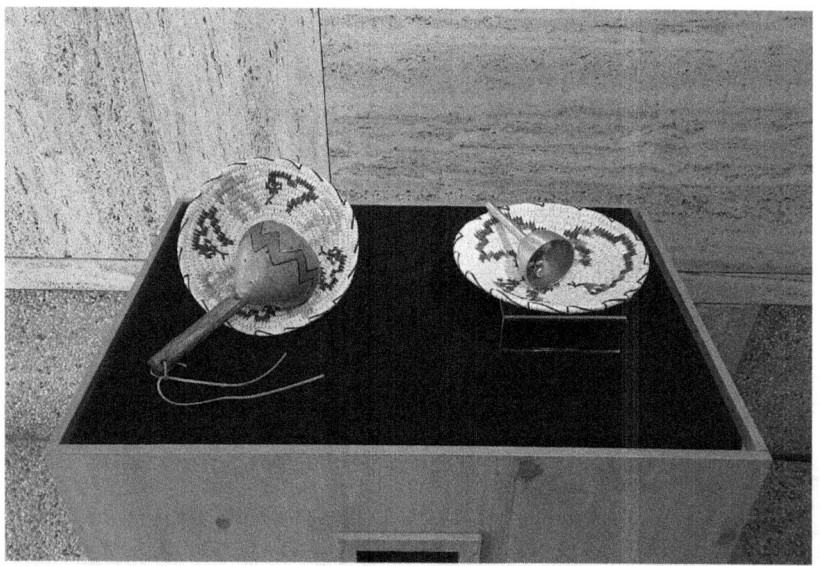

2.2 James Luna, "Chapel for Pablo Tac," detail, 2005. Mixed-media installation included in *Emendatio* at the Fondazione Querini Stampalia, Fifty-First Venice Biennale. National Museum of the American Indian, Smithsonian Institution, KF05ItalyA364. Photo by Katherine Fogden.

his growing artistic practice alongside his day job as a community college academic counselor. In 1977, Luna relocated to his ancestral lands on the La Jolla Indian Reservation, where he continues to live and work today.

Much like Durham's practice during the same period, Luna's parodic performances and installations strove to break the popular association of Native Americans with a premodern past. Specifically, Luna took aim at the romanticized archaeological and missionary record in California with humorous commentary on the harsh realities of contemporary reservation life. The basketry designs that populated his early canvases disappeared as Luna cast suspicion on "traditional" indigenous objects and practices appropriated by white anthropologists and New Age spiritual seekers. Notably, he stated that his most famous performance, *Artifact Piece* (1987), was "the beginning of a relationship between a museum and a living Indian who was there to make a statement; who wasn't there to grind corn, or weave a blanket, or do something quaint for the Saturday crowd. I don't even know how to fuckin' weave a blanket."[33] While I already discussed this paradigmatic work in the previous chapter alongside Durham's *On Loan from the Museum of the American Indian* (1985), I briefly recast my argument here to set the stage for Luna's "performing props." The artist lay in a display case in the San Diego Museum of Man surrounded by rock music cassettes, photographs, divorce papers, and labels pointing to scars from bar brawls (see plates 15–16 and fig. 1.6). Luna resisted the hardening lens of ethnography by forcing viewers to confront the fact of their bodily copresence with an "artifact" still living.[34] In other words, the logic of the performance rested on visitors' ability to recognize a gap separating Luna's breathing body and assorted contemporary belongings from his ancestors' bones, baskets, pottery, and tools. The latter were displayed as scientific evidence of prehistoric California throughout the museum.

In an analysis of Luna's performances, art historian Jane Blocker extended prior claims made by herself, Taylor, and Schneider that "performance and the body constitute unique epistemologies that might be radically or generatively deployed against hegemonic ways of knowing"—that is, against the archival logic I have discussed.[35] According to Schneider, performance need not disappear but can be an "act of remaining and a means of reappearance. . . . [We] are forced to admit that remains do not have to be isolated to the document, to the object, to bone versus flesh."[36] Building on Schneider's argument, Blocker explored how Luna's ancestors became entangled with archival logic through successive waves of colonization and globalization. His family members were rendered objects of scientific scrutiny, their bones dug up and their images recorded by amateur ethnographers in the nineteenth and twentieth centuries.[37] Blocker argued that in contrast to deadened museum displays, Luna uses his body to foreground the persistence of dynamic, multidimensional, contemporary Native Americans—flesh irreducible to bones. Her account locates Luna within a longer history of avant-garde performances in which, according to Amelia Jones, "the mobilization of the live body strategically destroyed the pretensions of objectivity on which the various institutions and discourses of Euro-American art based their authority."[38] However invigorating this strain of critique, its exclusive focus on the breathing, resisting body risks leaving the colonial division of archive and repertoire intact. I am concerned that in the rush to rescue live Natives from objectification, we inadvertently consign ancestral materials and histories to the grave.

There is a hint of this binary at play in Luna's prior installations of humorous "mestizo" objects that mock touristic and New Age appropriations of Native cultures. Three are particularly important precedents for "Chapel for Pablo Tac." In *California Mission Daze*, exhibited at Installation Gallery in San Diego in 1988, Luna collaborated with David Avalos, Deborah Small, and William E. Weeks to build a kitschy model mission complete with altar, gift store, schoolhouse, and graveyard (fig. 2.3). The curio shop, "Honest Injun," offers a clutter of baskets, postcards, racist banners, and a neon, feathered headdress worn by a grinning human skull. On the other side, an American flag, presidential portraits, and the Pledge of Allegiance dominate a grade school curriculum. Finally, visitors could pass through a fenced graveyard in back, filled with crosses and offerings of abalone shells and lit candles, indicating the presence of living kin. That same year, the group of artists created another mission-themed piece titled *Altaration of History*. They decorated an enormous altar with an image of Father Junípero Serra, the founder of the California mission chain, surrounded by mocking text: "canonization," "veneration," and a bit of pointed word play, "beatification." The bold exclamation "Bingo!" assures us that the proud mission legacy lives on in casinos. The entire façade rests on the backs of two Indian laborers silhouetted on hands and knees.

In *Chapel of the Sacred Colors*, exhibited in galleries in Saskatoon, Saskatchewan, and Santa Fe in 2000, Luna draped a room with curtains of red, yellow, and black. With the addition of bare white walls, the four "sacred colors" double as references to the racial coding of skin color, explored in an earlier photographic work, *Sacred Colors* (1992–94), now embedded above the altar.[39] In lieu of a crucifix, Luna placed a gleaming "High-Tech Peace Pipe." A piece

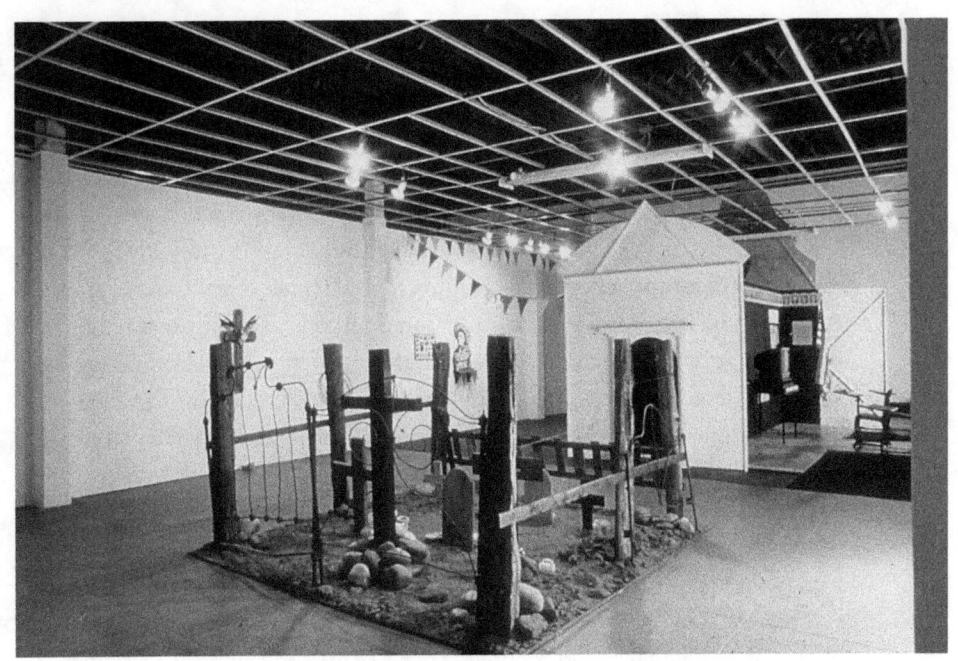

2.3 David Avalos, James Luna, Deborah Small, and William E. Weeks, *California Mission Daze*, 1988. Mixed-media installation, Installation Gallery, San Diego. Courtesy of James Luna.

of industrial plumbing decorated with beads and peace signs nestles atop a telephone receiver, awaiting the gods of the New Age to ring (plate 26). Other objects in nearby vitrines included a "wet dream catcher" (a befeathered tennis racket with condoms dangling from the strings) and an "electric rattle" (a beaded hot pink vibrator). Art historian Jennifer A. González summarized the work thus: "Ritual objects for not-so-traditional rituals were . . . on display, taking the form of material and visual puns, while mocking the viewer's desire for contact with 'authentic' Indian artifacts."[40] While the parodic mode may succeed in short-circuiting an ongoing process of colonial objectification, it does so by forcing a break between current lives and indigenous art forms and worldviews coded as the past. Baskets, rattles, pottery, and peace pipes—"traditional" objects that Native peoples continue to produce for use and sale today—function as the negative others against which Luna's absurd totems achieve their humor and fashionable brand of contemporaneity. Luna's prior mission-themed works join *On Loan from the Museum of the American Indian* and *Artifact Piece* in accepting the power of white institutions to categorize

Native histories as romantic relics. By extension, colonial ontologies that sever past objects from present subjects persist. Crucially, this hard line is in danger of relinquishing the agency of ancestors along with their bones.

The limitations of the parodic mode common to many AIM-generation artists' practices have gone largely unremarked to date. Yet several scholars laid the ground for my concern, challenging the recent preoccupation with bodily immediacy in the field of performance studies by analyzing the many forms of mediation that turn ephemeral acts into archival traces. Jones, for one, argued that performance art's frequent claim to presence is ironically secured by its documentation. Furthermore, live acts undermine immediacy by marking the body as a representation intended for an audience's gaze.[41] *Artifact Piece* is a prime example of this paradox. In the *Emendatio* catalogue appears an image of Luna in the NMAI in Washington, DC, standing before a lightbox installation featuring a photograph of *Artifact Piece*.[42] Scholars lauded the 1987 performance as an act of resistance thanks in part to its evocative media record. Luna subsequently reperformed the work, notably in 1990 for the blockbuster exhibition *The Decade Show: Frameworks of Identity in the 1980s* in New York discussed in chapter 1, and granted artist Erica Lord the right to restage it as *Artifact Piece, Revisited* in 2009.[43] Blocker additionally pointed out that performances such as *Artifact Piece* and "Renewal (A Performance for Pablo Tac)" "repeat" with a difference a longer transatlantic history of Wild West shows and other forms of colonial entertainment featuring live Native bodies as spectacles, a history I take up in detail in chapter 5.[44] In highlighting the unstable border between subjects and objects, Jones and Blocker hint that it is difficult, if not impossible, to fully disentangle the archive and the repertoire. I draw this specific lesson from their words: it is not adequate to rescue live Native subjects by severing them from historical materials. The fates of past and present humans and their stuff are far too enmeshed.

Exceeding a postmodern tool kit of irony and humor, *Emendatio* prompts a reappraisal of the relationship between Native bodies, historical material culture, and spiritual renewal. In particular, considering the exchange of materials across the performance and three installations points us toward a more constructive side of Blocker's equation: if live bodies are susceptible to objectification, objects can simultaneously participate in, and even undergo, subjectification. Luna's description of the mutability of materials in his work as early as 1985 indicates transit in both directions, "similar to the process and action of a transformer toy: A room changed to a church, objects to people, common utensils to ceremonial objects."[45] In a 2013 conversation with me he elaborated: "My affinity and my relationship with objects is a little different than somebody making something for sale or for beauty. I make things because they're a prop. . . . Props have become art objects, props have become performances. It just depended on the prop. They could start out [as] real simple things and they could get on a roll and start to be something more."[46] A consideration of "Renewal (A Performance for Pablo Tac)," the component of *Emendatio* that most closely follows the grooves of Luna's prior work, helps me to understand this "something more." During the opening week of the Venice Biennale, Luna danced in the interior garden courtyard of Fondazione Querini Stampalia for four hours on four consecutive days. Wearing jeans and a T-shirt imprinted with the words "You don't know me," he began by arranging a circle of stones, sachets of sugar, and insulin syringes, references to the health problems of contemporary Natives, alongside acorns, a staple of the indigenous California diet used to make a porridge called *weewish*.[47] The four "cardinal directions" were marked by arrows burrowed into the ground and tins of Spam, a favorite comfort food on the reservation. A colorful woven blanket lay in the grass, along with a box holding rattles and other accoutrements.

Luna proceeded to step in and out of the circle, changing between numerous costumes and wielding a variety of objects (plates 24–25). He shook a rattle and danced wearing stereotypical Plains Indian garb: a feather headdress, fringed buckskin, and beaded moccasins. In a leather vest and loincloth, he pretended to shoot a Winchester rifle, playing the cowboy *and* the Indian in a nod to "spaghetti westerns" discussed in chapter 1. The addition of a striped blue and white T-shirt and spiked leather jewelry transformed Luna into a punk gondolier, a kinky twist on the romanticized figure at the helm of the Venetian tourist industry. Luna also donned a metallic purple tuxedo emblazoned with a silhouette of James Fraser's iconic sculpture *End of the Trail*, created for the Panama-Pacific International Exposition held in San Francisco in 1915 (see plate 24). Fraser's visual argument about Native Americans doomed to disappearance has long been the victim of the contemporary artist's jokes—for example, when Luna straddled a sawhorse with a bottle of liquor in one hand for *End of the Trail* (1991). The sculpture was repurposed in "Renewal (A Performance for Pablo Tac)" as the ironic motif of his stock performance character, "Lounge Luna."[48] Not surprisingly, scholars and critics concluded that Luna was up to his usual tricks in Venice, a "mestizo mind" putting "ambivalence" to strategic use in the fight against racism.[49]

Yet in "Renewal (A Performance for Pablo Tac)," clothing and props—

loincloth, leather, rattles, Winchester, and Spam—"start to be something more": they are precisely what allows a hilarious, multifaceted, mestizo subject to come into being. Luna's metallic suit is as essential to his performance art as swords and *cheyat* are to the Quechnajuisom dances described by Tac. Materials furthermore seal relations between Luna and audience; the Venetian performance unfolded as a triangle of subject-object-subject relations in which props and bodies were equally busy performing. To return to "Chapel for Pablo Tac," we can see that the humble objects on view share something in common with the variety of props that make appearances in Luna's mock-ritual performances and installations. Sage and incense for odorous burning, chalices for communion, feathers and rattles for a ceremonial dance appear as potential performers, waiting to be lifted from vitrines by priests or indigenous initiates in shared ritual roles. Recognizing the interdependence of human bodies and mutable materials throughout *Emendatio* finally entails approaching the performance and installations as a continuous field of interaction, rather than belonging to discrete artistic genres.

Nonetheless, I find the subtle differences, even contradictions, between "Renewal (A Performance for Pablo Tac)" and "Chapel for Pablo Tac" telling. Commodities such as lounge suits and Spam arrive in viewers' space already coded as contemporary. The humor of the performance rests on their juxtaposition with loincloths, beads, and feathers. Far from generating a field of mestizo equals, it asks us to recognize the latter as anachronisms, locked out of claims to relevance in the present. While there are a few parodic elements in "Chapel for Pablo Tac"—namely, the inclusion of "A Whiter Shade of Pale" on the soundtrack and images of the kitschy Venetian resort in Vegas in the video montage—the treatment of material culture is markedly different. Framed by parallel stories of Tac's and Luna's travels, the juxtaposition of medicine pouches with Catholic liturgical tools forge living subjects' connection to, rather than freedom from, the past. A blanket—a class of object dismissed by Luna when he stated he didn't "fuckin' know how to weave" one in *Artifact Piece*, replaced with a garish serape in "Renewal (A Performance for Pablo Tac)"—appears at the front of the installation, now warmly embracing the threads of Tac's words. Blocker describes *Emendatio* as haunted by "the ghost of Pablo Tac, a conflicted figure if ever there was one."[50] But Tac appears surprisingly solid for a restless ghost. His words are made tangible in the skeins of textiles, and his silences are met with baskets, abalone shells, and chalices.

Elsewhere in *Emendatio*, Luna set objects and archives in motion, establishing other continuities between his courtyard performance and the in-

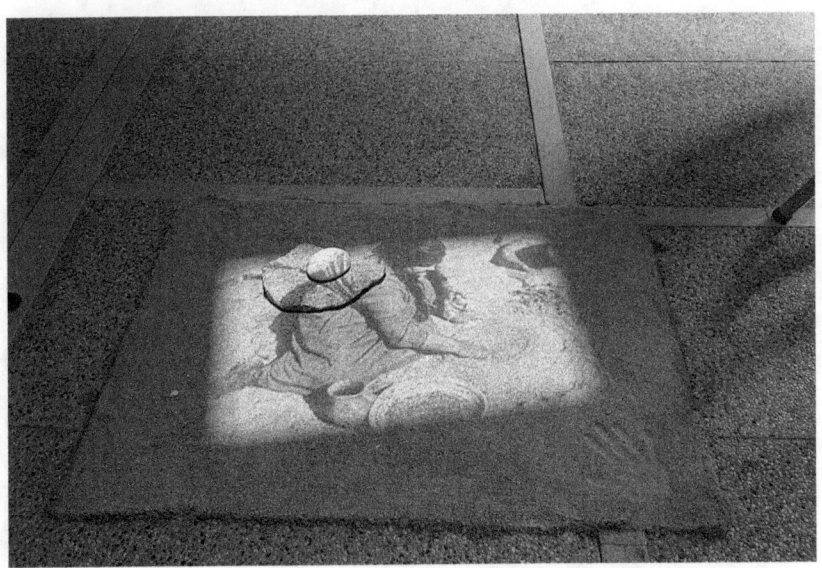

2.4 James Luna, "Spinning Woman," 2005. Installation of sound, moving photograph, sand, and stone, included in *Emendatio* at the Fondazione Querini Stampalia, Fifty-First Venice Biennale. National Museum of the American Indian, Smithsonian Institution, KF05ItalyB284. Photo by Katherine Fogden.

door installations. In the entryway to the Fondazione, visitors were greeted by title signage and a video of Luna's performance rehearsal from the NMAI, projected on a vertically hung Pendleton blanket. In "Spinning Woman," a smaller work in an adjoining room, Luna projected an archival photograph of a Native woman kneeling on the ground grinding acorns (possibly to make wee-wish) onto a bed of sand on the floor (fig. 2.4). Her image spins in a circle, first clockwise, then counterclockwise, in a dynamic, rhythmic motion. On one side lies a rock mortar and pestle. Stone and sand distort the smooth flow of the projection. They call attention to the materials pictured in intimate proximity to her photographed body, namely a pottery jug and a decorated basketry tray that bears the results of her labor.[51] The installation is accompanied by the recorded sound of a bull-roarer, a palm-sized, flat piece of cottonwood strung on a cord and twirled rapidly until it buzzes, used by the Payómkawichum to conjure spirits.[52]

"Apparitions (Past and Present)" similarly rematerializes digitized archival black-and-white and contemporary color photographs by projecting them on sheer, fluttering veils. In one photograph borrowed from the archives of the

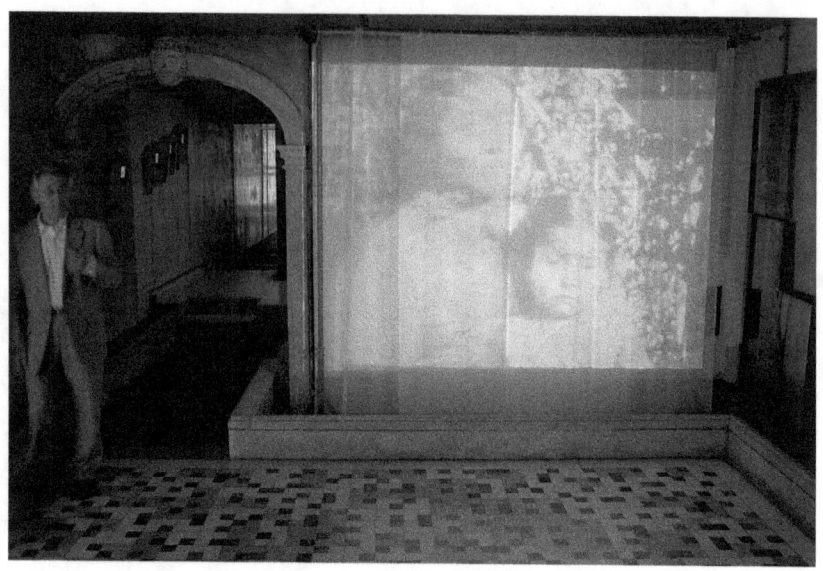

2.5 James Luna, "Apparitions (Past and Present)," 2005. Photographic installation included in *Emendatio* at the Fondazione Querini Stampalia, Fifty-First Venice Biennale. National Museum of the American Indian, Smithsonian Institution, KF05ItalyG110. Photo by Katherine Fogden.

San Diego Museum of Man, taken by the ethnographer Constance DuBois in 1906, Luna's great-grandmother, Maria Soledad Apish Trujillo, sits in calico dress with two of her children (fig. 2.5). Luna's projection superimposes a color photograph in which his niece, Jenny Nelson, and her daughter, both wearing tennis shoes, adopt the poses of their ancestors. Photographs form a crux of continuity between living and dead. Luna's archival installations connect, finally, to the montage of sound and images playing on the monitor embedded in the altar of "Chapel for Pablo Tac," including historical and contemporary photographs of California missions, the rhythmic beating of coastal waves, and the grand churches of Venice. In "Chapel for Pablo Tac," "Spinning Woman," and "Apparitions (Past and Present)," skepticism toward a colonized past shifts to respect for all that persists through it. These works foreground archival documents and material culture as bearers of indigenous histories, ancestral relations, and spiritual potencies across centuries and oceans. Luna grants objects an unprecedented capacity to perform alongside, and in interaction with, bodies. *Emendatio* is both archive and repertoire, and in it we are as likely to encounter breathing objects as stilled bodies.

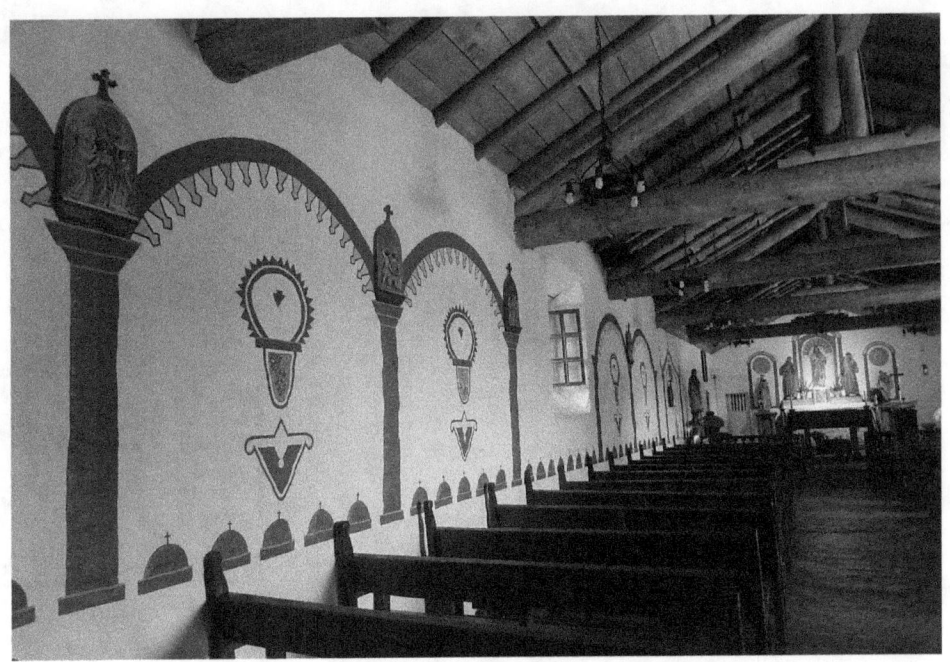

2.6 Mission San Antonio de Pala, Pala, CA, 2015. Photo by Jessica L. Horton.

Spirit and Letter

In what sense is the central installation of *Emendatio* a "chapel"? What room
is there for indigenous cultural knowledge in a space apparently circumscribed
by Catholicism? The diamonds and equal-armed crosses that march across the
temporary walls plunge us deeper into mission history for answers. Luna cited
a restored mural of likely indigenous design at Mission San Antonio de Pala,
a satellite chapel of Mission San Luis Rey, established by Peyri in 1816 (and
still active today), as inspiration (fig. 2.6).[53] Spaniards documented instances in
which Native peoples decorated crosses erected by missionaries with sardines,
deer meat, and broken arrows. The Christian cross apparently resonated with
the tall wooden poles used to demarcate territory and honor deities prior to
Spanish arrival.[54] Equal-armed crosses, repeated in the design of the basket
on the altar, point in the four cardinal directions invoked by Luna throughout
his oeuvre.[55] They appear on the surface of rocks, rattles, weapons, and textiles
throughout southern California. In his 1922 study "Basketry Designs of the
Mission Indians," ethnographer A. L. Kroeber identified eight distinct equal-

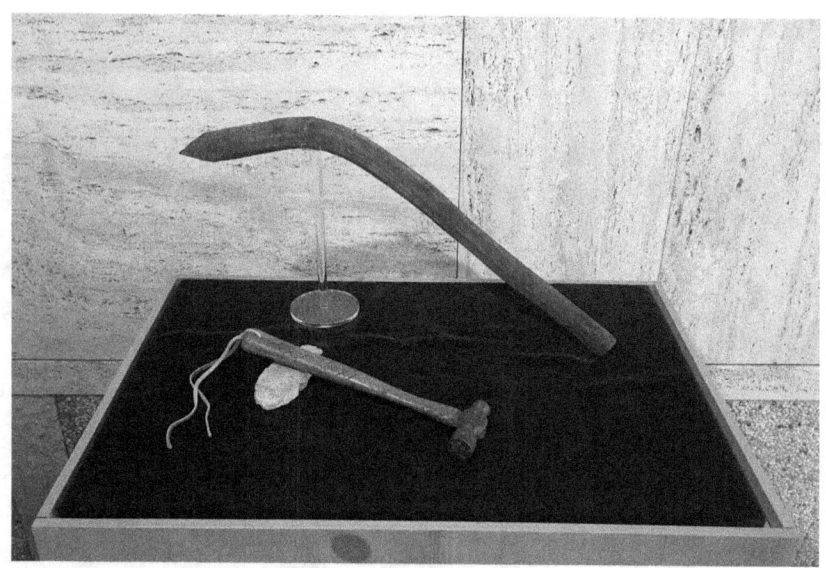

2.7 James Luna, "Chapel for Pablo Tac," detail, 2005. Mixed-media installation included in *Emendatio* at the Fondazione Querini Stampalia, Fifty-First Venice Biennale. National Museum of the American Indian, Smithsonian Institution, KFo5ItalyA397. Photo by Katherine Fogden.

armed crosses and five different diamond motifs, asserting that "the cross is a native design . . . simple diamonds are frequent," the latter perhaps referencing rattlesnakes, which are ubiquitous in the Southwest and frequently honored in indigenous art and rituals.[56] In a nearby vitrine, a diamond pattern appears etched on the handle of an aged ball-peen hammer, a tool of European manufacture to which Luna has attached a leather strap, transforming it into a makeshift tomahawk (fig. 2.7). Identical etchings cover a throwing stick of the kind Tac used in the Quechnajuisom ball game *uauquis*— or perhaps, as Luna suggested to me, "he was able to kill big rats in the Vatican gardens."[57] The symbolic vocabulary of "Chapel for Pablo Tac" bespeaks a history in which colonizer and colonized, sacred and mundane, spirit and letter, became thoroughly enmeshed.

Throughout the installation, Luna deployed basic conventions that bespeak chapel—altar, pews, liturgical tools—while drawing out an inherent flexibility in the laws and definitions governing Catholic religious space. According to the *New Advent Catholic Encyclopedia*, a chapel is defined less by architecture than by the activities that occur inside: "Any oratory where

Mass and Divine service were celebrated was called . . . chapel." Yet the word "chapel" can also name a private space of worship where no Mass is held. Here the stipulations of the Catholic Church are especially vague: "The . . . law of the Church, while placing no restriction on the erection of chapels that form part of a larger church, lays down very definite regulations respecting any that belong to the category of private chapels. This applies, however, only to those intended for the celebration of Mass; there is no restriction whatever as regards the setting apart of a particular chamber in a private house merely for purposes of private prayer and devotion."[58] The definition of *chapel* slips between the physicality of a structure and the activity for which it is built; between an institutional rulebook and individual intention; between gestures coordinated by Church authority, and bodies that might well bend the rituals of devotion to unexpected ends. Luna's "Chapel for Pablo Tac" embraces this ambiguity. No priest is present to direct the proceedings; no schedule of events hangs at the door. The pews and sound of ringing church bells invite visitors to gather for what is ultimately an unspecified purpose. This elasticity makes room for us to consider the perpetuation of indigenous knowledge—specifically, a framework of undivided earth—in the context of the enormous conversion project of the California missions.

Key here is historian David J. Weber's characterization of encounters between Spanish missionaries and indigenous peoples as a "struggle for sacred space." Weber stressed that for Native peoples of California at that time, "the whole world was sacred space," that is, undivided by missionary accounts of a distant heaven. Spirits of both benevolent and malevolent behavior inhabited clouds, trees, stones, lakes, and animals. Shamanic healing ceremonies, puberty rituals, and other activities focused on appeasing these spirits, enlisting their guidance, and generally establishing harmony with them. By contrast, the Spanish "prayed to an extraterrestrial being. Their god had created nature, but was not in nature."[59] Befitting its origins in post-Enlightenment Spain, the religious order depended—at least in theory—on a variant of archival logic: the rational appeal of "the word of God" could be gleaned through sermons and study. The friars believed that the Quechnajuisom, like Europeans, were able to reason their way to salvation. The Franciscan missionary project "rested upon the fundamental presupposition that although the Indians lived in blind idolatry and bondage to the devil, they were nonetheless rational human beings created in the image of God, capable of appropriating their redemption, and of becoming effective churchmen." Two steps were required to convert the heathens: first, iconoclasm, or the destruction of indigenous idols, dances, and other evidence of animist beliefs, and second, their replacement with "crosses, churches . . . preaching, teaching, and administration of the Sacraments."[60] According to historian David J. Silverman, "missionaries would struggle endlessly to convince Indians that religion should be a closed system of beliefs and rituals, that it should focus on the next world (heaven) instead of this one, that there was absolute good and absolute evil, and especially that they should halt their stream of interaction with the spiritual forces of the world."[61] While Weber and Silverman emphasized the Church's unchanging rulebook, they noted that in practice, conversions were filled with accommodations. So long as indigenous power remained multiply manifest in everyday environments, the Franciscans were hard pressed to abolish its many forms. They, too, broke the rules, appealing to the very idolatrous activities they verbally condemned in order to familiarize word of a distant God.

In a rare study of mission arts, art historian Clara Bargellini argued that missionaries likewise invested Catholic objects with an unusual degree of spiritual power in New Spain. Luxurious icons with miraculous powers could bolster the meager resources of the Franciscans, who vowed to live in poverty and convert indigenous populations without military force. The friars called urgently for the importation of patron saints and images of the Virgin Mary across vast seas and rugged terrains to adorn their missions. In 1769, when seven missionaries arrived from Spain to establish the first outposts in Alta California, they bore vestments and silver, seven sculptures of saints, and thirteen "paintings on copper of various advocations." Two years later, Father Junípero Serra, the Mallorcan priest responsible for the enterprise, learned that one such shipment was lost. He ordered five replacement paintings of saints from Mexico City's most renowned maker of icons, José de Paez. Bargellini explained that icons "protected the missionaries, who identified with them. They also participated in worship, they converted and cured indigenous people, they granted favors to those who implored them, and they shared the missionaries' fortunes."[62] Francisco Palóu, a mentee who authored a biography of Serra, told a story that dramatizes Spanish reliance on the power of images. When a group of warriors attempted to prevent Serra from establishing Mission San Gabriel in 1774, the Spaniards unveiled their most powerful cannon: a portrait of *Our Lady of the Seven Sorrows*, the sight of which caused the Natives to throw down their arrows in adoration.[63]

Although Palóu's story may involve a good dose of colonial fantasy, his suggestion that indigenous peoples recognized European icons as manifestations of power is not without grounds. The Quechnajuisom painted for ritual purposes prior to conquest, sprinkling natural pigments on the floors of cere-monial structures to create maps of the universe.[64] Rock art sites throughout southern California bear paintings of spirit beings who aid highly trained religious leaders, cosmological phenomena such as stars and moons, and ab-stract geometric forms like those repeated on the walls of "Chapel for Pablo Tac." Visions of potent other-than-human persons often came to those who ritually ingested datura. Persisting throughout the missionary endeavor, in-digenous understandings hold that properly educated humans may access spiritual presences in lived environments and influence their power for human good.[65] As Palóu's story hints, friars not only believed personally in the effi-cacy of certain objects and images; they also relied heavily on those materials to bridge an otherwise vast gap between Spanish and indigenous ways of conceptualizing the same earth. The pressures of mission life rendered the divided cosmos of the colonizers highly negotiable.

Some of the most compelling visual evidence for missions as a sacred "middle ground" occurs in Catholic icons painted by Native artists who were trained by friars.[66] Discussing a painting of Saint Raphael that hangs to-day at Mission Santa Inés, historian Steven Hackel noted that an unnamed Chumash artist incorporated unusual characteristics such as realistic fish and muscular wings. He speculated that the latter represent those of the Califor-nia condor, a bird of religious significance among the Chumash, who adorn their chiefly capes with its feathers.[67] Native Californians revered condors, eagles, and other birds of prey as powerful entities capable of passing between realms of sky and earth. An eagle features prominently in origin stories across California as told in the twentieth century, where he joins hummingbird and coyote as one of the First People (prototypical beings who lived before hu-mans), a leader responsible for generating human life on dry ground after a flood.[68] Likewise, the indigenous maker of saintly images relocated Christian symbols in a familiar, lived environment filled with spiritual entities.

If we placed this Chumash Saint Raphael, an angelic avian icon, at the center of a violently divided modernity, he might sit beside Paul Klee's *Angelus Novus* (1920) to whisper a different version of the story. In Walter Benjamin's famous interpretation, Klee's "angel of history" looks to the wreckage of the past, longing to "make whole what has been smashed," but a strong wind called "progress" propels her into the future.[69] By contrast, Saint Raphael withstands the gale, his message transformed through earthly encounters with humans who do not necessarily seek their salvation in another time and place. His power accrues through incarnation here and now, a process described by

Bruno Latour as "renewal, the rendering present again of this immanence."[70] In a reading sympathetic to global events of colonial conversion, Latour strove to recover the matter-of-fact materialism evident when Christians narrate their meetings with holy presences. He argued that the address of an angel "cannot be about anything other than what is present. It is about the present, not about the past nor about the future."[71] Such a case challenges prevalent interpretations of Christianity as belief in "transcendence, a Spirit from above"—a straining toward the future that hitches heavenly aspiration to secular progress.[72] Latour's angel instead recalls Benjamin's articulation of historical materialism in a different thesis: "A historian who takes [material] as his point of departure stops telling the sequence of events like the beads of a rosary. Instead, he grasps the constellation which his own era has formed with a definite earlier one. Thus he establishes a conception of the present as the 'time of the now' which is shot through with chips of Messianic time."[73] I am tempted to read Saint Raphael's muscular wings in precisely this light: the saint belongs neither in a distant Christian heaven nor in a receding indigenous past, but in embodied interaction with a receptive human in a land shared with condors. As palpable holy beings and human visionaries relate to each other on earth, the dogma of letter yields to a process of spiritual renewal that knits divided times and places back together. Latour finally shares Benjamin's determination to invest the angelic image with an earthly ethics, for only through a "more charitable and respectful definition of religion than the one provided . . . by secular and modernist interpretations" can we begin to "compose a common world."[74] Indigenous Californians share the earth not only with their Catholic colonizers, but with people worldwide who claim the sacred as an integral dimension of everyday experience.

In the absence of angels, Luna redirected visitors' attention to the efficacy of unassuming objects that play crucial roles in both Catholic and indigenous spiritual life. Among the humble liturgical tools is a chalice intended to bear the blood of Christ, glass vessels used for the administration of last rites, a gold-plated incense burner accompanied by a pot of incense, and a small copper bell (fig. 2.8 and plate 27; see also plate 23). Containers for sacred substances and material aids to rituals are essential and yet often overlooked components of Catholic sacraments; in the installation, they are elevated to the status of ritual performers and placed in dialogue with their indigenous counterparts. On the altar opposite the chalice stand two feathers resembling those of eagles, their shafts wrapped in strips of leather, nestled in a miniature woven basket tray and set inside a box once used to hold fine bottles of wine. Others

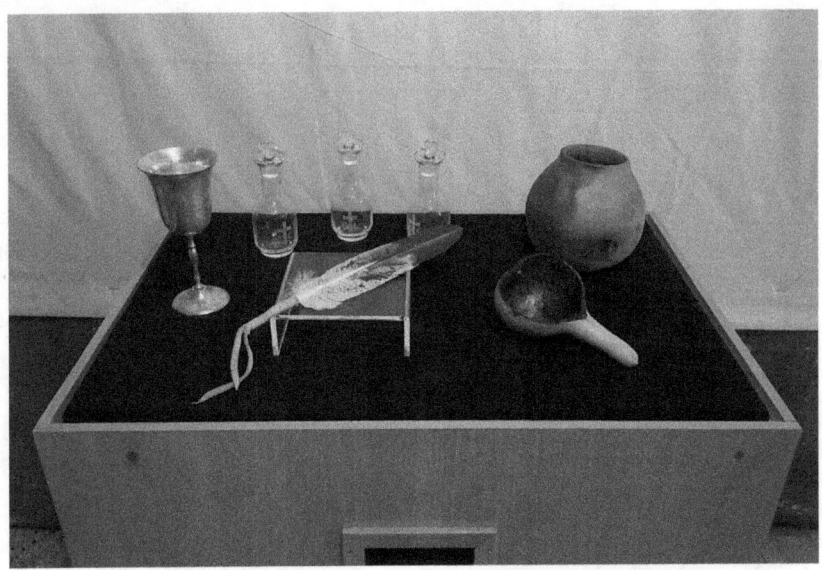

2.8 James Luna, "Chapel for Pablo Tac," detail, 2005. Mixed-media installation included in *Emendatio* at the Fondazione Querini Stampalia, Fifty-First Venice Biennale. National Museum of the American Indian, Smithsonian Institution, KF05ItalyA368. Photo by Katherine Fogden.

appear in the vitrines along the walls.[75] Feathers are metonyms for live animals, retaining a literal connection to potent beings that populate the planet; so too the small, fringed leather medicine pouches and abalone shells filled with ashes from a ritual burning (see plate 27). Luna intermingles and exalts the material underpinnings of Catholic and indigenous belief, revealing the surprisingly humble means through which spirit is manifested in dynamic relation to the living.

"Chapel for Pablo Tac" finally intervenes in a strain of modernism invoking churches and chapels as "models of installation and viewer involvement."[76] Art historian Alexander Nagel echoed Latour in arguing that Christian practices of devotion suspend key characteristics we typically attribute to post-Enlightenment European thought: progressive temporality; a rational, centered subject; and the increasing disenchantment of the material world. He showed that by borrowing from medieval forms and functions, a surprising number of modern and contemporary artists were empowered to give form to nonnormative temporal, spatial, and material concepts.[77] "Chapel for Pablo Tac" similarly foregrounds neglected indigenous makers and users who bent

Christian religious doctrine to a range of earthly ends. These diverse modernisms renew medieval and indigenous modalities in tandem, transforming the "struggle for sacred space" into shared ground.

Coiled Baskets

One object in "Chapel for Pablo Tac" especially gives form to the concept of undivided earth I have been discussing. Positioned at the apex of the installation appears a simple basket woven of golden plant fiber, bearing four stylized representations of eagle feathers in the shape of an equal-armed cross (see plate 23). Luna told me that he found the object in a jewelry shop in Albuquerque and immediately recognized its potential for *Emendatio*, given the strong cultural and historical ties between indigenous communities throughout southwestern North America.[78] His choice to replace the Virgin or crucifix with an anonymous coiled basket prompts me to reflect on the significance of Native basketry beyond the well-documented "Indian craze" for curios in the nineteenth and twentieth centuries.[79] Before and after European contact, baskets served a wide variety of functions such as food and water storage, cooking, carrying children, bearing valuables, holding ritual substances, and gifting to prominent persons. Never deemed idolatrous by the Spanish, the art of weaving flourished in New Spain. Missionaries indulged this attractive, useful, and seemingly secular activity, even commissioning Native women to weave for trade and diplomacy. In turn, weavers proliferated a range of new basketry forms that incorporated Spanish words and pictorial devices with geometric symbols of indigenous origin. Certainly, motifs such as eagle feathers in the shape of a cross suggest basketry's syncretic potential. I focus instead on the underexplored significance of the coiling method used to produce them. This technical dimension of weaving allowed for the coordination of material, pictorial, geometric, and even written elements into an indivisible whole. Elevating the art form to the highpoint of "Chapel for Pablo Tac," Luna calls our attention to baskets as models of undivided earth in miniature.

Coiled baskets consist of a foundation of plant rods in the shape of a continuous spiral from the center of the basket to the rim; each course of the spiral is referred to as a *coil*. The weaver wraps and stiches the coils tightly together with additional strands of plant fiber and the help of a bone awl. Decoration is most often a matter of introducing strands from different plant sources, some dyed by mud, sea life, or plant juices, in the course of connecting the coils. Pattern and image are thus fundamentally structural, not applied, requiring the weaver to envision the whole prior to the start.[80] Indeed, as contemporary weavers have assured me, the process of creating a basket begins long before coiling, with the harvesting, drying, splitting, and dyeing of suitable grasses.[81] As Jan Timbrook explained, plants, the literal foundation of basketry arts, are "everywhere in [Native] life, not only in daily activities but also in thought, philosophy, and ways of viewing the world."[82] Weaving represents vast botanical and geographical knowledge and necessarily unfolds in an intimate relationship to the environment.[83]

The resulting forms sometimes played significant political roles in transatlantic relations during missionization. In an extraordinary tray completed circa 1820 at Mission San Buenaventura, approximately 150 miles north of Tac's birthplace, Chumash weaver Juana Basilia Sitmelelene (1782–1838) created a central motif out of black mud-dyed juncus by combining reliefs from two different silver dollars produced in Mexico and circulated through the colonies (plates 28–30). In the "pillar" coin, a Spanish crown divinely anointed with a cross presides over a pair of overlapping globes—"Old World" and "New World" united—atop ocean waves flanked by Pillars of Hercules. The latter marked the entrance to the Strait of Gibraltar in Antiquity and signaled to Europeans the limits of their known world. In this case, pillars framing representations of the globe hint at newfound Spanish imperial confidence in the wake of American conquest. The central motif is surrounded by seven heraldry designs that closely resemble one stamped on the "portrait" dollar, bordered by a band of checkered diamonds that echo the wall motifs of "Chapel for Pablo Tac."

Weaving effectively levels the coin's message of political and economic dominion. Around the outside edge appears a curvilinear inscription: "La trabajó la Neofita Juana Basilia, deseosa de contribuir a las atenciones del Sor Govor SOLA p^a con su ilustre Mariscal del Campo el Sor D^n Jose dela Cruz" (She made it, the neophyte Juana Basilia, desirous of contributing to the attentions paid by Governor Solá to his illustrious Field Marshal Señor Don José de la Cruz). The last Spanish governor of California, de Sola apparently commissioned the basket as a gift for fellow royalist de la Cruz, just prior to Mexican independence.[84] Yet the object's diplomatic function—to communicate Spanish authority over American lands—was transformed when Sitmelelene turned authoritative text into pliable textile through an embodied, material process unique to indigenous California. Like Luna's blanket, her coiled form displaces the words from the top of a hierarchical system of signification to embed them in a variegated field of cultural expression. Signs of Spanish heraldry, religion, and cartography undergo a similar fate. In their translation from machine-impressed metal to handwoven textile, the images lose their legibility as symbols and are subordinated to the patterns created by the coiling technique. Sitmelelene converted hard, smooth lines into supple, serrated stiches; she replaced raised, undulating ocean waves with a flattened checkerboard; the constraints of her radiating coils deformed the contours of spherical globes. To create the silver coins, figures were impressed upon an unarticulated surface, thereafter physically and conceptually elevated above their ground. The process is an apt metaphor for the imposition of European colonial power on American soil. Through coiling, the images are interwoven with a surrounding field of golden sumac to form a single, nonhierarchical plane.

Through the lens of *Emendatio*, I speculate that weaving retained a tangible relationship to undivided earth under conditions of occupation. When the Chumash first encountered Europeans, they harvested weaving materials from the middle of three layered worlds that, unlike the Spanish heaven and earth, could be fluidly traversed by living persons who possessed adequate ritual knowledge, power objects, spirit helpers, and other essential tools.[85] While continuing to transform earth-dyed plants into coiled baskets under missionization, weavers from time to time deformed words and pictures from a distant Spain and its forceful colonizers, enveloping them in an intimately known geography.[86] Luna's choice to position a humble basket in place of a crucifix prompts us to consider that, like Sitmelelene, countless anonymous indigenous women quietly integrated elements of archive and repertoire, spirit and letter, beneath the watchful eyes of friars. In "Chapel for Pablo Tac," a coiled form replaces the Christian symbol of salvation as a purveyor of undivided earth. Instead of almighty God, an unnamed weaver has the last word.

Modernisms at the Venice Biennale

Emendatio performed its unique historical work at the interstice of a contemporary mega-exhibition's secular stage and the Catholic architecture permeating the island of Venice. From its beginning in 1895, the Venice Biennale followed the model of world fairs, where Western nation-states competed to exhibit their cultural sophistication, technical prowess, and colonial might.[87] Unique among biennial brethren, the event today still hosts seventy-seven national pavilions independently owned and curated by institutions—most often national governments—around the world. Additionally, it comprises a group exhibition curated by a major international commissioner (the "Arsenale") and a wide range of "collateral" events sponsored by organizations willing to pay a steep price to participate.[88] In 1995, Cree/Blackfeet Gerald McMaster first curated the work of Métis artist Edward Poitras in the Canadian Pavilion, prompting two decades of concerted efforts to secure Native representation at the oldest and perhaps most prestigious "global" art exhibition in the world. Commentators repeatedly contrast Canada's efforts with the failure of the United States to support indigenous artists abroad. It is a truism that an artist of Native American heritage has never been selected to exhibit in the proud neoclassical U.S. Pavilion, built with private funds in 1930 during a period of intensive nationalisms on both sides of the Atlantic.[89] Durham issued an especially rotten proposal in 2011: "I would like to be given the US Pavilion of the Venice Biennale. (I mean with no restrictions of course.) I propose a large dead bison on a Grand Cherokee Chief. As the carcass begins to reek maybe the entire area would be anointed with this 'Essencia America,' and art lovers would need gas masks. In the evening bats would help control the flies. We could bring in *zopilotes* [vultures] from Texas. (P.S. The concept of this project is copyrighted.)" (fig. 2.9).[90] Similarly hinting at a history of colonialist exclusion, a reviewer from *Art in America* dubbed *Emendatio* "the 'American' pavilion to [Ed] Ruscha's 'U.S.' pavilion."[91] Yet *Emendatio*'s framework of undivided earth transcends the competitive impulses that continue to shape the biennial, turning our attention to sacred dimensions of modernity irreducible to colonial nationalism.

Art historian Bill Anthes deemed 2005 a "breakthrough" year in the efforts to secure the visibility of Native American artists on a global stage.[92] Multiple events in Venice that year built on the foundations of McMaster and Apache scholar Nancy Marie Mithlo, who has tenaciously arranged group exhibitions of Native American artists since 1999 under the auspices of the Santa Fe–based Indigenous Arts Action Alliance, or IA3, with and without formal biennial representation. Mithlo stated that her goal was the creation of a "sovereign, culturally specific platform that is simultaneously engaged with larger art currents," invoking an indigenous island in a sea of biennials still largely governed by modern nations.[93] She took a hiatus in 2005 and 2007 as the NMAI celebrated the opening of a prominent new location on the National Mall in Washington, DC. With Ho-Chunk artist and curator Truman Lowe at its helm, the "museum different" channeled federal money toward sponsoring Luna and Edgar Heap of Birds to launch collateral events.[94] *Emendatio* joined Rebecca Belmore's video installation *Fountain*, the offi-

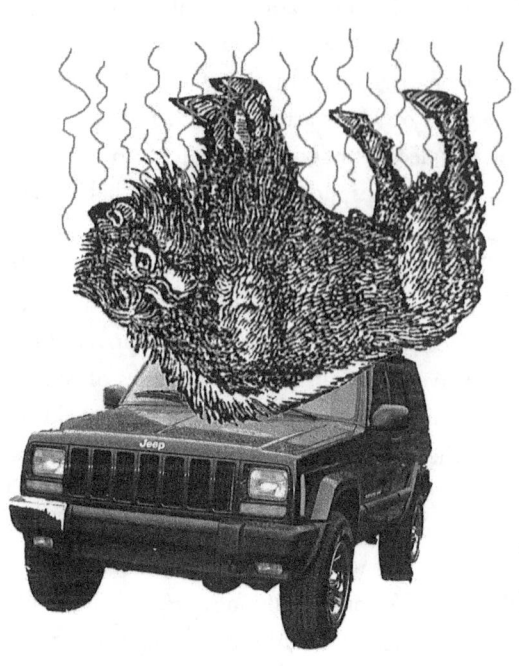

2.9 Jimmie Durham with
Abraham Cruzvillegas,
proposal for the U.S. Pavilion
of the Venice Biennale, 2011.
Courtesy of the artist.

cial 2005 selection for the nearby Canadian Pavilion. Both projects received
critical attention through the NMAI-sponsored symposium and publication
Vision, Space, Desire: Global Perspectives and Cultural Hybridity, featuring international scholars exploring "the role of Native artists within the global
cultural community."[95]

As Anthes discussed at length, assertions of the marginality of Native artists vis-à-vis the international art biennial circuit and an array of other arguments for inclusion permeate the North American literature on the topic. Jean
Fisher was among the first to address the issue in her introductory remarks to
the edited volume *Global Visions: Towards a New Internationalism in the Visual
Arts* in 1994. She described the "subordination of the non-white artist" to
"the philosophical parameters that govern both the historiography of art and
curatorial practice as the legitimating organs of cultural production."[96] Many
commentaries included in a volume of essays resulting from the *Vision, Space,
Desire* conference charged Native Americans with contesting a geopolitical
framework comprising "centers" and "margins," "insiders" and "outsiders," already evident in the artistic discourses of the 1980s discussed in the previous

chapter. Jolene Rickard urged the "simple recognition of our existence as discrete political and philosophical spaces throughout the world."[97] McMaster similarly wrote that Native artists can "help us to understand that centers include culture, language and family, among other loci."[98] Inviting indigenous and other marginalized voices to a conversation across national borders would, in this view, subvert Eurocentric systems of taste and value and make way for what Mithlo called "alternative knowledge systems."[99] Elegantly superseding this spatial imagination, Paul Chaat Smith stated, "The Indian experience is at the very center of how the world we live in today came to be.... James Luna tells . . . an Indian story, but it is also an Italian story." Smith viewed 2005 as part of "an ongoing effort for Indians to be present in the world." More important than visitor numbers or pavilion inclusion was the question of "whether we can build a new understanding of what it means to be human in the twenty-first century."[100]

I question the presumption that all Native American artists are outsiders to an internally coherent global art system. Mithlo has gone to great lengths to curate emerging and little-known artists in Venice, but she also included works by WalkingStick, an artist who has held numerous residencies in Rome, alongside other established artists. Meanwhile, Belmore, Luna, Heap of Birds, and Durham are among those invited by global gatekeepers to participate in mega-exhibitions and artists' residences abroad. In addition to Italy, Luna's career has taken him to Japan, Brazil, Britain, Australia, New Zealand, and Montenegro; Belmore's to Spain, Belgium, Australia, and Albania; Heap of Birds's to Australia, South Africa, and the Virgin Islands. Perhaps more so than any other artist of indigenous heritage, Durham is beloved of the biennial circuit and regularly invited to reside and exhibit in countries around the world.[101] Following the work of Miwon Kwon, Pamela Lee, T. J. Demos, and others, I submit that artists who move through a given cultural system likewise bear some responsibility for its production. It is precisely from this *inside* position that subjects retain a measure of agency within the vast purview of globalization, whether repeating its exclusionary privileges or addressing colonial legacies that haunt its present shape.[102]

In a related vein, Anthes argued that Native artists participate in the "'nomadic' model of artistic production" that currently prevails in the international art world.[103] Shifting the terms of *Vision, Space, Desire*, he proposed "a shift in emphasis away from issues specific to the history of settler colonialism in the US and Canada—land, treaty rights, and sovereignty; citizenship and

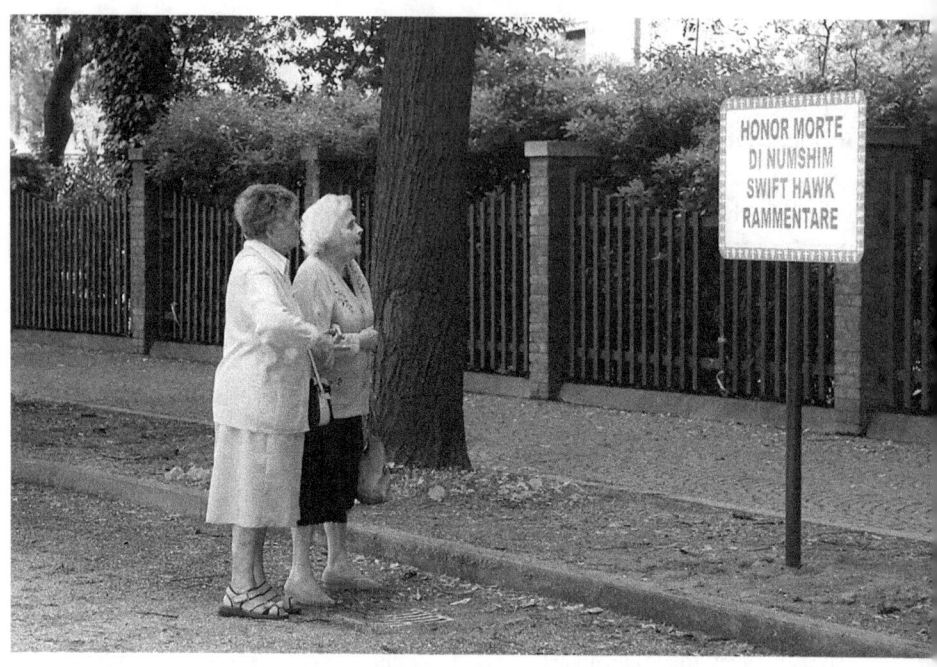

2.10 Hock E Aye Vi Edgar Heap of Birds, *Most Serene Republics*, detail, 2007.
Installation of metal signs exhibited at the Fifty-Second Venice Biennale in Venice,
Italy. National Museum of the American Indian, Smithsonian Institution (image #81).
Photo by Mara Tagon Comin.

the legal fictions of identity and blood quantum—to an engagement with
a transnational cohort of artists, critics, and theorists whose work examines
issues of travel and encounter, displacement, migration and exile from a
cosmopolitan—and what some critics and curators term a 'post-Indian'—
perspective."[104] I share Anthes's important observation that Native artists are
addressing a range of issues beyond "Indian" identity (while questioning the
"post-" in chapter 1). I furthermore maintain throughout this book that as
Durham, Luna, WalkingStick, and Houle travel abroad, their treatment of
"displacement, migration and exile" remains uniquely inflected by ongoing occupation in the Americas. *Emendatio* neither uncritically reiterates the terms
of nomadism that prevail in the biennial system today nor retreats to hermetic
conceptions of place and identity. By anchoring his travels to Venice in Tac's
prior journey to Rome, Luna reattached contemporary conditions of mobility
in which he willingly participated to a much longer history of displacements
resulting in complex entanglements of people, places, and things. *Emendatio*

holds the memory of European colonization that has reshaped the Americas while refocusing our attention on a continuity of creative responses. Luna furthermore shared his visibility on a global stage in Venice with the modernisms of Tac, Sitmelelene, and other indigenous agents from the past.[105]

In 2007, Heap of Birds carried on with this historical work in *Most Serene Republics*, his NMAI-sponsored collateral contribution to the Venice Biennale (fig. 2.10). Around the island of Venice he erected characteristic signposts in Italian, English, and Cheyenne, directing visitors to *rammentare* ("remember" in Italian) the Lakota performers who traveled with Buffalo Bill Cody's Wild West Show through Venice and other major cities in the late nineteenth century.[106] Like the other artists in this book, Heap of Birds situated his installation in the grooves of indigenous peoples who came before him, invoking what Bill Anthes called "a sense of temporal return . . . and histories as circularities" consistent throughout his oeuvre.[107] Such a project assures us that indigenous "breakthroughs" on European soil are not the exclusive domain of contemporary artists. Rather, they are a consistent feature of histories indigenous people shared and shaped in the wake of conquest, helping to establish a ground on which living artists might stand. While Heap of Birds's message relies on the power of signifying text for its political urgency, *Emendatio* invites our engagement with an unfinished story of modernity through material and spiritual means. The exhibition reintegrates archive and repertoire, spirit and letter, on an undivided earth—a framework of temporal, spatial, and material connections that must be renewed by the living. Lessons from Luna's Venetian project shape my approach to the ceremonial dance paintings of Fred Kabotie in the following chapter. Allied with the work of contemporary artists throughout this book, they withstood displacement in the U.S. Pavilion of the Venice Biennale in 1932 by inviting multisensory and embodied forms of engagement.

THREE "They Sent Me Way Out in the

Foreign Country and Told Me to Forget It"

FRED KABOTIE, DANCE MEMORIES, AND THE

1932 U.S. PAVILION OF THE VENICE BIENNALE

In 2011, as vaporetti bore throngs of art tourists to the sprawling events of the Fifty-Fourth International Art Exhibition of the Venice Biennale, I sat in the Historical Archives of Contemporary Arts, peering at a photograph dated 1932 (fig. 3.1). The middle ground of the image reveals oil paintings by well-known American artists adorning the walls of the neoclassical U.S. Pavilion, just two years after Grand Central Art Galleries in New York raised private donations to build it.[1] Three canvases by George Bellows line the center wall: in *The Sand Cart* (1917), laborers load a horse-drawn cart backed by golden hills on the shores of California; *Two Women* (1924) contrasts a heavily clothed female with her nude counterpart, the postwar "new woman"; in *Gramercy Park* (1920), a girl in white skips rope beneath a dense canopy of trees in Manhattan.[2] Scenes of a tradition-steeped American Southwest by members of the Taos Society of Artists flank the rightmost doorway.[3] Ernest L. Blumenschein's *Adobe Village—Winter* (1929) features a procession of Penitentes, members of a Roman Catholic sect active in northern New Mexico, advancing in the foreground of a tranquil, snow-dusted pueblo (plate 31).[4] In Walter Ufer's *Two Riders* (1930), a Pueblo man and woman on horseback are anchored in a vivid desert landscape (plate 32).[5] At first glance, the exhibition appears to offer a portal out of Venice, picturing the diversity of landscapes and people in the United States.

There is something else. Through the open doorway at right, glimmers of white disturb the telescopic effect of the canvases. Constellations of Pueblo

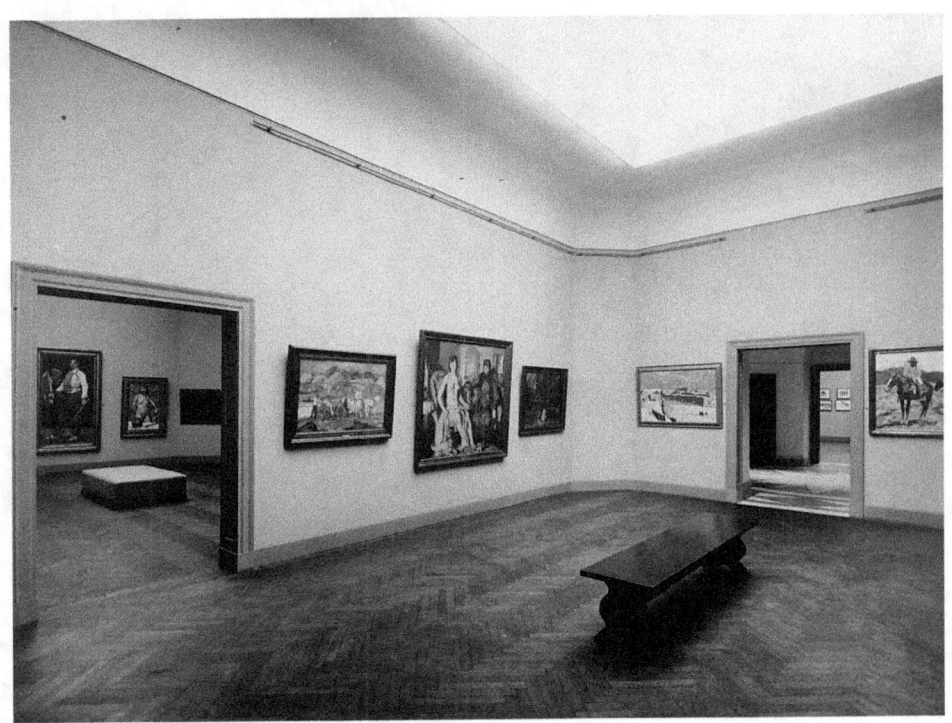

3.1 Padiglione degli Stati Uniti, 1932. © La Biennale di Venezia, Photo Library, Series "Attualità e Allestimenti," XVIII. International Art Exhibition, 1932, n. 1036.

dancers in elaborate dress float on the surface of four sheets of otherwise unadorned paper. Delineated in gouache by some of the first professional Native American painters of the twentieth century, the figures contrast starkly with the saturated scenes on either side of the doorway. Unlike the Pueblo riders and Penitentes, the dancers are not fixed in an elsewhere by a glue of continuous visual detail. They do not recede into a distant American landscape. Gazing at the photograph, I found myself pulled in two directions. The works in the middle ground transported me away from the canals, immersing me in early twentieth-century constructions of my nation of birth. But the figures in the background provoked a countermovement, arriving through the Pavilion doorway to join me in Venice.

The revelation of Pueblo watercolors among well-known American paintings in the U.S. Pavilion of 1932 was intellectually, as well as visually, destabilizing. As I described in the previous chapter, scholars have devoted much attention of late to the role of contemporary Native arts on a global stage,

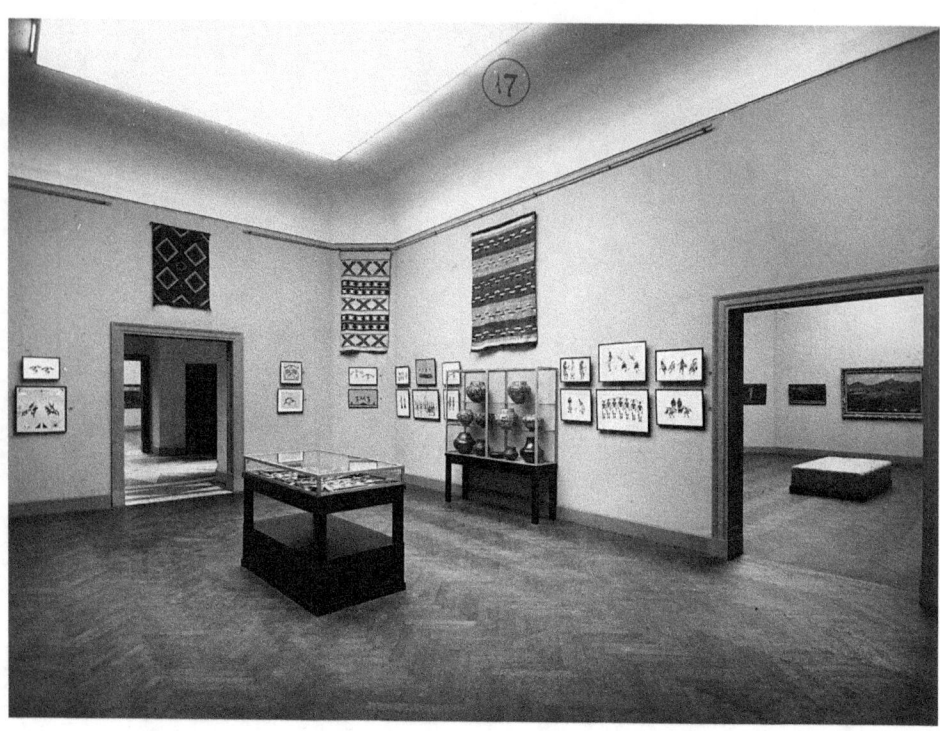

3.2 Padiglione degli Stati Uniti, 1932. © La Biennale di Venezia, Photo Library, Series "Attualità e Allestimenti," XVIII. International Art Exhibition, 1932, n. 1035.

especially the Venice Biennale, given that indigenous artists from the United States and Canada have consistently shown in various capacities since 1995.[6] Yet we are versed in a widespread truism that Native artists have never exhibited in the U.S. Pavilion.[7] A second installation photograph unearthed in Venice confronts this elision head-on (fig. 3.2). It reveals one of the four rooms of the Pavilion devoted to vitrines of turquoise jewelry, shelves of polychrome pots, and a fringe of textiles from the indigenous Southwest. Paintings of dancers and striped clowns hang in two rows at eye level, aligned with the canvases of non-Native contemporaries visible in adjoining rooms. While the potters, silversmiths, and weavers remain mostly anonymous, the names of the Native painters are listed in the Biennale catalogue: Ma Pe Wi, Santiago Cruz, Oqwa Pi, Tonita Peña, Awa Tsireh, Julian Martinez, Pen Yo Pin, Tse Ye Mu, Otis Polelonema, and Fred Kabotie.[8]

What are we to make of this doubly strange appearance of contemporary Native art at the Venice Biennale, some six decades earlier than convention attests? I argue that it is more than incidental that nobody remembers the display. The organizers of the Pavilion determined that the export of aesthetic nationalism failed that year. As European visitors gazed at contemporary Pueblo paintings, they apparently did not buy the Americans' claim that Native art was "an artistic treasury not only older but fresher and purer than anything Europe has to offer," providing deep aesthetic roots for the portraits and landscapes of Bellows, Blumenschein, John Sloan, Arthur B. Davies, and other American painters on view in the three adjoining rooms.[9] The Native American gallery marked the limits of the nation as an aesthetic and ideological frame. Equally, Pueblo paintings fell out of art history. Such forgetfulness highlights a lingering "methodological nationalism" in the study of historical Native arts.[10] Although colonial national boundaries are overtly contested in contemporary arts discourse, they often invisibly guide scholars' choice of materials from the past and, more profoundly, the questions we ask of them.[11]

As the work of AIM-generation artists underscores, a framework of modernisms prompts us to ask different questions of objects and histories we think we know. Scholars have already recounted the story of Pueblo artists without formal training who began to paint large numbers of ceremonial dances for sale throughout the 1910s and 1920s. In 1932, as Pueblo paintings hung in Venice, the movement was institutionalized with the opening of the federally funded Studio School at the Santa Fe Indian School. Reflecting the official reversal of federal assimilation policies that aimed to eliminate Native cultures, the white educator Dorothy Dunn encouraged students from around the country to paint exclusively from tribal sources.[12] Seen through the lens of nationalistic patronage, early Pueblo paintings have suffered a reputation as uniform, apolitical, and above all *static*. After the Studio School was replaced by the Institute of American Indian Arts in 1962, the early work was especially vilified by a younger, politicized generation of Native artists for its perceived conservatism. In an interview with *Art in America* in 1972, Navajo painter R. C. Gorman put it bluntly: "Stale. Overstated. Pretty. Gimmicky. Dumb. Lazy. I say, and I'm speaking to the young artists, leave Traditional Indian painting to those who brought it to full bloom."[13] My goal in this chapter is to set works by first-generation Pueblo painters back in motion. The story of the failed U.S. Pavilion highlights a gap between the aims of American patrons and Native artists. As the wrappings of national myth unraveled abroad, what other messages did the painted dancers deliver? Why did they refuse to stay in place? What were *their* terms of address?

I center my account on a reevaluation of the early work of Hopi artist

Fred Kabotie (c. 1900–1986), one of the earliest, most prolific, and influential Pueblo painters, whose works *Mountain Sheep Dance* (n.d.), *Snake Dance* (c. 1930), and *Hopi Rain God* (n.d.) were displayed in Venice (fig. 3.3).[14] Kabotie began to paint Hopi dances in what he called the "foreign country" of Santa Fe, New Mexico, while attending boarding school, as government-imposed education and widespread bans on ceremonial practices aimed to transform Native people into productive labor for the U.S. economy. Displacement was thus a primary condition of his painting. Kabotie's works from this period, as well as the words he repeated about them later in his life, reveal a persistent concern with materializing embodied memories of dance. I identify a kinship between Kabotie's paintings, musical notation, and other diagrammatic forms he encountered in Santa Fe, arguing that his spare images constitute visual solutions to the challenge of maintaining Hopi sensibilities at a distance. Their diagrammatic function withstands gaps in time as well as space, allying them with contemporary paintings, installations, and performances by Jimmie Durham, James Luna, Edgar Heap of Birds, Kay WalkingStick, and other Native artists at the Venice Biennale and elsewhere in Europe. Expanding the frame for painted dancers beyond period nationalism, I invite them to move us.

Displacement

Born in the village of Shungopavi on the Hopi Second Mesa around 1900, Kabotie traveled roughly three hundred miles in 1915 to attend the Santa Fe Indian School, a boarding school run by the U.S. government.[15] Between the passage of the General Allotment Act of 1887 discussed in chapter 1, and the appointment of progressive reformer John Collier as the commissioner of Indian affairs in 1933, federal officials parceled communal lands into private allotments, discouraged the practice of religious ceremonies, and attempted to acculturate youths through imposed education.[16] Like many resistant Hopi, Kabotie despised the day school he was forced to attend growing up in Shungopavi. About 1911 he ran away and hid on his family's land, where he tended cattle. In 1915, officials told Kabotie that if he completed three years of boarding school in Santa Fe, they would permit him to return to the mesas. In reality it was fifteen years before Kabotie moved back home.[17]

On arriving at the Santa Fe Indian School, Kabotie underwent military-style education, a key component of the government's larger campaign to

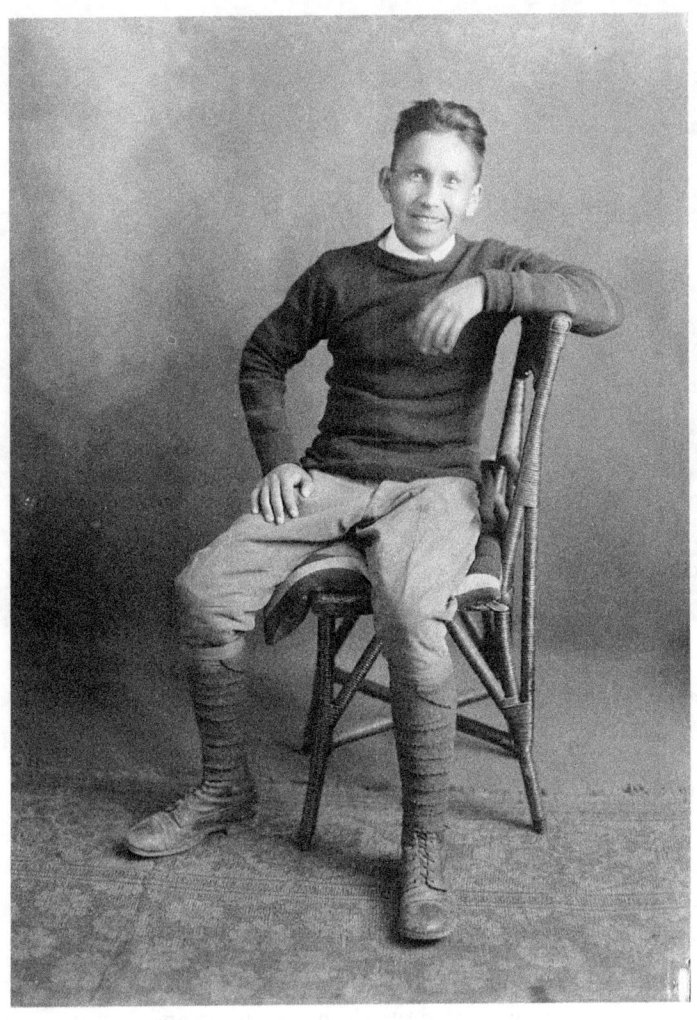

3.3 Hopi artist Fred Kabotie, c. 1930. Photo courtesy of Palace of the Governors Photo Archives (NMHM/DCA), 30714.

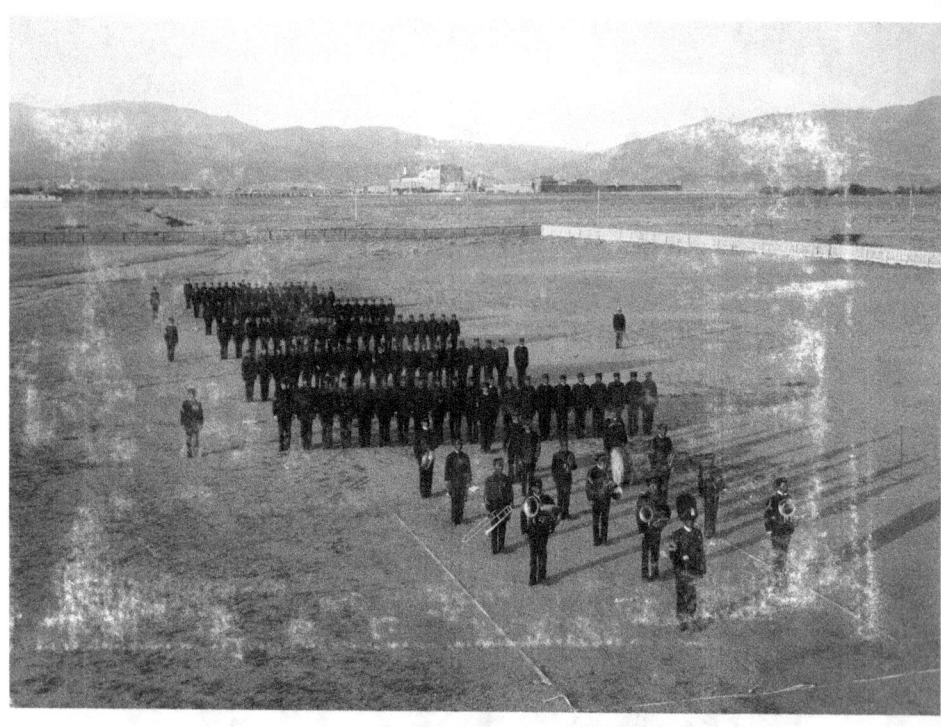

3.4 Indian boys at drill, U.S. Indian School, Santa Fe, NM, c. 1905. Photo courtesy of Palace of the Governors Photo Archives (NMHM/DCA), 3133.2.

assimilate Native minds and bodies to the U.S. labor economy (fig. 3.4). He was forced to speak only English and wear a uniform. He recalled, "The disciplinarian, Mr. Saenz, was short and stocky and had a loud voice. He always wore a military cap with a shiny band around it. In the morning when the bugle sounded reveille Mr. Saenz would yell, 'Roll out! Roll out! Everybody roll out!' We'd all jump up and run to the washroom. Then there'd be another bugle, and we would rush into a big room and line up for roll call."[18] At stake was not only the ideological inculcation of Native students, but also bodily forgetting, as neural pathways once primed to Hopi cultural rhythms conformed to regiments segregated by gender and age and marked with the letters *A*, *B*, *C*. Drills and bugles encouraged Native youths to "evolve" toward greater productivity. Superintendent of Pueblo Day Schools P. T. Lonergan explained in 1916, "It is our business to bring [the Indian] out of the past and put him in the twentieth century. It is our duty to make him efficient and we are making him efficient."[19] Boarding schools are a quintessential case of colonial biopolitics, enacting a widespread agenda to realign indigenous spatial and temporal sensibilities toward the nation's industrial progress.[20]

Kabotie obeyed the drills just as the U.S. government consolidated an attack against Pueblo dances. In 1915 Lonergan submitted a report to his superiors in Washington, DC, describing dances "so bestial as to prohibit their description."[21] Soon educators, government officials, missionaries, and social reformers launched a campaign to prohibit ceremonial dances by calling attention to their presumed sexual and moral excesses. In 1921, Commissioner of Indian Affairs Charles H. Burke issued a circular banning "any disorderly or plainly excessive performance that promotes superstitious cruelty, licentiousness, idleness, danger to health, and shiftless indifference to family welfare."[22] The attacks continued throughout the 1920s, perpetuating an image of Pueblo cultures as timeless, barbaric, and antithetical to the success of the nation.

Not all were sympathetic to the assimilation ethos. Much as it is today, Santa Fe was a crossroads for tourists, businessmen, government officials, anthropologists, artists, and laborers of Anglo, Native, and Hispanic heritage. Many white artists and intellectuals who went to the Southwest were deeply ambivalent about the values of industrial progress. They vehemently defended the aesthetic and spiritual properties of Pueblo dance—and, by extension, the painting movement they helped to launch—as an antidote to the alienating effects of modernity. When progressive educator John David DeHuff was appointed superintendent of the Santa Fe Indian School in 1918, he and his wife, Elizabeth, encouraged students to remember and record their cultural traditions. The DeHuffs likely followed the example of archaeologist Edgar L. Hewett, who encouraged painters and potters at San Ildefonso Pueblo as early as 1910 and in the 1920s bought works by Kabotie and others for the Museum of New Mexico. They arranged for Kabotie to be excused from vocational classes in the afternoons to paint in their parlor. Soon he was joined by fellow students Velino Herrera (a.k.a. Ma Pe Wi) from Zia Pueblo, Otis Polelonema from Hopi, and a few others. They exhibited alongside Awa Tsireh (a.k.a. Alfonso Roybal) from San Ildefonso Pueblo, whose uncle, Crescendo Martinez, started painting for Hewett around 1910, and Tonita Peña (a.k.a. Quah Ah), also from San Ildefonso, who was the lone female painter at the beginning of the movement.[23]

Given that Kabotie's figural mode of painting developed in close dialogue with Pueblo peers, the De Huffs, Hewett, and others, most scholars have focused on the power dynamics between painters and patrons. Building on the significant work of J. J. Brody, the art historians David W. Penney and Lisa

A. Roberts (now Lisa Roberts Seppi) offered a resounding critique of patrons' motivations, described as a "hegemonic prerogative to claim colonized cultures as national possessions for 'mankind.'" Patrons were often political activists working on behalf of the rights of Native communities in the 1920s, as Penney and Roberts acknowledged. Nonetheless, their preservationist attitude shared with the assimilationists an assumption that Native cultures were intrinsically linked to the past. Penney and Roberts concluded that Pueblo paintings "came to represent the image of American Indian culture that America wished to 'preserve': visible, accessible, aestheticized, and available for commodity consumption, yet concealing through the relentlessly applied image of 'authenticity' its accommodation to the colonizing culture that wished to claim it for its own."[24] Histories that begin and end with critiques of patronage, though foundational to my study, can inadvertently occlude the agency of painters. It is difficult to reconcile a narrative of acquiescence with Kabotie's own words: "I've been brought up and raised right out here, in Hopi. And then they sent me way out in the foreign country and told me to forget it, forget it. How could you forget it, when it is all imprinted in your mind?"[25] I follow the lead of scholars Michelle McGeough, Sascha Scott, and Jessica W. Welton, highlighting accounts by Kabotie and his relatives that point to meanings beyond the scope of patrons and nation.[26] Kabotie's grandson, Hopi/Tewa artist and musician Ed Kabotie, put it simply: "My grandfather's story to me is all about proactivity."[27]

The paintings themselves are also key actors in my story. I maintain that the dialectic of painted figures and bare page contains profound and unexplored lessons about displacement, encoding the artist's resistance to a progressive ethos in material form. Furthermore, as traveling objects, these works necessarily carry on "social lives" independent of their maker.[28] Following AIM-generation artists' lead, I demonstrate that focusing on material as well as human agencies can help us to recover overlooked meanings in historical objects. Specifically, I shift a discussion of Kabotie's practice away from the two poles that have guided much analysis of Pueblo painting. The first is an *ethnographic* reading of their relationship to Hopi culture: "They attempt to illustrate, in a fashion organized for didactic purposes, what is normally only enacted" (i.e., dance).[29] The second is a *modernist* formal analysis focused on visual innovations: "Already [Kabotie] has learned to work in the interstices of representation and abstraction"; "the novelty was total."[30] I propose a third possibility, a diagrammatic approach, which contains elements of the first two but more fully accounts for the paintings' complex engagement with memory, embodiment, and displacement. As I will show, diagrams are highly flexible tools, capable of transmitting the distinctive sensibility of Hopi dances (often neglected in modernist formal analysis) without transparently reproducing Hopi ceremonial life (often assumed to be the case in ethnographic readings).[31] While indebted to existing accounts of early Pueblo paintings, mine sees visual characteristics not as didactic or formal ends but, rather, as invitations to ongoing multisensory engagement in a manner that resonates with much contemporary installation and performance art.

Diagramming Dance Memories

Kabotie recounted, "Mrs. De Huff got me some drawing paper and water colors and I started painting things I remembered from home, mostly kachinas. When you're so remote from your own people you get lonesome. You don't paint what's around you, you paint what you have in mind."[32] *Katsinam* are powerful, benevolent beings who reside with the Hopi for roughly six months each year, returning to their homes in the San Francisco mountains after the summer solstice. Kabotie said, "They represent the whole thing, nature. Even the spirits of little birds and ants.... They are the messengers between the Hopi and the very high natural powers, like the clouds and the sun and even the moon and the stars."[33] Alph H. Secakuku wrote that Katsinam are honored in ceremonies "for the purpose of bringing good will and prosperity to all people of the earth, in the form of rain and abundant crops, as well as for maintaining the balance and harmony so necessary for preserving our very existence."[34] During public dances, children receive gifts from Katsinam as an important part of their Hopi education. According to Emory Sekaquaptewa, "Since the kachina has been so prominent in the child's life, most of the child's fantasies involve the kachina.... Children go around the corner of the house; they enact their feelings about the kachina, they dance and sing like the kachina. At this early age they begin to feel the sense of projection into this spiritual reality."[35] Katsinam were thus a powerful influence on Kabotie's painting. As I discuss later in this chapter, the artist was also aware of protocols to protect elements of this "spiritual reality" from both hostile and well-meaning outsiders. During his tenure in Santa Fe, Kabotie drew only from the public portion of lengthier rituals hidden from view in underground kivas.[36] As a non-Hopi, I focus on what his works respectfully communicate to those both outside and inside the culture, rather than attempting to decode esoteric meaning.[37]

In *Niman Kachina Dance* (1920), Kabotie divided the rectangle of water-color paper among nine figures drawn from the departure dance of the Katsinam (plate 33). Although the figures face different directions and adopt various poses, they are all identical in scale and placed at roughly even distances from one another. Kabotie dispensed with illusionistic shading. Discrete areas of vivid color articulate the elaborate dress of the Katsinam and the gifts of corn and melons that evince their "ideal goodness." Six black bodies, their heads delineated by stepped-cloud symbols painted red, white, and blue, are interspersed with three others in red and white capes, white deerskin boots, and the whorl hairstyle characteristic of unmarried Hopi women.[38] These self-contained figures and their gifts float on the surface of an otherwise bare page. Brody described several of Kabotie's early paintings as "shallow, linear compositions that have the potential for unfolding to infinity along their horizontal axes."[39] This is certainly true of *Niman Kachina Dance*, where we can imagine the contrapuntal wave pattern created by the two sets of figures continuing past the edge of the page.

However, the painting involves more than just optical experience. In interviews late in his life, Kabotie equated the physical act of painting with recollecting the sound as well as sight of *Niman Katsinam*. In particular, he described going on long walks in the mountains near Santa Fe and spontaneously hearing ceremonial music:

> Among the pines, the forest, when there is a breeze, you hear *katsina* music—like this Home [*Niman*] Dance *Katsina, Hemiskatsina*: "Mmmm Mmmm"—that way. . . . The music goes through the pines. And then you hear the bird call—it sounds just like a *katsina*. . . . That makes you feel that you just want to go ahead and paint something about them. . . . You hear that particular music, then you see the very *katsinas* who are using that music. And that always expresses happiness. . . . Sometimes when I am painting certain things, I can be humming that particular music that is what I am painting. That goes into my painting.[40]

The sounds produced by Hopi rattles, drums, and singing quote an existing repertoire available in the natural world—from birds, frogs, raindrops—and organize them into rhythmic patterns that match the exacting steps of dance.[41] As seen in *Niman Kachina Dance* and other paintings, turtle shells and gourd rattles attached to dancers' bodies correlate movement and sound. Kabotie indicated that he similarly coordinated humming and hand in order to complete paintings of dance. He suggested that the cochlear titillations of his environment (wind and birds), the vocal vibrations of a recollected Katsina song, and the manual brushstrokes of painting are conjoined on the page.

To more precisely understand the relationship of Kabotie's paintings to memory and music, I find it useful to contrast the precise, shallow distribution of discrete figures in *Niman Kachina Dance* with the fluid treatment of watercolors in John Marin's *Dance of the Santo Domingo Indians* (1929) (plate 34). Marin rendered a plaza filled with dancers, witnessed on a visit to Santo Domingo Pueblo in New Mexico in the summer of 1929.[42] Despite the abstraction of the scene, there is a discernible view: high, distant, and comprehensive, as if grasped from a hill at the edge of the village. Individual dancers are rendered in a few swift brushstrokes. Marin juxtaposed areas of color and varied textures produced by changing ratios of water and pigment. Individual swaths appear and recede, bleed and overlap, building a pulsing, unified field. Glimmers of bare ivory paper are absorbed into the scene and framed by linear brushstrokes. Critics of the period tellingly compared the painter's brush to a conductor's baton. Paul Strand, a photographer and avid supporter of American modernism, described "flowing color, interpenetrations of pigment, dry color dragged across paper texture, white paper counting as color. . . . Out of these he constructs ever more solidly his polyphonies of color, which may well be compared to the instrumentation of music."[43] Another commentator noted "the metallic timbre of the wood-winds, the clangor of the drums, the shrillness of flutes; in fact every conceivable instrument is employed by Marin to blend harmoniously into one grand contrapuntal creation in color."[44] These critics suggested that to look at a watercolor by Marin was not only to grasp a scene with the eyes, but also to hear it—that is, to experience sensations akin to listening to music.

To borrow their orchestral analogy, I submit that Kabotie was less a conductor than a composer. Next to the atmospheric renderings of Marin, his controlled method of applying paint on dry paper is especially pronounced. Instead of popular watercolor washes, Kabotie used gouache paints procured by his patrons. Larger pigment particles and inclusion of a binding agent are partly responsible for the discrete, opaque areas of color evident in *Niman Kachina Dance*.[45] Paint's potential to bleed and mix is further curbed by the hairlines that delineate Kabotie's dancers. "White" space does not just glimmer beyond their crisp edges, but persists as a stark, material expanse between them. The detailed fronts of individual dancers invoke an illusionism that is quickly short-circuited by their collective composition. In *Dance of Santo*

Domingo, a unified view of the plaza knits the dancers and their surroundings into a single ensemble. In *Niman Kachina Dance,* the figures are mapped from memory rather than viewed. As the cluttered ground falls away, distances between them are clarified and abstracted. Their distribution may correspond to that of live bodies on the Hopi plaza, but the absence of context invites them to relate to one another in a virtual space.

At first glance, this formal condition can be understood as an analogue to Kabotie's own exile. The figures without a ground may appear displaced, like the painter who conjured them: "When you're so remote from your own people you get lonesome. You don't paint what's around you, you paint what you have in mind."[46] Yet the composition does not necessarily consign the dancers to permanent limbo. Here it is critical to grasp how the works function diagrammatically. The potential for such a reading first struck me forcibly in the archives of the Venice Biennale, as unadorned paper gleaming in the photographs pulled the painted figures toward my space. To think through this experience, I borrow from what John Bender and Michael Marrinan call "the culture of diagram"—the capacity for a wide variety of visual materials to translate embodied forms of human experience first into two-dimensional renderings amenable to transport, then back into three dimensions. Here "white" space plays a critical role in correlating relationships between figures and receiver; it is "virtual space whose material presence . . . provides support for the composite play of imagery and cognition that is the motor-energy of diagram."[47] Understood diagrammatically, the unarticulated space between Kabotie's figures is neither a passive ground for figures nor a metaphysical void; it is a flexible material that invites the active participation of viewers.

Kabotie's life and words bear out my interpretation. In Santa Fe, the artist was intimately acquainted with one category of diagram in particular: musical notation.[48] He admired the work of John Philip Sousa, learned clarinet in a marching band in school, and played the saxophone in a professional swing and jazz band throughout the 1920s. He recalled experiencing a kinship during his walks in the mountains with "white people who are great musicians, they can go out in the woods and later, in homes, write."[49] As a musician, he relied on sheet music's ability to render the contiguity of live sound into an abstract visual language, characterized by discrete figures located at intervals across the page. Like the diagrammatic forms described by Bender and Marrinan, sheet music is portable; it can sustain human dislocation, permitting "transference of knowledge" despite "a separation between the creator [composer] and the performer [musician]."[50] The act of painting shifted Kabotie's role, from performer in a band to composer on the page: "humming that particular music that *is* what I am painting" (my emphasis).[51] While Marin's critics saw a painting such as *Dance of the Santo Domingo Indians* as akin to a fully realized orchestra, *Niman Kachina Dance* is better likened to a patiently waiting score.

My diagrammatic reading departs from existing ethnographic and modernist interpretations by proposing that the compositions are not ends in themselves. Diagrams are porous and relational; they materialize critical information about a live phenomenon so that a subject can re-create the experience in a new time and space. Specifically, an embodied viewer must "play" what has been composed. "White" space acts as a suture, drawing the viewer into a triangulated "arena of potentiality" with images.[52] Grasping the link between static images and sonorous, moving dancers requires sustained cognitive and bodily engagement, an imagined stretching of the expanse between the figures into the actual space and time of reception. In effect, this encounter mirrors Kabotie's description of creative process. Just as the artist coordinated mind and body to materialize the sound and movement of Katsinam, viewers of his painting must do the same in order to activate static images. In this manner, diagrammatic paintings transpose multisensory experience across the significant space-time gaps separating Kabotie, the Hopi mesas, and far-flung audiences who continue to encounter his works.

I emphasize that the formal composition of *Niman Kachina Dance* makes sense only in the context of displacement. Secakuku writes that the Hopis regard their land, *tuuwanasavi*, as "the spiritual center of the earth."[53] A diagrammatic function is extraneous at tuuwanasavi, where site-specific art such as painted rock sites and subterranean kiva murals create an essential link between humans, particular places, and sacred powers.[54] Knowledge related to the symbols can be dangerous unless it is maintained by highly trained individuals of proper hereditary descent in the context of Hopi sacred space.[55] Pueblo communities' concerns about religious secrecy became especially acute and politicized in response to outsiders' incursions into their ceremonial life, which accelerated following the arrival of railroads, anthropologists, and tourists in the 1880s.[56] Kabotie was well aware of shifting Hopi protocols when he left the mesas in 1915. His spare, groundless forms implicitly acknowledge that sacred places, like the coded religious knowledge activated at these sites, are not reproducible beyond the mesas. While the works of some peers, including some by Awa Tsireh and Herrera, resemble iconography found in kiva murals and Pueblo pottery, Kabotie's exclusively figural work grew increasingly distant from Hopi painting conventions throughout the 1920s (fig. 3.5).[57] For

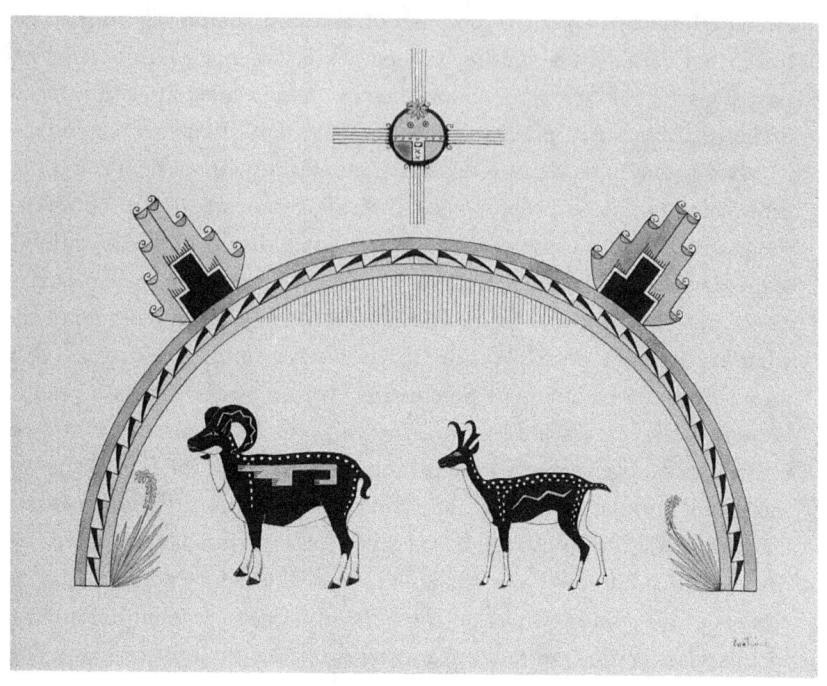

3.5 Awa Tsireh, *Ram and Antelope*, c. 1925–30. Watercolor and ink on paper. Smithsonian American Art Museum, Corbin-Henderson Collection, gift of Alice H. Rossin, 1979.144.50.

example, his *Ahöla Kachina* (c. 1920s), a Katsina who appears at the winter solstice, incorporates European techniques of shading, proportion, and a hint of contrapposto (fig. 3.6).

It is likely that each of the early Pueblo painters arrived at a different balance between protecting and communicating indigenous cultural values.[58] I propose that Kabotie's particular solution was to transmit the distinctive *sensibility* of dances as he knew them growing up. During public dances, the combined effects of music, vivid regalia, and movement immerse participants—uninitiated Hopi and sometimes non-Hopis who are permitted to attend—into what Secakuku called a "great and meditative wholeness."[59] Attendees are invited to glean bodily awareness of Hopi cultural values, even as deeper levels of significance are withheld. Kabotie's paintings convey this tacit, rather than coded, knowledge. His diagrammatic solution is to render select slices of choreographies that coordinate sights, sounds, and gestures, without compromising the integrity of Hopi ceremonial life. The paintings offer a glimpse of the complex temporal and spatial structures underlying

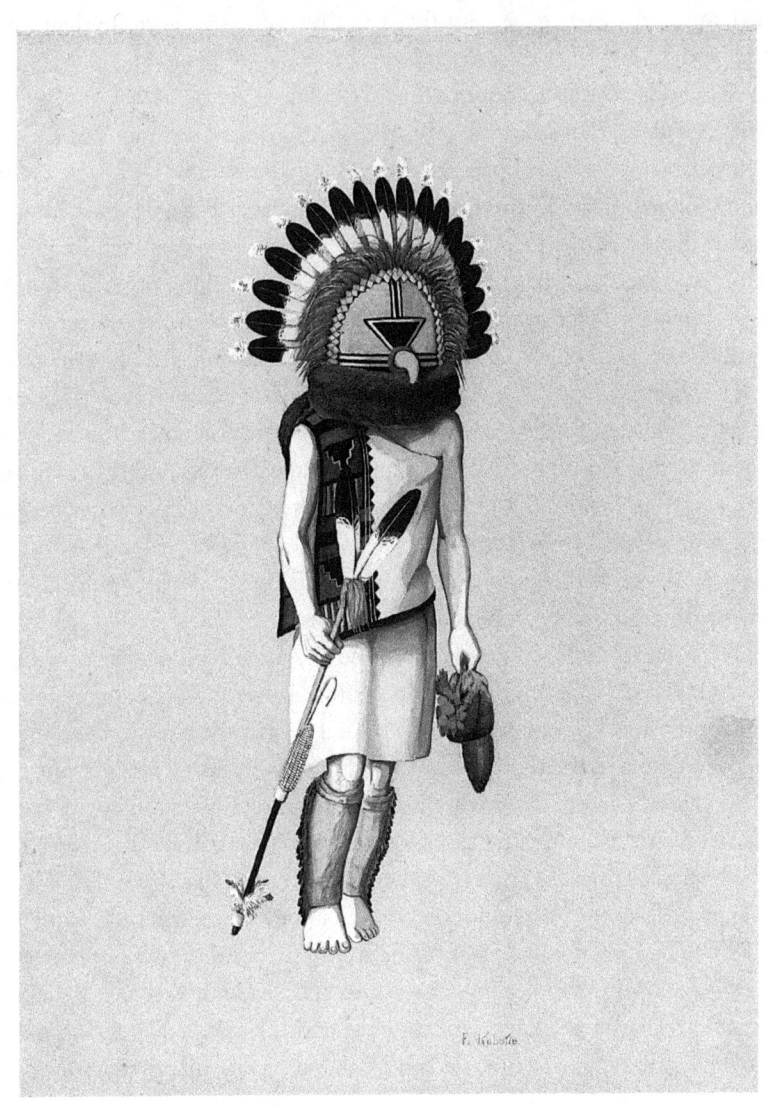

3.6 Fred Kabotie, *Ahöla Kachina*, c. 1926–29. Watercolor on canvas, 21½ × 17½ in. Fred Jones Jr. Museum of Art, The University of Oklahoma, Norman; The James T. Bialac Native American Art Collection, 2010.

dances, hinting at deeper levels of Hopi epistemology and training that inform participants' encounters with the "wholeness" of the world. The embodied, multisensory engagement that paintings solicit is far more than superficial and far less than transparent.

Kabotie's formal solutions to this challenge are as varied as the dances they recollect. In a pair of paintings depicting respective men's and women's dances, his figures form precise, self-contained ensembles. They call to mind textbook geometry illustrations such as those that Kabotie must have studied in Santa Fe. In *Hopi Basket Ceremony* (1921), women stand equidistant from two stacks of baskets at center, creating an ellipse around an expanse of bare paper. The formation of bodies echoes the rounded perfection of the individuated baskets held in each woman's hands (fig. 3.7). The geometry is even more pronounced in *Young Men's Spring Ceremony* (1920–21), featuring a public dance of the Wuwtsim, one of four Hopi men's societies. While I mention this painting due to its significance within Kabotie's oeuvre and to my argument below, the Hopi Cultural Preservation Office requested that I not reproduce it. In its place I offer *Hopi Butterfly Dance*, a later depiction of a social dance with a similar composition (fig. 3.8).[60] Forty figures appear as interlocking elements of a rectangular prism.

Virginia More Roediger wrote of the analogous conformity of dancers at Zuni Pueblo, "No corps de ballet in white tarlatan and pink slippers could be more uniform. The stiff white kilt is folded around the body to the same point above each knee, the shining black hair hangs to the same straight line at each waist, and the tail of each swinging foxskin clears the ground by the same few inches."[61] Yet Kabotie's figures cohere beyond naturalism. The patterns and feathers adorning the *tablitas* of the dancers create diagonals that cut across the page. Like the dotted lines used in diagrams to indicate the hidden walls of a polyhedron, the bodies of the figures in the far row peer out between the heads of those in front. Such directional cues lead our eyes in a visual circuit around triangles of blank paper at both ends of the rectangular form.[62] The "white" space that fills out the spherical and rectangular formations in *Hopi Basket Ceremony* and *Hopi Butterfly Dance* functions as potential volume, waiting to be pulled by a viewer back into three dimensions.

Kabotie was enrolled in Santa Fe Public High School when he painted *Young Men's Spring Ceremony*, delaying his initiation into Wuwtsim until his permanent return to Hopi in 1930.[63] As I have established, however, dance was a critical part of his education long before geometry and drills. Such paintings materialize foundational Hopi experiences, offering an exercise in the collec-

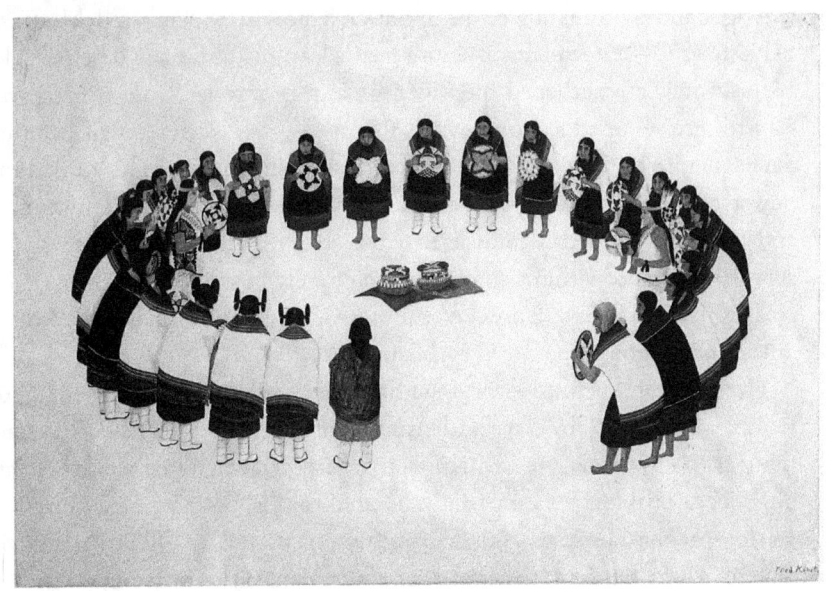

3.7 Fred Kabotie, *Hopi Basket Ceremony*, 1921. Gouache on paper. Courtesy of Museum of Indian Arts and Cultures, 35485/13.

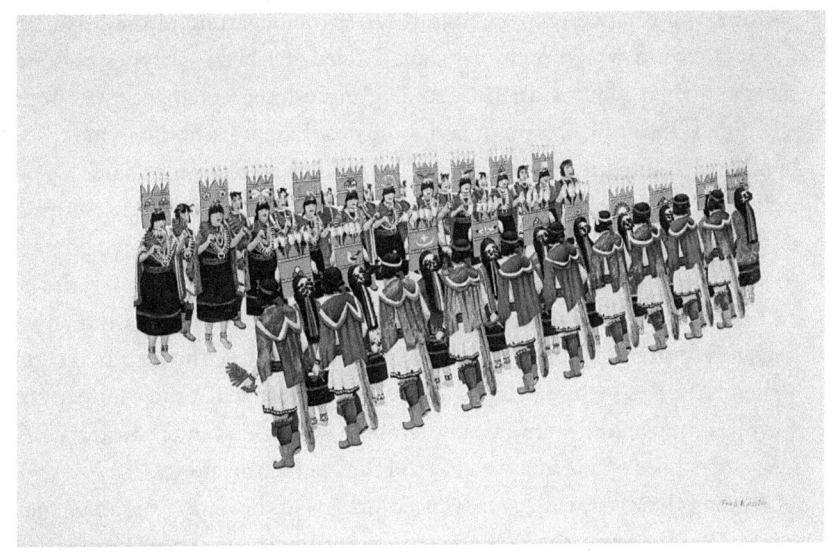

3.8 Fred Kabotie, *Hopi Butterfly Dance*, c. 1928. Lithograph, 14 × 21¾ in. Courtesy of the School for Advanced Research, IAF.P22. Photo by Jennifer Day.

tive rigor and coordination of the initiation dances he remembered. Matthew Sakiestewa Gilbert explained, "Hopi pupils learned to think and behave like Hopis, which strengthened their identity as they traveled from the reservation to receive an education beyond the mesas."[64] Kabotie's act of painting dance memories resonates with Gilbert's assertion that "students 'turned the power' at Indian boarding schools in the nineteenth and twentieth century, and their achievement demonstrated the ability of Indian pupils to adapt, survive, and excel within a foreign and culturally hostile environment."[65] By creating recollections of embodied culture, Kabotie worked against the federal government's goal of enforced forgetting.

Here we can begin to clarify the broader political significance of Kabotie's paintings. As they traveled beyond Santa Fe, they intervened in a far-flung economy of misrepresentations that returned real, often violent effects on Pueblo peoples. It is especially notable that Kabotie painted countless versions of the Hopi snake dance throughout the 1920s. Of all the Pueblo dances, it was the most celebrated and simultaneously reviled by outsiders. In the 1880s, as the railroad opened the Hopi mesas to a flood of outsiders, representations of the snake dance circulated widely. Commentators focused almost exclusively on a snapshot of the public portion of a nine-day ceremony performed every two years in August (after the departure of the Katsinam): the moment in which men in regalia circled the plaza carrying poisonous snakes in their mouths. In 1884, soldier and ethnographer John G. Bourke recounted "the crowning point being the deadly reptiles borne in mouth and hand, which imparted to the drama the lurid tinge of a nightmare."[66] A decade later, anthropologist Jesse Walter Fewkes published detailed descriptions of five variants of the dance in order to "consider the question which one of them is most primitive."[67] On returning from a snake dance in 1924, the poet and novelist D. H. Lawrence wrote sarcastically, "The hopping Indian with his queer muttering gibberish and his dangling snake—why, he sure is cute!"[68] When Kabotie's mature painting *Snake Dance* arrived in Venice in 1932, some European audiences were already familiar with German art historian Aby Warburg's tales of a formative visit to Hopi in 1896 (plate 35).[69]

Among the most widely reproduced images of the dance was an oil painting by Taos Society artist E. Irving Couse, entitled *Moki Snake Dance—Prayer for Rain* (1904) (plate 36). The Santa Fe Railway purchased the work, featuring it on postcards and in a souvenir book distributed to travelers on Southwest tours with the Fred Harvey Company. As with most other images of the period, Couse focused on the moment in the ceremony when priests carry snakes in their mouths. Nonetheless, the painting privileges atmosphere over clarity of detail, foreshadowing the unity of Marin's *Dance of the Santo Domingo Indians*. Behind the pair of dancers in the foreground, bodies and snakes appear as a teeming jumble at one with each other, the tilting rooftops, and the rough red earth. There is no order, no discernible choreography. In this portion of the painting, Couse provoked a confusion of figure and ground, suturing Hopi, beast, and land. At front, the delineated body of a priest leans left, one knee raised, echoing the sinuous curve of the snake in his mouth. Couse's image bolstered the souvenir book's thesis that Hopi priests were not bitten because they "understood" this primordial beast.[70]

In marked contrast to Couse's *Moki Snake Dance*, Kabotie's *Snake Dance* is all figure, no ground. The artist chose a moment that was equally familiar to non-Hopi audiences, but comparatively less spectacular. The priests are picking the snakes up just prior to their final procession. Rather than mimicking serpent bodies, most are bent at the waist, forming a tent to contain the irregular, twisting forms. Building on this relatively orderly composition at front, Kabotie includes a graceful, upright, white-clad line of antelope dancers, one of several key elements that Couse omitted in order to focus on the more striking phenomenon of snakes-in-mouth. At right, two corn maidens stand at rigid attention, their offerings alerting viewers to the importance of the dance as prayer. In contrast to outsiders' derision of beastliness and excess, *Snake Dance* presents an orderly and rule-bound choreography, hinting at the ways in which the dance manages reciprocal relations between humans and "natural forces."[71] The circle of snake priests and line of antelope dancers combine geometric elements of *Hopi Basket Ceremony* and *Hopi Butterfly Dance*, poised to spring into three dimensions. *Snake Dance* diagrams the complex coordination of human and serpent roles necessary for the ongoing creation of the world. Inviting the copresence of painted figures with widespread audiences, the painting maps an evocative alternative to outsiders' images—both derogatory and romantic—that sutured the Hopi to a primordial past.

Kabotie painted *Snake Dance* on the eve of his permanent return to the Hopi mesas, following a stint working at the Fred Harvey Company's gift shop in the Grand Canyon.[72] There he may well have sold reproductions of Couse's *Moki Snake Dance* to tourists en route to the mesas. Yet Kabotie had long since grasped the power of replicating and circulating images. One of his earliest paintings of a snake dance was intended for his Danish carpentry teacher at the Santa Fe Indian School, who sent Kabotie's works to Denmark, because "at that time Europeans were more interested in the Indians than the white people here in America."[73] Kabotie painted multiple versions of the basic composition visible in *Snake Dance* throughout the 1920s, one of which was reproduced in Hewett's 1922 article "Native American Artists" for the prominent publication *Art and Archaeology*.[74] Five additional works by Kabotie and several by Awa Tsireh and Herrera supplemented the text, transmitting dance sensibilities well beyond Santa Fe.

Exporting Nationalism

Pueblo paintings arrived at the center of the New York art scene in 1920, when the painter John Sloan, president of the Society of Independent Artists, who had spent the summer of 1919 in Santa Fe, arranged to include a grouping in the society's Fourth Annual Exhibition at the Waldorf-Astoria Hotel in New York.[75] That same year, New York–based artist and writer Marsden Hartley published the first of three prominent articles in which he argued, "The red man is the one truly indigenous religionist and esthete of America. . . . Throughout the various dances of the Pueblos of the Rio Grande . . . the same unified sense of beauty prevails, and in some of the dances to a most remarkable degree." He concluded, "As Americans we should accept the one American genius we possess, with genuine alacrity. We have upon our own soil something to show the world."[76] His second article appeared alongside the reproductions of Pueblo paintings in *Art and Archaeology*. By then New Yorkers could shop for an original on Madison Avenue, thanks to the opening of a nonprofit gallery of Indian art run by Amelia Elizabeth White, a newspaper heiress who split her time between New York and Santa Fe.[77]

Hartley's promotion reveals the extent to which educated Americans' concern over national identity in the arts fueled their resistance to the federal dance bans.[78] Pueblo painting was presented as source material for a distinctly American art with deep aesthetic and spiritual roots untouched by classical training in the "Old World." For those who wished to heal the industrial sores of a nation still reeling from World War I, Native arts as patrimony trumped Native bodies as labor. In this context, Kabotie's spare gouache works and John Marin's fluid washes of paint could be construed as brethren. Strand declared that watercolor works by young American artists such as Marin and Georgia O'Keeffe were "an affirmation that a truly indigenous expression is as possible in America as it is in Europe."[79] Strand's use of "indigenous" signaled independence from Europe. "Indigenous" also expressed the value of a liberated creativity, an untutored form of expression suited to a young country. Promoted at the Society of Independent Artists and elsewhere, the lightness, fluidity, and mobility of watercolors promised to free Americans from the weighty conventions attending oil painting in the great academies of Europe. As non-Native watercolorists moved through the art colonies of Santa Fe and nearby Taos, watercolors became associated with the American West—its supposedly independent spirit and open horizons.[80]

Educated Americans' search for a wholly homegrown national aesthetic thus bolstered the political motivations for beautifying Pueblo dance. Yet as the government eased its attack on Pueblo dances in the late 1920s, patrons of painting increasingly focused on these works' striking surface qualities, such as linearity and bold colors. In 1931, Sloan joined anthropologist and author Oliver La Farge to curate the *Exposition of Indian Tribal Arts*, a blockbuster show of some 650 historical and contemporary objects, including more than 40 paintings. After opening at Grand Central Art Galleries in New York, subsequent versions of the exhibition toured fifteen other American cities.[81] In the introduction to the accompanying catalogue, Sloan and La Farge championed "the first exhibition of American Indian art selected entirely with consideration of esthetic value." Their goal was to convince the American public that Indian art was "Modernist" even though it was "steeped in an ancient tradition."[82] More than three thousand people saw the exhibition on its opening day in New York, leading Christian Brinton, president of the College Art Association of America, to declare triumphantly in a radio address, "The battle for American aesthetic expression has now been won. But it has not been won by our typical foreign-trained man with his ill-digested Parisian artist table-d'hote." His declaration that the United States had "an artistic treasury not only older but fresher and purer than anything Europe has to offer" borrows from the paradoxical new definition of Native arts as ancient and rooted in American soil, yet wholly modern—and ready to travel.[83]

Kabotie's painted dancers were thus framed by nationalism when they came face-to-face with European crowds in Venice, some six thousand miles from Shungopavi. With the aim of exposing a broad public to American artistic patrimony, Walter L. Clark, director of Grand Central Art Galleries, arranged the building of a permanent U.S. Pavilion at "the most important of all international exhibitions" in 1930, despite the American government's patent lack of interest in the project.[84] The newly defined modern Indian art was one of the first artistic expressions to grace its walls. After the successful opening of the *Exposition of Indian Tribal Arts* in New York, Clark agreed to send at least two dozen Pueblo paintings alongside more than one hundred

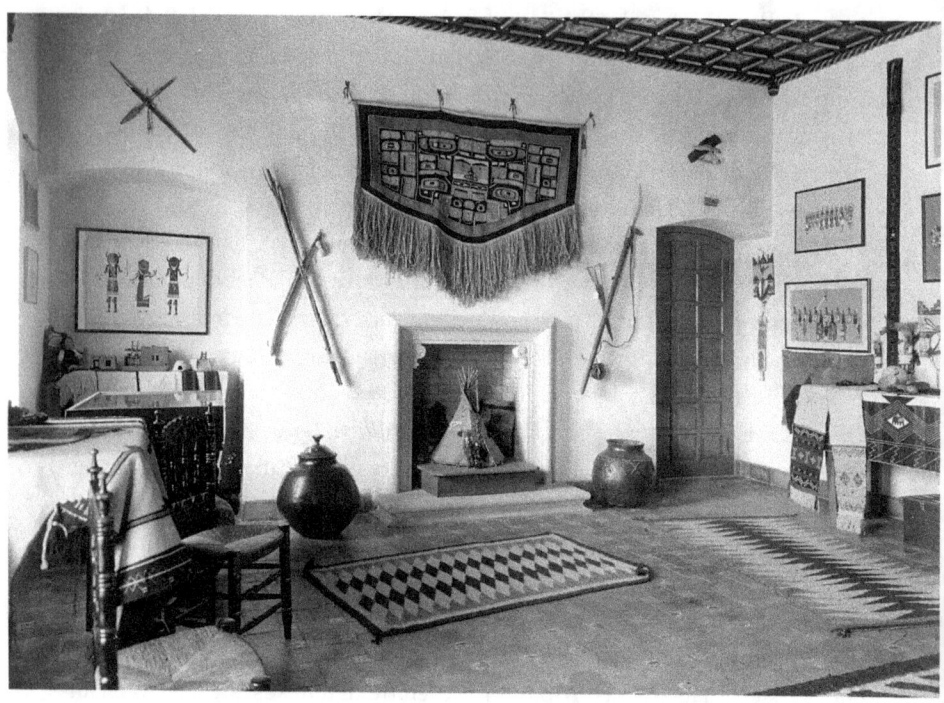

3.9 American Pavilion of the International Exposition in Seville, 1928. Courtesy of the School for Advanced Research, Amelia Elizabeth White Photo Collection, AD18.386.

other Native works to Venice. While John Sloan is formally credited with the selection, letters attest that his wife, Dolly Sloan, in coordination with White, did most of the work. Their efforts were part of a larger endeavor to expose European audiences to Native American painting. White arranged and accompanied a significant exhibition at the widely attended International Exposition in Seville in 1928 (fig. 3.9).[85] Subsequently works went on view at the International Congress of Folk Arts in Prague in 1929 and were translated into limited-edition *pochoir* prints published in 1929 and 1932 by L'Edition d'Art C. *Szwedzicki* in Nice, France.[86] An author for *Art News* championed the effort in Venice: "Since this country so frequently comes to a real evaluation of her own assets through European approbation, the showing of Indian art across the sea will prove doubly valuable."[87]

But reality disappointed rhetoric. An urgent letter sent by Italian commissioner and sculptor Antonio Maraini to Clark on December 13, 1931, suggests that he viewed the American newcomers as amateurs in need of firm guidance.

I am awfully sorry to have to press you to answer me, but I really must do so because time is getting short, and all the other foreign Representatives have already communicated to me their plan.

Of course it is for you to suggest to me the names of the artists whose place and number in general has been marked on the map of the pavilion already sent to you. But let me add here that for the retrospective Exhibition we should like some of your very great artists like Whistler; and as for the living ones we should allow a room for Manship as Sculptor, and Stern, or some others, as painters.[88]

On December 24, Grand Central Art Galleries manager Erwin S. Barrie issued a vague reply: "We are giving this matter our concentrated effort at this time and are planning to devote probably two galleries to the works of three or four American artists who have died within the last ten years." He mentioned John Singer Sargent and Winslow Homer, neither of whom made appearances in the final exhibition.[89] It is likely that Maraini suffered some sleepless nights until the delinquent New York contingent sent news in January 1932 that the American expatriate Martin Birnbaum had been appointed commissioner of the Pavilion. In the same letter, Barrie also announced Grand Central Art Galleries' decision to devote a room to Native American art. It must have been a surprise for the Italian commissioner to learn that his request for America's "very great artists like Whistler" was to be met with textiles and silver by hitherto unheard of American Indian artists. Here Sloan's aesthetic credentials were used to grant legitimacy to the choice. Barrie assured Maraini, "This room will be assembled by the noted American artist, John Sloan, who is also the leading authority on Indian art in this country."[90]

After living abroad for fifteen years, Birnbaum shared neither Clark's nationalist ambitions nor Sloan's conviction of the unique aesthetic qualities of every American Indian object. This is made abundantly clear in the American commissioner's catalogue introduction, which skips the glorified rhetoric of nationalism in favor of an *apology*. Birnbaum wrote, "With the most profound regret, we must defer to another occasion an exhibition of American watercolors that would go from the magnificent works of Winslow Homer, from the exquisite works of Whistler and from the wonders in this type of painting by John S. Sargent, to the truly outstanding works of our living artists. However, the choice is made."[91] His subsequent discussion of the virtues of Native American art rings insincere in light of the message that America's "truly outstanding works" are absent. The expatriate clearly did not receive the message that Pueblo painters and the country's great watercolorists were "indigenous" brethren. Later in the introduction, he wrote of the rise of artistic nationalism with scarcely veiled sarcasm. "The Nationalists feel they must at all costs find an American school. . . . Their late inspired teacher Robert Henri, and John Sloan the ardent realist—it is to his enthusiasm and knowledge that we owe choice of the Indian collection—belong to this group."[92] Here nationalism is not naturalized; instead it is presented as a perspective shaping the choice of work in the American Pavilion that need not be shared by all.

The final appearance of the Native American room reflects a compromise between the organizers' conflicting agendas. The mostly anonymous, three-dimensional works appeared close together in cases with little distinction as to age or provenance. Navajo textiles hung high in the room filled the expanse of walls that was left bare in adjoining galleries to isolate the paintings. While not quite the panoply of goods on view in Indian trading posts and "Indian corners" of Victorian homes in prior decades, their display nonetheless coded them as "craft"—different in status than the canvases.[93] Pueblo paintings, in contrast, occupied a privileged position at eye level. They were visually set apart from the silver and textiles and placed in conversation with the contemporary works on view in the adjoining room. The installation photograph with which I began this chapter suggests the deliberate nature of the choice (see fig. 3.1). Blumenschein's *Adobe Village—Winter* and Ufer's *Two Riders*, the only works by Taos Society artists in the Pavilion, seem carefully situated to frame the Pueblo paintings visible through the doorway. No doubt the fulsome, peopled landscapes were intended to supply a topography for the placeless dancers. Surrounded by an exotic Southwest, the Pueblo figures might be seen as "steeped in an ancient tradition," "upon our own soil."[94] Yet as I have indicated, the juxtaposition works through contrast rather than supplement. The layers of oil paint seem thicker, the visual details more continuous, the rich palettes enhanced beside bare paper. Likewise, the gouache dancers seem lighter, more mobile, and insistently *present* next to the scenes of a distant America. The appearance of Native paintings short-circuits the logic of the display, baring the paradoxes at the core of Americans' search for a national aesthetic.

Textual evidence supports my visual analysis, indicating that the U.S. Pavilion undermined the export of nationalism. Clark wrote to Maraini on June 2, "We have seen some accounts of your exhibition in the foreign press, but unfortunately, it did not come out in the New York papers, which was a disappointment to us."[95] Clark's chagrin indicates that the success of Native American art in Venice depended in part upon elusive domestic headlines. On June 13, 1932, Birnbaum wrote an unusually candid letter from London to Maraini's wife, British author Yoi Maraini. The triple underlines he penned in black chart their own emotive score on the page: "I have seen nothing in English or American papers, except the London Times—America seems to ignore the Biennale which is the most beautifully arranged exhibition one can hope to see. The fact that our artists are not all great men is not Signor Maraini's fault—nor mine! I do not feel responsible because I did not send the works shown,—i.e. not one third of those hung—and here after I shall have the power to choose all or none."[96] Here Birnbaum clarified that while he accepted responsibility for *arranging* the rooms, he wanted nothing to do with two-thirds of the content—roughly, the portion devoted to little-known American Indian artists. The indifference of the American press apparently spurred these frank revelations, confirming the trepidation evident in Birnbaum's catalogue introduction.[97] In his estimation, Native American art abroad failed to represent the nation *to* the nation.

Not surprisingly, the response abroad was even less supportive of American nationalism. Italian correspondent Francesco Monotti wrote belatedly in the *New York Times* on August 28 that even the fussiest European critics were "suddenly taken aback—though they ended by insisting that the importance of the Indian show is more scientific than artistic."[98] He suggested that for European skeptics, Native paintings, pots, and weavings failed to provide the modernist aesthetic encounter promised by Sloan. A much lengthier article by esteemed Italian critic Emilio Cecchi from 1932 overtly resisted the newly formed national myth in a canny assessment of the Americans' recent institutionalization of Native painting. After asserting his credentials by telling of his own travels in the southwestern United States, Cecchi observed, "Ethnographical interest is now turning into, in America, artistic interest. Some universities are starting organic courses around a figurative tradition that is the only original one on American soil."[99] Like Birnbaum, Cecchi acknowledged the constructed and increasingly institutionalized nature of the nationalist program. His assessment of the paintings likewise cut across American patrons' romantic language. "At Tesuque, Taos, etc., the walls of indigenous houses are papered with tri-color [magazine] covers, with portraits of movie stars, and advertisements for toothpaste and cigarettes. Modern art works on the Indian taste through these models."[100] Here the Italian critic foregrounded a contemporaneity that Hartley, Sloan, La Farge, and others could only obliquely acknowledge. He implied that Pueblo painters were savvy consumers of American visual culture and positioned their work as products of historical contingency, rather than deep-rooted American traditions.

Yet Cecchi concluded that Pueblo watercolors were "a crude and mixed tradition," thereby reasserting a dominant system of aesthetic valuation.[101] We must consider that, like Hartley's and Sloan's in the United States, his words were shaped by nationalistic political preoccupations. They suggest his position as an Italian navigating the increasingly fascist climate leading up to World War II, where America was often construed as a shallow, commercial culture. There is a hint, in Cecchi's critique of the American art scene in 1932, of the conflicting ideologies that led Grand Central Art Galleries to withdrawal from the biennial in 1936 and prompted the Italians to use the Pavilion to exhibit their own prints and drawings. Under the direction of Maraini, the biennial would soon become an instrument of the state. The very participation of the United States beginning in 1930 reflects intensified nationalism on both sides of the Atlantic.[102]

If there were visitors to the U.S. Pavilion who activated the space between Kabotie's figures, they did not write polemical articles in major outlets of the day. However, I think the invitation was there. Kabotie's painting *Mountain Sheep Dance* (n.d.) is visible in one installation photograph of the American Indian room and is the only work by a Native artist reproduced in the biennial catalogue (plate 37). In this work, a mature version of the approach he honed throughout the 1920s, the carefully proportioned Katsinam gather around a central fir tree "planted" in an absent ground. Their guide, a hunter, attends them at a measured distance. Kabotie later described the live dance: "Leading into the plaza is a row of small piñon trees and Douglas fir trees. As the sheep approach one tree after another, they circle and utter guttural sheep calls."[103] Secakuku's in-depth narrative of Angk'wa night dances (when mountain sheep Katsinam make appearances) describes a sense of connectedness in space and suspension in time:

Turtle shells clack and clatter, bells jingle, and with a loud and deep chorus of singing the dance begins like a huge cloudburst of sound and motion, a burst of prayer for all life forms.

In the village kiva, the same events are taking place at the same time, accompanied by the same music and synchronous dancing, and using the same bright ceremonial dress and dance objects (such as bows and arrows, rattles, and evergreen). All combine to create a great and meditative wholeness. For those present, focused as they are on this powerful and harmonious dance, time disappears. Then, with the shake of a rattle, the dancing, singing, and drumming abruptly cease, and in the peacefulness and quiet the beauty and spiritual uplift of the songs echo in one's mind.[104]

Kabotie's painting renders the "echo" described by Secakuku diagrammatically, in two dimensions. The "bright ceremonial dress and dance objects" are maximally visible; the rattles attached to the Katsinam appear as visual metonyms for their "clack and clatter." The unarticulated space separating the figures functions as a material hook for a participant, inviting her to activate the "huge cloudburst of sound and motion" that marks the arrival of dancers.

These painted figures did not side with the conflicting nationalisms that framed them. They occupied a clearing somewhere between American patrons' intentions and the U.S. Pavilion's malfunction in Venice, between a reigning ideology that claimed them as primordial Americana and an Italian critic's assessment of their crude commercialism. In the United States, the Native American gallery in the 1932 pavilion was forgotten as quickly as it was conceived. The organizers' initial plans to travel the works to other European cities dwindled in the wake of disappointing press coverage and Depression-era financial constraints.[105] Birnbaum had his way: contemporary Native art was not seen again in the U.S. Pavilion. In a telling parallel, the Whitney Museum of American Art acquired *Basket Dance* by Tonita Peña from the display in Venice for a record sum of $225.[106] The painting has since vanished from the museum's collections, along with all records pertaining to the sale. As Pueblo paintings slipped beyond the nation, they fell out of history.

Contemporaneity

When I engage the painted dancers in the photograph that opens this chapter, at once coeval and irreconcilable with the southwestern landscapes next door, they simultaneously move in *my* time and space. Lessons from *Emendatio* and other AIM-generation artworks have undoubtedly conditioned my response. The contemporary works in this book supply an additional context for Kabotie's dancers that extends well beyond the walls of the failed U.S. Pavilion. When Durham, Luna, and others exhibit alongside their peers in art biennials today, they conjure "radical disjunctures of perception," a defining feature of our contemporaneity, according to art historian Terry Smith. He argued that accelerating conditions of economic and cultural globalization after 1989 produced "actual coincidences of asynchronous temporalities," which artists from around the world are poised to navigate, communicate, and alter.[107] Yet the diplomacy of Attakulakula, the translations of Pablo Tac, and the paintings of Kabotie indicate that divergent perspectives on a shared modernity were negotiated in London in 1733, Rome in 1834, and Venice in 1932. Their varied modernisms are legacies of a world shaped by colonization, filling grooves that contemporary art continues to cut in the context of global capitalism today. Perhaps what Smith calls contemporaneity is not new so much as renewable, like "a huge cloudburst of sound and motion" grasped suddenly, bodily, in Venice.

FOUR "Dance Is the One Activity That I Know

of When Virtual Strangers Can Embrace"

KAY WALKINGSTICK, CREATIVE KINSHIP,

AND ART HISTORY'S TANGLED LEGS

In 1998, while on a residency with the American Academy in Rome, Kay WalkingStick secured a special appointment to view Codex Vaticanus A in the vast rare books collection of the Vatican Library (fig. 4.1). After an interview with a priest during which the artist wore her crucifix in plain sight, she had a rare opportunity to spend time with the "original," rather than the facsimile at hand.[1] The object confounds the descriptor. It is thought to be a copy of a translation of a compilation of lost Aztec pictorial manuscripts, heavily annotated by Europeans sometime after 1569.[2] Among the 101 bound folios, Italian text interprets (and often confuses) the significance of an ancestral king and culture hero, Topilzin Quetzalcoatl, and Quetzalcoatl, the plumed serpent deity associated with wind, creation, and fertility. We are told that Topilzin Quetzalcoatl was born of a virgin and sent by his father to reform a sinful world. In the course of his life, the hero saved his people from famine, "survived the flood," drew "his own blood with thorns and other forms of penance," and disappeared into the "red sea."[3] Upon his death, he rose into the sky as the Morning Star and promised to return to earth when a bearded people would rule the land.[4]

Eloise Quinoñes Keber argued for understanding Codex Vaticanus A as a "unique production," a "blend of indigenous lore, analogies made between Indian and European/Christian traditions, and oftentimes fanciful speculations on their meanings."[5] Aztec knowledge is reconstituted in Western book form, apparently for the enlightenment of an unnamed Italian patron.

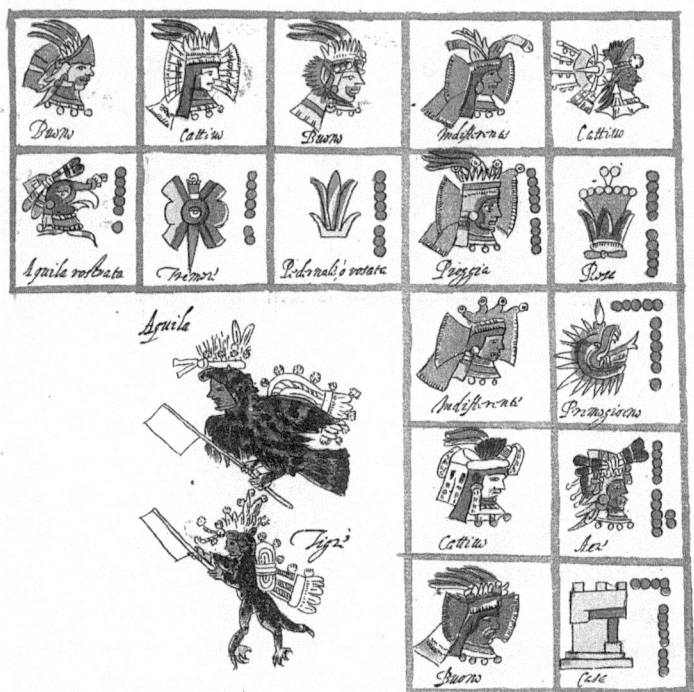

4.1 Messicano Vaticano No. 3738_024r. Codex Vaticanus 3738, Loubat facsimile. Courtesy of Ancient Americas at Los Angeles County Museum of Art.

European writing surrounds stilted renderings of kings and deities, replacing the oral recitations of the Aztec priesthood that mediated between indigenous readers and the divine. In the process, famines and floods plague the precontact landscape and our hero combines episodes from the lives of Topilzin Quetzalcoatl, Moses, Noah, and Christ. Codex Vaticanus A thus hails from what Walter Mignolo called "the darker side of the Renaissance," during which the "rebirth" of classical arts and philosophy in Europe and the violent conquest of the indigenous Americas informed each other across the ocean.[6] It provides a glimpse of the familiar and often familial frameworks through which Europeans and indigenous Americans made sense of one another for roughly the first century of their entanglement.

WalkingStick described her artistic experience in the Vatican that day as "a great adventure unlike anything else I have ever encountered."[7] She resumed the four-centuries-old process of selective creative translation, sketching vibrantly colored paintings in swift, sure black lines on cream-colored paper (figs. 4.2–4.3). Wedged between a figure of Quetzalcoatl and the body of an eagle with human hands and face (a representation of the Aztec warrior class), drawn from separate pages of the manuscript, appear her words, "pictures of corn, birds, eagles, jaguars, reptiles . . . serpents flowers men & women in elaborate headdresses. lots of eagle dances [sic]." Reordering the profusion of images and replacing the Christian text with a contemporary artist's commentary, she claimed Codex Vaticanus A on the pages of her growing collection of visual memories abroad. The figures take up residence alongside more familiar Renaissance and classical themes we might expect to find in a traveler's sketchbooks from Rome, including a fish-tailed Neptune, fawns, angels, "lion bird women," and numerous risen bodies of Christ (fig. 4.4 and plate 38). Each is elegantly rendered in black lines and occasional splashes of watercolor. Through the process of translation, resemblances among varied beings that disobey the modern, biological boundaries of bodies to sprout plumes, hooves, claws, or scales and move between earth, sea, or sky come to light. Like the creators of Codex Vaticanus A, WalkingStick drew equivalences.

The copious sketchbooks made by the artist during repeated trips to Italy between 1996 and 2012 picture a vast history of art anchored in worldly Italian collections. In this chapter I explore resonances between WalkingStick's sumptuous artistic practice abroad and a culture of similitude that shaped the imagination of the globe for roughly the first century of conquest.[8] Instead of assuming essential differences, sixteenth-century European artists and intellectuals often made sense of their encounters with plants, animals,

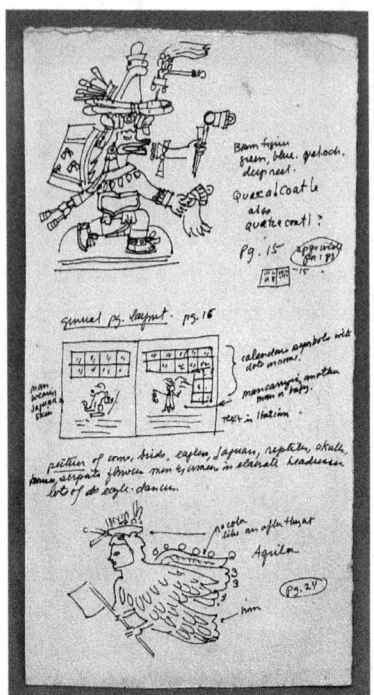
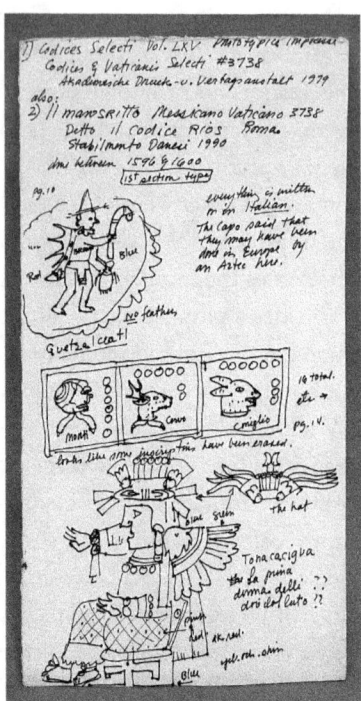

4.2–4.3 Kay WalkingStick, sketchbook from Rome, 1998. Collection of the artist. Photo by Jessica L. Horton.

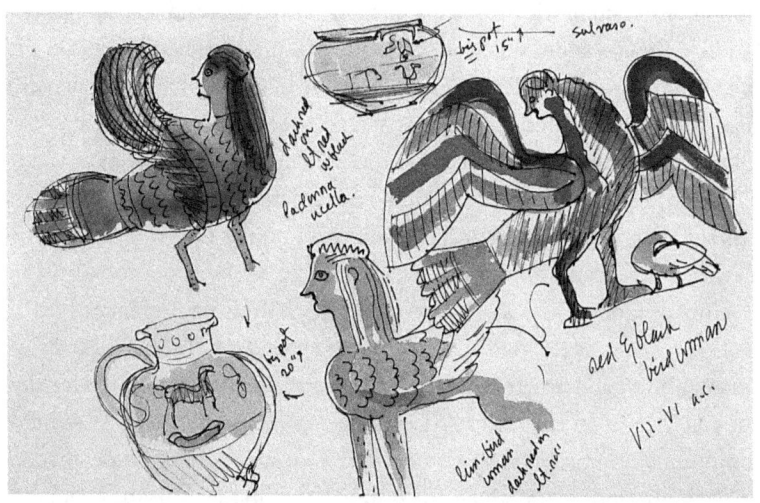

4.4 Kay WalkingStick, sketchbook from Rome, 1998. Collection of the artist. Photo by Jessica L. Horton.

and peoples of the "New World" by enveloping them into a vast family of resemblances, premised on familiar narratives from Antiquity and the Bible.[9] In
turn, indigenous people—such as *tlacuiloque*, highly educated Aztec painter-
writers—negotiated foreign impositions by absorbing them into existing
frameworks of belief and practice, bending likeness to the ends of survival. In
the same instant, both parties conceived new subjects and objects that made
the search for distinct origins impossible, before the quest to do so had even
begun. I see a strong echo of this process across the whole of WalkingStick's
Italian work. In particular, she translated sketches of the vast archive of early
contact into vibrant, gleaming works on paper in which themes of fertility,
bodily transformation, and dance take shape.

The resulting creative body circumvents art history's core assumptions of
difference. The discipline developed in nineteenth-century Europe alongside
emerging biological classifications of race and anthropological definitions
of culture. The same period gave rise to studies of indigenous kinship and
national-legal calculations of blood quantum used to determine racial ancestry in the United States. Art history has borrowed its cultural categories
from the contours of the scientifically governed body as much as from for-
malist preoccupations, a line both crossed and managed through discourses
of primitivism in the twentieth century. The pursuit of Native American and
European arts as discrete fields of inquiry has never suited WalkingStick,
whose complex and elective creative affiliations challenged the isolation of
artists of Native heritage, beginning in the 1970s. At that time, prompted
by pan-Indian cultural politics of the American Indian Movement and the
death of her Cherokee father, WalkingStick began to explore the excised
indigenous roots of her modernist training in archetypal forms. Her painted
diptychs pairing abstract symbols with semirepresentational landscapes negotiated constructions of "distance and difference" that the postcolonial vetting
of modernist primitivism both exposed and hardened in the late twentieth
century.[10] To slightly restate an argument from chapter 1, critical discourses
of the period left little room for artists to explore kinship with the long record of indigenous images, let alone the varied modernisms that took them
up. While some of her AIM-generation peers responded with postmodern
parody from the margins, I suggest that WalkingStick did not give up the
possibility of belonging to both—or, more specifically, to their many historical
intersections. Still, her diptychs were structured by formal differences, modern
building blocks that continued to shape aesthetic and affective possibilities
in supposedly postmodern climes. By exploring similitude historically, I seek

to understand how WalkingStick's Italian journeys open back up possibilities for shared genealogies of art that seemed foreclosed, like so much else, in the wake of AIM. The resulting works on paper substitute a network of creative kin for the modern biological determinism that has quietly persisted in underwriting differences between Native American and European arts as well as bodies. The racially ambiguous, androgynous legs of WalkingStick's dancers, tangled in vines drawn from Etruscan vases, make way for many ancestors. In turn, WalkingStick's use of sensuous figuration to explore complex affiliations can help us to picture an undivided art history.

Sketching Renaissance Similitude

A longtime arts educator and visitor to the Metropolitan Museum of Art (MET) and the Museum of Modern Art (MoMA) in New York, Walking-Stick was highly fluent in the canon of art history when she first taught in Cornell University's Art in Rome program in 1996.[11] Upon her arrival she began filling sketchbooks with every manner of god, human, beast, and plant drawn from Italian collections of "worldly goods" dating to the Renaissance.[12] WalkingStick's own eccentric gathering of swift black lines on cream paper disregards the discrete cultures and periods that typically organize the study of art history. She was especially drawn to fertile mutable bodies found throughout the arts of Greek and Roman antiquity, the European Renaissance, and the indigenous Americas: a "female satyr with bambino" and "lady lion" from the Villa Sciara, copulating couples from pottery at the Museo Archeologico Nazionale Tarquiniense, votives of pregnant women at Subiaco and Orvieto, a black devil birthing a human from the Pinacoteca Nazionale di Bologna, the feathered serpent god Quetzalcoatl from a precontact Mesoamerican statue in the Museo Etnologico of the Vatican, a fish-tailed Neptune, ancient god of sea and earthquakes from the Villa Giulia, and Christian angels with enormous wingspans, including one playfully entitled "Angel Hailing a Cab in Rome" (see fig. 4.4 and plate 38).[13] The artist's sketchbooks entail both the discovery and creation of resemblances among transformational beings, drawn together in a nonhierarchical field of relations. They record her intimate and highly affective reintroduction to a vast and promiscuous history of art. "I was in love," WalkingStick recalled of her first days in Rome. "I was absolutely, madly in love with it."[14]

I propose that WalkingStick's sketchbooks reprise an imagination of the globe mapped through expanding Renaissance trade and conquest. For a time,

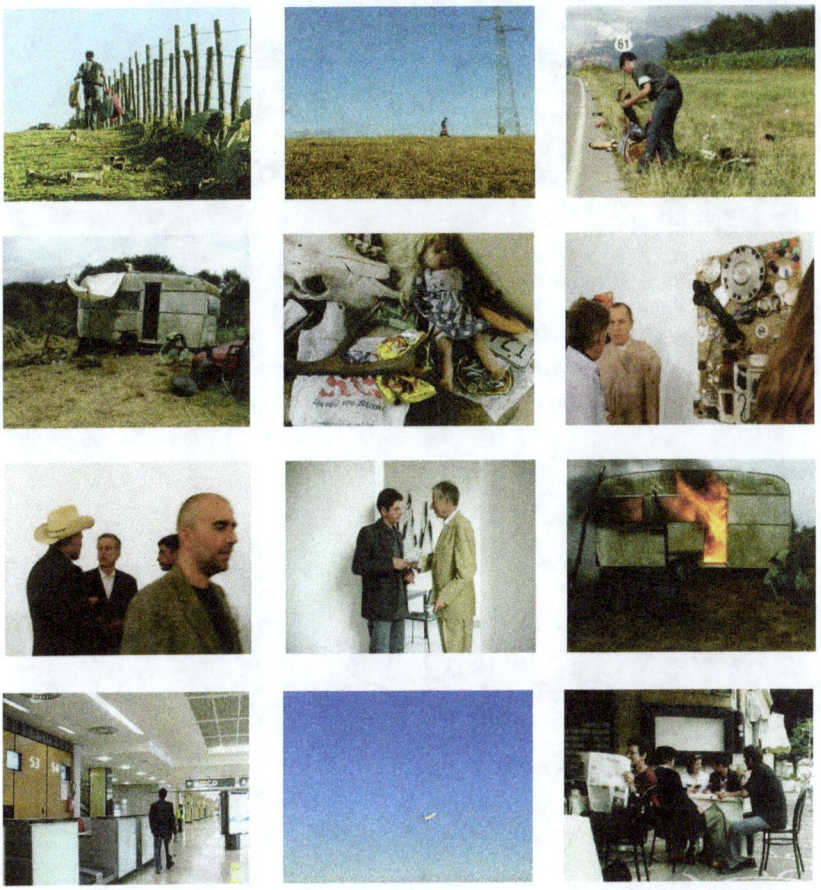

PLATES 1–12 Jimmie Durham, stills from *La poursuite du bonheur*, 35 mm film transferred to DVD, 13 min., 2002. Courtesy of the artist.

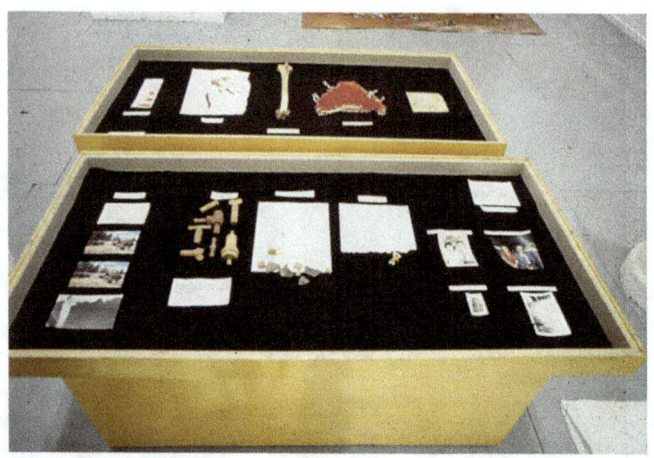

PLATE 13 Jimmie Durham, *On Loan from the Museum of the American Indian*, 1985. Mixed-media installation at Kenkeleba Gallery in New York. Courtesy of the artist. Photo by Maria Thereza Alves.

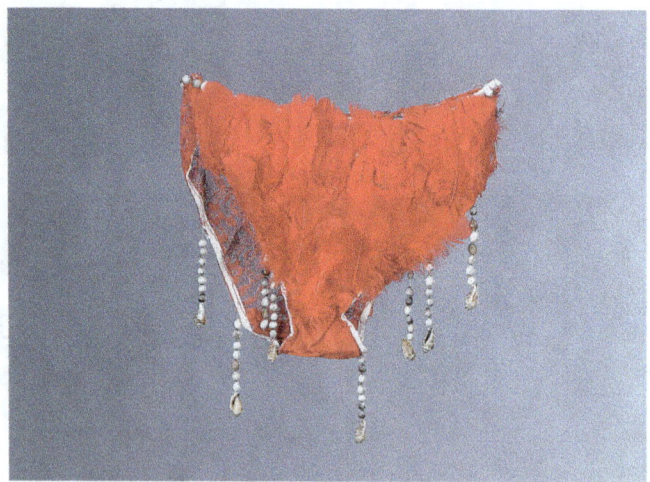

PLATE 14 Jimmie Durham, "Pocahontas' Underwear," 1985. Feathers, beads, fabric, fasteners, 31 × 25 cm. Element from *On Loan from the Museum of the American Indian*, mixed-media installation at Kenkeleba Gallery in New York. Private collection, Belgium. Courtesy of the artist.

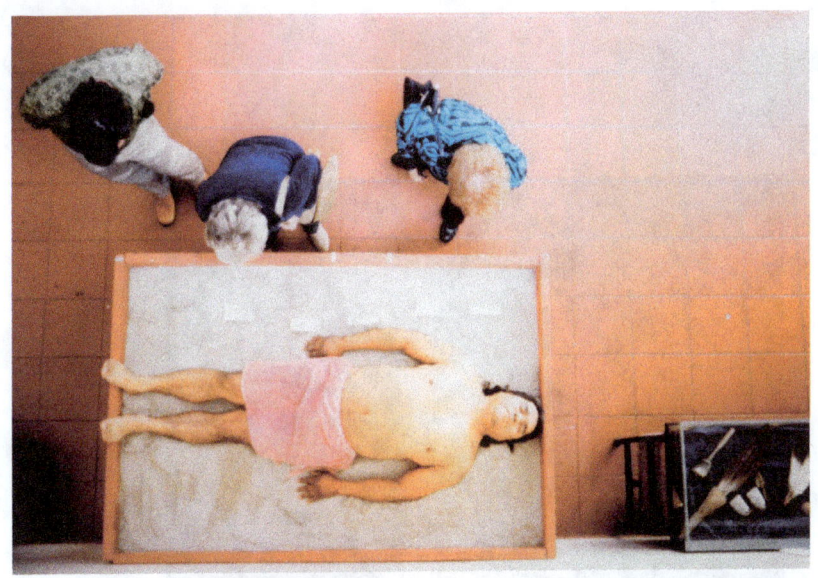

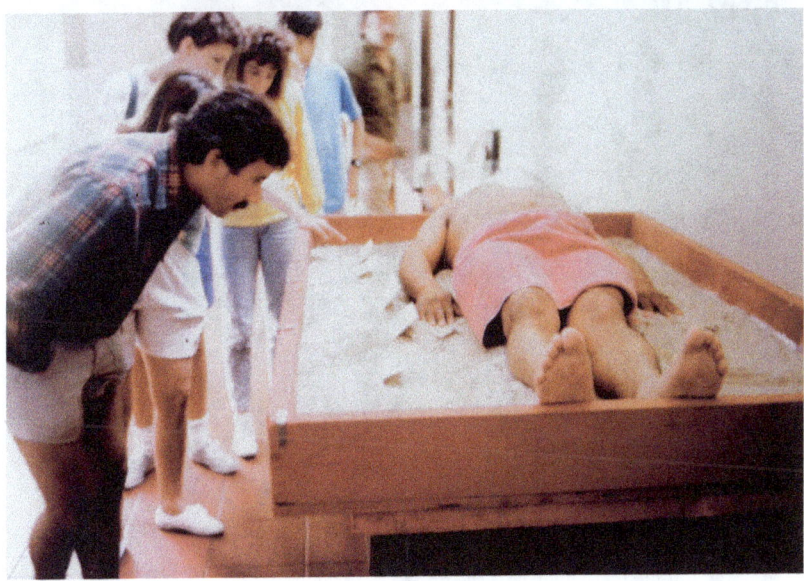

PLATES 15–16 James Luna, *Artifact Piece*, details, 1987.
Performance and installation at the San Diego Museum of Man.
Courtesy of the artist.

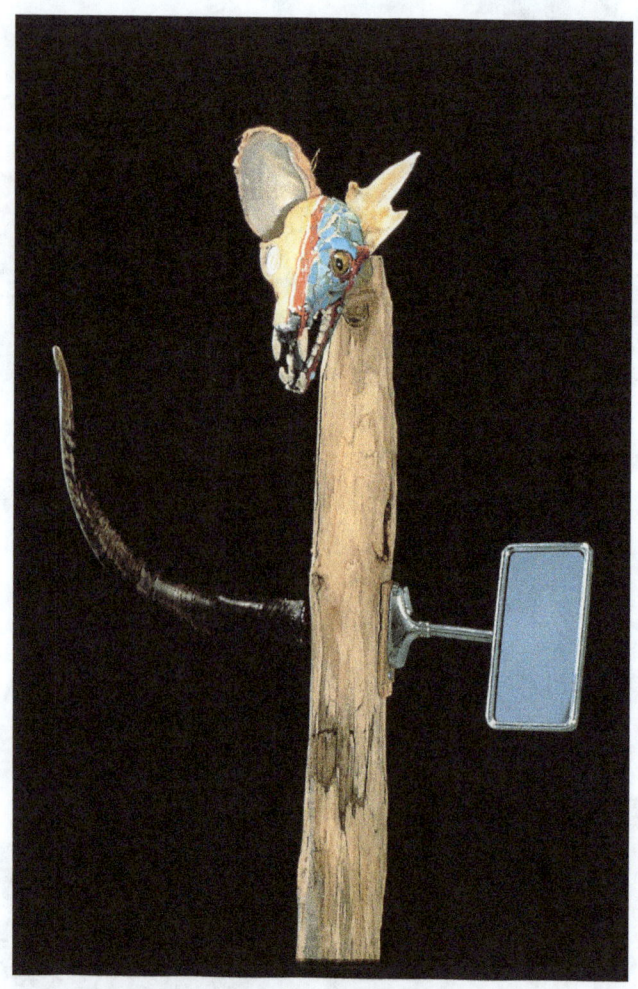

PLATE 17 Jimmie Durham, *Not Joseph Beuys' Coyote*, 1990.
Coyote skull and mixed media, 63 × 28 × 29 (location unknown).
Courtesy of the artist.

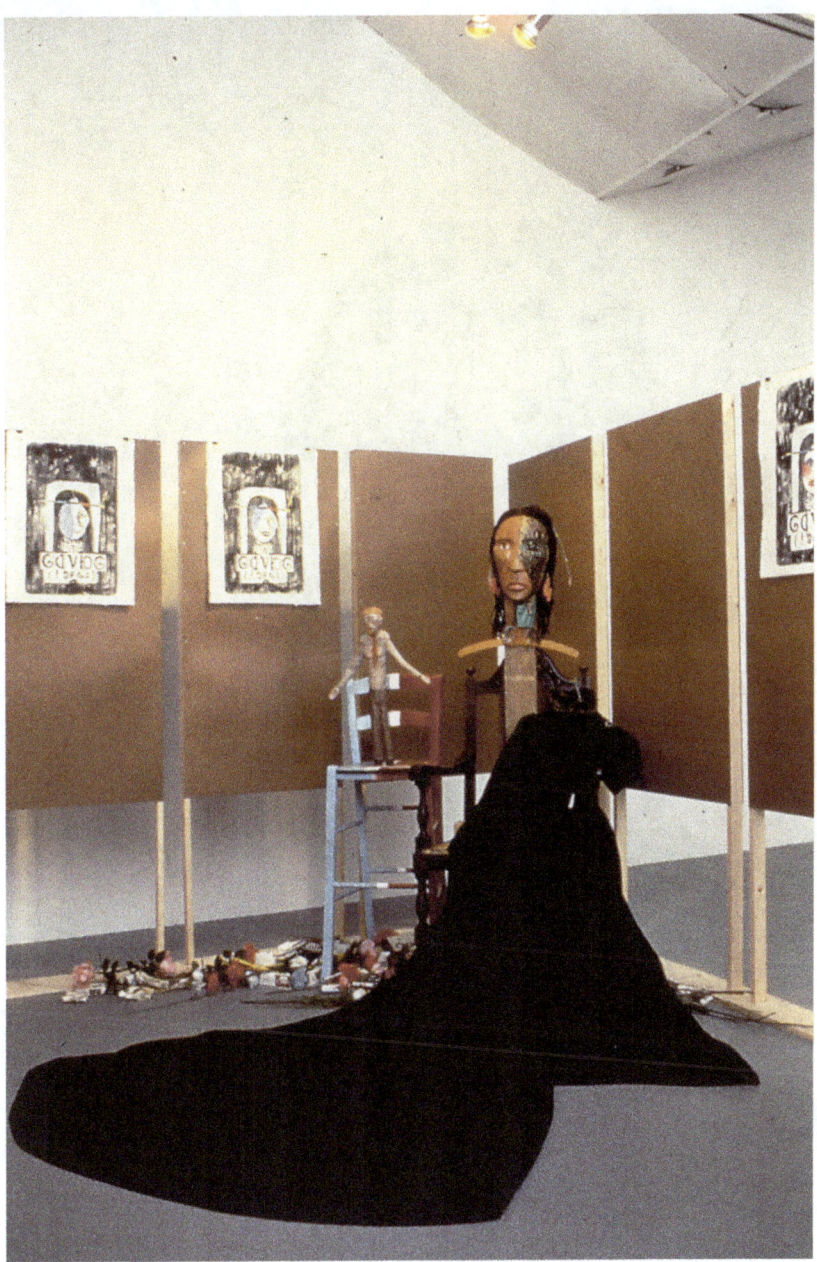

PLATE 18 Jimmie Durham, *Mataoka Ale Attakulakula Anel Guledisgo Hnihi (Pocahontas and the Little Carpenter in London)*, detail, 1988. Mixed-media installation. Courtesy of Matt's Gallery in London.

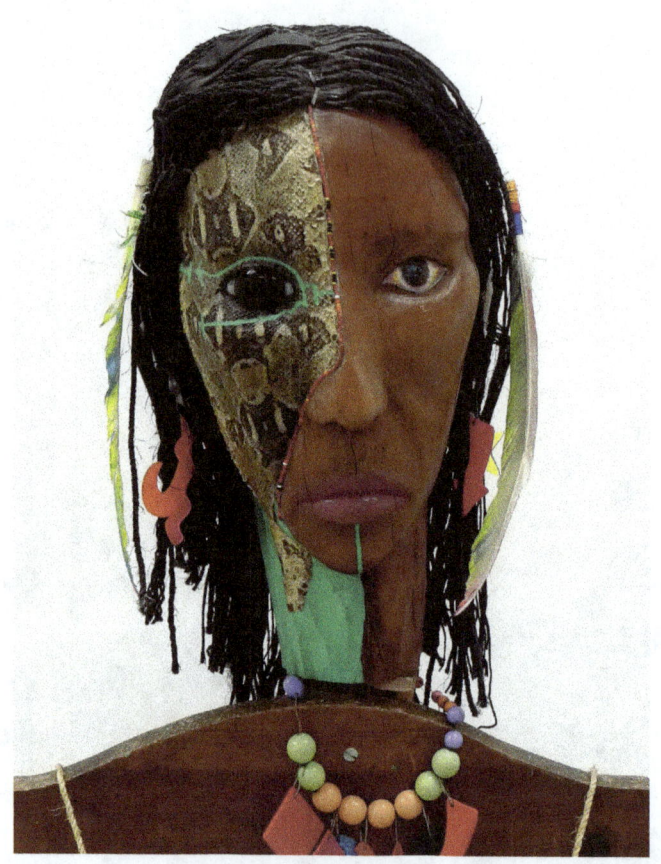

PLATE 19 Jimmie Durham, *La Malinche*, 1988–91. Wood,
cotton, snakeskin, watercolor, polyester, metal, 168 × 56 × 84 cm.
Collection of S.M.A.K., Ghent. Courtesy of the artist.
Photo by Jessica L. Horton.

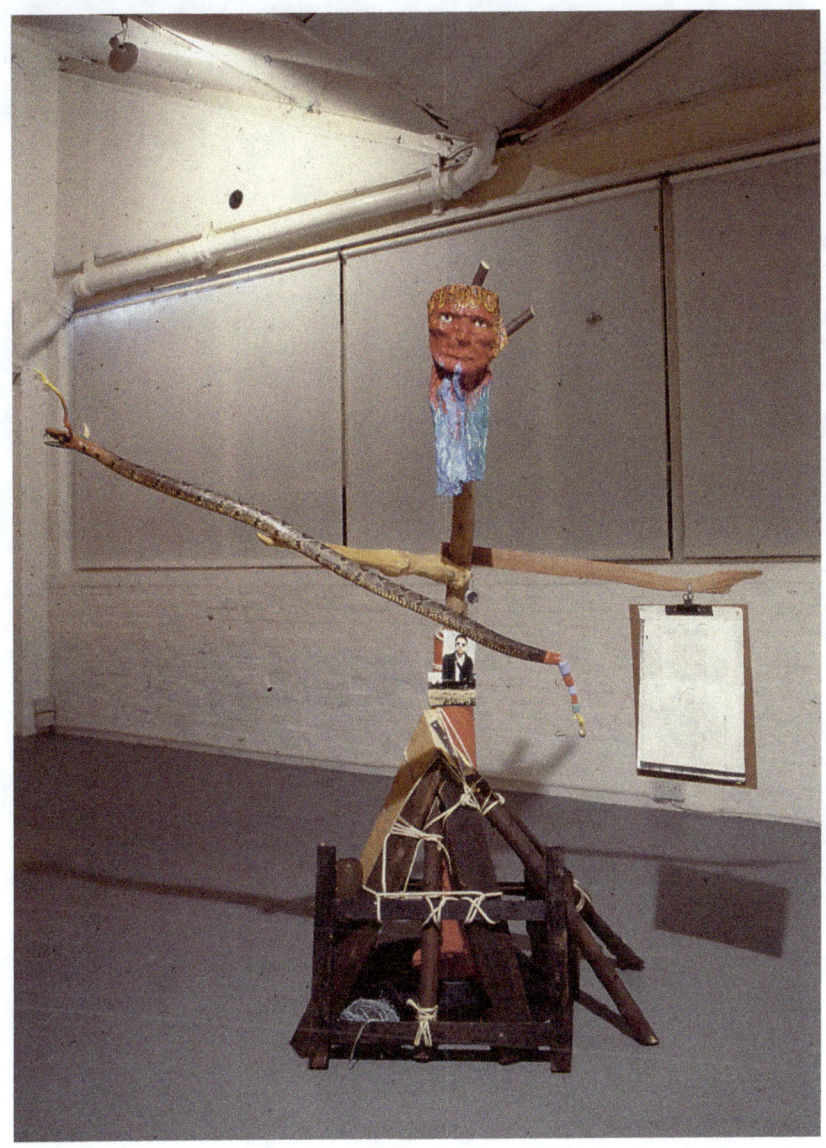

PLATE 20 Jimmie Durham, *Mataoka Ale Attakulakula Anel Guledisgo Hnihi (Pocahontas and the Little Carpenter in London)*, detail, 1988. Mixed-media installation at Matt's Gallery in London. Courtesy of Matt's Gallery.

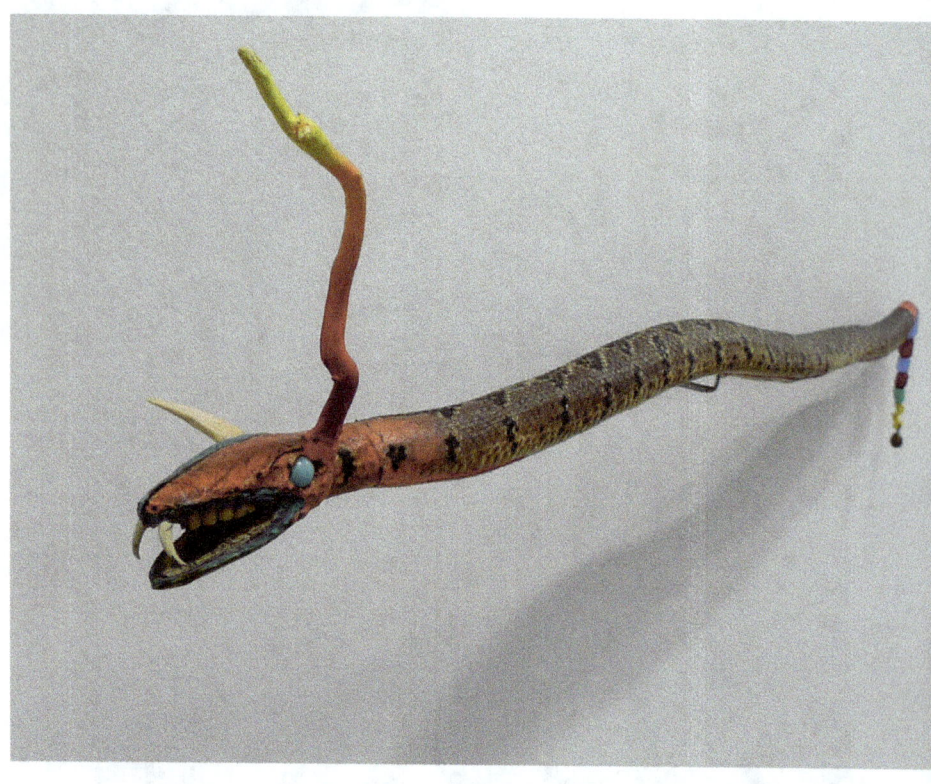

PLATE 21 Jimmie Durham, "Attakulakula," 1988. Snakeskin and mixed media, element from *Mataoka Ale Attakulakula Anel Guledisgo Hnihi (Pocahontas and the Little Carpenter in London)*. Collection of Danielle Fiard, Geneva. Photo by Jessica L. Horton.

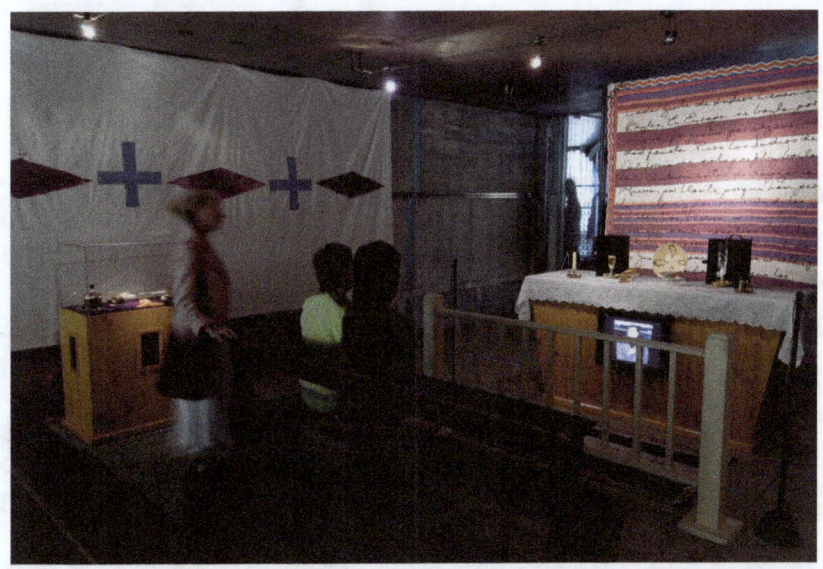

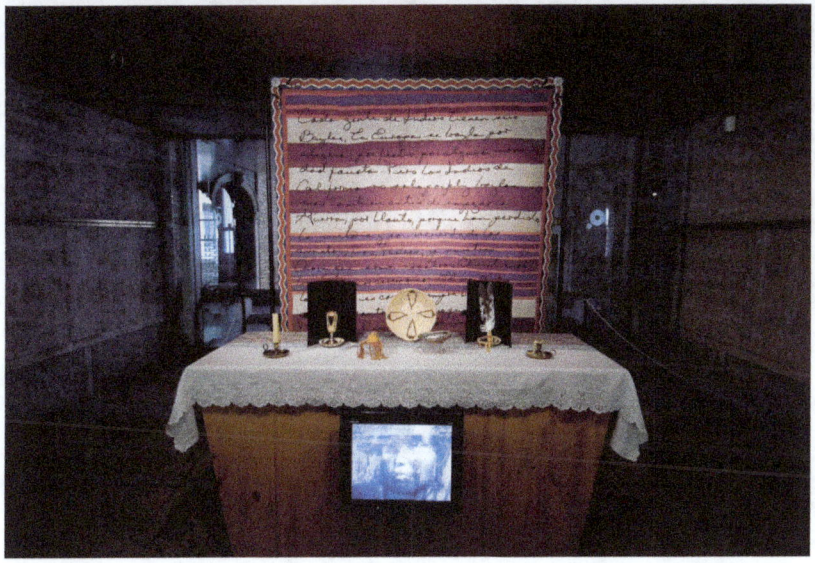

PLATES 22–23 James Luna, "Chapel for Pablo Tac," 2005. Mixed-media installation included in *Emendatio* at the Fondazione Querini Stampalia, Fifty-First Venice Biennale. National Museum of the American Indian, Smithsonian Institution, KF05ItalyG134. Photos by Katherine Fogden.

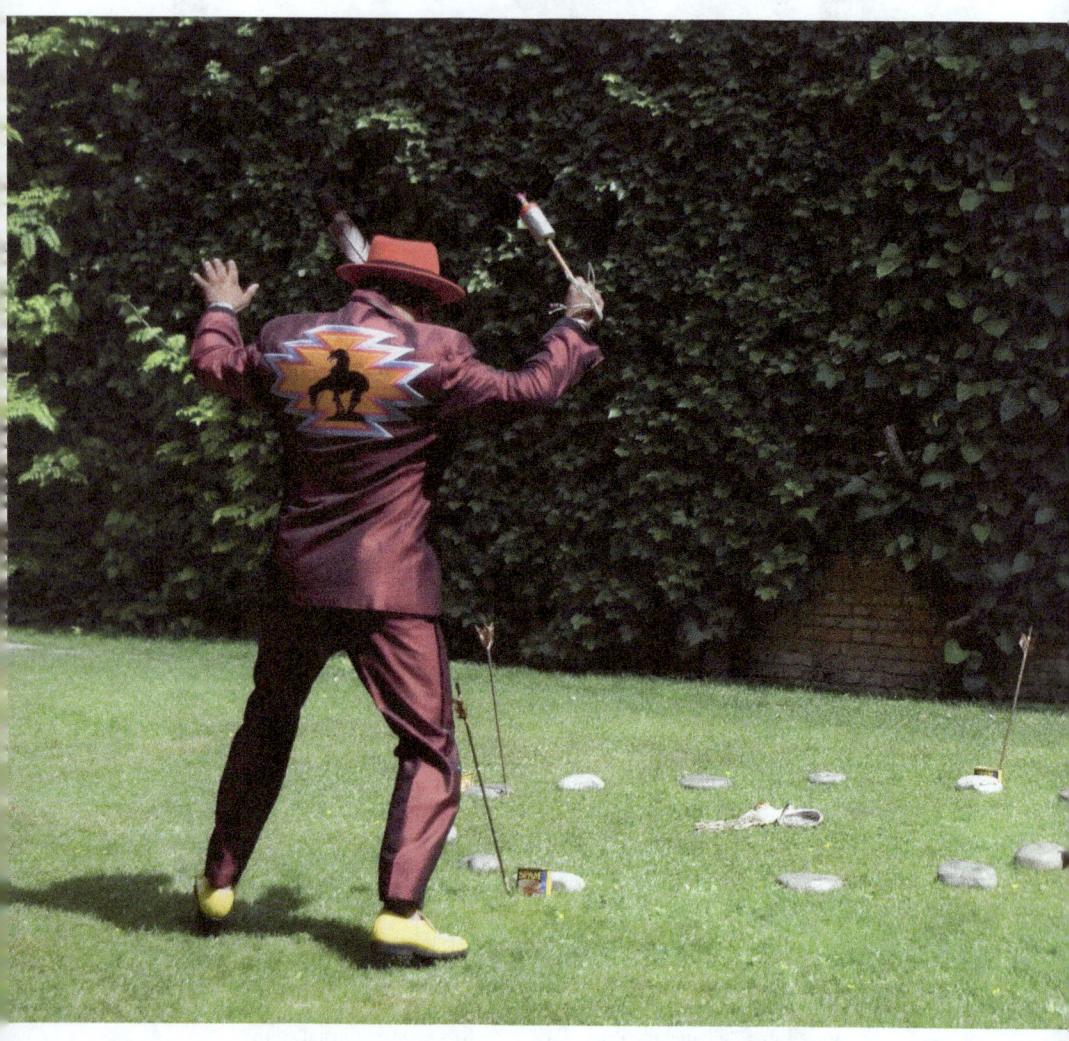

PLATES 24–25 James Luna, "Renewal (A Performance for Pablo Tac),"
2005. Performance included in *Emendatio* at the Fondazione
Querini Stampalia, Fifty-First Venice Biennale. National Museum
of the American Indian, Smithsonian Institution, KF05ItalyF356.
Photos by Katherine Fogden.

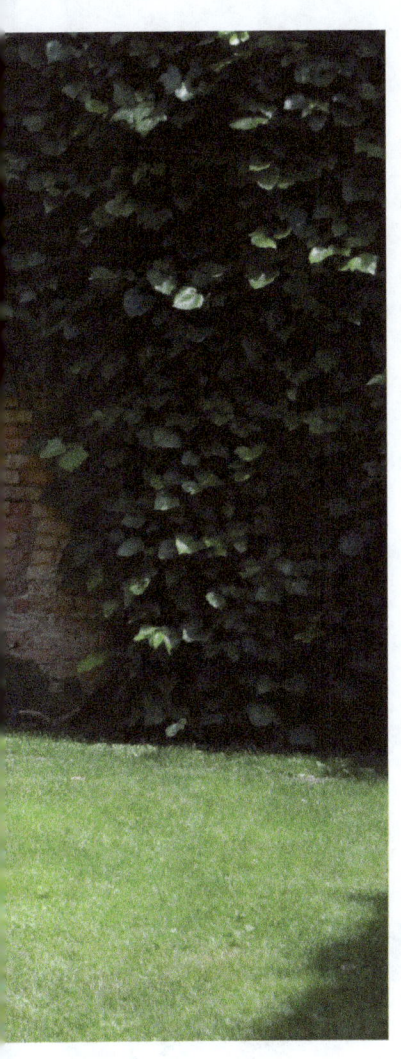

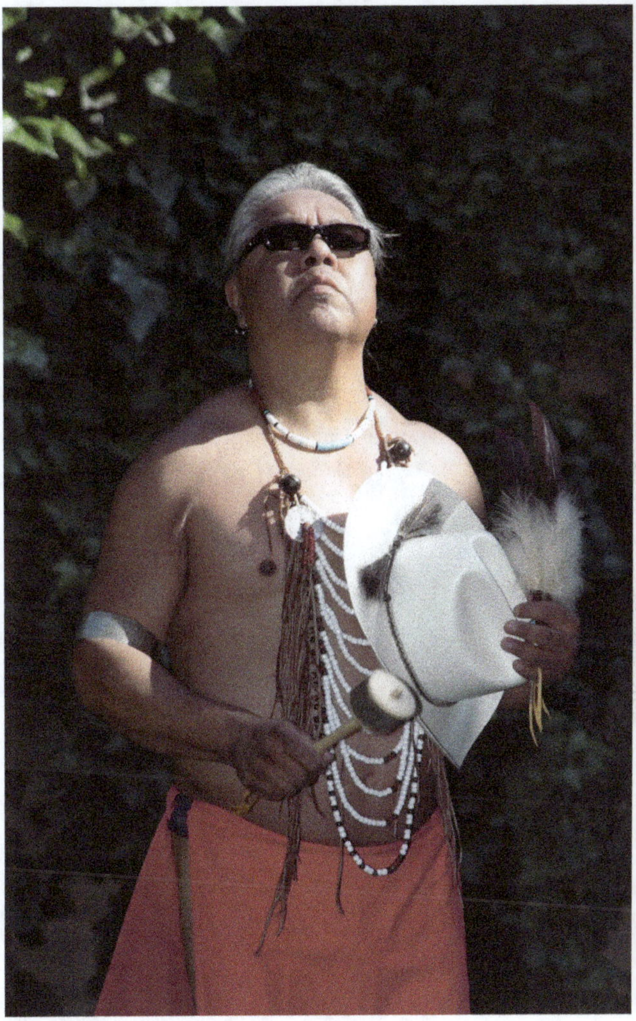

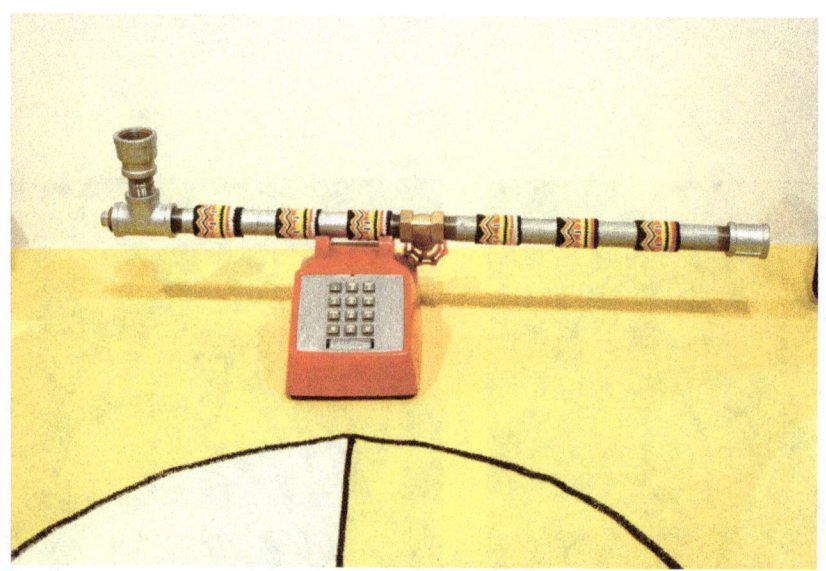

PLATE 26 James Luna, "High-Tech Peace Pipe," 2000. Mixed-media element from *Chapel of the Sacred Colors*. Courtesy of the artist.

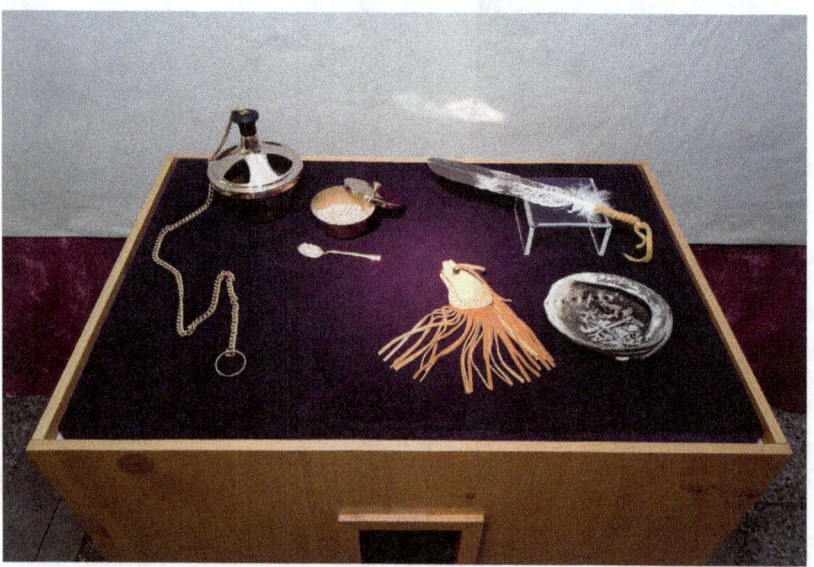

PLATE 27 James Luna, "Chapel for Pablo Tac," detail, 2005. Mixed-media installation included in *Emendatio* at the Fondazione Querini Stampalia, Fifty-First Venice Biennale. National Museum of the American Indian, Smithsonian Institution, KF05ItalyA376. Photo by Katherine Fogden.

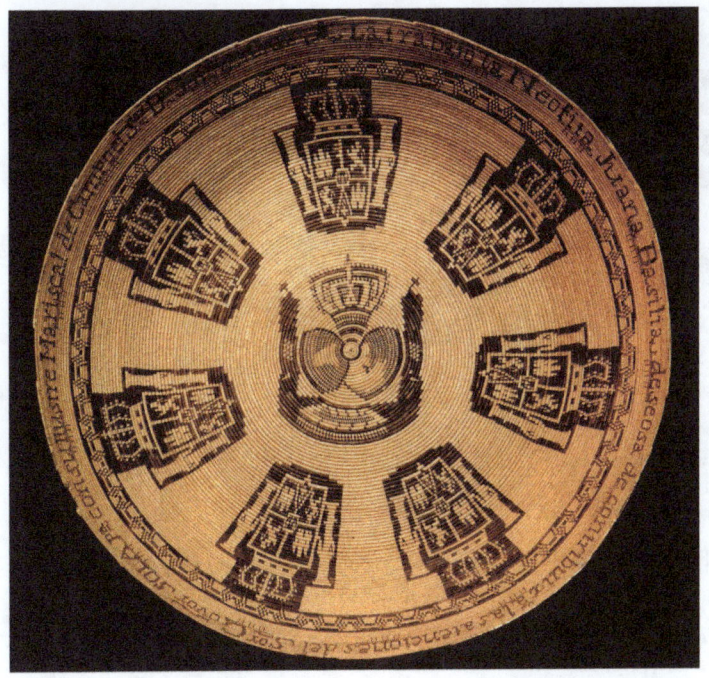

PLATE 28 Juana Basilia Sitmelelene, *Basket Tray with Inscription and Heraldic Designs*, c. 1820. Plant fibers, 24 in. diameter by 4 in. height. Gift of Anna Blaksley Bliss. Courtesy of the Santa Barbara Museum of Natural History, NA-CA-CH-4F-3.

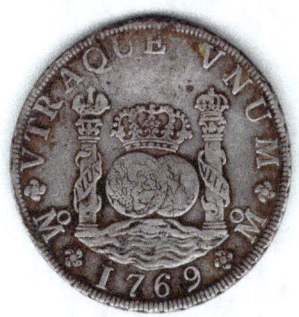

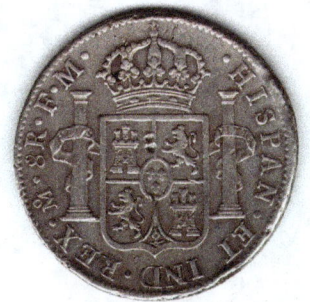

PLATE 29 Pillar dollar (obverse). Milled silver eight-real coin, a type minted in Mexico City, 1732–72. Courtesy of the Santa Barbara Museum of Natural History. Photo by Jan Timbrook.

PLATE 30 Portrait (or Bust) dollar (reverse). Milled silver eight-real coin, a type minted in Mexico City, 1772– c. 1823. Courtesy of the Santa Barbara Museum of Natural History. Photo by Jan Timbrook.

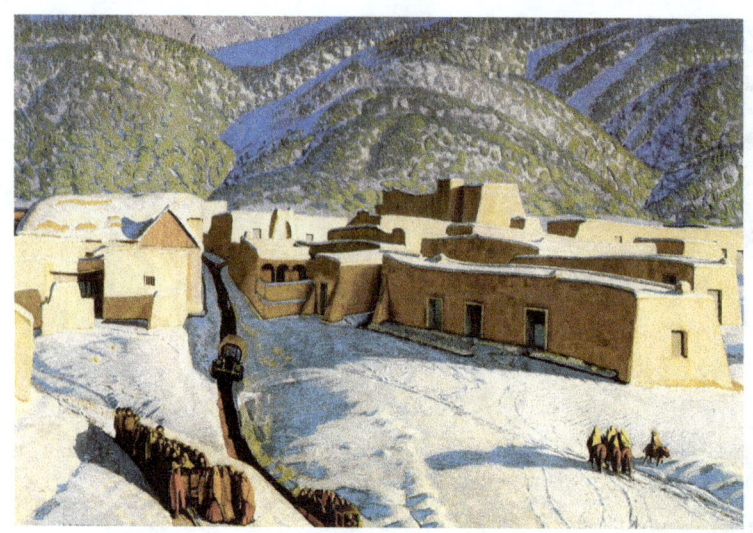

PLATE 31 Ernest Leonard Blumenschein, *Adobe Village—Winter*, 1929. Oil on canvas, 34 × 50 in. (location unknown). Reproduced from William C. Foxley, *Frontier Spirit: Catalog of the Collection of the Museum of Western Art* (Museum of Western Art, 1983), 144.

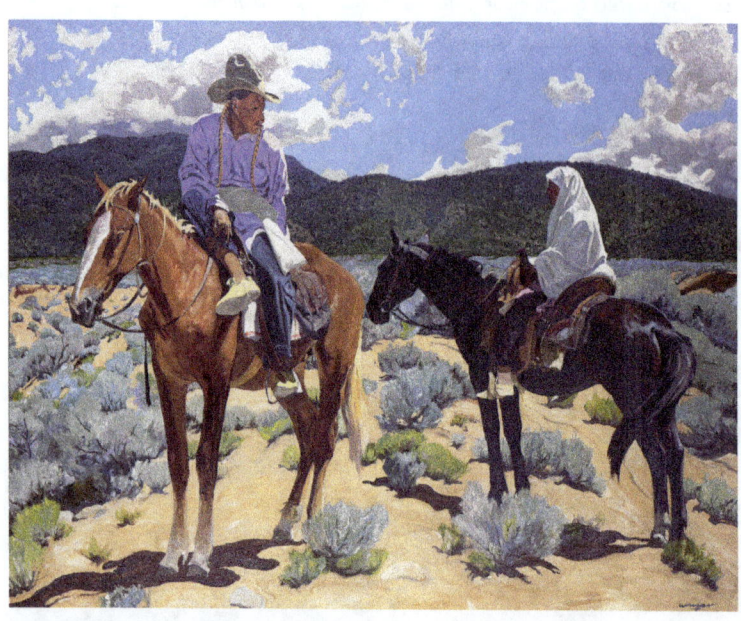

PLATE 32 Walter Ufer, *Two Riders*, 1930. Oil on canvas, 40 × 50 in. Stark Museum of Art, Orange, Texas, 31.5/8.

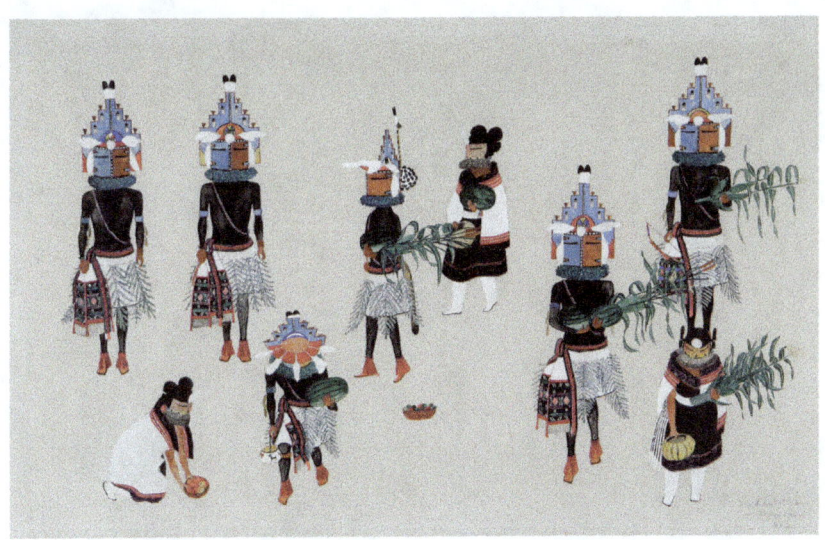

PLATE 33 Fred Kabotie, *Niman Kachina Dance*, 1920. Gouache on paper, 22.75 × 32 in. School for Advanced Research, IAF.P22. Photo by Addison Doty.

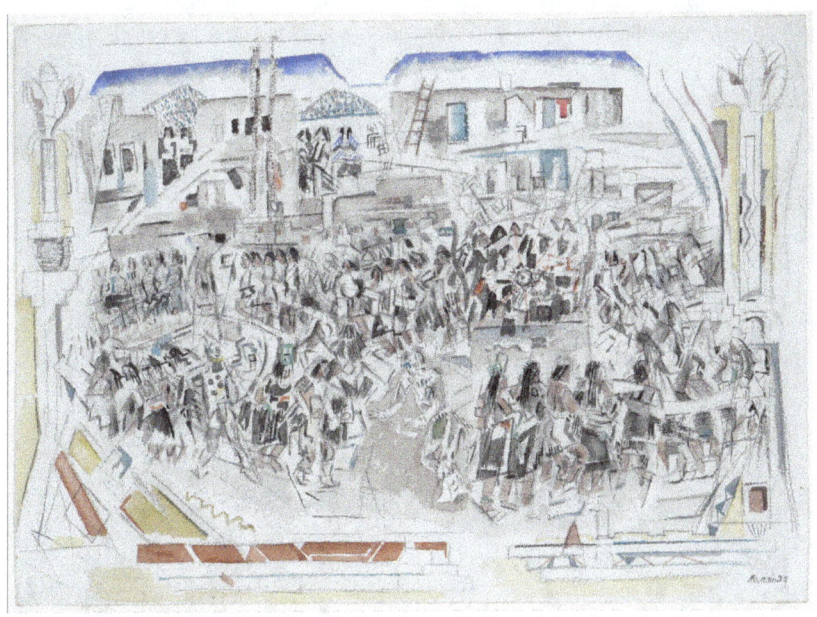

PLATE 34 John Marin, *Dance of the Santo Domingo Indians*, 1929. Watercolor and crayon on paper, 22⅛ × 30¾ in. Alfred Stieglitz Collection, 1949, 49.70.227. Courtesy of the Metropolitan Museum of Art. © 2014 Estate of John Marin / Artists Rights Society (ARS), NY. Image source: Art Resource, NY.

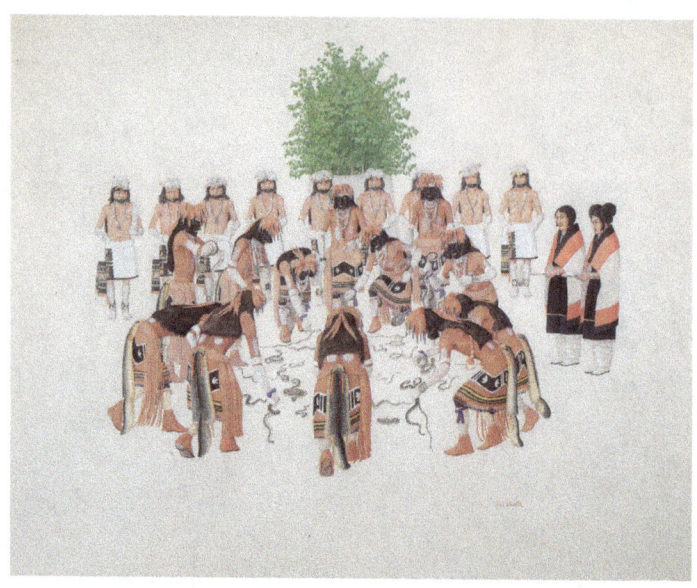

PLATE 35 Fred Kabotie, *Snake Dance*, c. 1930. Gouache on paper, 57.5 × 48 cm. National Museum of the American Indian, Smithsonian Institution, 22/8647. Photo by David Heald.

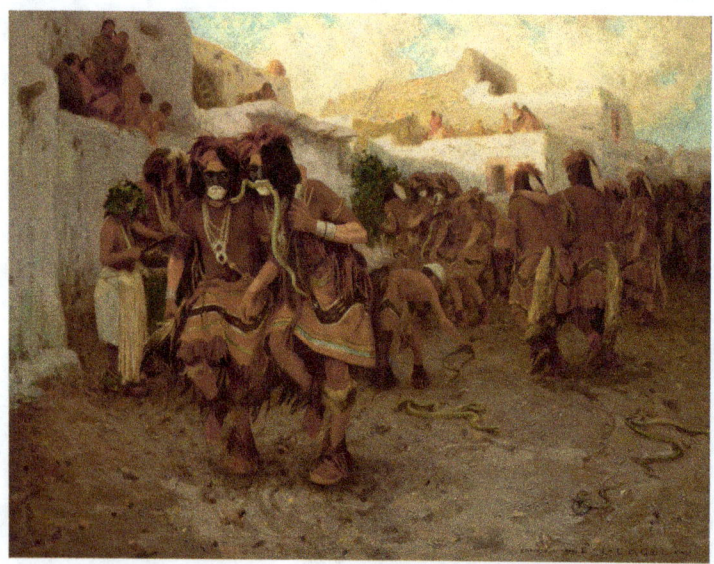

PLATE 36 E. Irving Couse, *Moki Snake Dance—Prayer for Rain*, 1904. Oil on canvas, 36 × 48 in. Courtesy of the American Museum of Western Art—The Anschutz Collection. Photo by William J. O'Connor.

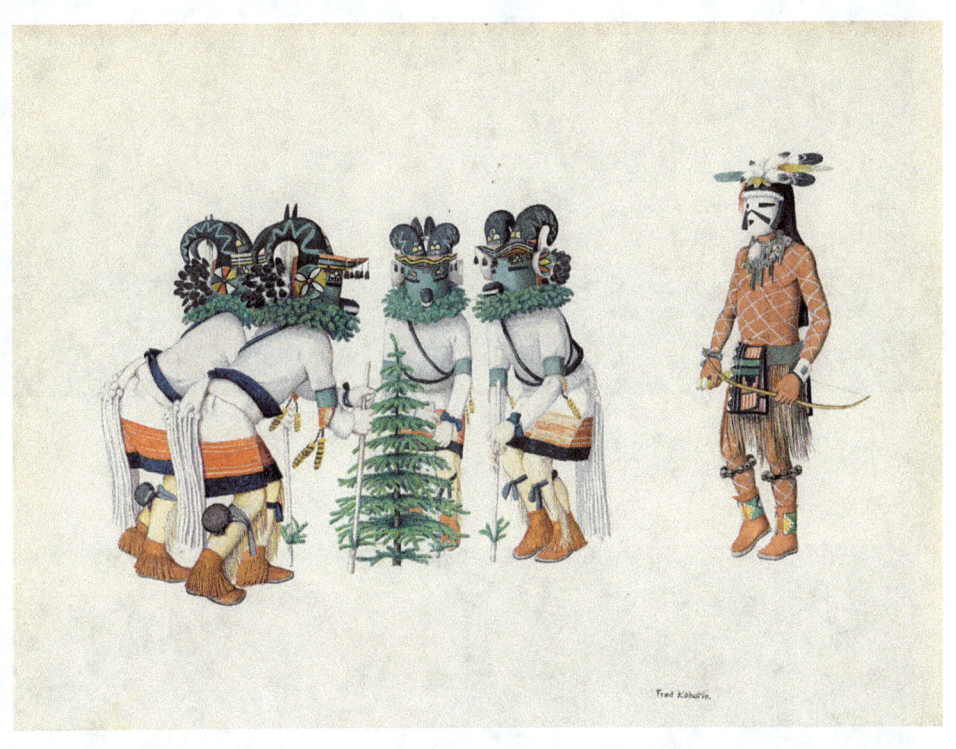

PLATE 37 Fred Kabotie, *Mountain Sheep Dance*, n.d. Gouache on paper, 16⅜ × 20⅝ in. National Museum of the American Indian, Smithsonian Institution, 22/8646. Photo by Ernest Amoroso.

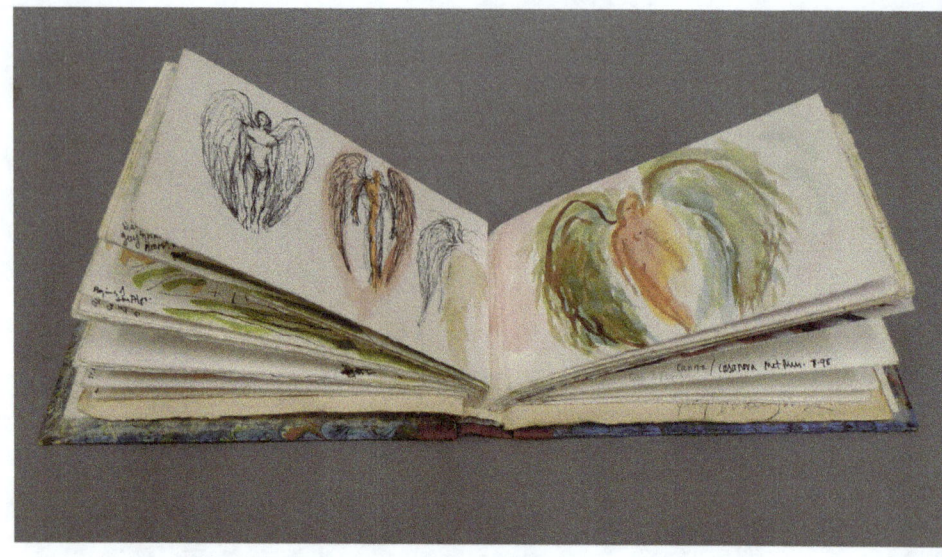

PLATE 38 Kay WalkingStick, sketchbook from Rome, 1996. Ink and watercolor. Collection of the artist. Photo by Jessica L. Horton.

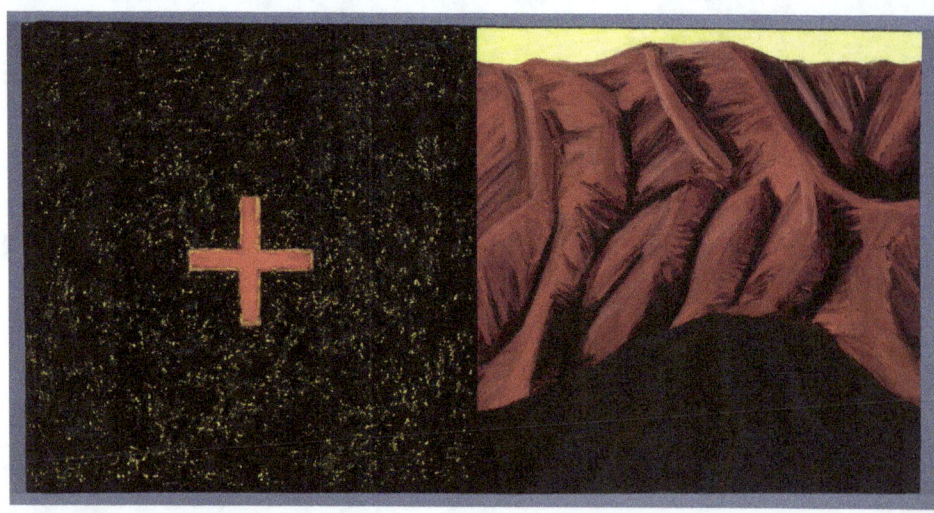

PLATE 39 Kay WalkingStick, *With Love to Marsden*, 1995. Acrylic, wax, sparkles, and oil on canvas, 32 × 64 in. Collection of the artist.

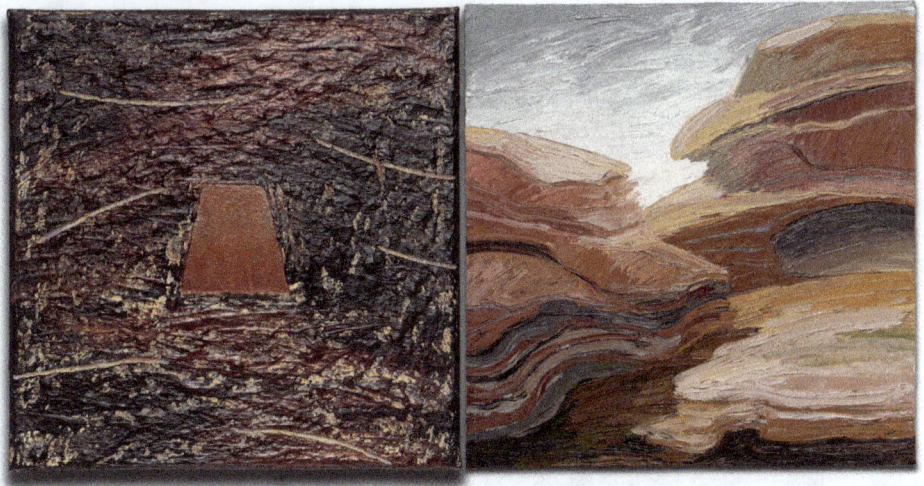

PLATE 40 Kay WalkingStick, *Hovenweep #331*, 1987. Oil on canvas, 20 × 20 in.,
W: 20 × 20 in., D: 3 × ½ in. each. Peabody Essex Museum, Salem. Gift of
Katrina M. Carye, 2011. 2011.29.72.1–2.

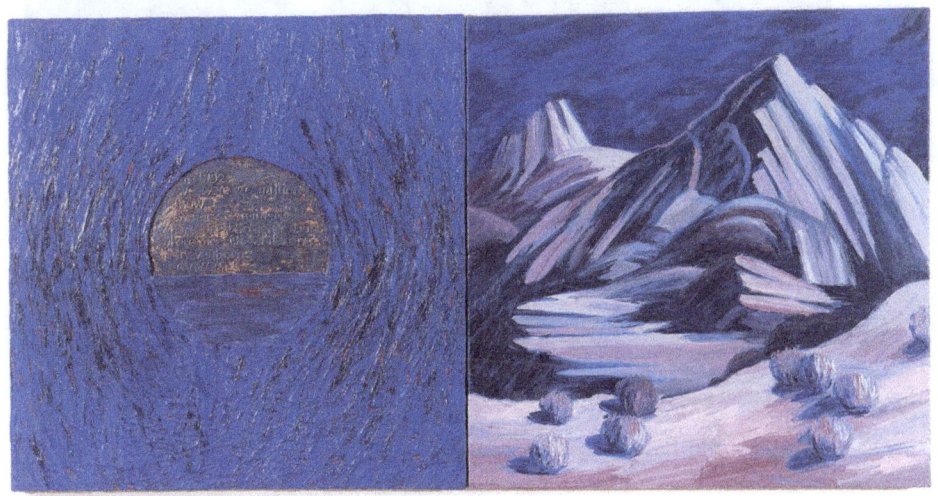

PLATE 41 Kay WalkingStick, *Where Are the Generations?*, 1991. Acrylic, wax, copper, and oil
on canvas, 28 × 56 × ½ in. Collection of Jim and Keith Shaw. Photo by Lee Stalsworth.
Courtesy of the National Museum of the American Indian, Smithsonian Institution.

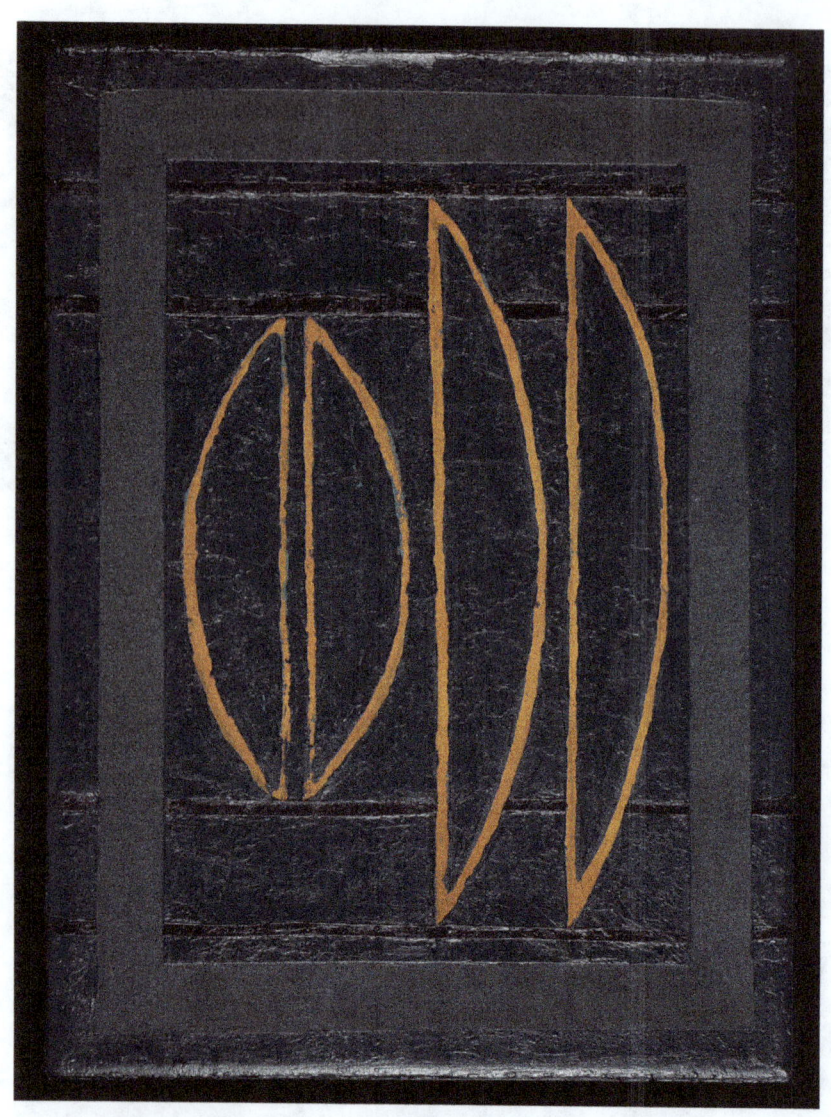

PLATE 42 Kay WalkingStick, detail from *Chief Joseph* series, 1974–76. Acrylic, wax, and ink on canvas. Each panel, 20 × 15 in. (36 total). Collection of the National Museum of the American Indian, Smithsonian Institution (Panel 16, 5366.016). Photo by R. A. Whiteside.

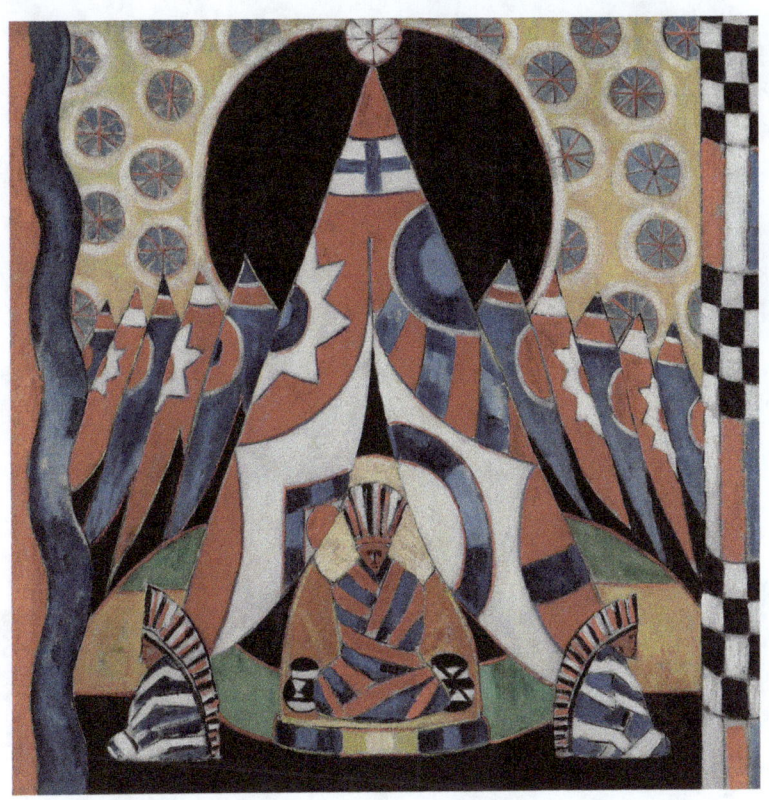

PLATE 43 Marsden Hartley, *American Indian Symbols*, 1914. Oil on canvas, 39 ³⁄₁₆ in. × 39 ³⁄₁₆ in. Amon Carter Museum of American Art, Fort Worth, Texas. 1999.8.

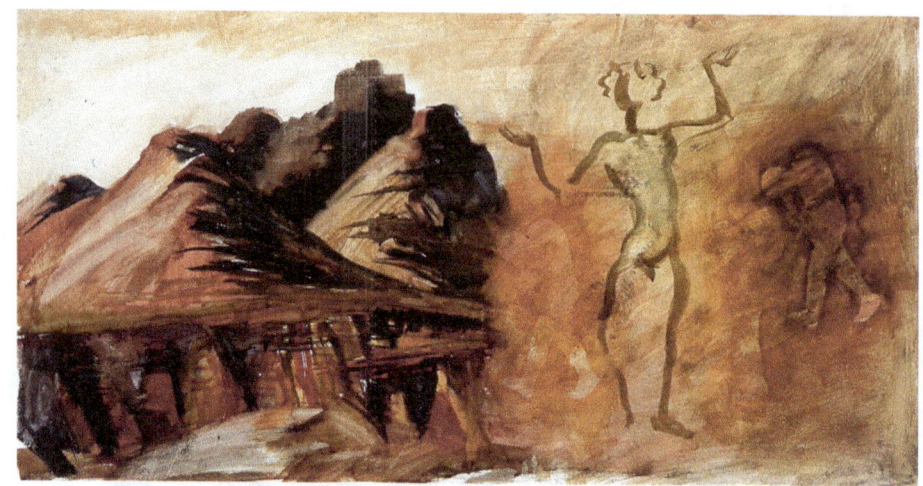

PLATE 44 Kay WalkingStick, *Mountain Men*, 1996. Gouache on paper, 19½ × 38 in. Collection of the artist.

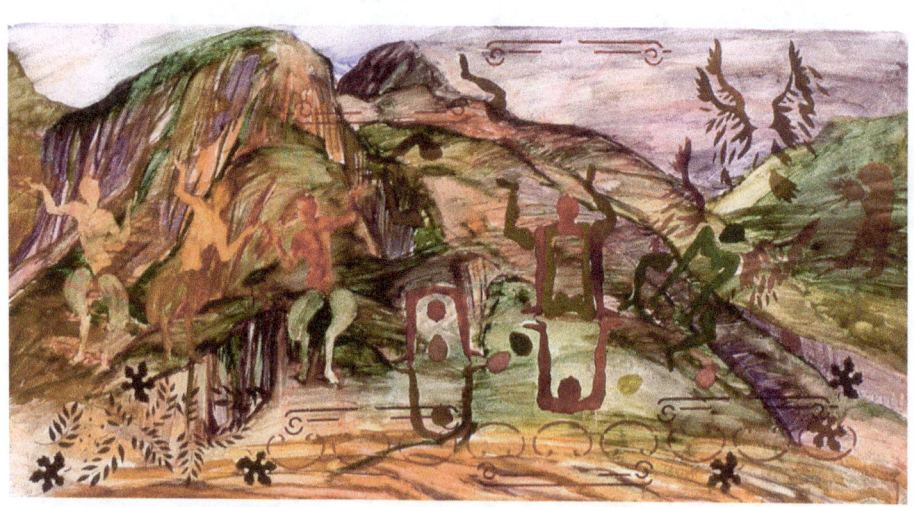

PLATE 45 Kay WalkingStick, *Narcissus*, 1996. Gouache, acrylic on paper, 19½ × 38 in. Collection of the artist.

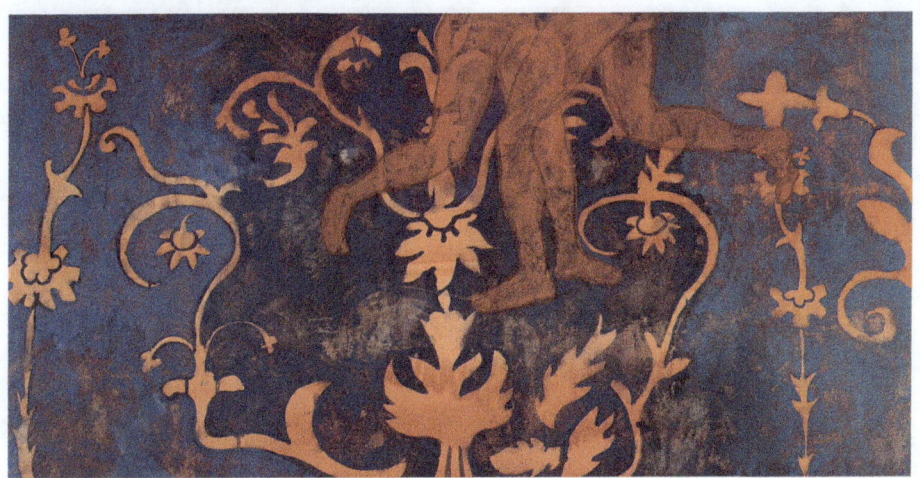

PLATE 46 Kay WalkingStick, *ACEA V*, 2003. Gouache, Conté crayon on paper, 19 × 38 in. Collection of the artist. Courtesy of the National Museum of the American Indian, Smithsonian Institution. Photo by Lee Stalsworth.

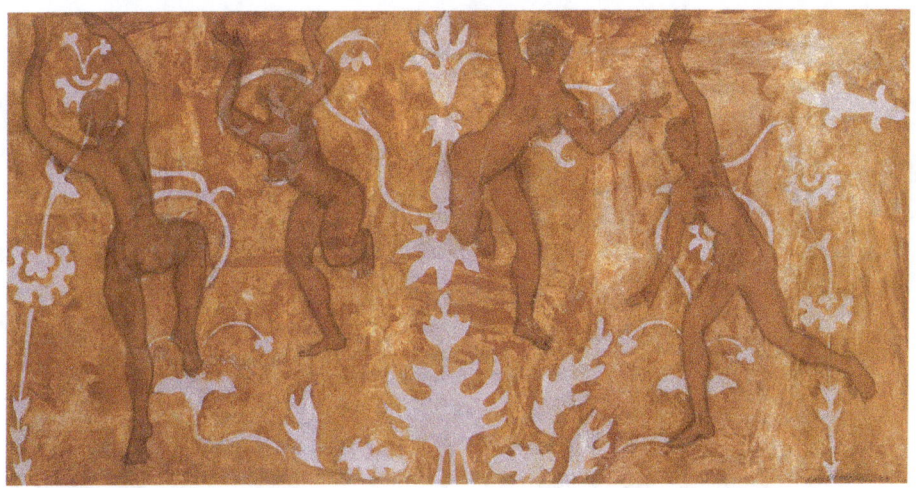

PLATE 47 Kay WalkingStick, *ACEA VI—Bacchantes*, 2003. Gouache, Conté crayon on paper, 19 × 38 in. Collection of the artist. Courtesy of the National Museum of the American Indian, Smithsonian Institution. Photo by Lee Stalsworth.

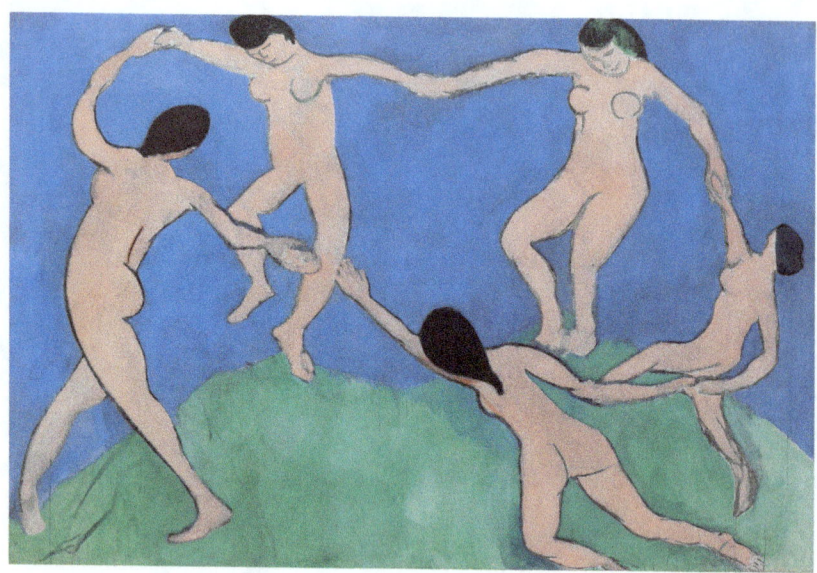

PLATE 48 Henri Matisse, *Dance (I)*. Paris, Boulevard des Invalides, early 1909. Oil on canvas, 8 ft. 6½ in. × 12 ft. 9½ in. (259.7 × 390.1 cm). Gift of Nelson A. Rockefeller in honor of Alfred H. Barr, Jr., The Museum of Modern Art, 201.1963. © 2017 Succession H. Matisse / Artists Rights Society (ARS), New York. Digital Image © The Museum of Modern Art / Licensed by SCALA / Art Resource, NY.

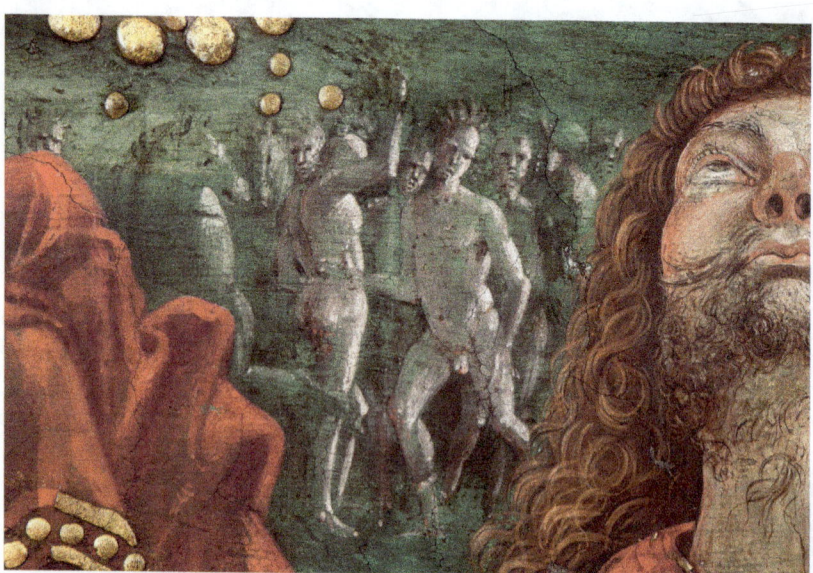

PLATE 49 Pinturicchio (Bernardino di Betto) workshop, detail of *The Resurrection of Christ*, 1492–94. Fresco in La salle de Mystères, Borgia Apartments of the Vatican. Photo © Vatican Museums. All rights reserved.

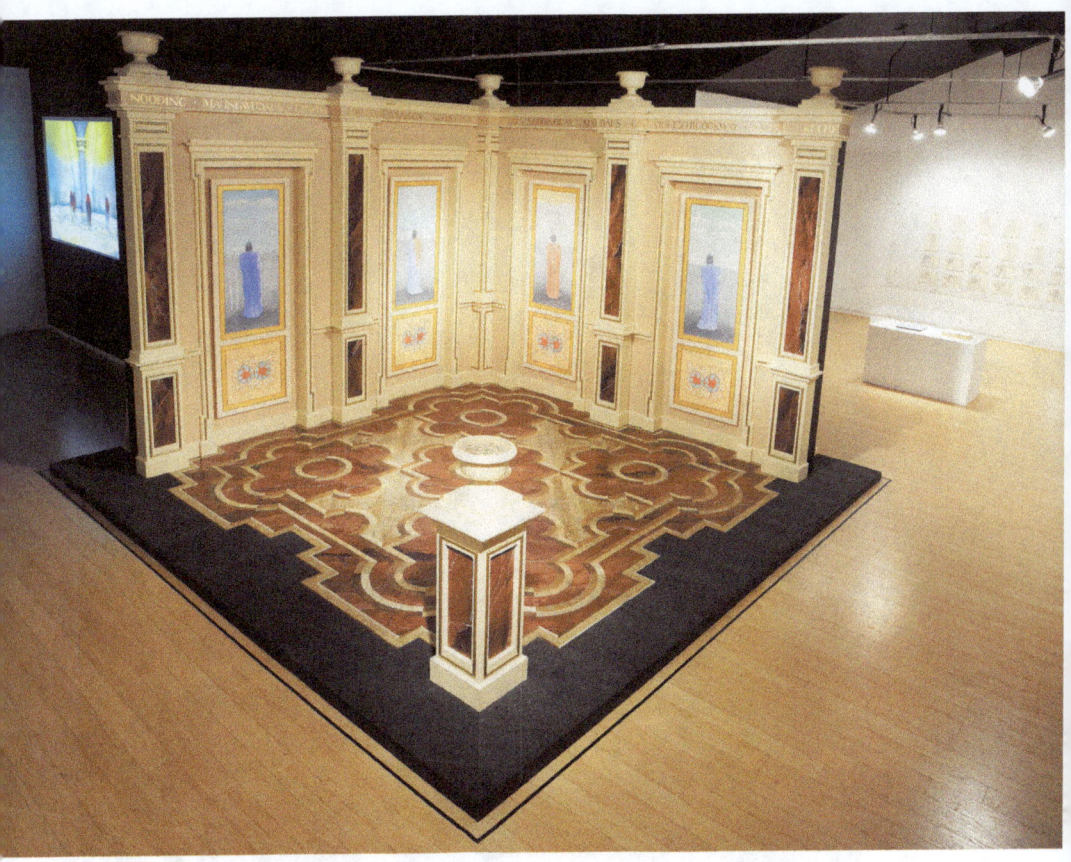

PLATE 50 Robert Houle, *Paris/Ojibwa*, 2010. Multimedia installation. Installation view, Art Gallery of Peterborough, 2011. Collection of the artist. Photo by Michael Cullen, Trent Photographics.

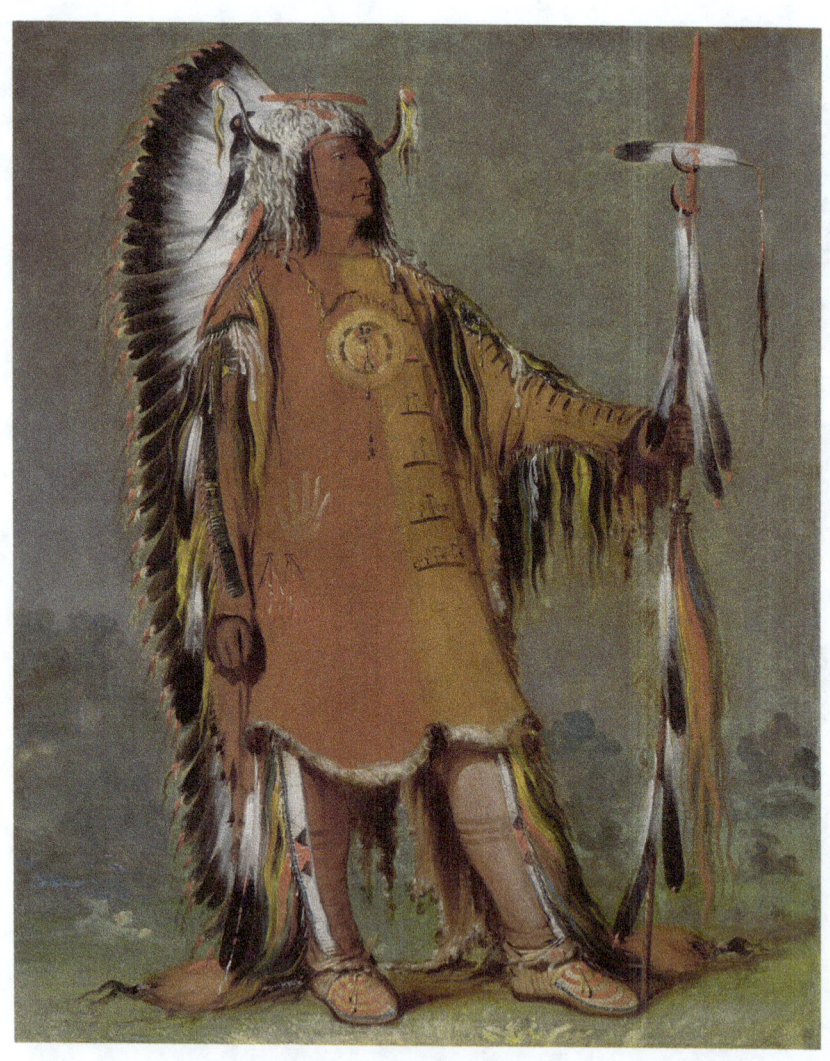

PLATE 51 George Catlin, *Máh-to-tóh-pa, Four Bears, Second Chief, in Full Dress*, 1832. Oil on canvas, 73.5 × 61 cm. Smithsonian American Art Museum, gift of Mrs. Joseph Harrison, Jr. 1985.66.128.

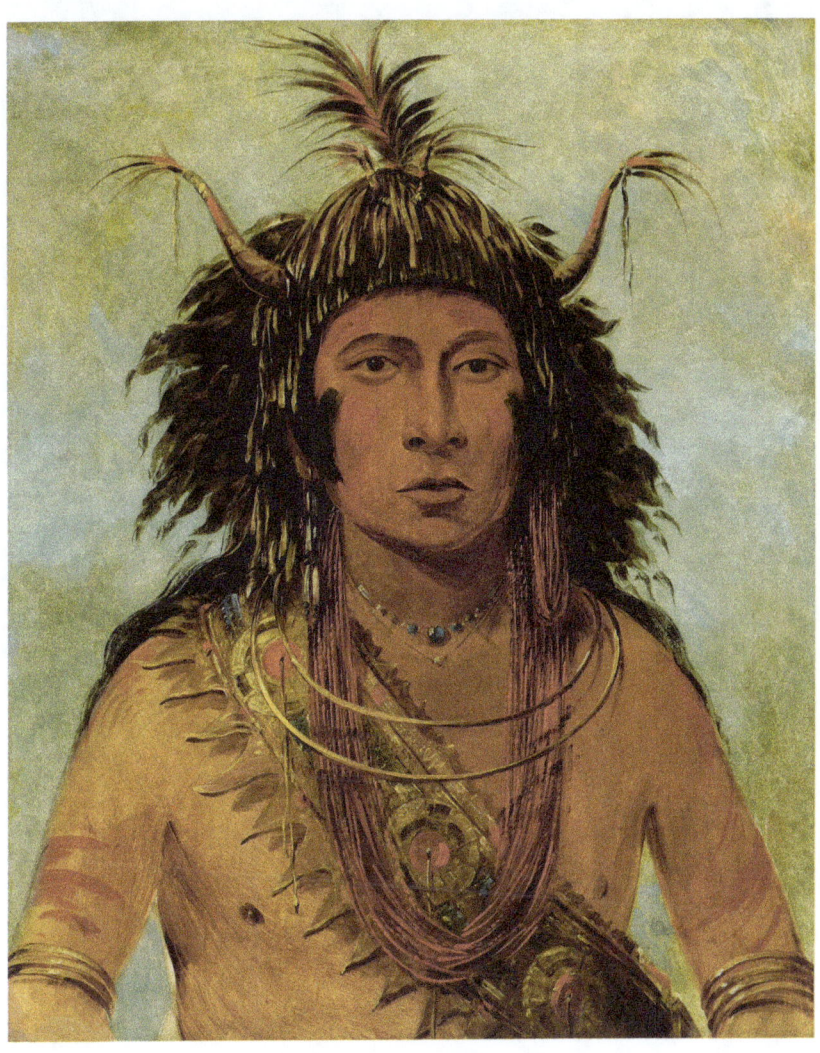

PLATE 52 George Catlin, *Say-say-gon, Hail Storm, War Chief*, 1845. Oil on canvas, 73.7 × 60.9 cm. Smithsonian American Art Museum, gift of Mrs. Joseph Harrison, Jr. 1985.66.532.

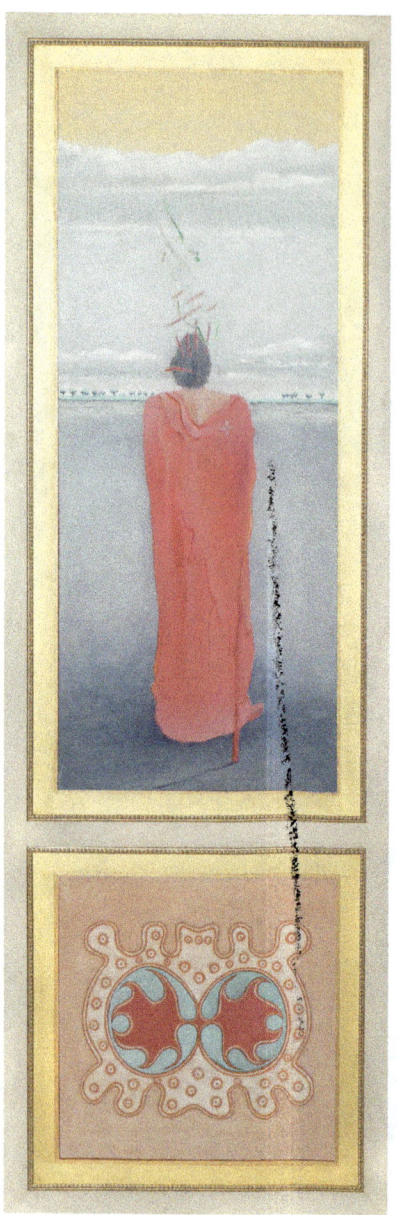

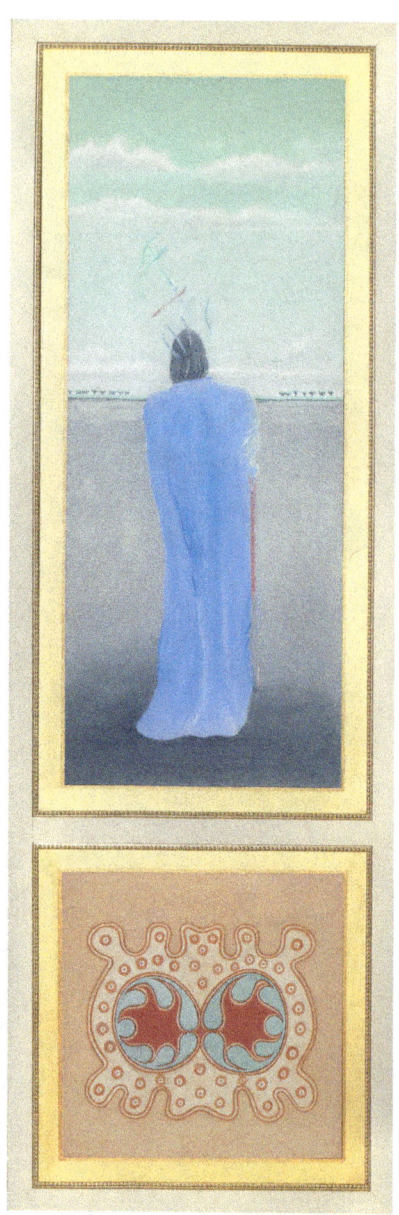

PLATE 53 Robert Houle, "Dancer," 2010. Framed oil on canvas, 71.5 × 214 cm, element from *Paris/Ojibwa*. Collection of the artist. Photo by Michael Cullen, Trent Photographics.

PLATE 54 Robert Houle, "Healer," 2010. Framed oil on canvas, 71.5 × 214 cm, element from *Paris/Ojibwa*. Collection of the artist. Photo by Michael Cullen, Trent Photographics.

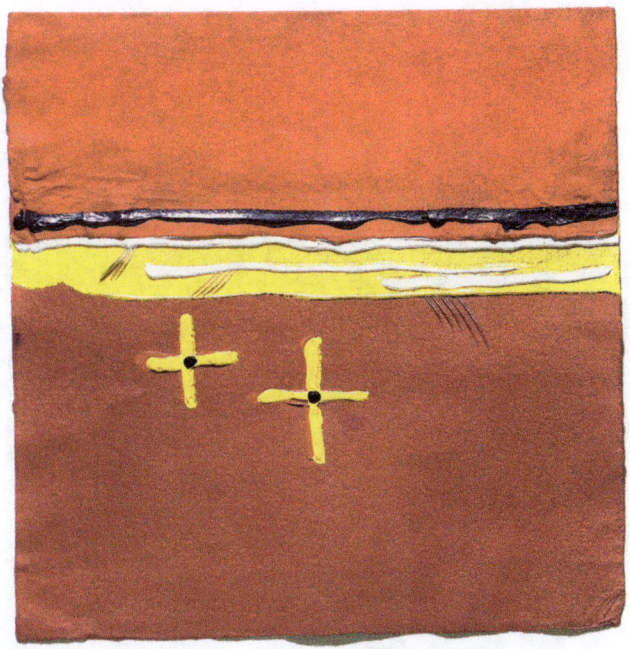

PLATE 55 Robert Houle, *Parfleches for the Last Supper #5: Philip*,
1983. Acrylic and porcupine quills on paper, one of a series of
thirteen, each 56 × 56 cm. Collection of the Winnipeg Art Gallery.
Photo by Ernest Mayer.

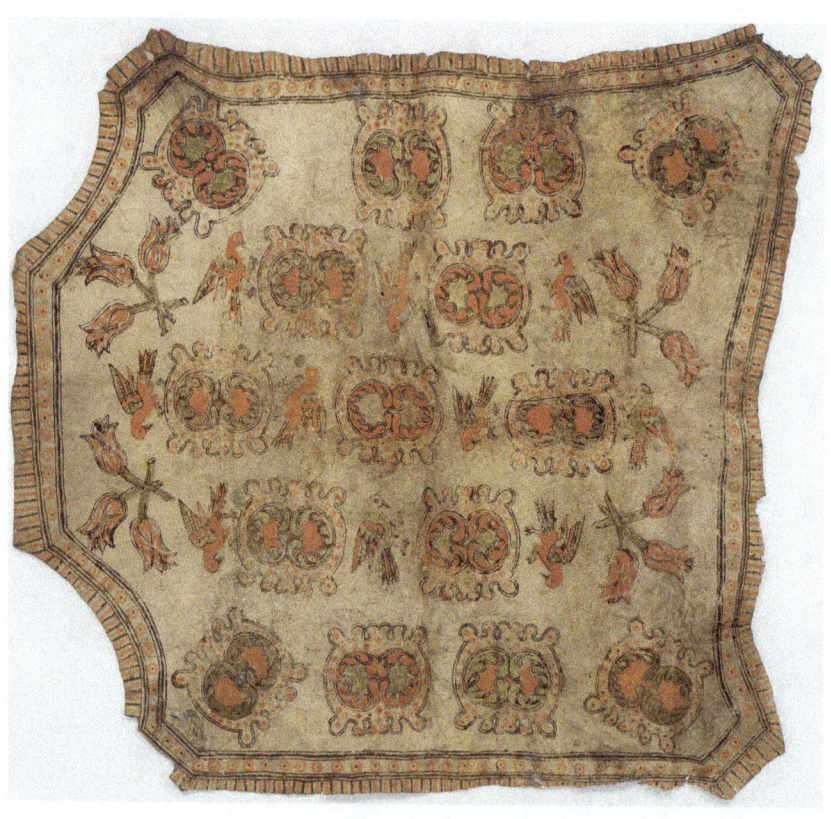

PLATE 56 Cape, date unknown. Painted hide, 107 × 100 × 2 cm. Collection of the Musée du quai Branly, Inv.71.1878.32.161. Photo by Parick Gries / Valérie Torre. Courtesy of Musée du quai Branly / SCALA / Art Resource, NY.

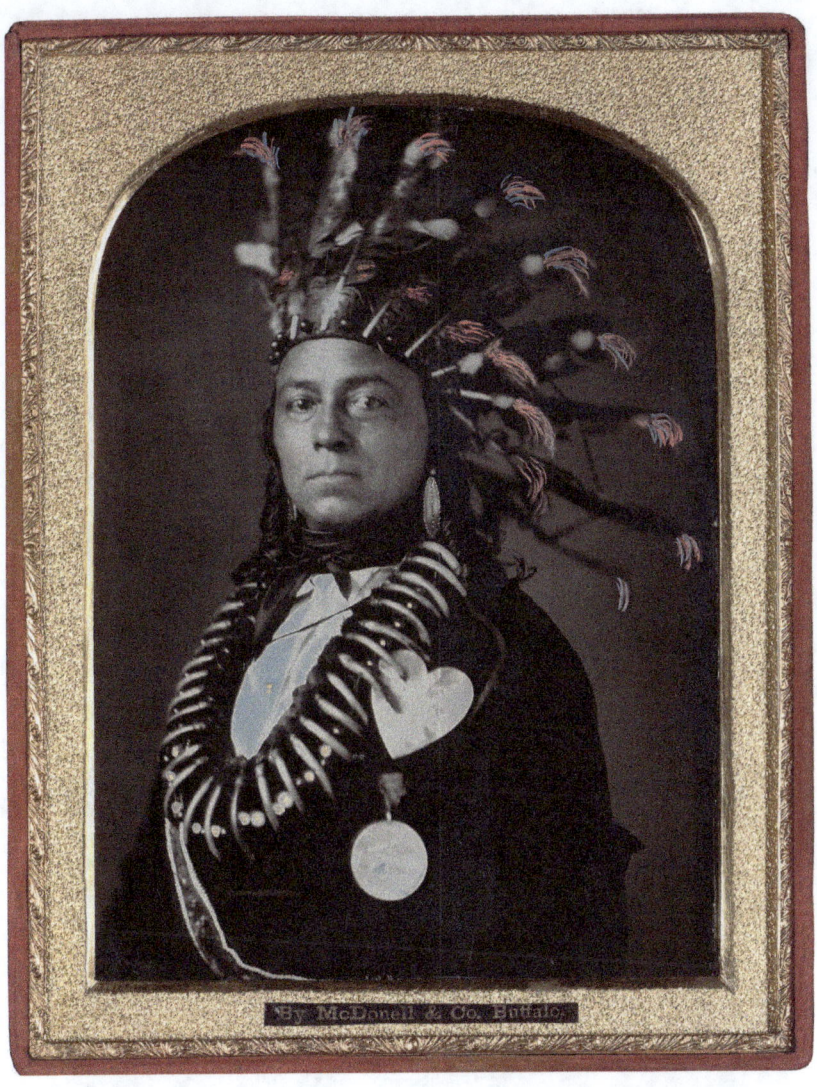

By McDonell & Co. Buffalo.

PLATE 57 Donald McDonnell, *Indian Chief Maungwudaus, Upper Canada*, c. 1850–51. Daguerreotype, 12.1 × 9.2 cm. The Nelson-Atkins Museum of Art, Kansas City, Missouri. Gift of Hallmark Cards, Inc., 2005.27.20. © Nelson Gallery Foundation. Photo by Thomas Palmer.

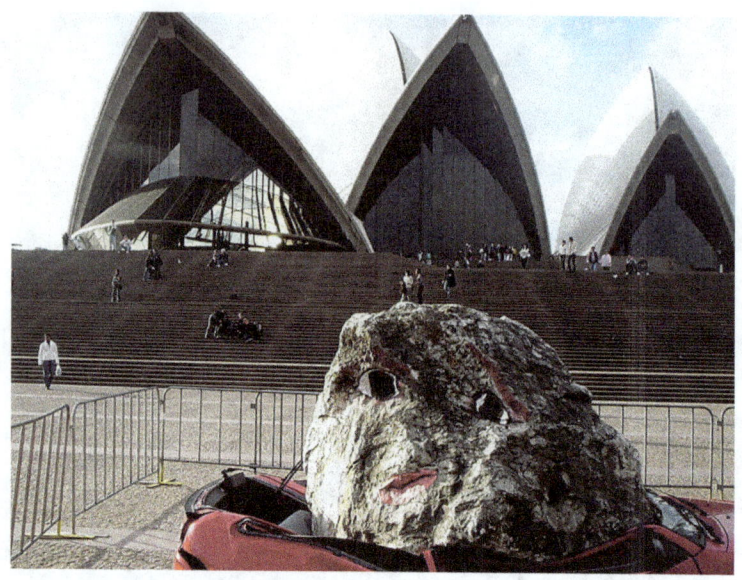

PLATE 58 Jimmie Durham, *Still Life with Stone and Car*, 2004. Stone, car, acrylic paint. Installation for Fourteenth Biennale of Sydney, *On Reason and Emotion*. Photo in public domain.

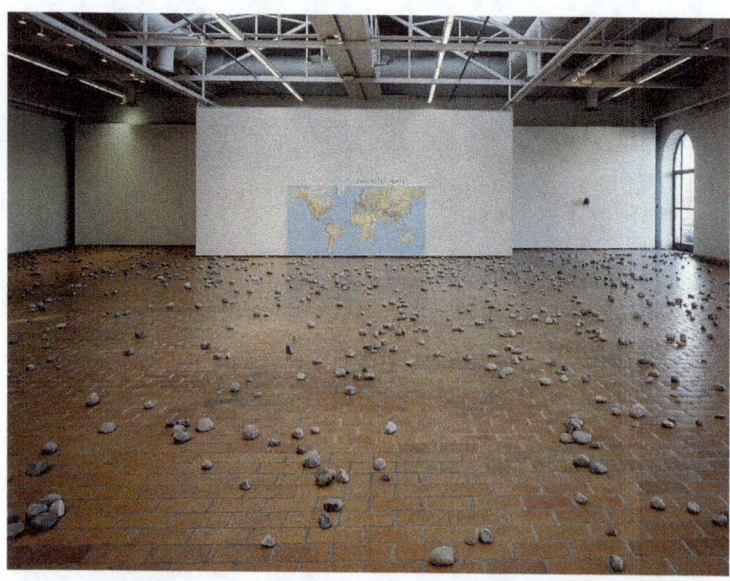

PLATE 59 Jimmie Durham, *The Center of the World at Chalma*, 1997. Mixed-media installation, Pori Art Museum, Finland. Courtesy of the Pori Art Museum.

Europeans enveloped Greek and Roman antiquity as well as foreign places and peoples into a continuous landscape, rather than positing their essential "distance and difference."[15] Michel Foucault, for one, described a "logic of similitude" governing sixteenth-century thought: "It was resemblance that organized the play of symbols, made possible knowledge of things visible and invisible, and controlled the art of representing them."[16] Plants, animals, and peoples were understood to imitate one another from one end of the universe to another; "the world is linked together like a chain."[17] Space and time could be creased to reveal "twin" forms at great distances from one another, drawn close inside an envelope of emulation not yet torn by modern classifications of science and culture. This folded space contained the whole of God's creation, including the Father himself, who had not yet wholly departed from the world of matter to reside in a distant heaven.[18] Importantly, language was thought to reside in the world, "among the plants, the herbs, the stones, and the animals."[19] Signatures, figures that included both material and linguistic signs, were everywhere visible in the landscape, God's way of giving voice to mute similitude so that humans could apprehend it. Foucault wrote evocatively, "And the space inhabited by immediate resemblances becomes like a vast open book; it bristles with written signs; every page is seen to be filled with strange figures that intertwine and in some places repeat themselves."[20] Knowledge involved deciphering the material language of things by creating a further play of signs. Humans both read and wrote the open book, participating in an ongoing interweaving of words, images, and world.

Freehand sketching of older works of art, a medieval practice with a long modern afterlife, calls our attention to the active creation, rather than passive reception, of similitude.[21] In a sermon first published in 1493, Dominican monk Girolamo Savonarola declared, "The master draws from his mind an image which his hands trace on paper and it carries the imprint of his idea. The pupil studies the drawing, and tries to imitate it. Little by little, in this way, he appropriates the style of his master. That is how all natural things, and all creatures, have derived from the divine intellect."[22] The final sentence clarifies that both copy and "original," less than affirming the inventive genius of a human artist, perpetuate a chain of resemblances whose ultimate source is the hand of God. As Carmen C. Bambach noted in her study of drawing in Renaissance workshops, this was by no means the only attitude available in the period. But even the words of Leonardo di Vinci, who is credited with voicing a shift away from reproduction, underscore the familial framework that Foucault attributes to similitude: "I say to painters that no one should ever imitate the style of another, because he will be called a nephew and not a child of nature with regard to art."[23] Rather than abnegating the value of copies, he advocates that they directly interpret the signatures of nature; the artist should bypass the uncle to imitate the father. WalkingStick, by contrast, assumed the role of niece, emulating the signatures of numerous human "uncles" from a Renaissance pictured as transcultural milieu. In her sketches of Topilzin Quetzalcoatl from Codex Vaticanus A and Christ's risen body from Raphael's *Transfiguration*, also in Vatican collections, bodies are encircled by a ring of wavy lines, suggesting radiating light and power. They forge additional likenesses between sacred, sky-bound heroes whose identities were already thoroughly entangled by the end of the sixteenth century. In mirroring the organization of Renaissance thought, WalkingStick's sketchbooks point to the productive agencies, the field of signatures created in the wake of conquest that actively folded foreign places and peoples into new formations of resemblance.

As Codex Vaticanus A suggests, modern classifications of race, culture, and kinship do not map neatly onto early colonial developments. Vanita Seth argued that Renaissance humans were as politically and culturally heterogeneous as they are today, but notably lacked a concept of a rational, sovereign European self required to posit a primitive other. The disciplinary policing of the boundaries of the human body, a biological determinism underlying the modern epistemology of difference, did not adhere in the first decades of conquest. Seth furthermore emphasized that the Renaissance entanglement of bodies and origins was conceptually possible because time and space were not yet ironed into secular, historical notions of progress, which would become essential to denying indigenous peoples a coeval claim to modernity.[24] Hence, "the New World was rendered into a very old world, because it was enveloped into a pre-existing world—one malleable to commensurability through reference to ancient texts, biblical scriptures, and popular travel stories."[25] Europeans debated the possibilities for shared heritage with indigenous peoples. Were Native Americans descendants of Adam, the lost tribes of Israel, or Vikings?[26] One annotator of Codex Vaticanus A was certain that Aztecs were descended from Hebrews due to striking correspondences in their baptismal rites.[27] When Spaniards absorbed the realization of a well-formed indigenous pantheon during their march across Mexico, they drew equivalences with the gods and goddesses of Antiquity everywhere present in the efflorescence of classicism back home. Perhaps the most famous example is the sixteenth-century Florentine Codex, a partnership between Franciscan friar

Bernardino de Sahagún and missionary-educated *tlacuilos* who survived the conquest, in which representations of Aztec deities are anthropomorphized to resemble classical figures and explicitly paired with the names of their Greek and Roman analogues.[28] In other European illustrations of the period, the gods sprout cloven hooves and tails, mimicking mischievous Roman fauns and Christian devils like those that appear in WalkingStick's sketchbooks.[29] Native Americans were projected into a heterogeneous past just as they were giving birth to the mixed offspring of conquest.

Contemplating shared ancestry did not pause the brutality of the Spanish conquest. On the contrary, it may have served the ends of colonial power. It is probable that likenesses were drawn to aid missionaries in identifying and abolishing idolatry. Keber, for one, concludes that missionaries who preserved and "copied" Mexican manuscripts were "inspired as much by the desire to dominate as by the need to understand."[30] While they drew admiring parallels between Roman and Aztec empires, imitation of Roman might motivated some of the most violent acts of Hernán Cortés and his army, who razed the Aztec capital of Tenochtitlan in 1521.[31] The replication of signatures across time and space may even have reinforced the air of divine purpose surrounding colonial atrocities, as witnesses claimed to see the plagues of Egypt and the fall of Jerusalem repeated in the Spanish conquest.[32] Fratricide was an all-too-common practice in this "family of resemblances."

But as I have emphasized throughout this book, totalizing views of colonization as "covered ground" occlude the agency of Native contributors and prevent understanding of the complex affiliations that mark its historical—and art historical—record. Europeans were not the only ones to envelop that which was new and strange inside familiar, even familial frameworks; indeed, such practices were essential to the perpetuation of indigenous knowledge in the wake of conquest. Diana Magaloni-Kerpel argued that the Nahuatl-language portion of the Florentine Codex "established the conditions necessary for human existence to continue into the new Nahua-Christian era . . . by replicating ancient Nahua [Aztec] rituals and myths."[33] The Native authors told of eight precontact omens that predicted the Spanish invasion, interpreting what was ostensibly new and cataclysmic inside "patterns of mythic, cosmic time" in a manner not unlike European accounts of "New World" floods drawn from the Bible.[34] Furthermore, in postcontact codices and other arts, a thorough entanglement of heritages frustrated missionary efforts to replace the indigenous pantheon with a single Father. Recall the body of an eagle with human hands and face, conjuring the feather-covered dress worn by members of the Aztec military, that WalkingStick sketched from the pages of Codex Vaticanus A. In the manuscript he is paired with a jaguar, and both of them wear elaborate headdresses of heron feathers and eagle down (see figs. 4.1–4.2).[35] Together, the human-animals, related to respective celestial and earthly spheres, express the prestige and supernatural power granted to Aztec warrior orders. Surely signatures of indigenous might would be the first suppressed by conquistadors, yet "the parallelism with Old World symbols of royalty, the eagle and the lion . . . facilitated the convergence of heraldic meanings in the colonial period."[36] A divine messenger from the sun among the Aztecs, eagles were also associated with the god Jupiter in European antiquity and mobilized long after as symbols of authority with roots in the imperial armies of Rome.[37] Hybrid jaguars and eagles bear a striking resemblance to sketches of lion-bird-women that WalkingStick encountered on Etruscan vases from the Villa Giulia during the same residency in 1998 (see fig. 4.4). Broken scallops delineate the feathers of like-bodied fowls, repeating the Renaissance alignment of heraldry and heredity. These and other examples suggest that similitude was the stuff not merely of European cooptation, but of indigenous survival.

WalkingStick's sketches direct the Renaissance repertoire of resemblances away from unilateral conquest and toward creative multiplicity. Drawing the before and after of colonization together, they hint that a pure European or Native American art history never was, and never will be. The permutations of porous, fertile bodies that populate the whole of her sketchbooks perpetuate long-standing heterogeneity on both sides of the Atlantic. Alessandra Russo wrote of a feathered altar cloth from postcontact Mexico, "Its lineages intersect so much that it seems impossible to identify any of its 'ancestors.' . . . [It] invites us to start from zero."[38] By contrast, WalkingStick's copious lines make room for many possible ancestors, for "strange figures that intertwine and in some places repeat themselves" without a clear origin or end point.[39] She simultaneously traced her lineage to this unorthodox art historical family and gave birth to it through the labor of sketching.

"Distance and Difference"

WalkingStick negotiated an energizing yet polarizing culture of critique in the wake of AIM. While I have already discussed key issues in relation to the practices of Jimmie Durham and James Luna, here I will cast that history in slightly different terms. As WalkingStick developed her painting practice in the 1970s and 1980s, difference had hardened into a seemingly incontrovertible framework dividing European and Native American art histories, following the contours of the racially governed body. Foucault and Seth agreed that similitude faded from Europeans' self-conception after the sixteenth century, eventually replaced by an autonomous, rational (white, male) subject who commanded a world of lesser beings and mute matter.[40] For Seth, nineteenth-century racial science dealt similitude a final blow, rendering the human body "a stable, transparent, and measurable object of knowledge—a body that is knowable precisely through its meticulously raced, sexed, and sexualized classification."[41] Such a body could not readily sprout wings or encounter a twin on the other side of the ocean; its genealogy was no longer subject to the temporal, spatial, and material promiscuity evident in the Renaissance arts of resemblance. Walter Benjamin famously observed the waning of "the gift of producing similarities—for example, in dances, whose oldest function was this." He continued, "Modern man contains only minimal residues of the magical correspondences and analogies that were familiar to ancient peoples."[42] For others, what Benjamin termed "sensuous similarity" did not decline so much as retreat to the domain of primitivism.[43]

Modern anthropology reserved a particular term to describe the bonds among indigenous humans who claimed coyotes as brethren, embodied snakes, and donned mountain sheep horns: *kinship*. Though the concept was deployed primarily to describe social constructs, kinship's many recent critics agree that it was rooted in the assumption of "a set of natural facts" under "the ruling sign of biology" in the nineteenth century.[44] Accounting for blood ties and cultural difference went hand in hand, securing a modern epistemology of difference anchored in the racialized body described by Seth. While strains of self-reflexive critique have long been a part of anthropological engagements with kinship, Mark Rifkin traced the migration of the term into national legal-political contexts. Identifying indigenous deviance from the rational, national norm of the nuclear, land-owning family justified "the coordinated assault on native social formations that has characterized US policy since its inception, conducted in the name of 'civilization.'"[45] As we have already seen in chapters 1 and 3, bans on Pueblo ceremonies deemed "so bestial as to prohibit their description" in the 1910s and 1920s and the identity-policing Indian Arts and Crafts Act (IACA) of 1990 evince the long arm of the General Allotment Act of 1887, in which blood and paperwork replaced "lots of eagle dances" as the sanctioned mode of establishing ancestry. Indigenous communities have alternately adopted and resisted this "code of assimilative patriotism."[46]

Equally, anthropological and national-legal deployments of kinship affected art historical engagements with indigenous arts. A discipline formally born and bred in Europe in the nineteenth century, art history increasingly borrowed from anthropological discourses and collections as a means of cultural redress in the twentieth. As we saw in chapter 3, widespread critiques of industrial modernity as a force of alienation between the wars produced nostalgia for Native American art as an endangered connective tissue holding an otherwise divided world together. The image of a people still intimately bonded to nature fueled Marsden Hartley's romance with the "red man," who "knows every form of animal and vegetable life adhering to our earth, and has made for himself a series of . . . stirring dances to celebrate them, and his relation to them."[47] Simultaneous with federal assimilation measures anchored in kinship deviance, white artists and intellectuals sought an *indigenous* American modernism, in which John Marin and Fred Kabotie were briefly construed as brethren. Native arts were thus charged with bearing Europeans' lost gift for producing likeness into modernity's darkest hours.[48] This romance was repeated in 1984 in MoMA's hotly debated exhibition *"Primitivism" in 20th Century Art: Affinity of the Tribal and the Modern*, as I will explore in a moment. Such a changeable discourse of kinship has underwritten and occasionally undermined difference across multiple domains of knowledge, as similitude was torn from its European roots and redeployed to manage (rather than enlarge) the modern boundaries of belonging.

The literature on kinship criticism is far vaster than I can account for in this chapter, much of it still deployed within the discipline of anthropology. While it may be tempting to relegate the concept to the dustbin of deconstruction, a number of scholars concerned with queer, feminist, and Native studies have argued that it continues to mark a commonly intelligible category that can be reclaimed and reconfigured beyond biological determinism.[49] WalkingStick's oeuvre in particular prompts me to consider an alternative, art historical application for the term, through her reintegration of Native American and European arts back into a larger family of resemblances. Before Renaissance similitude, modernism's mixed heritage of archetypal forms was her chosen field of engagement. In 1995, on the eve of her departure to Italy, WalkingStick created a diptych suggestively titled *With Love to Marsden* (plate 39). In it she paired the iconic russet mountains of the Southwest lovingly painted by Hartley with a bright red equal-armed cross resembling indigenous maps of the cosmos, repeated throughout both artists' oeuvres (as well as the work of Luna and Robert Houle).[50] Befitting the critical climate of the late twentieth century, WalkingStick might well have dismissed Hartley's conviction, "The red man is the one truly indigenous religionist and esthete of America," as a deleterious fetish.[51] Instead, she chose to traverse the distance between them with familiar, even familial affection. Her paintings picture modernity through complex figurations of belonging, giving rise to what I call *creative kinship*.

Nonetheless, it is important to recognize how assumptions of difference reified in late twentieth-century critiques of primitivism shaped the aesthetics of WalkingStick's practice prior to her Italian sojourns. Although she had exhibited work in New York City and taught college-level art classes in New Jersey for quite some time, my story picks up on the eve of her graduation from the Pratt Institute, when indigenous concerns seeped quietly into her work.[52] Until that point, WalkingStick described her upbringing as devoutly Protestant and her education as "completely Male-Eurocentric."[53] An enrolled member of the Cherokee Nation of Oklahoma, she grew up off-reservation with her mother and siblings in Syracuse, New York. While WalkingStick's Cherokee father was largely absent from their lives and died in 1970, her white mother instilled pride in the children's indigenous heritage. Emboldened by second-wave feminism and AIM activism airing on the news, the artist elected to dig into personal and political histories in her work. In *Messages to Papa* (1974), she made an eight-foot-tall tepee of wood and painted canvas, a pan-Indian symbol filled with feathers and letters addressing their fraught relationship from what she called "my white view, the white side of myself."[54] She also began giving honorific titles of historical Native figures to her monumental abstract paintings, such as *Sakajeweha, Leader of Men* (1976).

In an epic series of thirty-six canvases, *Chief Joseph* (1974–76), she embarked on a thorough exploration of the compositional possibilities of an upright arc using a familiar modernist grid (plate 42). The title invites a relationship between the self-imposed constraint and rigor of her formal investigation and analogous qualities in indigenous political leadership. Chief Joseph headed a contingent of resistant Nez Perce toward safety in Canada while pursued by the U.S. Army in 1887, eventually surrendering less than forty miles from the border. For WalkingStick, he represented "the height of human accomplishment . . . a truly moral person."[55] The work soon caught the attention of Salish artist Jaune Quick-to-See Smith and others who invited her to join a growing network of Native artists across the United States and Canada, with whom she exhibited for years to come.[56] At the same time, WalkingStick's choice to associate the formal journeys of an arc with the trial-tested moral

backbone of a historical leader was shadowed by white modernist predecessors who borrowed such forms from Native art. The same shape can be
seen, for example, in the repeating tepee covers of Hartley's *American Indian
Symbols* (1914), or in the toothy mouth of Adolf Gottlieb's *Pictograph-Symbol*
(1942), described by Gottlieb as "recollections of our prehistoric past" (plate
43).[57] The reception of WalkingStick's work correspondingly recycled classic
primitivist tropes, evident, for example, in the assertion, "In the heavy opaque
tones slashed with raw colors of these paintings, we can find intimations of
the strength, stoicism, and violence inherent in such a [Cherokee] people."[58]
WalkingStick later noted wryly, "If I showed with women then the arcs in the
paintings were vulvas, if I showed with Indians the arcs were bows."[59]

Histories of modernist primitivism received their first truly postcolonial
vetting in the decade following *Chief Joseph*. A crucial benchmark was the
controversial 1984 exhibition at MoMA, *"Primitivism" in 20th Century Art:
Affinity of the Tribal and the Modern*.[60] Curator William Rubin emphasized
that European and American modernists valued "virtually any art *alien* to the
Greco-Roman line of Western realism that had been reaffirmed and system-
atized in the Renaissance" (emphasis mine).[61] His account mapped dichoto-
mies of civilized European selves and naturalized indigenous others onto the
aesthetic poles of representation and abstraction. In a highly critical review of
the show, Hal Foster argued that modernism's "primal scene," Pablo Picasso's
wedding of prostitutes and African masks in *Les Demoiselles d'Avignon* (1907),
was driven by "desire for mastery [of woman, primitive other] and fear of
its frustration. . . . Picasso transgresses . . . in order to mediate the primitive
in the name of the West."[62] Echoing this theme, Abigail Solomon-Godeau
responded to the traveling Paul Gauguin retrospective that opened at the National Gallery of Art in Washington, DC, in 1988 by defining primitivism as
"a white, Western and preponderantly male quest for an elusive object whose
very condition of desirability resides in some form of distance and difference,
whether temporal or geographical."[63] Stripped of its innocence, the history of
abstraction was now seen to encode a colonial relation. Modernist primitivism
evacuated mutual histories of entanglement by enshrining tribal bonds in a
time and place distinct from Europe, a "distance and difference" traversable
in only one direction.[64]

We have already seen that in light of such critiques, a number of Walking-
Stick's AIM-generation peers treated the formal language of modernism as
"covered ground." Durham, Luna, and others initially addressed their displacement from the field of representation with mockery from the margins.

Beginning with Fritz Scholder's generation, the spare figural paintings of Fred Kabotie and the subsequent "Studio Style" that followed his lead were vilified for their perceived conservatism.[65] Even Houle's abstract canvases, which "infect" modernism with Native materials and histories, initially took the form of a postmodern rescue mission, as I will discuss in chapter 5. In the 1980s, to reappropriate a language of archetypal forms borrowed from indigenous cultures without irony or interruption was to risk being found guilty of self-primitivizing. Such discourses affected a double displacement from the history of indigenous arts and the diverse modernisms that took them up. Although WalkingStick publicized her concern with a "mass-culture value [that makes] indigenous people appear remote, generalized, savage, nonhuman, and nonthreatening," I suggest that she did not abandon the possibility of belonging to both.[66] The diptychs she began making in New York in the mid-1980s sought "that unity of the totally dissimilar" by bridging the alien relationship that Rubin posited between European perspectivism and indigenous "pictographs."[67] The artist frequently invoked dance and poetry to describe a fluid relationship between halves: "There is a quality of movement—dance—that expresses physicality and human presence," and "the parts, like stanzas of a poem, complement and resonate with one another."[68]

In a work that exemplifies these properties, *Hovenweep* (1987), self-contained squares abut, one half semirepresentational landscape and one half abstraction (plate 40). On the right, we see a view of cliff sediments at Hovenweep National Monument in Colorado, home to six ancestral Puebloan villages that were abandoned around 1300 AD. Here land "means" according to the perspective held by a single, centered subject—or rather, camera, as Walking-Stick often painted views from photographs taken during her travels. At the same time, the representation dissolves into interlocking lines, as angles of sediments mirror those of the abstract polygon in the center of the leftmost panel. In contrast to the relatively flat landscape panel, the neighboring square consists of a thick layer of shiny paint on a canvas that protrudes several inches. WalkingStick applied the combination of acrylic and wax directly with her hands, creating a sculptural, even architectural presence. The central pyramidal form cut into layers of canvas echoes the shape of towers at Hovenweep, suggesting a figure to both populate and harmonize with the landscape at right. Yet it also opens onto a mysterious, potentially vast scale independent of the human body, hinting at other, nonanthropocentric approaches to dwelling in land. In the context of Pueblo history and culture, the leftmost panel also suggests the art of inscribing symbols directly onto the surfaces of sacred sites to elicit contact with unseen spiritual agents, thereby affecting reciprocity among humans and their environment.[69] *Hovenweep* invites a visual dialogue between different kinds of mark-making and their associated systems of perception and meaning. Figure and ground move toward one another, crossing the distance (but not necessarily the difference) between sides.

A number of binary terms have been invoked in discussions of Walking-Stick's work to date: short- and long-term memory, the physical and the spiritual, and the artist's own biracial heritage.[70] Although the paintings certainly make room for these interpretations, I am wary of romantic or ahistorical claims sometimes made on their behalf: for example, that they reflect the artist's "inborn abiding passion for the land" or they are "primitively personal."[71] My alternative approach is to consider how the diptychs carefully negotiated the rigid terms of modernist primitivism in the 1980s, while reaching toward the excluded multiplicity of art history. Here it is especially notable that the American Southwest, a region where Native and non-Native peoples have intermixed and influenced one another since the arrival of Spaniards in the sixteenth century, features prominently in WalkingStick's diptychs.[72] The dual aesthetics of *Hovenweep*, *With Love to Marsden*, and other related works recall paint on cliff walls, pottery surfaces, mission churches, and canvases by a range of historical makers, from Anasazi water jars to landscapes by Georgia O'Keeffe, equally admired by WalkingStick.[73] As I discussed in chapter 3, the complex aesthetic results of such exchanges intensified in the twentieth century as white pilgrims and patrons sought an "indigenous" source of modernism in red rock mesas and Pueblo arts. Fred Kabotie, Tonita Peña, Maria Martinez, and many others approached the white culture of primitivism not as a unilateral appropriation, but as an opening in which to produce distinctive modernisms of their own. As Ruth Phillips elegantly stated, aesthetic primitivism created "portals which allowed traffic to flow between cultural and social worlds, changing contexts for the production of art on both sides."[74] WalkingStick's diptychs point to the inseparability of those sides and make palpable the traffic between them. Her paintings plant their feet in a more promiscuous history of art than late twentieth-century debates about modernist primitivism permitted.

Nonetheless, a simple but salient point remains: however much they move toward a shared midpoint, WalkingStick's diptychs are made of self-same squares. That is, they are formally structured by the binary terms of difference that connect Hartley's preservationist plea, Rubin's alien aesthetics, and Solomon-Godeau's critique. Whether negotiated or parodied, these would remain the modern building blocks of legibility in supposedly postmodern climes. The constraints embedded within formal relations furthermore mirrored those in social and political spheres, limiting available forms of attachment and belonging. As Jonathan Flatley wrote of the United States in the second half of the twentieth century, a society organized according to binaries of selves and others—capitalism and communism, homosexual and heterosexual, white and black (or red)—negates the "space we share with others," including "possibilities of emotional engagement" that accompany the discovery and production of likeness.[75] Love or hate? Kin or colonizer? These were the hard choices that the dividing line of difference demanded.

Approaching the five-hundred-year anniversary of Columbus's landing, the poles of affect stretched wider than the ocean he crossed. Recall from chapter 1 that around this time WalkingStick joined Durham in publicly voicing her opposition to the IACA, declaring that "the numbering and registering have returned to haunt us."[76] She noted at the outset of a measured 1991 essay in *Artforum* that her own grandfather, Cherokee lawyer Simon Ridge WalkingStick, was instrumental in registering Oklahoma-based Native peoples in keeping with the General Allotment Act of 1887, establishing the necessary basis for contemporary Cherokee to "prove" their tribal heritage. WalkingStick nonetheless viewed his collusion with federal assimilation policy as a well-intentioned mistake with consequences that are still unfolding. After reviewing arguments from both sides, she validated those who viewed the IACA as a perpetuation of federal policing of indigenous social networks and communal landholdings, "a foreign, bureaucratic imposition *alien* to [Native American] traditions of thought" (emphasis mine).[77] The participation of some Indian peoples in establishing and implementing the IACA underscored ongoing ideological fault lines dividing indigenous affiliations, in art as in politics.

In contrast to the IACA, WalkingStick emphasized the importance of what Cherokee literary scholar Daniel Heath Justice calls "what we do, what we create, as much as what we are."[78] Elsewhere, she insisted that choices about what and with whom to paint and exhibit uphold "much broader ways to identify as Native American" than allowed by the exclusionary history of tribal registry.[79] Challenging "Indian arts and crafts" as a fixed, inherited, and legislated category, she emphasized elective, affective, and productive dimensions that gave rise to an alternative kinship network. Quick-to-See Smith, Durham, Houle, Luna, and others of the AIM generation who showed together beginning in the 1980s were members of a "large extended family" who "love each other and respect each other's work."[80] Here it is worth pointing out the obvious: few artists included in group shows of Native American art claimed that they shared biologically determined inheritance with one another. If the category of "Indian arts" encoded in the IACA is a colonial fiction bolstered by a trail of blood and paperwork, elsewhere it has named a changeable network of allies forged and maintained through practices of making and exhibiting in the wake of AIM.

WalkingStick's commentary aligns with a number of scholars who argue that policing identities according to racial inheritance reproduces colonial ideology. Richard William Hill wrote, "Our way out of this trap [of colonial definitions of race] is not to think of our heritage as set in the blood and constantly in jeopardy of contamination, but as culture—not something we are obliged to mimetically reproduce, but rather, a tool box of strategies for being in the world from which we can actively and reflectively choose and develop."[81] Justice similarly argued for decolonizing indigenous relational networks through creative acts of storytelling. Echoing Hill, he defined kinship "as a verb, rather than a noun, because kinship, in most indigenous contexts, is something that's *done* more than something that simply *is*." He emphasized "an understanding of common social interdependence . . . that link[s] the People, the land, and the cosmos together in an ongoing and dynamic system of mutually affecting relationships."[82] Justice shifted attention from the identities of the participants to the *form* of relationships, in which interdependence is a given but acknowledgment and care remain matters of choice and responsibility. His analysis recalls the relational philosophies described by Vine Deloria, Durham, and others in chapter 1, as well as the phrase "all our relations," widely used in North American indigenous communities today to signal kinship among humans and other-than-human persons.[83] Justice's verb form has unacknowledged implications: by appropriating an anthropological notion of kinship on behalf of literary storytelling and redefining it as an open, ecological system, rather than a biologically fixed category, he removed any absolute boundary determining where an "indigenous context" begins and ends. In his definition of kinship, difference gives way to a fluctuating field of relationships that demand recognition and maintenance.[84] As we have seen, the allied process of creative kinship upheld in WalkingStick's practice at times stretches well beyond the AIM generation to embrace Raphael and Hartley, thereby acknowledging entanglements between Europeans and indigenes for some five centuries.

Circa 1992, however, the "vast open book . . . filled with strange figures that intertwine and in some places repeat themselves" with which I began this chapter was tightly shut. Like many of her peers, WalkingStick addressed the profound loss of lives and worldviews following the arrival of Columbus "the slave trader" in several overtly political artworks included in Quincentennial exhibitions of Native American art across the United States and Canada, including the melancholic codex *The Wizard Speaks, the Cavalry Listens*, discussed in chapter 1.[85] Similarly, the lament of *Where Are the Generations?* (1991) offers a counterpoint to the embrace of *With Love to Marsden* (plate 41). The diptych weds a nighttime desert landscape with a luminous copper disc embedded and partially covered in deep blue paint, suggestive of a lunar eclipse. Hammered in repoussé on the exposed portion of the circle appear the words "In 1492, we were 20 million. Now, we are 2 million. Where are the generations, where are the children? Neverborn." Below, WalkingStick signed her own name using the Cherokee syllabary she was then learning, perhaps a small sign of the survival of indigenous worldviews.[86] Yet the reduction of kinship to the dictates of biological race and census counts overshadows the creative multiplicity promised by her sculpted and painted forms. Recourse to written language further implies the circle's inability to produce meaning on its own. It is a failed fertility symbol, deformed by diminishing numbers and mournful words.

Fertility and Figuration

Borrowing from the fluid properties of paint, fertility assumes a markedly different valence in works on paper resulting from WalkingStick's first trip to Rome just a few years later. Images of lust, consummation, and procreation linking human bodies, mythological creatures, and fecund mountains are the foundation of the alternative art history that unfolds across the pages of *Terra Corpo*, a watercolor sketchbook completed by the artist in 1996. The final folios offer a summation of lessons gleaned from WalkingStick's visits to collections assembled during the Renaissance, an homage to similitude handwritten in Italian and English:

> The ideas in this book grew out of my realization that the landscapes in my paintings are a stand-in for the human body. It records my thoughts concerning the similarity of various myths of human kind concerning the tie between the body and the fertility of the earth.
>
> The fawn/satyr figure is based on a sculpture found in the House

of the Fawn in Pompeii; the hunch-backed male figure is Kocopelli who is found repeated in the petroglyphs of the American southwest [*sic*]. Both are fertility symbols and exist in the mountains of their respective lands. The other figures in this book are based on those found in paintings and sculptures in Rome, Florence, and Naples, as well as from my own memory. The landscapes are based on photos taken in Arizona & Montana in 1995 and sketches made in southern Italy in 1996.

Many varied peoples see mountains as holy places. Gods live in mountains. A commonly held ancient view is that the continuation of the fertility of the land is dependent on the fecundity of its inhabitants, and of course, the reverse is true also. Our mythic tie to the earth is a close one. Every culture has stories of mysterious mountain apparitions. Kocopelli and Fawn are only 2 of them.[87]

In this inaugural volume, as in all of the artist's Italian work, "the physically sensual or sexual body and spiritual experience are connected," wrote art historian Lisa Roberts Seppi.[88] Throughout, WalkingStick visually quoted sources from European antiquity, Renaissance classicism, and Puebloan arts, as well as her own imagination (fig. 4.5). Kokopelli is the popular name for the hunchback flute player, a sacred prankster who "beguiles us with his erect flute," found in ancient and contemporary Pueblo arts.[89] Fauns and satyrs, respectively associated with the Roman god Faunus and Greek god Dionysus, likewise embody carnal desires, while the related figure of Pan seduces nymphs into liaisons with music.[90] WalkingStick created handmade stencils from her initial sketches of these "mountain men," a symbol for a copulating couple, and an hourglass figure inspired by Greek amphorae that she referred to as "mitochondrial Eve," the popular name for genetics research tracing the most recent common female ancestor of modern humans to Africa.[91] The bathing nymph who stares boldly out at viewers from the foreground of Domenichino Zampieri's *Diana and Her Nymphs* (1616–17) makes an appearance, as does Donatello's effeminate *David* (c. 1440s).[92] Perspectival mountains occupy other pages, their distinctive color palettes distinguishing western United States and southern Italy, while diagonally stacked lines of bleeding watercolor paints grant them structural similarity.

In a series of related works on paper from the same year, this panoply of signatures interacts with purple, red, gold, and green mountains of varied origin. In *Mountain Men*, the memory of diptychs like *Hovenweep* lin-

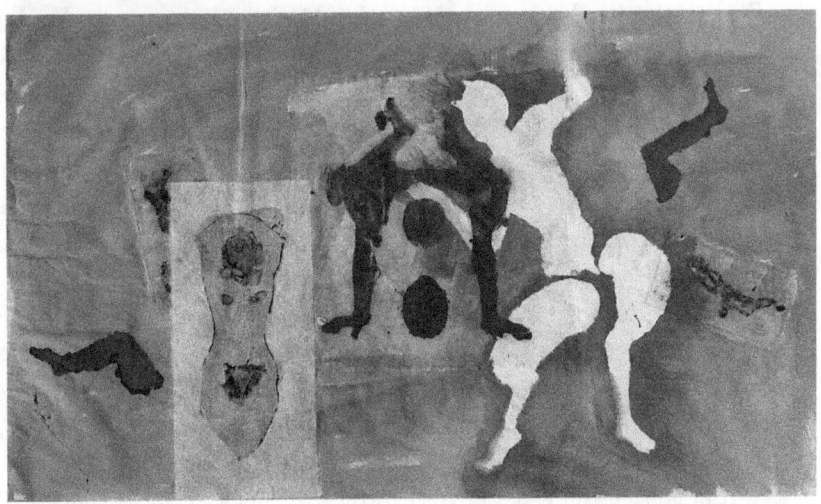

4.5 Kay WalkingStick, *Terra Corpo*, detail, 1996. Watercolor sketchbook. Courtesy of the artist. Photo by Jessica L. Horton.

gers, formally (plate 44). The paper maintains the dimensions of two perfect squares now joined in a continuous field. Mountains—Arizona—give way roughly halfway across to a mystical space. There a free-form watercolor faun and a procession of Kokopelli stencils stamped with paint meet, recalling the Renaissance propensity for mixing of Roman and Native pantheons on both sides of the ocean. In *Narcissus*, the entire page is covered with bristling signs. Rather than juxtaposed in relations of difference, symbols overlap and fuse with landscapes (plate 45). Figure and ground merge into palimpsests, transforming mountains into "pubic-thatched gullies and breast-like peaks," in the words of David Penney.[93] Components of the copulating couple stencil join and separate; one female half has sprouted the wings of an angel or an eagle. Oval heads multiply like eggs and appear to roll across the hills at front. Disembodied legs and feathers float upward, as if shed or birthed from the orgiastic intermingling below. This time a trio of fauns and a solitary Kokopelli flank the grouping. Instead of a sovereign subject surveying the land, conjured by figureless landscapes in the "snapshot" portion of WalkingStick's diptychs, here bodies emerge from it and are everywhere reflected in it. They appear as hybrids of parts and traits subject to disassembly, replication, and recombination as well as ongoing connectivity to a corporeal landscape that births and nurtures them. Repeating brushstrokes and stencils form chains of human and other-than-human likeness and lovemaking in a folded time and space.

To slightly alter Justice's verb form, kinship is something that Walking-Stick *paints*. Here paint is the reproductive element that realizes the fertility of any single figure, multiplying it in a range of permutations with others. In this account of creative kinship, I suggest that paint replaces the metaphor of blood anchoring legal-political discourses of ancestry, creating a fluid material interface that at once connects and separates the land and bodies depicted. WalkingStick arrived at the idea of using stencils after seeing an exhibition of Nancy Spero's collage panels, *Black and the Red III* (1994), in Rome. Spero's hand-printed dancers contain the echo of figures on ancient Greek vases, an instance of art historical kinship that WalkingStick elected to extend when she adopted and adapted Spero's means of figuration. Painted stencils allowed her to repeat body parts in various colors and combinations that are neither exactly the same nor entirely different from their neighbors.[94] Layers of gouache on gessoed paper further articulate the material base that bodies share with each other and land. While establishing their condition of commonality, distinct applications of paint still maintain subtle boundaries between figures and ground. In this sense, paint has more in common with flesh than blood. Feminist philosopher Kelly Oliver considered flesh "an in-between element, the flesh through which we are kin, the flesh through which we are at the same time strangers."[95] In WalkingStick's work, flesh-like paint appears as a permeable interface that delineates the contours of bodies and permits them to touch, and be touched by, the world. In *Eve Energy* (1996), six delineated hourglass figures in skin tones of peach and terra-cotta intersect with diagonal brushstrokes of brown and green, replacing solitary biblical Eve with a chain of earthly mothers. A separated head and a pair of legs from the copulating couple stencil emerge from, or perhaps make love to, the land (fig. 4.6). Instead of assessing blood quantum or population statistics—the basis for lamenting generations of Native Americans "neverborn"—WalkingStick actively engenders attachments through promiscuous applications of paint. Figuration is, I suggest, the basis of this work's claim to creative kin, a process of repeating and varying stencils and brushstrokes to simultaneously trace and produce a vast art historical ancestry.

Dancing with Strangers

In the early 2000s, WalkingStick's figures began to dance. She told me, "Dance is the one activity that I know of when virtual strangers can embrace. It has this intimacy that is usually socially controlled."[96] In chapters 2 and 3, I dis-

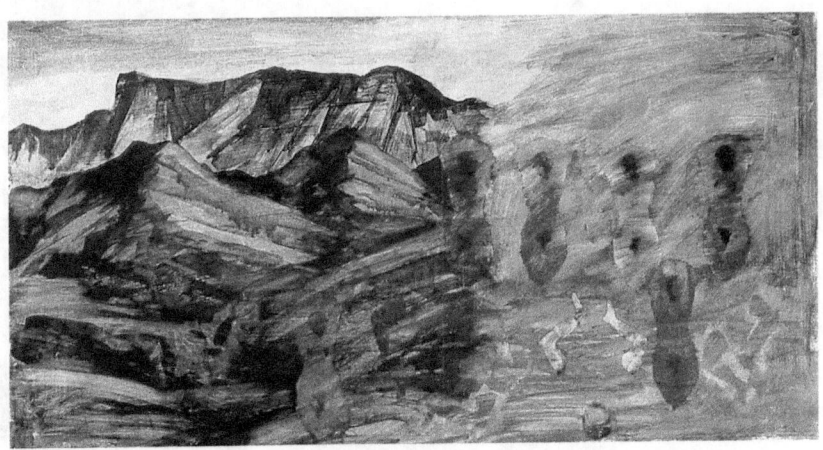

4.6 Kay WalkingStick, *Eve Energy*, 1996. Gouache on paper, 19 × 38½ in.
Collection of the artist.

cussed dance as a means of maintaining indigenous sensibilities amid the
displacements engendered by Spanish missionization and U.S. assimilation.
I now return briefly to this theme to build on earlier significances, through
WalkingStick's practice of painting kinship with a range of art historical
"strangers." It seems especially appropriate to preface this discussion with an
account she wrote in 1999 of a transformative experience: attending Angk'wa
night dances at Shungopavi, Fred Kabotie's home village on Hopi Second
Mesa. Accepting an invitation from a friend at the Heard Museum in Phoenix, she found herself to be the only non-Hopi inside the kiva. At first she felt
conspicuous, but soon she became absorbed in the slow drumbeat and beauty
of the dancing Katsinam, realizing "we were participants . . . not watchers."
At the close of the evening, a Katsina gifted her an apple, underscoring her
growing recognition that the ceremonies were "not only for the Hopi people,
but for the entire world, so that we may all eat."[97] In the early 2000s, WalkingStick followed Kabotie in painting dances capable of crossing oceans. But
unlike his efforts to render the specific sensibility of Hopi ritual at a distance
through a dialectics of bare page and discrete figures in detailed regalia, her
unadorned limbs caught in a web of paint are culturally and racially indeterminate. They belong to Europe and the indigenous Americas at once.

Across her ACEA series of seven works on paper from 2003, a tangle of
vines replaces perspectival mountains (fig. 4.7). The plant motif first appeared
in the artist's sketchbooks in 2001, drawn from a first-century-BC mosaic

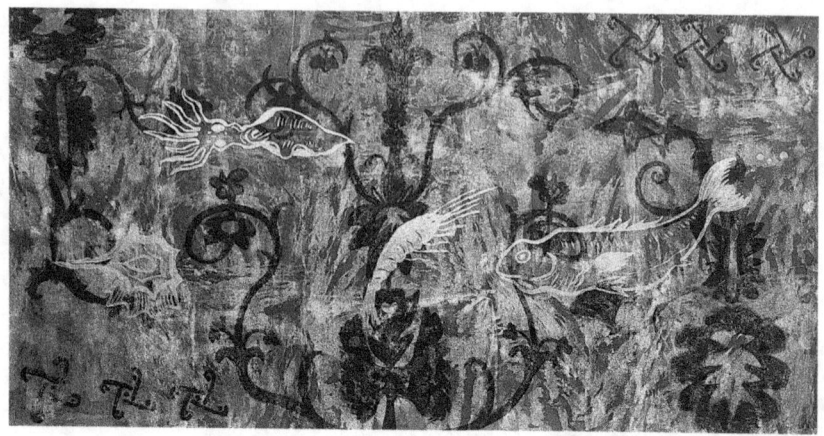

4.7 Kay WalkingStick, *ACEA 1*, 2003. Gouache, acrylic on paper, 19 × 38 in. Collection of the artist. Courtesy of the National Museum of the American Indian, Smithsonian Institution. Photo by Lee Stalsworth.

displayed at the Azienda Comunale Energia e Ambiente (ACEA) museum of antiquities on the outskirts of Rome. It was later repurposed to mingle with sea creatures, marble busts, and dancing legs drawn from the same collection and the artist's imagination on scuffed surfaces of gouache, acrylic, and Conté crayon. The vines form a loose organic grid, uniting asymmetrical halves of the paper more thoroughly than the central seam of the diptychs. In several of the works, muscular legs that appear to be sourced from classical statues are roughly centered and cropped by the top edge of the paper (fig. 4.8 and plate 46). No longer observable in their ideal totality, their identities are rendered androgynous and multiple, like the limbs that float across WalkingStick's earlier mountains. In *ACEA VIII*, they merge at the waist. More than a binary pairing of discrete bodies, it is possible to imagine several permutations from the tangle of legs, evoking the fertile possibilities of figuration evident in her related series from 1996.

Lacking a perspectival ground, the ACEA dancers appear to have churned up the whole page with their movements. The plant motif does not lie passive beneath their implied activity; vines shimmy up the semitransparent columns of paint-flesh, caressing them, tugging gently. We are made vulnerable to the dancers' limbo in a number of ways. As WalkingStick pointed out, we receive a similarly truncated view of our own bodies when looking down while having sex or dancing.[98] Bare limbs of unspecified race and gender invite us to project

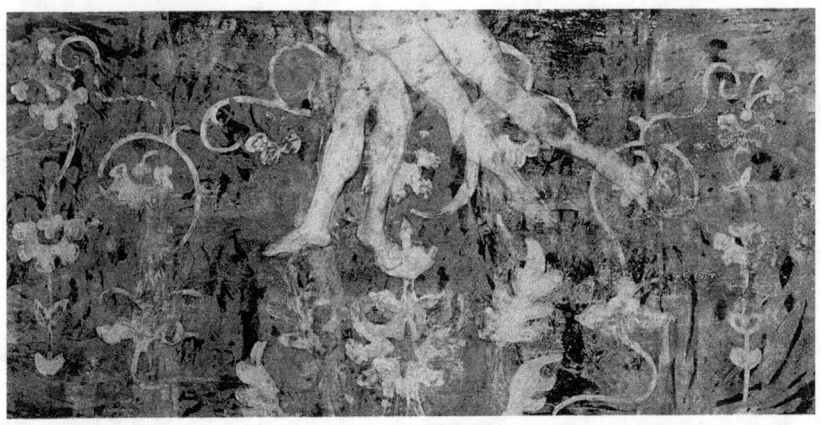

4.8 Kay WalkingStick, *ACEA VIII*, 2003. Gouache, Conté crayon on paper, 19 × 38 in. Collection of the artist.

our own bodies into the fleshy image, a sensation that is enhanced by the tactility of the abraded surface. But even when the limbs of coupled bodies are nowhere visible, looking feels a bit like dancing. The same pleasurable precarity is apparent in the swaying towers of flora and pirouettes of vegetal tendrils in *ACEA I* (see fig. 4.7). To gaze at the wayward structure of vines is to experience a slight loss of equilibrium, to be made suddenly vulnerable to the strange embrace of flora and mollusks. While Kabotie's diagrammatic solution left expanses of unadorned paper that functioned as a material hook for viewers, WalkingStick loaded up the surface with pattern, producing a different kind of allure that anthropologist Alfred Gell called "cognitive stickiness." He explained that when we look at repeating designs in wallpaper, textiles, and other decorative arts, we only ever grasp a fragment of an implied whole that extends far beyond the limits of the human eye.[99] Pattern generates a material web that entraps and decenters us within its vast and seemingly inexhaustible world. It also has a social function, as its filaments wrap us into relationships with distant humans who have likewise become attached to the work. By repeatedly excerpting the Roman mosaic, WalkingStick made work that enthralls us in a mesh that is material, social, and even transhistorical, encompassing the *ACEA* series, the past art forms cited within, and the strangers (ancient Romans, the artist) who made them.

In one additional work from the *ACEA* series, *ACEA VI—Bacchantes*, full-bodied female figures multiply and form a loose semicircle across the page (plate 47). Delineated in a deep orange Conté crayon matched to their surroundings, they are named for the followers of the Roman god of winemaking and ritual excess, Bacchus, driven to ecstatic dance. Creamy white vines thread through their arms and caress their breasts, like the streams of milk that the Bacchantes scratched from the earth at will in Euripides's famed version of the myth.[100] WalkingStick's rendering also points us toward the long afterlife of classical mythology in art history, as it became entwined with primitivism in twentieth-century paintings by Europeans and Americans. The interlaced duality of reason and revelry, found throughout the Greek and Roman pantheon and reinterpreted in the work of nineteenth-century German philosopher Friedrich Nietzsche, appealed to members of a transatlantic avant-garde who simultaneously sought the mythic underpinnings of a divided world in indigenous arts.[101] Images of muscular nude dancers formed ambivalent alliances between classical and Native bodies throughout the canonical history of modern art, confusing Rubin's clear delineation of Renaissance and indigenous art heritages. Henri Matisse's famed *Dance (I)* (1909), for one, shares with ACEA VI—*Bacchantes* a basic composition of dancing female nudes in red (plate 48). In his monumental panel, five figures clasp hands to form a circle against color-blocked fields of green and blue, suggesting elemental earth and sky. Yet, while the cropping and flattening of perspective draws them near, the closest dancers turn their backsides to us, implying closure of the circle. They exist apart from us, performing a spectacle for our separate gaze.[102] In ACEA VI—*Bacchantes*, the dancers face us in a horizonless maze of paint and flora. Instead of clasping hands in a sealed circuit, their raised fingertips brush tangled vines or the edge of the page; one arm reaches past it, recalling the cropped legs of ACEA V and ACEA VIII. More than a metaphysical vision, their appeal is tactile and corporeal. They embrace us in a jubilant choreography of plants and humans that crosses the "distance and difference" separating art historical periods, cultures, and bodies.

Fleshy paint and sticky pattern are the material means by which WalkingStick both elected and made creative kin. By sending love to Marsden, facilitating meetings between "mountain men," and inviting classical figures to dance with vines and fish, her chosen network suggests a critical role for the arts in picturing an undivided earth, founded in "the interconnectedness . . . of all life."[103] I have argued that investigating similitude historically, through worldly collections of Renaissance art, prompted WalkingStick to circumvent modern terms of difference dividing Native American and European art heritages along the lines of the racially determined body. Her efforts to negotiate the limits of this model from within it are reflected in the binary structure of her diptychs. In the wake of the embittered divisions of the IACA and the Columbus Quincentennial, the artist's repeated trips to Italy gave rise to a new body of works on paper that recall and reprise a Renaissance family of resemblances. WalkingStick drew equivalences among varied beings in her sketchbooks, reintegrated fertile bodies and corporeal landforms in fleshy paint on paper, and, finally, invited her figures to dance. This trajectory does not, I suggest, entail relinquishing the bonds forged among some indigenous artists in the wake of AIM, so much as it reintegrates them with neglected kin outside the narrow, colonial-national terms of permissible heredity.

I close by positing one final group of painted dancers as potential ancestors of the muscular, porous bodies that move across the ACEA series. According to Columbus's letter of 1493, the Arawaks living on the present-day Caribbean islands, whom he mistook for South Asians, were "well built and of handsome stature. . . . They do not hold any creed nor are they idolaters; but they all believe that power and good are in the heavens. . . . They are . . . of a very acute intelligence."[104] In other words, the "Indians" were Greek-like of mind and body, and predisposed toward Christianity. As we have seen, for nearly a century after Columbus's geographical mistake was corrected, Europeans continued to debate the possibilities for shared heritage with indigenous peoples. During a 2006 restoration of *The Resurrection* (1492–94), a fresco created by artists in Pinturicchio's workshop in the Vatican apartments, the art historical equivalent of Columbus's letter came to light (fig. 4.9 and plate 49).[105] At the center of the painting, commissioned by the Spanish pope Alexander VI (pictured kneeling in prayer at left), a cluster of nude figures with feathers in their hair emerged, dancing directly below Christ's sacred feet, from the grime of centuries. The pale, classicized bodies mingle with a pair of ghostly white horses, all partially transparent to the green ground beneath them. Apparently created from imagination after Columbus's news circulated in Italy, they hover in an indeterminate space, somewhere between Jerusalem on the horizon and the Vatican in the foreground.[106]

Scholars have emphasized that Pinturicchio's workshop painted to bolster papal power during a period of expanding global consciousness and vulnerability in Italy, especially before the threat of Muslim Turks assaulting Christendom from the east.[107] Pope Alexander VI, more famous for his spoils than for his scruples, sought to expand his political fortunes via a "crusade against the infidels."[108] In 1493, while the frescoes were under way, he granted possession of the "Indies" to his native Spain, "wherein dwell very many peoples living in peace. . . . And it is hoped that, were they instructed, the name of

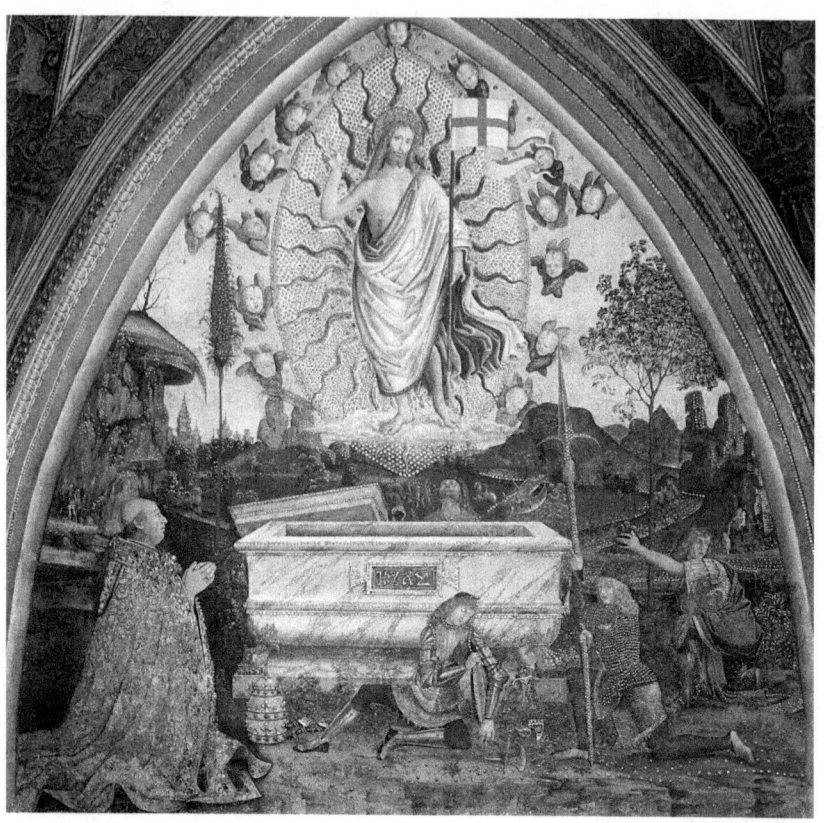

4.9 Pinturicchio (Bernardino di Betto) workshop, *The Resurrection of Christ*,
1492–94. Fresco in La salle de Mystères, Borgia Apartments of the Vatican.
Photo © Vatican Museums. All rights reserved.

the Savior, our Lord Jesus Christ, would easily be introduced into the said
countries and islands."[109] The flag Christ holds, associated with the warrior
Saint George and the crusades, hints at the earthly work to be done, while
promising the eventual triumph of friars and fighters. The pope gazes piously
upward, his elaborate garment gleaming in a reflection of God's glory—or
perhaps the "incalculable gold" promised by Columbus, poised to fall in coin-
like drops on the heads of the natives.[110] Knowing how this story played out
for the indigenous Americas, it is tempting to graft ominous intent onto
the painting of nude figures, pushing them firmly to "the darker side of the
Renaissance."[111]

WalkingStick did not see the tiny group of Native Americans clustered beneath Christ's feet on her trips to the Vatican between 1996 and 2012, as it was only unveiled to the public in 2013. But I think the ACEA dancers are nonetheless appropriate heirs to figures that look like classical statues set in motion.[112] Like the artists in Pinturicchio's workshop, WalkingStick painted bodies with multiple ancestors and provenances. Perhaps we are looking at art history's tangled legs, which, throughout five centuries of colonization, cannot be divided with ease—and certainly not with love.

FIVE "They Advanced to the Portraits of

Their Friends and Offered Them Their Hands"

ROBERT HOULE, OJIBWA TABLEAUX VIVANTS,

AND TRANSCULTURAL MATERIALISM

In 1846, the French painter Eugène Delacroix (1798–1863) sketched a party of traveling Ojibwa performers in Paris. *Cinq études d'Indiens* depicts men wearing robes and headdresses in various states of repose (fig. 5.1). Robert Houle (b. 1947), a Saulteaux curator, artist, and critic from Canada, recalled encountering the loose but sure lines for the first time during a residency at Cité des Arts in 2006:[1] "Seeing the sketch at the Louvre's Pavillon de Flore, le department des arts graphique was like traveling back in time to when [Delacroix] first drew it, looking fresh, every line an immediacy of romantic passion. Foreign and coming from a former colony, I sat at a large table in a salon with a gilded ornate ceiling, putti holding garlands at the cornices, and drew directly from the study. The moment was intimidating and inspirational, surrounded by empire and glory, art as a frontier without cultural borders."[2] Houle attested to feeling the presence of the Ojibwa everywhere in Paris: on the streets, at galleries, and in Delacroix's airy figures, which he drew over and over again (fig. 5.2). The resulting sketches provided source material for four painted panels, which the artist embedded in the bas-relief walls of his architectural installation *Paris/Ojibwa*. Together with the raised faux-marble floor and abbreviated freestanding colonnade, the panels bring to mind the grand salons of "Paris, capital of the nineteenth century," where Ojibwa and French elites entertained one another in 1846 (plate 50).[3] At the Canadian Cultural Center in Paris, where *Paris/Ojibwa* was first exhibited in 2010, visitors could walk around the façade to witness exposed wooden beams suggestive of a

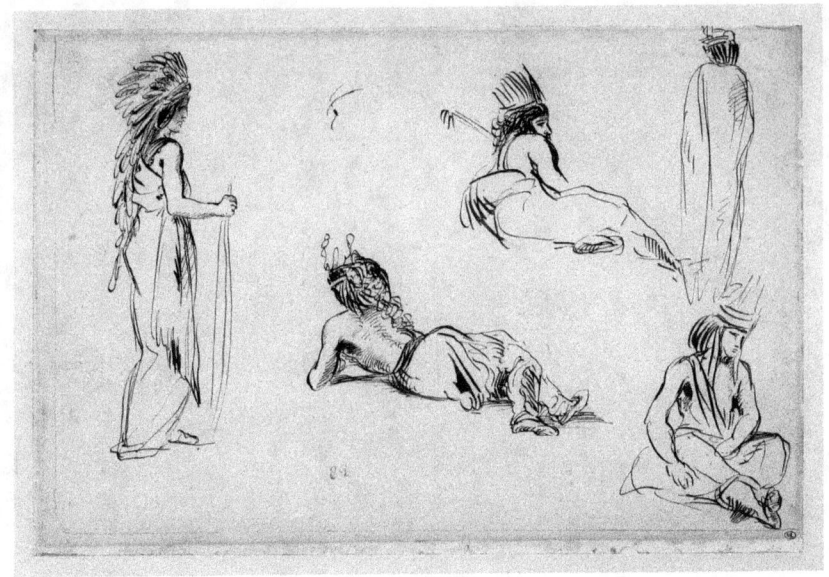

5.1 Eugène Delacroix, *Cinq études d'Indiens*, 1845. Pen and brown ink on vellum, 11.5 × 19.5 cm. Photo: Thierry Le Mage. Musée du Louvre. © RMN-Grand Palais / Art Resource, NY.

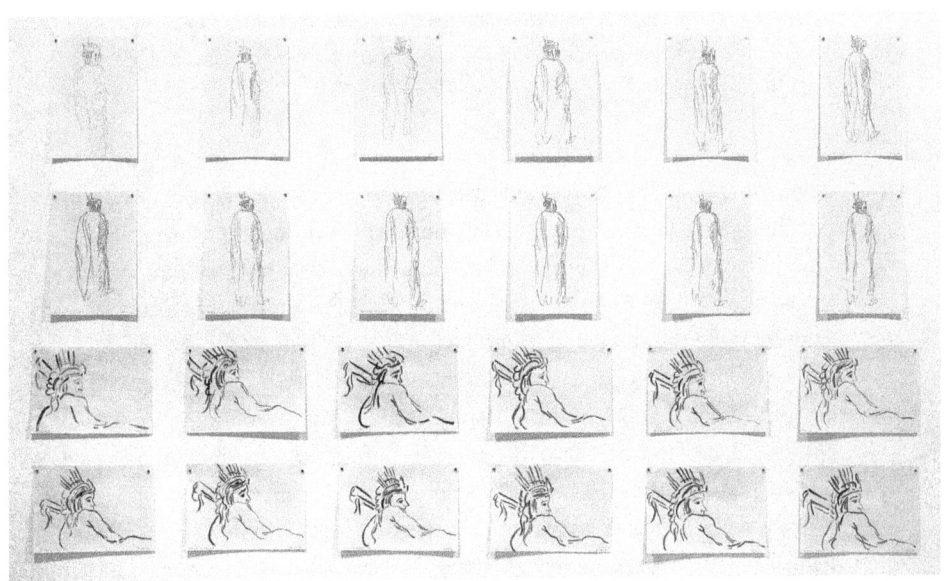

5.2 Robert Houle, *Paris/Ojibwa Studies*, 2006. Graphite on paper, watercolor on paper, each 27.9 × 21.6 cm. Collection of the artist. Photo by Michael Cullen, Trent Photographics.

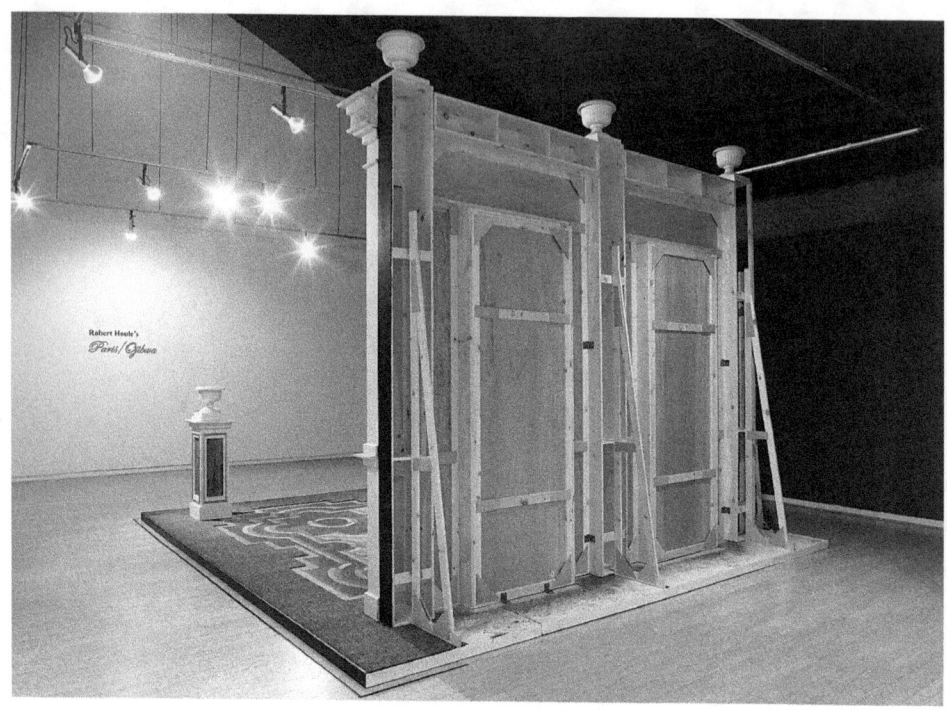

5.3　Robert Houle, *Paris/Ojibwa*, 2010. Multimedia installation. Installation view, Art Gallery of Peterborough, 2011. Collection of the artist. Photo by Michael Cullen, Trent Photographics.

stage set (fig. 5.3).[4] They could also browse nearby displays of preliminary sketches, reproductions of artworks, and historical documents that informed Houle's process. *Paris/Ojibwa* is simultaneously a salon, a theater, and an archive. The painted Ojibwa populate the otherwise empty stage, encouraging us to imagine that pictures might perform.

Paris/Ojibwa reformulates the history and function of tableaux vivants, a pastime in which human actors assume static positions to mimic scenes culled from painting and literature. Popular in public theaters and private parlors on both sides of the Atlantic in the eighteenth and nineteenth centuries, tableaux vivants appealed to American artist and entrepreneur George Catlin, who was in the business of picturing Natives. When he toured his famed Indian Gallery across Europe from 1839 to 1846, he hired groups of British actors, followed by three traveling parties of Iowa and Ojibwa performers, to stage variations on his painted portraits and scenes of Native Americans.

Today the Indian Gallery is widely recognized as an archetype of salvage ethnography, representing Catlin's attempt to preserve cultures that he believed were disappearing due to the advent of modernity—a "beguiling veil of primitivism that he cast across the American West," in the words of William B. Truettner.[5] Catlin's European exploits ended with the deaths of seven performers from smallpox, including the four represented with their backs to us in Houle's panels. Much like Pocahontas in London, the Lakota who performed with Buffalo Bill's Wild West Shows, and countless other Native peoples who contracted deadly diseases during trips to Europe beginning in 1492, the legacies of the Ojibwa and Iowa are firmly associated with colonial exploitation, objectification, and demise. We are left to mourn their memory in two dimensions, primarily through the wide circulation of Catlin's many words and pictures.

Paris/Ojibwa looks to tableaux vivants to enliven a different story. When indigenous men, women, and children performed alongside the Indian Gallery, they were painted and sketched by Catlin, Delacroix, and other European artists, participating in an unsettling chain of bodies-turned-pictures-turned-bodies-turned pictures. As I will explore, tableaux vivants gave shape to what Bruno Latour terms "quasi-objects," hybrid forms that mediate between modern, European categories of human and nonhuman, nature and culture. Furthermore, *Paris/Ojibwa* helps us to see that indigenous performances of tableaux vivants incorporated an Ojibwa understanding of the potential liveliness of images and objects. Embodying complex indigenous notions of personhood, tableaux vivants reversed the ambitions of nineteenth-century ethnography: instead of turning living Natives into static pictures, they made way for the reanimation of paintings. By inviting contemporary visitors to realize this potential, *Paris/Ojibwa* restores sociability to the archive of Ojibwa representations and makes visible "the possibilities hidden on the canvases, invisible in public records, and therefore hidden from history."[6]

As *Paris/Ojibwa* crosses the historical distance between 1846 and 2010, as well as the ontological distinction typically drawn between live bodies and static pictures, the installation prompts timely questions about the "new materialisms" that have lately preoccupied scholars across disciplines.[7] Is the currently popular notion that material entities share liveliness and agency with humans really so "new"? What happens to the European "we" of Latour's *We Have Never Been Modern*, perhaps the most influential book theorizing the role of material agents within modernity to date, when the perspectives of indigenous performers in Paris are taken into account?[8] The transcultural phenomenon of Ojibwa tableaux vivants demands a materialist framework bigger than the "new" and the "we."[9]

Commentators describe an academy "in thrall to things" with varying degrees of enthusiasm.[10] The essays in one major collection, *New Materialisms: Agency, Ontology, Politics* (2010), promise to nudge poststructuralism from its prime position in Western scholarship of the late twentieth century by drawing attention to nonhuman agencies. Editors Diane Coole and Samantha Frost write optimistically of "a radical reappraisal of the contours of the subject, a reassessment of the possibility and texture of ethics, an examination of new domains of power and unfamiliar frames for imagining justice, and an exploration of the sources, quality, and dimensions of agency."[11] A slightly more cautious note is struck in the introduction to the panel *Objects, Objectives, Objections: The Goals and Limits of the New Materialisms in Art History* at the College Art Association Annual Conference in 2014. Organizers Bibiana Obler and Benjamin Tilghman described a recent scholarly shift "from an understanding of the world centered on people and texts, and toward a reconsideration of the interrelationships among all things, including humans." They invited debate about how art historians "attuned to the specificity and uniqueness of our objects of study, can enrich and productively complicate New Materialist ideas," and "whether New Materialism offers anything different from earlier philosophical trends."[12]

I approach the subject with enthusiasm tempered by two objections. For scholars of Native American art, a subfield with roots in anthropology as well as art history, the possibility of sharing concern with material agencies across disciplines feels overdue. As the citations throughout this book attest, our recent studies are indebted to poststructuralist theory, which aided a thorough critique of ethnographic and primitivist constructions of "animistic" cultures that effectively denied colonized peoples an equal claim to modernity. But while such a focus on discourse draws Eurocentrism into view, it remains anthropocentric, leaving us again poorly equipped to account for "the interconnectedness . . . of all life" foundational to many indigenous philosophies.[13] I see in recent materialist trends the potential to find shared ground, where indigenous precepts are respected as intellectually challenging propositions about a cohabited planet rather than romanticized as the beguiling beliefs of others. If ethics and justice are to lead this inquiry, as Coole and Frost suggested, then we are compelled to take seriously Native peoples who attest to the persistence, recurrence, or recovery of materialisms that are very old. To this end, I eschew the modifier "new."

It is for a similar reason that I focus attention on the "we" in *We Have Never Been Modern*. At stake in Latour's oeuvre, along with much recent materialist literature, is an urgent, ecological need to respect relations between human and nonhuman agents. Latour is concerned not only with ontological boundaries that divide nature from culture, but also with a temporal order that granted "we moderns from the Western world" vanguard status in a global hierarchy.[14] I suggest that *We Have Never Been Modern* expands the "new" but maintains boundaries around the "we." Latour applied an anthropological vision, normally fixed on tribal cultures in distant locales, to the moderns in question. He held up a mirror to reveal a squirming, teeming mass of quasi-objects, a gesture of self-reflexivity that might begin an equitable planetary dialogue. Yet his mirror stops short of reflecting those he persisted in calling others: colonized subjects long and profoundly entangled with Europeans.[15] I cultivate a potential unrealized in *We Have Never Been Modern* by relating Latour's quasi-objects to Ojibwa conceptions of material agency on the shared ground of modernity. Through the lens of *Paris/Ojibwa*, I envisage a common project that bridges persistent divisions of time, culture, and geography: a transcultural materialism suited to an undivided earth.

George Catlin's Indian Gallery

George Catlin is best known for his Indian Gallery of painted portraits, ceremonies, and scenes of everyday life, the labor of eight years of travel among forty-eight Native North American communities. The project reflects what Joshua J. Masters called a "mania for inscription" that transformed the land and peoples of "'the American West' [into] mythic constructs in the national imaginary."[16] Catlin wished, as he stated in the catalogue, "by the aid of my brush and my pen, to rescue [the Indians] from oblivion . . . and set them up in a *Gallery unique and imperishable*, for the use and benefit of future ages."[17] Frontal portraits and scenes display an abundance of ethnographic detail, transforming Native physiognomies, rituals, and environments into fixed objects of knowledge. Catlin's will to memorialize was premature and preemptive. He recorded the living as if they were already dead, naturalizing the colonization of indigenous lands while omitting active protests by affected communities.

Despite Catlin's repeated sales pitches, Congress declined to purchase his Indian Gallery. While politicians at the time saw little worth preserving in indigenous cultures, Catlin swore that Europe would love what America disdained.[18] In 1839, he sailed from Washington, DC, to London in the company of more than five hundred portraits and scenes of American Indians, an enormous Crow lodge, trunks of artifacts, two live grizzly bears, and a pair of assistants.[19] The spectacle drew crowds from London to Paris, attracted to "those interesting races, many of whom are now, alas! nearly extinguished, under the civilizing influences of fire-water, small-pox, and the exterminating policy of the Government of the United States," as one *London Morning Post* reviewer described.[20] As British and French colonial power waned in North America, Catlin's Indian Gallery provoked sentiments of anti-Americanism and "imperialist nostalgia." European audiences could assume their innocence by playing sympathetic host to the memory of abused Indians.[21]

But Catlin soon discovered that the "imperishable" nature of the gallery that he touted wasn't always good for business. However much crowds enjoyed the "lifelike" details of his paintings, they wouldn't pay to see unchanging objects more than once. Faced with hefty venue bills and a dissipating audience, Catlin turned to tableaux vivants as novel and singular supplements to his Indian Gallery. He hired around twenty British men and boys, chosen for "some striking Indian character in their faces or figures, or action," and adorned them with face paint, wigs of horse hair, and Native garb from his collections. Catlin then instructed his actors "with almost infinite labor . . . through the Indian mode of walking, with their 'toes in,' of using their weapons of war and the chase, and of giving their various dances, songs and the war-whoop."[22] Three nights a week, after the galleries closed, Catlin called on this cast to illustrate his lectures on Indian life through a series of nineteen distinct tableaux: eleven war scenes and eight domestic scenes.[23] In an account of his European tour that he self-published in 1848, he stated without modesty, "I have no hesitation in saying, that when I had brought this difficult mode to its greatest perfection, I had succeeded in presenting the most faithful and general representation of Indian life that was ever brought before the civilized world."[24]

Catlin's descriptions touch on two characteristics that must have made tableaux vivants compelling for European audiences in the mid-nineteenth century. First, prior to popular photography, tableaux vivants promised to make present an otherwise absent source, whether a famous work of art in a nearby city or the customs of Natives on a distant continent. Catlin explicitly aligned his scenes with the documentary qualities afforded tableaux, rather than the inventive narrative arc of theater (although his occasional incorporation of action and speech in English was unorthodox). His comments about "Indian life" suggest that he wished the resemblance between tableaux and painted scenes from his Indian Gallery to be understood within an economy of ethnographic depiction; the proposed "originals" in both instances were authentic Natives. Second, Catlin's success depended on comforting his audiences with the illusion of access to an enlightened understanding of indigenous peoples, superior to that of the young American nation. Europeans' ability to see this "truth" rooted them firmly in their own national cultures. This power was literally inscribed in the bodies of British men and boys who mastered the gestures of imagined warriors and healers, only to shed their costumes at the end of the night.[25]

Catlin's descriptions of specific tableaux give us an additional glimpse of their character. "War scenes" such as the following were scheduled for the first night in Egyptian Hall in London: "*Group of Warriors and Braves, in Full Dress*, reclining around a fire, regaling themselves with the pipe and a dish of *pemmican*. In the midst of their banquet the chief enters in full dress; the pipe is lighted for him—he smokes in sadness, and breaks up the party by announcing that an enemy is at hand—that a number of their men have been scalped whilst hunting the buffalo, and they must prepare for war."[26] In a second night's program, "domestic scenes" such as the following appeared: "*The Blackfoot Doctor, or Mystery-man*, endeavoring to cure his dying patient by the operation of his mysteries and songs of incantation"; and "*Mr. Catlin at his Easel, in the Mandan Village*, painting the portrait of *Mah-to-toh-pa*, a celebrated Mandan chief. The costumes of the chief and the painter the same that were worn on the occasion."[27] In *Group of Warriors* and *Blackfoot Doctor, or Mystery-man*, Catlin drew from and reinforced an existing storehouse of Indian tropes: pipes, buffalo, scalps, chiefs, warriors, and shamans. The occasional appearance of a strange word in italics suggests just how familiar he expected the majority of the fare to be. These generic scenes were probably chosen less for their veracity than for their capacity to reinforce the most pleasing conceptions of Natives held by Europeans.[28]

Among the nineteen tableaux described, *Mr. Catlin at His Easel* stands out for its unusual and ultimately unsettling inclusion of the artist. The scene mimicked a painting of the same subject that Catlin had already completed, widely reproduced in Europe as the engraved frontispiece of his book *Letters and Notes on the Manners, Customs, and Condition of the North American Indians* in 1841 (fig. 5.4). In the latter Catlin and Mah-to-toh-pa stand before Plains tepees rather than the spherical houses characteristic of agricultural Mandan communities. Christopher Mulvey argued that given these idiosyn-

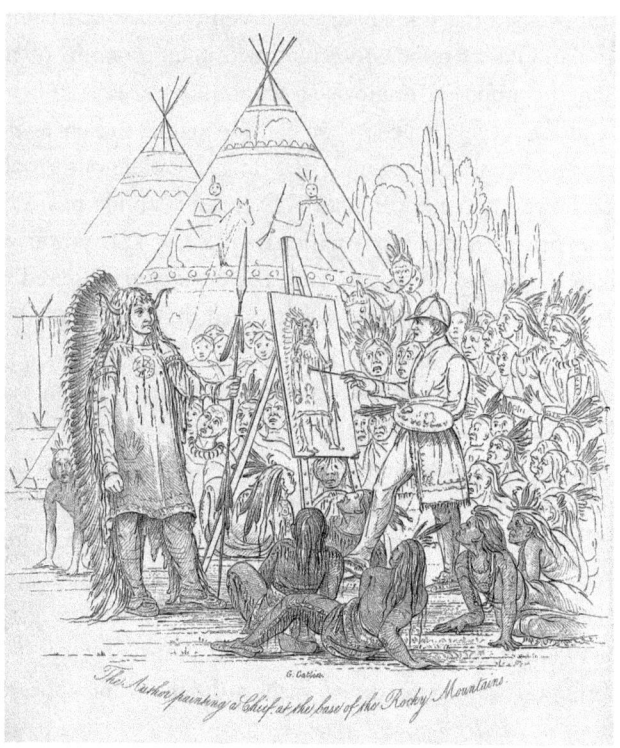

5.4 George Catlin, *The Author Painting a Chief at the Base of the Rocky Mountains*, 1841. Engraving reproduced as the frontispiece of *Letters and Notes on the Manners, Customs, and Condition of the North American Indians*, vol. 1 (London, 1841).

crasies, Catlin must have intended the image to function as a metarepresentational icon of his life project.[29] The image acquired a particular poignancy as European newspapers reported (inaccurately) that only one year after Catlin's visit, "the whole of this nation was swept away by the smallpox; not an individual man, woman or child survives."[30] Catlin appears as savior of the memory of disappearing Natives.

Yet *Mr. Catlin at His Easel* simultaneously exposed the mediated nature of ethnographic portraiture and the threat posed by tableaux vivants to the very notion of an original.[31] Given that the artist could only paint himself through an act of imagination, the image that inspired *Mr. Catlin at His Easel* foregrounded the subjectivity of the painter, rather than authentic Natives, as origin. It contrasts with Catlin's realized portrait of Mah-to-toh-pa in the Indian Gallery, which excludes the painter to facilitate an illusion of access to the chief (plate 51). On performance evenings, the doubling of the artist implied by the self-portrait was actualized in the flesh, as the American leapt from lectern to stage. As Truettner emphasized of the artist's escapades in Europe, "Catlin became, in effect, as much of a show as his collection."[32] The insistent repetition of this theme—*the artist is present*—wrenched one of the tableau's referents from the American West and located him firmly in the room. The figure of Mah-to-toh-pa underwent a similar displacement, as the British performer in Native garb could hardly stand in a village overseas while he posed for the in-the-flesh painter's canvas. Amid the lively copresence of bodies, Catlin's brush was poised to transform the "chief" back into a picture, returning him to an ethnographic context. But the reconstitution of the portraiture theme as a tableau vivant suspended this promise indefinitely, preventing its realization. *Mr. Catlin at His Easel* set in motion a cycle of bodies-turned-pictures-turned-bodies-turned-pictures without a final resting point in time or place. The figures became caught in a limbo of ontological uncertainty.

Mr. Catlin at His Easel resonates with Latour's influential notion of "quasi-objects," described at length in *We Have Never Been Modern*. He outlined an unspoken constitution, a rationalist rulebook premised on a "total separation of humans and nonhumans" that nonetheless grants modern European subjects autonomy from and power over the external world. Through the discourses of reason—ethnography chief among them—the moderns in Latour's book fantasize that knowledge is transparent and that they can enjoy unmediated access to "things in themselves," including nature and "primitive" peoples existing in a premodern state. Occluded from this worldview are countless instances of "mediation, translation, and networks" whereby the moderns become implicated in the "others" they seek to know and control.[33] We can imagine the various components that converged in *Mr. Catlin at His Easel* as links in the chain described by Latour. First Catlin painted Ma-to-toh-pa in-the-flesh, then imaginatively re-created the encounter as a self-portrait of the artist painting an ethnographic portrait, then reconstituted the scene through a live performance in which he assumes dual roles as painter and painted subject, thereby facilitating a circuit of transactions between persons, pictures, and world that undermine his own claims to autonomy and objectivity. Latour insisted that while denying their complicity in such chains, the moderns go about proliferating monsters: "We have . . . mixed together much greater masses of humans and nonhumans, without bracketing anything and without ruling out any combination!"[34] Latour termed the products of mediation "quasi-objects," inseparable hybrids of human and nonhuman, nature and culture.

In Latour's account, the unseemly offspring of translation remain in disguise, hidden beneath the constitution's assurances of purity. Hence Catlin confidently claimed that tableaux vivants provided a "faithful" account of Indian life in the midst of a self-conscious period of modernization on both sides of the Atlantic.[35] Yet there is some evidence that their pleasurable titillation and deeper disturbance lay precisely in their contamination of the European categories of human and nonhuman, engendering a palpable confusion of the representational and the real, the social and the material. For example, one reviewer for the *Morning Post* described a visit to the Indian Gallery during which the audience was "startled by a yell, and shortly afterwards by the appearance of a stately chief of the Crow Indians . . . armed to the teeth and painted to the temples." But readers were not permitted to sustain this fantasy for long, as the author then noted that the performer was Catlin's own nephew, whose "warlike appearance and dignified movements seemed to impress the assemblage more strikingly with a feeling of the character of the North American Indian than all the other evidences which crowded the walls." Soon the performer reappeared wearing a "costly and magnificent [Mandan] head-dress" (possibly the same worn by Mah-to-toh-pa and collected by Catlin), on which "'the horns of power' assume a conspicuous place." The reviewer's obvious delight in the scene may have rested precisely in the vacillation that occurred between picture and world, in which the aura of authentic regalia became mixed with the affectations of a performance that represented distant Natives as "the most proud and picturesque similitude that can be conceived."[36]

Tableaux vivants thus destabilized Catlin's ethnographic conceit, a challenge that is made far more explicit on the introduction of live Native subjects. In 1843, the first group of nine Ojibwa performers arrived in England of their own volition. Like subsequent parties of Iowa and Ojibwa, they left communities suffering acute poverty, disease, alcoholism, and confinement on reserves, as the northeastern fur trade dwindled and colonial authorities aggressively pursued religious conversion and assimilation.[37] Once abroad, they sought Catlin's patronage and performed alongside his traveling Indian Gallery. Catlin gladly swapped out the British actors, whose novelty was well-worn. He relates, "The cry of—'Indians! Real Indians!' was started in Manchester, which soon rung through the kingdom."[38] Here were the "originals,"

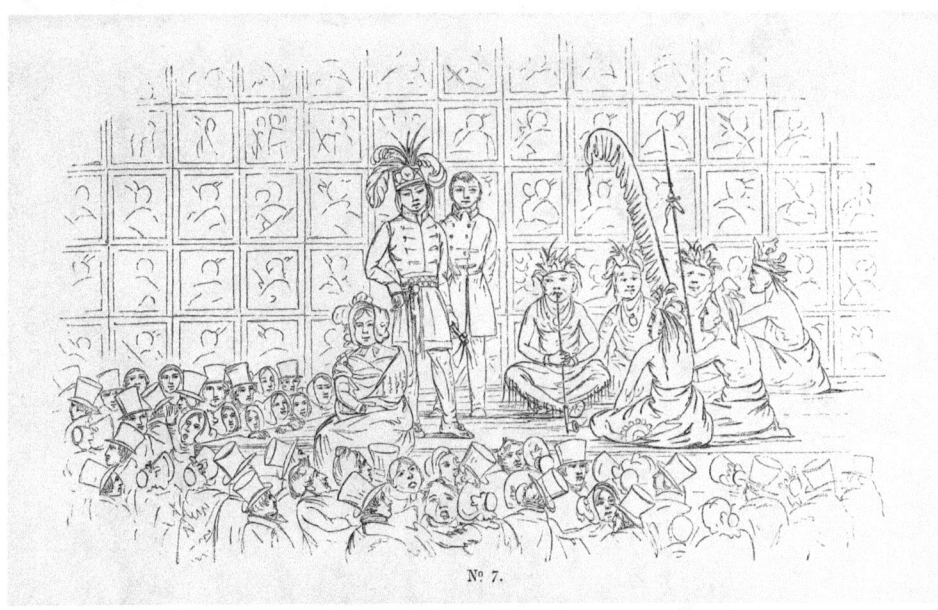

Nᵒ 7.

5.5 George Catlin, *Ojibwa Performing at Egyptian Hall in London*, 1848. Lithograph reproduced as plate 7 in *Catlin's Notes of Eight Years' Travels and Residence in Europe with His North American Indian Collection*, vol. 1 (London, 1848).

performing themselves (fig. 5.5). Catlin's account, not surprisingly, grasps the nature of the scenario as self-evident: the arrival of "real Indians" relieved him of the burden of illusion, for these performers needed no coaching. However, it seems that the Ojibwa were not invested in the noble portrait-ready image of Indians that Catlin longed to preserve. Newspaper accounts report that they "ran wild in the streets, drinking and brawling, carousing on the roof-tops."[39] Charles Dickens, who witnessed their audience with Queen Victoria, maintained that she was sorely insulted, as they were "squatting and spitting on the table ... mere animals and wretched creatures."[40] Though riddled with stereotypes, these accounts hint at the breakdown of manicured performance when dimensional subjects came to town. Unlike the British, who shed their cardboard identities at the end of the night, the Ojibwa remained on view from stage to street to salon.

Through the departure of the Ojibwa and the arrival of fourteen Iowa in London in 1844, Catlin struggled to tame live Natives with further words and pictures. He added their portraits to the Gallery and repeatedly referred to their appearance as "picturesque," that is, ideal for sketching and painting

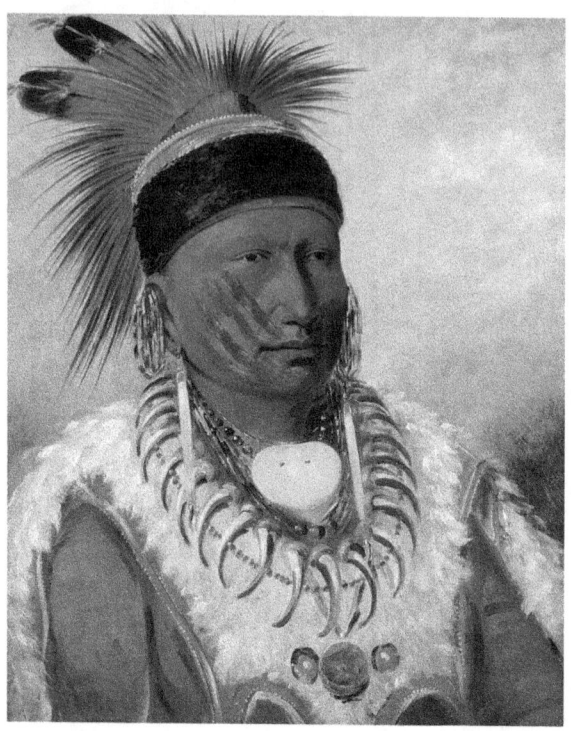

5.6 George Catlin, *The White Cloud, Head Chief of the Iowas*, 1844/1845. Oil on canvas, 71 × 58 cm. Paul Mellon Collection, National Gallery of Art, no. 1965.16.347.

(fig. 5.6).⁴¹ Ignoring the scandal of the newspaper reports, he wrote, "I am proud, for the character of the abused race which I am yet advocating, that ... I never discovered either of them intoxicated, or in a passion with one another, or with the world."⁴² The logic of the Indian Gallery depended on a distance between tamed pictures and unruly bodies, premature mourning and persistent life, that tableaux vivants too readily crossed. Catlin's attempts to police the line between picture and person, first introduced in the form of costumed Europeans, collapsed entirely in 1845. Following the deaths of an Iowa woman and child due to illness, the remainder of the party relocated with Catlin to Paris and performed before returning to the United States in the late summer. They were soon replaced by the Methodist-educated Ojibwa leader Maungwudaus (christened George Henry, c. 1807–c. 1851), accompanied by his wife, three children (soon augmented by the birth of a fourth), and six other Ojibwa, who sought Catlin's patronage during their stay in Paris. This time, however, Catlin's reputation for showmanship undermined his marketing of "real Indians"; he reported that Parisians determined that "they were paying their francs to see their own countrymen aping the Indians of America."[43] He was hard put to dispel the rumor, which drove down attendance for the duration of their stay. Catlin could no more control the living than he could make a living off their image.

The Indian Gallery came closest to Catlin's preservationist ideal when death consumed it. In 1846, Catlin and the Ojibwa left the Gallery installed in the Louvre in Paris and traveled to Belgium, where two performers died of smallpox. When other ill members of the group recovered, Catlin sent them to London, where he hoped they would make a fast departure to America. There the warrior Say-say-gon died. Maungwudaus chose to stay on tour in Britain, only to suffer the death of his wife and three children the following year.[44] The portraits in the Indian Gallery resumed their memorial function, as names and faces associated with the living could now definitively be lamented (plate 52). Catlin was overwhelmed with the magnitude of loss, which ultimately included the illnesses and deaths of his own wife and son in Paris. The cumulative emotional and financial blows folded the business and eventually sent him to the debt collector.[45] Though the Indian Gallery metaphorically embalmed Native Americans, Catlin protested the objectification of their actual remains. He rightly assumed that Europeans would dig up the bodies of performers buried in Europe as exotic specimens. The final pages of his *Notes* tell of a visit to London, during which he was invited to inspect the preserved skeleton of Say-say-gon. Catlin felt "indignation" and "disgust" at the inhumanity of this "mercenary" gesture. He correlated the unfeeling osteo-pursuits of science with "thousands of Indian graves I had seen on the frontier thrown open by sacrilegious hands for the skulls and trinkets they enclosed."[46] Exhumed bodies and frozen portraits: did Catlin finally recognize their resemblance?

Infecting Abstraction

Paris/Ojibwa reinterprets the archive of Ojibwa tableaux vivants in Europe in a manner that resonates with, yet shows the limits of Latour's theory of quasi-objects. But understanding this process first requires a detour through another, specifically art historical narrative: modernism as a sequence of developments in abstraction, in which art history and ethnography have long been entangled. I begin by defining abstraction in conventional terms as the emptying out—to varying degrees—of the referent. The painted panels of the installation pointedly omit references to the fulsome details of Catlin's portraits as well as European artists' contemporaneous paintings of Natives, such as Delacroix's iconic *The Natchez* (1835), dramatizing the fate of the Natchez during the eighteenth-century French and Indian War, and French court painter Karl Girardet's image of the Iowa performing for King Louis Philippe in 1845 (fig. 5.7).[47] Such saturated paintings of dark-skinned peoples functioned, in Linda Nochlin's words, as "a stage for the playing out, from a suitable distance, of forbidden passions—the artist's own fantasies."[48] Instead, Houle chose to foreground Delacroix's spare and comparatively undervalued drawing of the performers in Maungwudaus's troupe, a work exhibiting a high degree of abstraction that heralded modernism for some, even as it participated in a French academic tradition of freehand drawing from models (see fig. 5.1).[49] *Cinq études d'Indiens*, and to a greater degree Houle's sketches, evacuate desirable details of indigenous physiognomy upheld in both ethnographic and romantic conventions of the period. Houle repeatedly sketched the figure with the least information of all: a man viewed from behind, wearing a robe that shields his body from view, whose head is cropped by the top edge of the page (see fig. 5.2). As Houle translated his own sketches into oil paint, he exacerbated the abstraction already evident in the French artist's lines (figs. 5.8–5.9 and plates 53–54).

Paris/Ojibwa builds on Houle's prior engagement with modernisms' multicultural heritage. As I explored in the last chapter, modernist primitivism received a thorough vetting during the 1980s. Scholars disparaged art history for valorizing the formal innovations of primarily white avant-gardes in Europe and the United States, many of whom drew inspiration from the arts of indigenous peoples, while relegating Native makers to the parallel, self-contained discourse of ethnography. In a position allied with that of WalkingStick, Houle rather saw the "openness" of Jackson Pollock to Navajo sandpainting and Barnett Newman to Native Northwest Coast formline design as prompts for recovering elided indigenous contributions to the history of abstraction.[50] In the 1980s, his own work merged celebrated characteristics of paintings by Kasimir Malevich, Piet Mondrian, Newman, and others with Native iconographies, materials, and histories. Mark Cheetham usefully analyzed Houle's grids and color field paintings using a metaphor of contamination, arguing that they "infect" the classic Greenbergian account of twentieth-century painting as an evolution toward "optical purity." Reversing

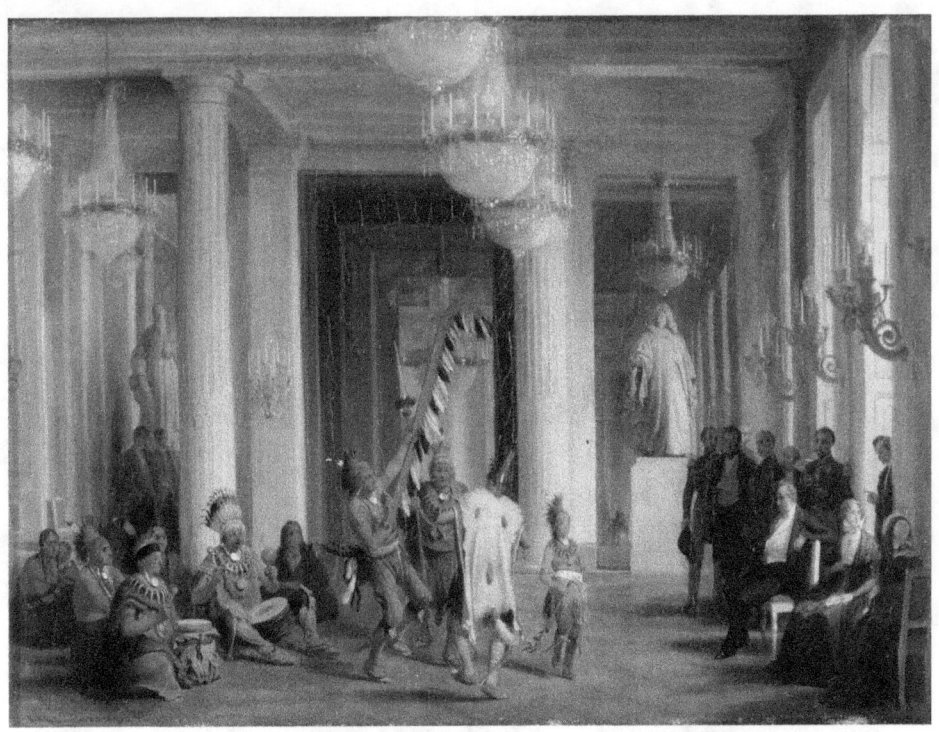

5.7 Karl Girardet, *Louis-Philippe assistant dans un salon des Tuileries à la danse d'Indiens hovas. 21 avril, 1845*, 1845. Oil on canvas, 39 × 54 cm. MV6138. Chateaux de Versailles et de Trianon. © RMN-Grand Palais / Art Resource, NY.

the process whereby the canvas is emptied of outside referents, Houle deployed abstraction to *fill in* what was missing from a dominant art historical genealogy, namely the agency of indigenous subjects and objects.[51] For example, Houle's series *Parfleches for the Last Supper* (1983) visually and thematically evokes Newman's *Stations of the Cross* (1958–66), except that monochrome fields and colored lines cover simulated *parfleche*, the French name for painted rawhide bags made by the women of nomadic Plains communities to carry food, belongings, and sacred medicines (plate 55).[52] Newmanesque "zips" of color meet the penetrating diagonal stitches of porcupine quills, such as those that decorated northeastern Native clothing and containers.[53] Cheetham argued that by "infecting" recognizable modernist forms—in this case by an American painter who admired the metaphysical properties of Native American art—Houle's canvases promise to open up invisible colonial wounds for healing.[54]

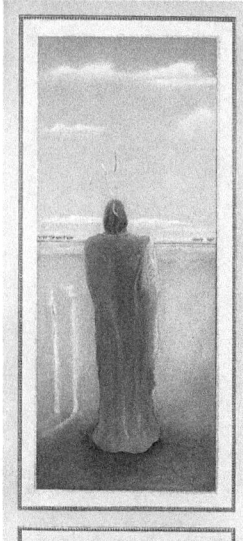
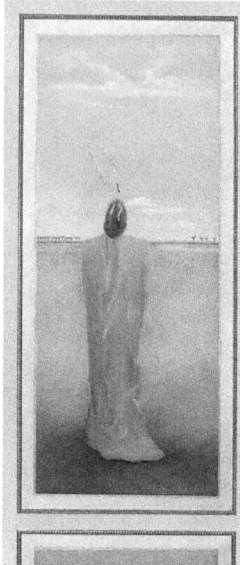
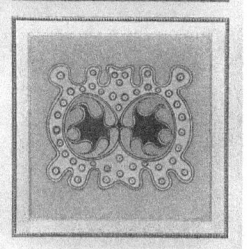
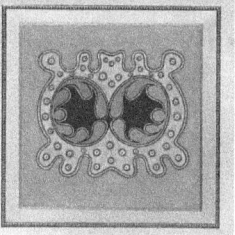

5.8 Robert Houle,
"Shaman," 2010. Framed
oil on canvas, 71.5 × 214 cm,
element from *Paris/Ojibwa*.
Collection of the artist.
Photo by Michael Cullen,
Trent Photographics.

5.9 Robert Houle,
"Warrior," 2010. Framed
oil on canvas, 71.5 × 214 cm,
element from *Paris/Ojibwa*.
Collection of the artist.
Photo by Michael Cullen,
Trent Photographics.

Houle's redress in paint developed in intimate proximity to a range of Canadian institutions. He grew up with the trauma of an abusive residential school system designed to edify Aboriginal children through a Christian curriculum, active in Canada until 1996.[55] At the same time, he spent weekends on the Sandy Bay First Nation Reserve in Manitoba, where he received an education in Saulteaux spirituality and oral culture.[56] Notably, the artist earned a BA at the University of Manitoba in 1972 on the eve of the AIM occupation of Wounded Knee in South Dakota, discussed in chapter 1.[57] Following the formal establishment of AIM in Minneapolis, the activist network included communities across Canada, whose struggles against widespread racism and government policies of confinement, relocation, and assimilation paralleled those in the United States.[58] By the time Houle earned a BEd from McGill University in 1975, arrests of Native friends at the hands of armed forces on campus had become commonplace. Houle told me that while First Nations communities retooled AIM to fit local and national concerns, it "provided a way to frame our resistance. It gave us a language to use in our struggle for equity and also a way of pointing out political injustice."[59] Activists' struggles for space informed a generation of artists, curators, and critics who sought to decolonize indigenous representation in the arts in Canada, often in close dialogue with peers in the United States.

In 1977, Houle was appointed the first curator of contemporary Indian art at the Canadian Museum of Man (now the Canadian Museum of History), only to resign three years later.[60] He protested the institution's treatment of historical and contemporary Native art as "extensions of the ethnological collections, without any appreciation of their esthetic values." He recalled spending his last day sketching in the galleries: "Surrounded by all those objects, presented in a context that isolated them from life and reality, all I could think of was that I wanted to liberate them. How do I do that? I am leaving. What can I do to breathe life into them, to show that they still matter? In desperation I sketched these lifeless objects, and decided that this would be my project for the next little while. Up until last year [1987] I concentrated on making parfleches and warrior staffs, trying to rehabilitate those objects I left behind."[61] If quills were agents of infection in Houle's early work, paint in turn promised recovery. He saw in painting the potential to restore life to indigenous materials left for dead inside ethnographic museums. In *Parfleche #5: Philip*, for example, from the series *Parfleches for the Last Supper*, equal-armed yellow crosses float across color fields (see plate 55). Though resonant with the Christian cross, these familiar indigenous maps of the cosmos point in four cardinal directions with an opening at the center, a passageway traversable by spiritual agents.[62] Abstractions formed by the meeting of quills and paint create a social link between humans and unseen forces in their environment. Houle further elaborated on his vision that contemporary art might revitalize indigenous objects "despoiled through curatorial greed" when he cocurated the influential exhibition *Land, Spirit, Power: First Nations Art at the National Gallery of Canada* in 1992, the year of the Columbus Quincentennary. In the accompanying catalogue he wrote that the eighteen artists who showed, including James Luna, Kay WalkingStick, Jimmie Durham, and Edgar Heap of Birds, were heirs to "the spiritual legacy of the ancient ones," poised to "make use of the powers evoked by this historic backdrop in their own artworks."[63] Houle called for a contemporary practice that "should begin with [artists] honoring their birthright," rather than an avant-garde emphasis on breaking with the past.[64]

Paris/Ojibwa brings these ideas to fruition and takes a step beyond them.

Houle's prior artistic and curatorial efforts privileged living artists as agents responsible for "rehabilitating" the past from a present vantage point. Echoing Durham's *On Loan from the Museum of the American Indian* (1985) and Luna's *Artifact Piece* (1987), Houle implicitly accepted the power of Western institutions and discourses to render historical materials "lifeless," awaiting salvation. His postmodern rescue mission left the parallel pasts of ethnography and modern art intact without touching. In *Paris/Ojibwa*, Houle freed his own practice of abstraction from responding to the progressive development of the Euro-American avant-garde by conversing with nineteenth-century representations. Translating between the "spiritual legacy of the ancient ones" and Delacroix's drawing, the installation locates indigenous aesthetics and meanings at the beginning rather than the end of the modernist queue, reminding us that art history and ethnography have long been mutually "infected." By drawing out possibilities that were present in the archive all along, the contemporary artist becomes the recipient, as much as the purveyor, of historical lessons. As Houle translated sketches of Delacroix's drawing into oil paint, headdresses worn by the Ojibwa disintegrated into a confetti of bright wavy lines (see figs. 5.8–5.9 and plates 53–54). It is as if the ghostly extraneous squiggles found elsewhere on Delacroix's page, likely contours begun and abandoned, migrated and concentrated above the heads of the Ojibwa. As I will elaborate, abstraction fills in what Catlin and Delacroix could not see: the presence of an Ojibwa spirit world manifested in images and objects. The lines suggest powers of vision beyond the average human eye, underscoring the spiritual capabilities that Houle ascribed to the figures by titling them "Shaman," "Healer," "Dancer," and "Warrior" (generic English translations of the Ojibwa concepts *medáwenene*, *nóojemowenene*, *nahmidwenene*, and *megahzoownene*).[65] Rather than *look at* the figures (as Catlin's Indian Gallery and French Romantic canvases compel us to do), we are invited to *see like* them.

Other-Than-Human Persons

The complex of marks hovering around the four figures' heads brings to mind the "wavy or castellated ... power lines" that historian of Native American art Ruth Phillips identified surrounding representations of supernatural beings, or manitous, on Ojibwa twined bags from the eighteenth century.[66] Similar abstract renditions of powerful cosmological beings appear on a wide range of Ojibwa objects before and after European contact, including painted robes,

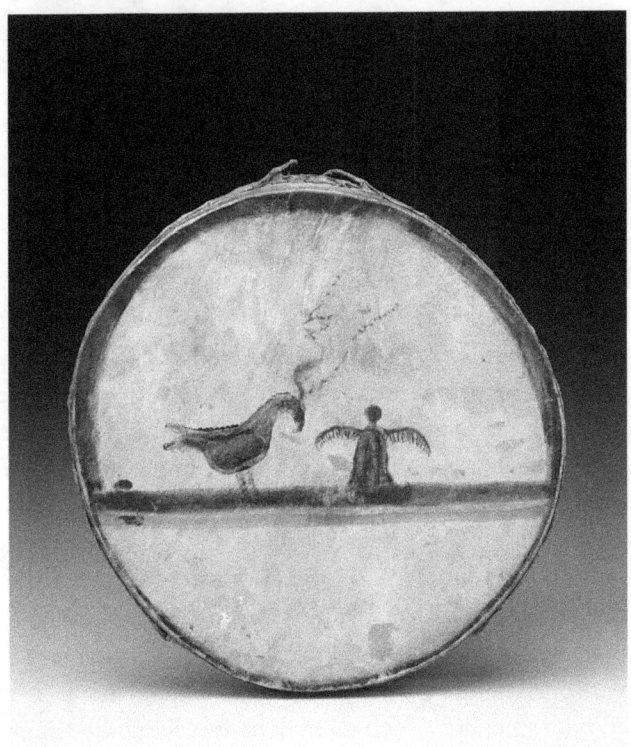

5.10 Drum, Chippewa culture, c. 1840. Wood, deerhide, pigment.
Detroit Institute of Arts, gift of Deborah S. and Richard A. Pohrt, Jr.
Courtesy of Bridgeman Images, DTR660940.

quillwork pouches, parfleche, birchbark scrolls used by shamans of the still-active Midewiwin Society, and musical instruments used to communicate with spirits (fig. 5.10). The motifs range from highly personal visions encountered in dreams, to symbols corresponding to a shared Ojibwa vocabulary, such as the equal-armed cross.[67] Phillips explained that "such representations were not merely mementos of [an individual's] vision, they were imbued with a part of the power he had received."[68] Images are an extension of the *manitous*, or spiritual helpers, on whose goodwill the Ojibwa depend for mental and physical thriving. This begins to explain why objects understood to be wholly static in a European worldview are classified as animate in the Ojibwa language. Anthropologist Irving A. Hallowell summarized this difference in a respected essay first published in 1960: "The concept of 'person' is not, in fact, synonymous with human being but transcends it.... 'Social relations' between human beings and other-than-human 'persons' are of cardinal significance."[69] One characteristic that all persons share is a vital part, a soul, which is detachable from the body and may reappear in a new form in another time and place.[70] Representations are privileged sites within the larger class of materials imbued with soul, providing formal means for humans to directly influence the manitous. Ojibwa "living pictures" inscribed on clothing, pouches, and drums invite spiritual guardianship for precarious life journeys.[71]

Hallowell's description helps us to see how Ojibwa conceptions of material agency both align with and depart from Latour's account of quasi-objects. Mediators between modern, European binaries—human and nonhuman, nature and culture—quasi-objects are relegated to a "yawning gap" between opposing categories that Latour insisted is denied by rational discourse.[72] By contrast, other-than-human persons occupy a range of positions that are fully conceptualized in Ojibwa thought, linking language to the lived world. Social relations between a variety of persons, human and otherwise, are recognized, respected, and even utilized in this framework, rather than systematically repressed. The Ojibwa subjects who informed Hallowell's writing and Houle's installation dwelled knowingly within the very networks of material agency that Latour aimed to recover. The distinction notwithstanding, I emphasize, as I have done throughout this book, that indigenous understandings of an undivided earth are not other to colonial modernity. Rather, they have proven flexible enough to encompass it. By the mid-nineteenth century, the missionization of the Ojibwa led many—Maungwudaus, for one—to revise Ojibwa spiritual practices to accommodate Christian ideas and stories, while stopping short of full religious assimilation.[73] The testimonies that Hallowell gathered from Salteaux individuals in the 1930s describe a physical world alive with other-than-human transactions, undivided by missionary accounts of a distant heaven.[74] *Paris/Ojibwa* likewise attests that Ojibwa philosophies have persisted, absorbing new meanings through colonization, to offer valid perspectives on a modernity shared with Europeans.

As I have already hinted, the installation shares this "spiritual legacy of the ancient ones" with visitors in the form of a visual lesson. The abstract lines that congregate over the figures' heads simultaneously deflect ethnographic curiosity and redirect our gaze over their shoulders, toward a shimmering horizon. Houle's figures recall the backsides of those that populate the romantic landscapes of German painter Caspar David Friedrich (1774–1840). In the latter, the presence of a figure mediates our encounters with the "sublime," a force field of awe and terror lurking beyond the limits of human knowledge, indicating the glory of a Christian God.[75] Rather than the earthly work of a distant, all-powerful creator, the lands that open beyond Houle's figures manifest a range of spiritual intercessors in dynamic, reciprocal relationships with humans. The mottled color-field skies echo the backdrops of Catlin's portraits, but beneath Houle's hand they grow and command attention. While the blue skies of "Warrior" and "Shaman" appear naturalistic, the green and orange expanses opening beyond the clouds in "Healer" and "Dancer" hint at the celestial origin narratives of the Ojibwa.[76] A narrow treed horizon line, repeated in all four panels, separates vivid skies from the liminal fields of gray in which the figures stand. The horizon has a physical referent: it is a view of the prairie from the First Nations cemetery near Lake Manitoba, where Houle's grandfather harvested marsh grasses for his cattle and horses. The equal-armed cross visible in *Parfleche #5: Philip* reappears above the horizon lines in the "Warrior" and "Healer" paintings, calling to mind the meeting of Christian crosses and indigenous cosmologies at Native burial sites (see fig. 5.9 and plate 54). The artist photographed and painted the horizon many times; one small canvas appears among the exhibited research materials of *Paris/Ojibwa* (fig. 5.11). When recycled in the panels, the view becomes a physically impossible one. Houle painted Ojibwa subjects who didn't make it home alive, but rather faced their lands from a cemetery across the ocean. To glimpse the same green horizon snapped by Houle's twentieth-century camera, they—and those of us peering over their shoulder—must look beyond the limits of the body, across temporal and spatial boundaries, over the very threshold of death.

This possibility is figured in Ojibwa philosophies of the afterlife that have persisted, often in syncretic form, through Christianization that was well under way in the mid-nineteenth century. Testimonies from Saulteaux individuals gathered by Hallowell in the 1930s described a physical world rife with spiritual transactions; that is, an earth undivided by missionary accounts of a distant heaven. Ojibwa life after death corresponds to an actual geography: the spirits of the dead, or *djibaiyak*, travel a long road to the south to the land of *djíbaiaking*, where they carry on lives parallel to those of their living relatives, though with more plentiful resources and without threat of death. Knowledge of this locale, at least as described by twentieth-century Ojibwa, is experiential rather than dogmatic; the living catch glimpses when, in rare circumstances, individuals transcend mundane flesh during severe illness, dreams, or ceremonies to travel south for a visit with the dead and then return to tell of their experience.[77] Medáwenene, nóojemowenene, nahmid-

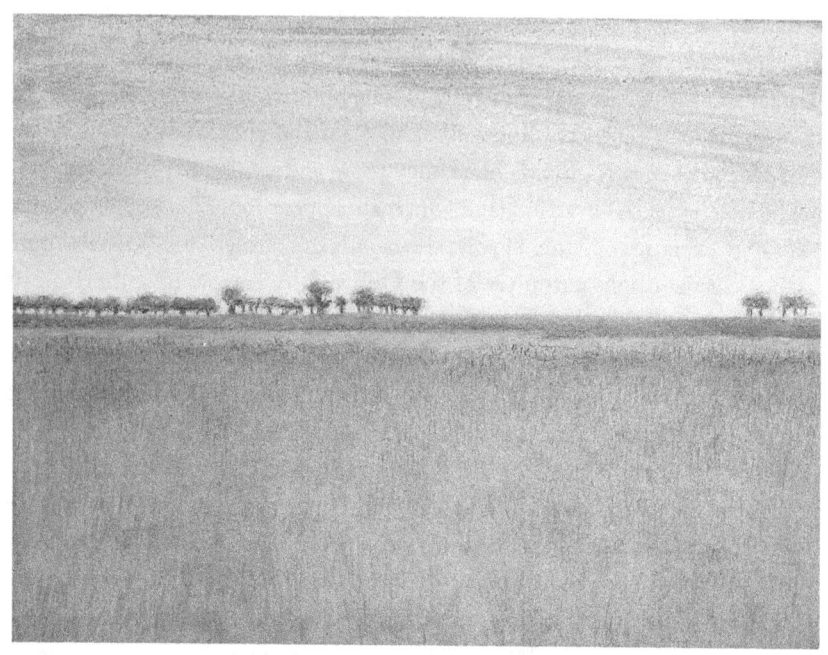

5.11 Robert Houle, *Sandy Bay*, 2007. Oil on Masonite, 22.9 × 29.8 cm.
Collection of the artist. Photo by Michael Cullen, Trent Photographics.

wenene, and megahzoownene are especially powerful communicators across
the permeable and occasionally reversible boundary between living and dead.
Humans may also contact ancestors by leaving offerings of food, tea, and
tobacco at their graves. When travelers encounter these sites, they are invited
to enjoy the offerings as they would during a hospitable visit with the living,
thus carrying on a relationship with the deceased. In turn the djibaiyak may
occasionally return in physical form to their burial sites, retaining a friendly
interest in their living kin.[78] This materialist tradition is invoked in *Paris/
Ojibwa* by a tobacco offering, visible in the urn atop the shortened column
that marks the fourth corner of the stage (see plate 50).[79]

   In addition to food, drink, and smoke, music travels easily from north to
south. The djibaiyak are happy when they hear human drumming, and in
turn they sing, dance, and drum at night. The deceased may be sent to the
grave with a drum as company in the afterlife; the Ojibwa sometimes call
the drum "grandfather," a flexible term used for ancestors, in recognition of the
liminal qualities of traveling sound.[80] Recorded drums permeate the stage of
Paris/Ojibwa. They are entwined with the voices of the powwow band Kick-

ing Woman Singers performing a traditional Grand Entry song, and carry forward the rhythmic sound of water striking stone that begins the looping soundtrack.[81] This unusual mix was initially produced for *Morningstar,* Houle's 1989 installation for the Manitoba Legislative Building. Two years prior, Houle had traveled with his father, media artist Ken Gregory, and Shirley Madill, a curator at Winnipeg Art Gallery, by boat to a Saulteaux sacred site on an island in the Manitoba Narrows. Houle explained the significance of the sound they recorded: "The water beating against the resonant limestone cliff and pounding along the pebbled shore creates the sound 'ke michomis-na-ug' (literally, 'our ancestors'), believed to be the voice of Manitou. It was and still is a sacred place, a power place whose hierophantic messages compel Saulteaux who continue to live nearby to offer tobacco; and many travel to it seeking renewal, as a Muslim will travel to Mecca. To the Saulteaux, the Narrows are known as Manito-waban, meaning the 'divine straights' or 'the place where god lives.'"[82] He described a flexible religious framework in which the voice of Manitou, the Ojibwa creator and most powerful spiritual entity in the cosmos, is manifested in the physical environment along with the manitous. The holy dwelling place is a contact zone between humans and the ancestral/spiritual complex that renews them. When Houle undertook his pilgrimage, few could recall the exact location of the Ojibwa sacred site. The recording translated the alchemy of water and stone onto magnetic tape, later rendered as digital audio, so that it could be transmitted at a distance. The sound of *Paris/Ojibwa* extends the centuries-old role of the drum, a social link between humans and other-than-human persons, across the ocean.[83]

Smallpox and Steamboats

The affirmative sound and images of *Paris/Ojibwa* are shadowed by a figure aligned with death in both European and Native imaginations: the smallpox virus. The appearance of the disease is critical to Houle's treatment of indigenous performers in Europe, given that it has powerfully shaped their legacy as victims of colonial objectification. Below "Shaman," "Healer," "Dancer," and "Warrior" are square paintings of fleshy pink containing identical turquoise ovals with scalloped edges and vivid, spiny splashes of red at center (see figs. 5.8–5.9 and plates 53–54). Together with the painted Ojibwa, they form a vertical diptych; neither can be read without the other in mind. The graceful, stylized forms call to mind images of the peanut-shaped microorganism tinted and viewed through the lens of a microscope (fig. 5.12). Houle's

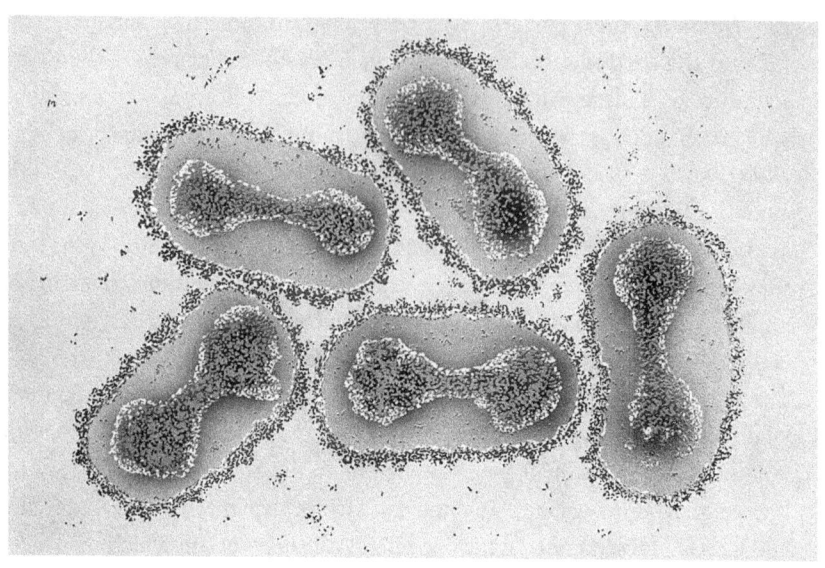

5.12 Color-enhanced transmission electron micrograph of the smallpox virus (*Poxviridae*). Magnification: 42,000×. Photo by Chris Bjornberg / Science Source, AP2IOA.

motif merges this ominous reference with yet another that connotes indigenous flourishing: an abstract design repeated across the surface of a buffalo robe he encountered in the collections at the Musée du quai Branly in Paris, reproduced in the archival section of the installation (plate 56). Although little is known about the buffalo robe's ovoid motif, Houle refers to it as a "mnemonic style of painting" traditional to his culture. Given that it is entwined with French-influenced designs of tulips and parrots, he joins French curators in speculating that the robe's provenance is east of the Great Lakes, perhaps from the Convent of the Ursulines in Quebec, where Algonquian girls first studied from 1599 to 1672.[84] Painted hides like this were traded or gifted between nations, communicating the political sovereignty, cultural survival, and adaptability of Native groups. When National Museum of the American Indian curator George P. Horse Capture first visited this and other robes in Paris in 1993, he wrote, "I carefully touched each robe four times, and their power reached out, leaving me humble.... I felt grateful to the robe ... and the artist. To me, this joining was a sign that we would meet again and influence each other somewhere down the road."[85] Can the ancestral power adhering in aged robes be reconciled with smallpox, a disease long associated with colonial exploitation and the decimation of indigenous communities?

Smallpox devastated Native populations across the Americas from the earliest moments of European contact. When the National Museum of the American Indian in Washington, DC, opened in 2004, it featured an iconic exhibit, *Our Peoples: Giving Voice to Our Histories*, which focused on guns, Bibles, and disease as key weapons of colonization.[86] Though exact numbers are difficult to ascertain, the Ojibwa were hit especially hard in the eighteenth century; an estimated 50 to 75 percent of the Ojibwa living west and north of Grand Portage (including Manitoba) died in the great epidemic from 1780 to 1783. Another wave struck the Ojibwa and their neighbors in Manitoba, Saskatchewan, and Alberta in 1837, although vaccination campaigns significantly reduced the death toll.[87] Ojibwa historical accounts regularly blamed the French and British colonialists for deliberately spreading smallpox to the Indians, as the mixed-heritage author William Warren notes in his *History of the Ojibway Nation*, first published in 1885.[88] Houle invoked this history in a nine-canvas series titled *Palisade* (1999). Eight canvases in shades of green broken by white "zips" are followed by *Postscript*, a collage of historical texts detailing the infamous personal communications of General Jeffrey Amherst, commander of the British military in North America during the French and Indian War (1754–63), outlining a plan to distribute smallpox-infested blankets to a peaceful First Nations delegation, as well as the Pontiac Confederacy's subsequent takeover of eight British garrisons from the Great Lakes region (1763–66).[89] As Cheetham argued, *Postscript* functions as a legend, encouraging the viewer to return to the seemingly neutral canvases with failed diplomacy and infected trade blankets in mind.[90] While historians are still debating whether Amherst followed through with his idea, Houle's *Palisade*, as well as his mention of "the distribution of infested blankets, the first germ warfare in North America," in his essay for the *Paris/Ojibwa* catalogue, suggest how deeply understandings of biological warfare shape contemporary Native views of colonial history.[91] Recall from chapter 1 that Jaune Quick-to-See Smith's *Paper Dolls for a Post-Columbian World with Ensembles Contributed by the U.S. Government* (1991–92) includes "matching smallpox suits for all Indian families after U.S. gov't sent wagon loads of smallpox infected blankets to keep our families warm."[92]

But the archive of the Ojibwa in Europe suggests an alternative to the neat bifurcation of life and death in familiar smallpox narratives.[93] In the materials exhibited alongside the stage of *Paris/Ojibwa*, Houle included a travelogue that Maungwudaus authored and published in 1848. The educated leader showed great promise as a missionary among his people following his conversion to Christianity in 1825, deemed "a good divine, a tolerable poet, and an excellent translator," by one Anglo reverend (plate 57).[94] But he abruptly left the church following a disagreement with his half-brother, respected missionary Peter Jones, in 1840. To Jones's consternation, Maungwudaus inserted Ojibwa spiritual concepts into his translations of Christian hymns, a willful "cross-pollinization of cultures" that he continued by organizing a dance troupe to travel in Europe four years later.[95] Upon his return, Maungwudaus put his pen to work, offering a counternarrative to Catlin's mournful travelogue of the same year. In a terse thirteen pages, he described the travels, illnesses, and deaths of his Ojibwa family and friends in Europe. Yet he lavished surprising detail on an account of peering, for the first time, into a microscope at a piece of cheese and a drop of water. He saw "hundreds of living creatures swimming in it: some like beasts, some like snakes, some like fish; some had wheels on each side of their bodies, and with these they were moving about like steamboats, hooking, chasing, fighting, killing and eating one another."[96] The microscope reveals an unexpected, lively world beyond the everyday appearance of materials. Here a tool of science, capable of powerfully augmenting human vision, doubles back on itself, undermining the objectivity of the thing studied. Mediated by the microscope, cheese, that most mundane of French consumables, turns out to be a quasi-object.[97] Maungwudaus aptly linked swimming microscopic organisms with the colonial vehicles that moved cheeses and diseases around the Americas and across the Atlantic.[98] He focused on the unfixed nature of things, their transport across permeable boundaries between cultures and places as well as life and death.

In *Paris/Ojibwa*, Houle similarly channeled viral imagery through a lively, traveling Ojibwa form, the buffalo robe. Stylistically, the motif suggests continuities between the paintings of the Woodland School from Canada, a movement begun by Ojibwa artist Norval Morrisseau (1932–2007) in the late 1950s, and the "spiritual legacy of the ancient ones."[99] Houle's respect for and debt to Morrisseau, whom he knew personally during the 1970s, is expressed in *Parfleche for Norval Morrisseau* (1999).[100] Morrisseau drew inspiration from sacred birchbark scrolls incised with pictographic designs, creating vivid, starkly outlined color-block images of animals and spirits.[101] *Paris/Ojibwa* repurposes Morrisseau's most famous motif, the divided circle, visible, for example, across the whole of his monumental *Psychic Space* (1996).[102] Morrisseau is credited with "inventing" this basic symbol in two dimensions, yet he almost certainly drew from a much older storehouse of Ojibwa decorated rattles and drums.[103] Some visitors to the Canadian Cultural Center in Paris in 2006 may have recognized the affinities between Houle and Morrisseau; the French press dubbed the older painter the "Picasso of the North" after he exhibited in the famous exhibition *Magiciens de la Terre* at the Centre Pompidou in 1989.[104] Yet by placing his own and Morrisseau's work in a continuous pictorial legacy with an anonymous seventeenth-century painter of buffalo hide, Houle rejected the avant-garde emphasis on radical newness indicated by the comparison with Picasso.

The smallpox motif joins the cast of Ojibwa living pictures, embedded in the stage alongside the upright figures of "Shaman," "Healer," "Dancer," and "Warrior," who see across the ocean and beyond the threshold of death. Ojibwa motifs appearing on painted drums, buffalo robes, and contemporary paintings attest that ancient ones may persist and reappear. As Hallowell explained, Saulteaux temporal orientation treats past and present as "part of a whole because they are bound together by the persistence and contemporary reality of mythological characters not even now grown old."[105] Likewise, Houle wrote, "The lack of a linear chronology in myth, storytelling, and dreams [recorded in art], the interchangeable grammar and the interchangeability of perception is what makes wonderful, rhythmical patterns of thought in the oral traditions of the ancient ones."[106] Humans may recall the upheavals of colonialism, acknowledge the horrors of disease, and mourn the death of loved ones. But they can also bring ancestors near again by performing songs and stories, touching a robe, or painting a line.

From Animism to Transcultural Materialism

In *Paris/Ojibwa*, other-than-human persons survive objectifying displays and smallpox deaths to inhabit the same modernity as Latour's quasi-objects. The phenomenon of Ojibwa tableaux vivants calls for a dialogical field of representation generous and flexible enough to include indigenous peoples and their spiritual and material realities. Yet the "new" and the "we" present ongoing barriers to conceptualizing an interconnected world that includes more than five hundred years of entanglements between Natives and Europeans. The source of the problem is revealed in German curator and critic Anselm Franke's two-part global traveling exhibition and essay collection *Animism* (2005 and 2012), perhaps the most thorough and provocative application of *We Have Never Been Modern* to recent contemporary art discourses.[107] Underlying Franke's otherwise skeptical attitude toward European rationalism is a belief in the power of modern institutions to desacralize indigenous objects. He began by usefully exposing the roots of the term "animism" in nineteenth-century anthropology. Following Latour, he turned his gaze away from colonized cultures and back upon Europe, arguing that the category of fallacious and irrational beliefs ascribed to "primitive" people best functions as a mirror of modernity:

> For most people who are still familiar with the term "animism" and hear it in the context of an exhibition, the word may bring to mind images of fetishes, totems, representations of a spirit-populated nature, tribal art, pre-modern rituals, and savagery. These images have forever left their imprint on the term. The expectations they trigger, however, are not what this project concerns. *Animism* doesn't exhibit or discuss artifacts or cultural practices considered animist. Instead, it uses the term and its baggage as an optical device, a mirror in which the particular way modernity conceptualizes, implements, and transgresses boundaries can come into view.[108]

Importantly, it is not just "expectations" that Franke discarded. While acknowledging its European invention, he also deployed animism descriptively, to argue that non-Western arts and related practices are antithetical to representation, exhibition, and objectification (a triad of all-powerful synonyms): "[An] exhibition about animism that upholds a direct signifying relation to its subject is doubly impossible: Animism is a practice of relating to entities in the environment, and as such, these relations cannot be exhibited; they resist objectification." Franke's use of "resist" is disingenuous, for he concludes that any exhibition framework effectively "de-animates animate entities."[109] In relation to indigenous materials, Franke reifies the nature/culture binary that he, like Latour, set out to overcome: Natives are relegated to the "environment," a space distinct from Europe, separate from modernity, and outside of representation. Only Europe transgresses this boundary, while gazing at its unitary reflection in the mirror. Notably, Franke did include Durham's *The Dangers of Petrification I & II* (2007) in the exhibition as well as an essay about it by Richard William Hill, and another on Amerindian cosmology by Brazilian anthropologist Eduardo Viveiros de Castro; I discuss Franke's reading of the artist's stonework in the epilogue.[110]

While the second installation of Franke's *Animism* exhibition was traveling the world, a Paris auction house pursued the power of objectification to its logical, capitalist end point. On April 12, 2013, seventy sacred objects that were removed from Hopi, Zuni, and other Pueblos under mysterious circumstances in the early twentieth century, many of them related to the Katsinam ceremonies discussed in chapter 2, were sold by auctioneer Gilles Neret-Minet to an array of collectors for $1.2 million. Answering protests from the Hopi government and activist supporters that the so-called masks were sacred, living beings requiring care by ritual leaders, Neret-Minet told the Associated Press, "I am also very concerned about the Hopis' sadness, but you cannot break property law. These are in collections in Europe: they are no longer sacred. When objects are in private collections, even in the United States, they are desacralized."[111] Neret-Minet bluntly confirmed Franke's lurking bias: when other-than-human persons pass through the doors of modern institutions, they are stripped of their potency and left for dead. I maintain that we cannot grant the museum or the auction house such totalizing power. When these men indicate that objectification is a superauthority adhering in institutions, they strip agency from humans—themselves included—as much as the things in question. They prevent us from seeing the deanimation of objects as the outcome of a relationship, an interaction between ordinary subjects and "the environment"—including galleries and showrooms. Furthermore, if institutions alone determine the outcome of human-material encounters, it follows that the contemporary artworks in the *Animism* show must be as impotent as the artifacts Franke dismissed. Yet not surprisingly, he maintained that these privileged artifacts are more than mere mouthpieces for the monoliths that frame them. They "will help unpack the 'riddle of modernity' in new ways," presumably in dialogue with diverse and discerning visitors.[112]

Franke's description of animism as a practice of "relating to entities in the environment" contains the seed of an alternative perspective that opens institutions back up to the possibility of mutually affecting encounters between humans and materials. Recall that Houle reported feeling the presence of past Ojibwa everywhere in Paris. He described enlivening relationships with a drawing at the Louvre and a robe at the Musée du quai Branly. His account hints that manifestations of agency do not occur exclusively in subjects or objects; rather, they result from relationships that ultimately confound the neat distinction between either category. This process furthermore occurs in an "environment" that does not arbitrarily stop at the institutional front door. Houle's stated wish to "liberate" objects in museum collections, to "breathe life into them, to show that they still matter," finds an ally in the culminating scene of Anishinaabe (Ojibwa) writer Gerald Vizenor's novel *Shrouds of White Earth* (2010). The narrator, mixed-heritage painter Dogroy Beaulieu, visits the

Musée du quai Branly with his lover, Cimone, intending to critique the romantic primitivism at work in that state-sponsored storehouse of other-than-human persons in the center of Paris. Instead, they are surprised to encounter the brush of string instruments, the crack of wood split by a carver, and the murmur of ancestral voices. The sounds grow louder as they approach particular objects: a feathered headdress from the Great Lakes, a heraldic totem pole from the Tsimshian. Cimone cries and sings before a hide decorated with paint and porcupine quills, recognizing that "the Mandan painter survived [the smallpox epidemics of the nineteenth century] in the voice of his bison ceremonial robe."[113] Beaulieu relates, "The native voices were not bound by the museum. I am convinced we heard the voices of an earlier time."[114]

In an interview published in volume 1 of *Animism*, Latour told Franke, "Museums have never been modern, either."[115] Contemporary artists pass on lessons that linger already in the archive, that collection of entangled materials where indigenous persons, human and otherwise, await renewed engagement. I conclude these thoughts by offering Ojibwa tableaux vivants as models of transcultural materialism, a process by which Europeans' own impurities meet those of colonized peoples and undergo translation inside modern institutions. In his travel notes, Catlin describes the first time Ojibwa performers encountered his Indian Gallery installed in Egyptian Hall in London, a scene with all the characteristics of a tableau vivant: "As they entered the hall, the portraits of several hundred of the chiefs and warriors of their own tribe and of their enemies were hanging on the walls and staring at them from all directions, and wigwams, and costumes and weapons of all constructions around them: they set up the most frightful yells and made the whole neighbourhood ring with their howlings; they advanced to the portraits of their friends and offered them their hands; at their enemies, whom they occasionally recognized, they brandished their tomahawks or drew their bows as they sounded the war-whoop."[116] Catlin hints that the response of the Ojibwas stemmed from their naive confusion of bodies and pictures; they mistook paintings for friends and enemies in the flesh. At the edges of the salon stood the mayor of London and his newspapermen, invited by Catlin to record the spectacle. The Ojibwas' behavior flattered his abilities as an ethnographic painter and offered yet another "primitive" spectacle. Yet the scene perpetuated a chain of transactions that Catlin had already exposed by staging tableaux vivants with British actors, quasi-objects whose pleasures likely lay in their contamination of European categories of human and nonhuman, culture and nature. The Ojibwa introduced another, critical link in the chain, making it impossible to ignore indigenous perspectives on the very pictures they came to embody. I think the performers knew exactly what they were looking at: powerful representations in which the spirits of friends and enemies reside, other-than-human persons who demand social engagement in the form of a greeting. We can finally imagine Latour's "translation, mediation, and networks" stretching to include indigenous people, present and participating in the gallery designed to represent them in the middle of Paris.

I have argued that Houle drew this potential out of the archive of the Ojibwa in Europe to share it with us, translating the abstraction of Delacroix's lines into paintings of an undivided earth continuously enlivened by spiritual exchanges. Let us finally bring the four painted figures of *Paris/Ojibwa* back into focus. They stand at the border between a Manitoba landscape and a Parisian stage/archive/salon. Facing them from the other side, visitors confront choices about what to see and how to listen. We may resume Catlin's ethnographic prompt to locate the Ojibwa in "their" world, assumed to be culturally, geographically, and temporally distant from ours. In this case the stage remains empty, a site for mourning Native bodies razed by smallpox and the animist beliefs buried with them. Alternatively we might follow Houle's lesson and offer them *our* hands. Now the stage expands in both directions, enveloping the figures and us in relationships linking pictures and bodies, Manitoba and Paris, Natives and Europeans, the nineteenth century and the present. The entire site of exhibition becomes a tableau vivant, a generous space for a transcultural materialism that discards the "new" and broadens the "we."

EPILOGUE Traveling with Stones

One sunny afternoon in 2004, while strolling with a throng of fellow tourists past the Sydney Opera House, I came face-to-face with a boulder (plate 58). She confronted me with a quizzical look, her painted eyebrows poised at rakish angles, her pink lips pursed. She was settled atop a red car transformed by her significant weight into a shiny heap of metal. I scanned the scene for further clues. Had she fallen from the sky or leapt from a nearby building? Was the car moving when it was struck? What had it done to deserve her attention, and what, in turn, did she think about the situation? Without recourse to a human maker, a characteristic of the ensemble was all the clearer: here, stone had done the sculpting. She had somehow sprung to life to ground that archetype of modern mobility, the Ford automobile, manufactured and sold in Australia and other former dominions of the British Empire since the first decades of the twentieth century.[1] In turn, the wide-eyed boulder on her custom-made love seat transformed the palatial forecourt of the Opera House into a stage for comic theater. The eggshell peaks of the proud national symbol seemed suddenly fragile, bringing to mind a childhood ditty, "Humpty Dumpty sat on a wall. Humpty Dumpty had a great fall . . ." The rhyme was my only ready reference for the movement of a material typically associated with inertia: "stone dead," "stone deaf," "stone faced."

This was my introduction to the work of Jimmie Durham, although I didn't know it at the time. *Still Life with Stone and Car* was commissioned for the Fourteenth Biennale of Sydney, *On Reason and Emotion* (2004). Durham ordered a two-ton stone quarried from the Australian Central Coast and matched its size to that of the hatchback, a 1999 Ford Festiva chosen from a local used-car dealer. He then painted a crude face on it—"like a clown's with a hangover," wrote Michael Taussig—and directed the slow lowering of the rock by crane before the eyes of bystanders and the biennial opening crowd.[2] The discrete event temporarily highlighted the artist's role as orchestrator. But the life of *Still Life with Stone and Car* continued to unfold through a series of encounters with locals and visitors like myself, departing from the memorializing qualities of the genre referenced in the title.[3] Following Durham's relocation to Europe in 1994, uncut stones of every size and shape, usually quarried near their resting places, trailed in the wake of his worldwide travels. Pebbles and boulders pelted the front of a refrigerator, busted the seat of an antique armchair, splattered paint on a gallery wall, sank a boat, split an airplane in two, adopted the guise of bacon and pecorino, and masked the artist's visage. Indigenous to nearly every place on earth, they supplanted the bones of coyotes, rabbits, and bears fused with shells, feathers, and paint that dominated his earlier U.S.-based practice. Durham repeatedly unleashed the latent power of stones to act on their surroundings, participate in stories, and forge alliances with disparate humans, often long after the artist departed the scene.

Still Life with Stone and Car, like all of the other projects foregrounded in this book, belongs to an art world tangled up with economic and cultural globalization. Here it is worth repeating T. J. Demos's phrase "crisis globalization," referring to an expanded operation of state power that "divides the uninterrupted transmission of goods and capital from the controlled movements of people," the majority of whom are stripped of their legal rights and displaced against their will.[4] While Demos emphasized the uniqueness of the post–Cold War global order, I have devoted this book to recent work that takes a much longer view of mobility and its discontents. Durham, James Luna, Edgar Heap of Birds, Kay WalkingStick, and Robert Houle excavate the creative strategies developed by indigenous people to negotiate a wide range of willed and coerced movements across five centuries of colonial occupation. On the one hand, their archival projects insist that the uneven effects of contemporary globalization contain the memory of historical empires, by pointedly retracing the grooves created by European expansion. At the same time, they refuse to accept the totalizing power of a modern "constitution" that divides the earth along capitalist and colonial lines, often marshaling long-standing indigenous resources to pose alternative constellations of time, space, and material.[5] Recognizing that alliances must be simultaneously conceptualized and enacted, they invite us to practice a larger "we."

Durham's words and work are ideal bookends to my study. The phrase "places to stand," invoked in this book's introduction, answers the impasse he so eloquently described in 1988, by picturing a modernity of complex entanglements spanning multiple periods and locations. As this book goes to press, artists of the American Indian Movement generation discussed on its pages occupy a range of disparate positions. Durham has settled permanently in

Europe and is widely celebrated outside the United States; Luna continues to call ancestral lands on the La Jolla Indian Reservation home, while traveling far and often for work; Heap of Birds teaches at the University of Oklahoma and participates in his nearby Cheyenne-Arapaho nation; WalkingStick recently renovated a house and studio in Easton, Pennsylvania; Houle lives and works in bustling Toronto. From such varied locales, each artist's work has been informed by both deeply painful and privileged experiences of mobility. Following the debut of *Mataoka* in London, Durham continued to model critical and constructive responses to the long incubation of crisis globalization. His rockwork suggests additional ways for displaced humans to take such lessons with them wherever they go. In the final pages of this book I offer stones as steadfast wayfinders in dire times, that collectively map a temporally, spatially, and materially connected world.

Readymade Storytellers

I begin with a closer look at the operation by which Durham transferred a measure of creative agency to material. This process is made especially clear in *He said I was always juxtaposing, but I thought he said just opposing. So to prove him wrong I agreed with him. Over the next few years we drifted apart* (2005), a work that both cites and departs from the canonical history of the readymade. A small, finely sculpted marble head lies in the rubble from the smashed rim of a porcelain urinal mounted on the wall (fig. E.1). Durham staged a classical head, embodying humanist ideals of rationality and subjectivity, in the ignoble aftermath of the smashing of a lowbrow urinal. The work recalls the fixture that Marcel Duchamp famously turned upside-down, signed "R. Mutt," and titled *Fountain* in 1917. Duchamp's signature and pithy title granted human acts of nominalization and recontextualization the power to transform an object from a mundane matter of bathroom plumbing to a celebrated work of art. He erased the former identity of object and its singular history of use, inserting it into a new framework allegedly unburdened by past associations.

In a study of the readymade's "aesthetics of exile," Demos tied Duchamp's persistent concern with the mobility of objects to the precarious political situation of human subjects in the first decades of the twentieth century. In particular, the violent nationalisms of World War I compelled Duchamp to emigrate from France to the Americas. Duchamp's gesture of moving objects across the carefully policed border between commodity and artwork freed them from the stasis of *belonging* to enter a more fluid and open-ended state

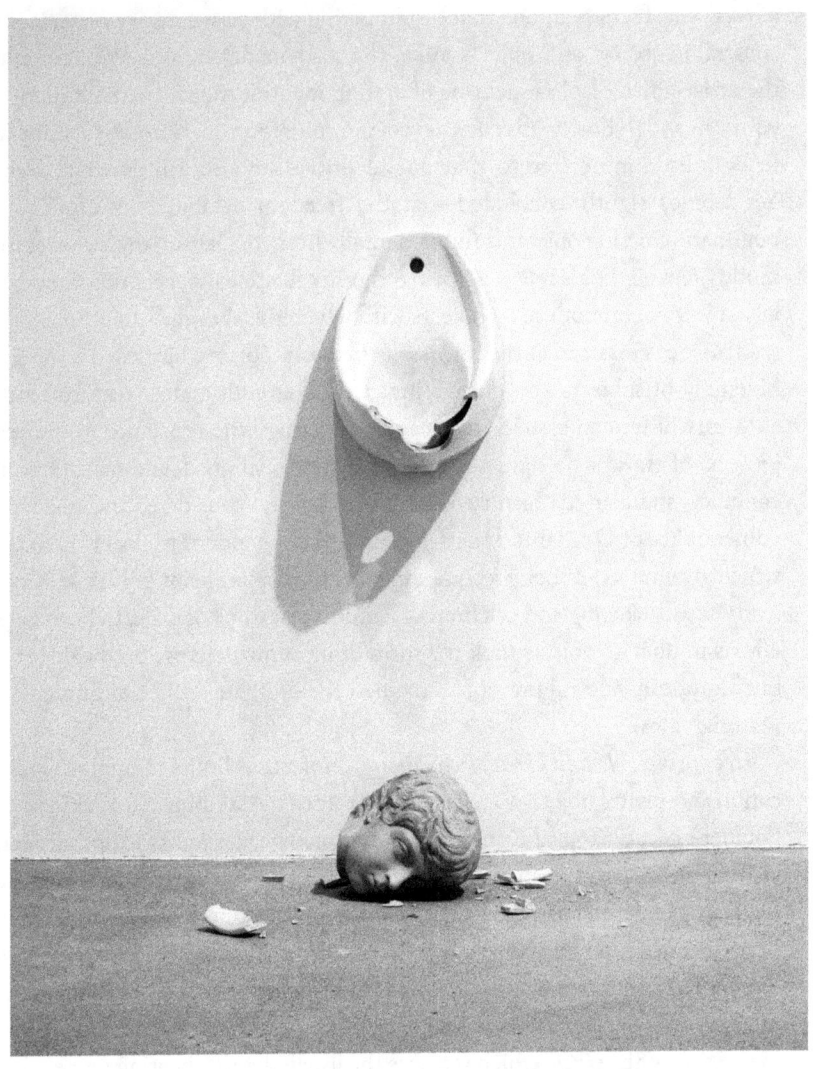

E.1 Jimmie Durham, *He said I was always juxtaposing, but I thought he said just opposing. So to prove him wrong I agreed with him. Over the next few years we drifted apart*, 2005. Installation of marble head and porcelain urinal. Courtesy of the artist.

of *becoming*. Demos argued that by tampering with classificatory systems that constrain subjects and objects alike, the readymades helped to rehabilitate the artist's own displacement by liberating identification.[6] Durham likewise wrote in 1995, shortly after his reverse immigration to Europe, "I want art to be a little more free so that our identities are also a little more free."[7] Yet Demos rightly concluded that the freedom exhibited by Duchamp's boundary-crossing objects is fundamentally limited. Despite their conceptual fluidity, the materials retain a "formal rigidity that meant accepting the physical objectification of the . . . objects with which they began."[8] In other words, readymades cross categorical divisions between objects, but leave a modern hierarchy of subjects and objects intact. *Fountain* ultimately reaffirmed the authority of human systems of meaning, offering little resistance to the projections of those who have variously exhibited, critiqued, and celebrated its canonical status in the history of art. In chapter 1, I considered the analogous vulnerability of Durham's bone sculptures to postmodern trickster discourse, which attempted aesthetic recompense for the displacement of Native Americans by repackaging and celebrating a modernist trope of exile. In both cases, efforts to liberate objects took the form of movement across fixed categories, but European cultural precepts remained the ultimate arbiter of human and material fates.

In contrast, *He said I was always juxtaposing* poses limits to human signification and invites objects to tell their own stories. Assuming a role akin to the boulder in *Still Life with Stone and Car*, sculpted head acted as sculpting agent, visiting an irreversible change upon the surprisingly fragile porcelain urinal. Delivering clues to us in the form of rubble and aftermath, the installation indexes an encounter between things that occurred in an otherwise elusive past. We are left to ask questions of the materials' histories, thereby relinquishing a measure of authority to know and to narrate. The key difference is borne out in the title of the piece, which replaces the usual identity-bearing name with a fragment of a story told in the past tense. The characters "he" and "I" suffer from a confusion of identities as they attempt to converse. Opposition—emphasizing the discreteness of identity through difference—bleeds into juxtaposition—allowing for the possibility of intermingling and contamination. A clear ontology is further confounded if we attempt to relate the text to the objects. An encounter between "he" and "I" might just as easily refer to urinal and head, classicism and the readymade, Durham and Duchamp, and/or visitor and work. The title falls short of promised nominalization, undermining the authority of (English) language to order the world. To piece this story together, we must instead heed the semantics of dust—that is, strive to listen to a story told *by* objects, rather than *about* them. Having leapt or tumbled from our familiar categories, boulders and marble heads reclaim a measure of agency by implicating us in a narrative that we can't quite command. While it is perhaps inevitable that we will resort to the conventions of one language or another to make sense of this encounter, our translations must begin with objects as protagonists and acknowledge the significant role they played in shaping events. We are thereby made aware of the precarious position of humans in an entangled earth where materials can be deadly and allies essential to flourishing.

Allies

The notion of stones as allies in dire political times appears throughout Durham's anthology *Columbus Day: Poems, Drawings and Stories about American Indian Life and Death in the Nineteen-Seventies* (1983). Stones bear witness, offer solace, and sometimes join forces with plants and animals to forge larger networks of kinship and solidarity with humans. In a poem about the decimation of brothers and fathers by warfare, Durham wrote, "But in dances come from anguish / Expressible only by bodies / We held council with the universe / The stars, eagles, loons and coyotes / Sang, 'Time is with you.' / 'History is on your side.' / Trees gave seeds / And rocks encouraged."[9] On finding an armadillo skull in Texas, Durham asked "rocks and other things around" whether a hunter killed the creature with a .22 rifle. "It was probably that way, they said."[10] *They Forgot That Their Prison Is Made of Stone, and Stone Is Our Ally* references the incarceration of American Indian Movement leader Russell Means. Durham told his readers that the stones speak "the language of the Sioux—what other language could a South Dakota stone speak?"[11] They say to the imprisoned man, "Friend, does your chest hurt? Your friends are with you."[12] Durham continued in verse, "Even cut stones / sing honoring songs / For wolf brothers, / And lend their strength / As thunder spirits gather."[13] Conversing with rock walls bolsters Means's capacity to keep objectification at bay in the prison, a disciplinary center of the modern state.[14]

Durham translated friendly Sioux words into English but otherwise set up a polarizing conflict between colonial authority and imprisoned activist. Stones side with the latter. In nearly all his early poems and stories, they participate in coded alliances with Native Americans, forging an exclusive "we" in opposition to colonial warmongers and state officials. In contrast, *The*

Center of the World at Chalma (1997) at the Museum of Contemporary Art in Pori, Finland, one of Durham's first works with stone in Europe, issues an open call for participation (figs. E.2–E.5 and plate 59). His handwritten text appears on the wall:

> There is a spring and an ahuahuete tree that mark the center of the world. They are near the village of Chalma, in the state of Morelos in the southern part of North America.
>
> Everyone should make a pilgrimage to the sacred tree, but those who become discouraged and give up along the way are turned to stone.
>
> On the chance that they should be lost souls which might recover themselves upon arrival at the tree, we are asked when on the pilgrimage to kick stones in the direction of Chalma.

Durham hung a two-meter-tall map of the world on the back wall of the gallery. He drew a handy, albeit rather crooked, arrow in black ink across the ocean, linking Pori with the village of Chalma in central Mexico.[15] He then scattered a truckload of softball-sized stones across the floor of the museum. They spill across architectural boundaries, into the bathroom, through the gift shop, and onto the sidewalks outside. The custom of pilgrimage, still practiced today, predates the arrival of colonizers, missionaries, and the Mexican nation.[16] For many European visitors, Durham's project might appear to concern the "animist" beliefs of distant others. Yet by insisting matter-of-factly that "everyone" should make a pilgrimage to Chalma, the "center of the world," Durham wrote that particularity into a continuous, shared geography.[17] We (itinerant art audiences) are called on to activate the latent lives of each rock with a decisive kick in the direction of Chalma, following the "suggested route." Lurking in the humor of Durham's hand-drawn directions is a certain request for humility. We are asked to pause on our journeys to consider that other centers might be valid, make global demands, and reorient us. We are invited to engage the story of every rock, in case it might be an ally or an exhausted fellow traveler in need of revitalization.

As pebbles and boulders confront Durham's far-flung, multilingual audiences following his relocation to Europe, they no longer speak a specific human language or side with a designated ethnic group. Eventually Durham omitted painted features, such as those adorning *Still Life with Stone and Car*, which lend stone the reassuring familiarity of a face. In one photographic work, *Self-Portrait Pretending to Be a Stone Statue of Myself* (2006), the artist is

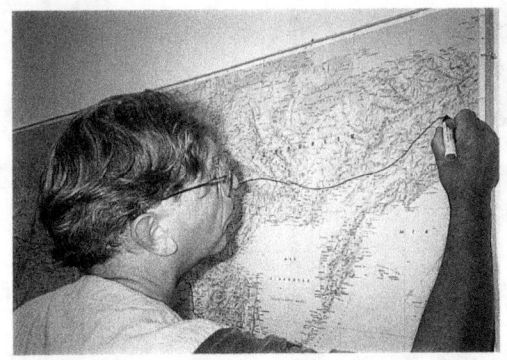

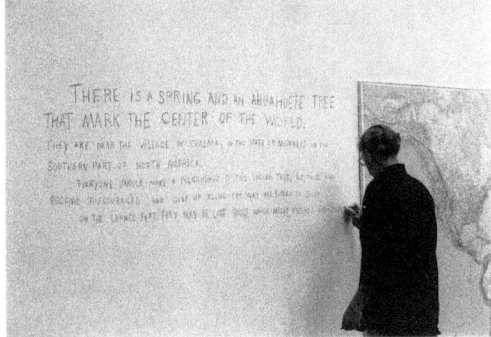

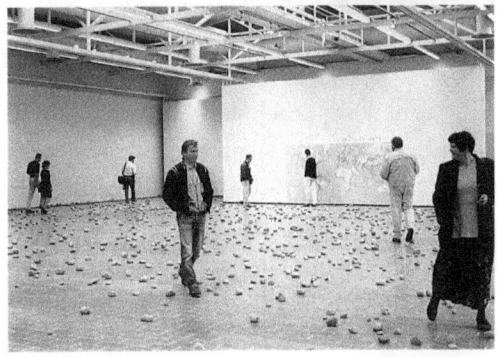

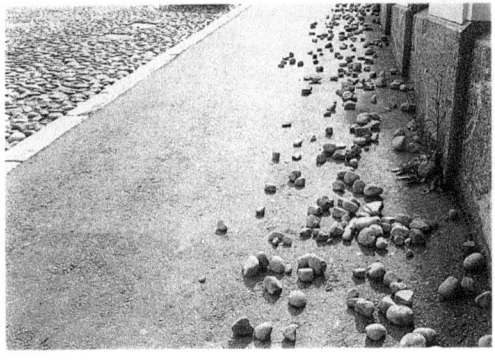

E.2–E.5 Jimmie Durham,
The Center of the World at Chalma,
details, 1997. Mixed-media
installation, Pori Art Museum,
Finland. Courtesy of the artist.

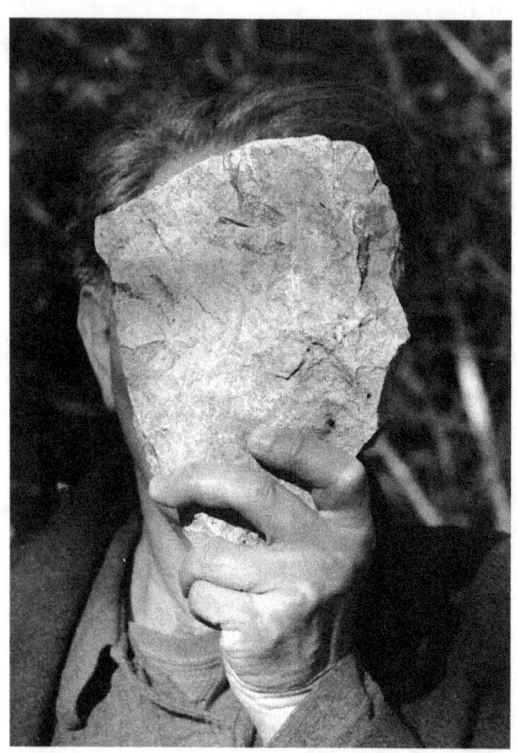

E.6 Jimmie Durham, *Self-Portrait Pretending to Be a Stone Statue of Myself*, 2006. Dimensions variable. Courtesy of the artist. Photo by Maria Thereza Alves.

pictured holding up a jagged chunk of fleshy peach substrate to block his face (fig. E.6). Durham's pretend masquerade both acknowledges and frustrates our temptation to project human qualities onto facets of rock. Absent anthropomorphizing, stones are freed to relate to humans as unpredictable actors on their own, material terms. In *Encore tranquillité* (2008), an unadorned boulder exhibited a political and ethical orientation specific to the challenge at hand (fig. E.7). The work began when Durham staged the lowering of the rock onto a single-engine airplane in an abandoned airfield outside Berlin. According to the artist, the antiquated ex-Soviet plane was deemed unsafe by European standards and slated for sale in Africa.[18] Exhibiting a brute force to match the global goliath of the market, stone comes out on top, nearly splitting the fiberglass aircraft in two. Relocated to the foyer of the Musée d'Art Moderne de la Ville de Paris for Durham's 2009 retrospective, *Rejected Stones*, the pair came to reference an encounter that took place in the past.[19] Visitors were left to scan the scene for clues: Did the stone fall from above or sail through the air? Was it local to Europe or a hit man from Africa? Was the plane it

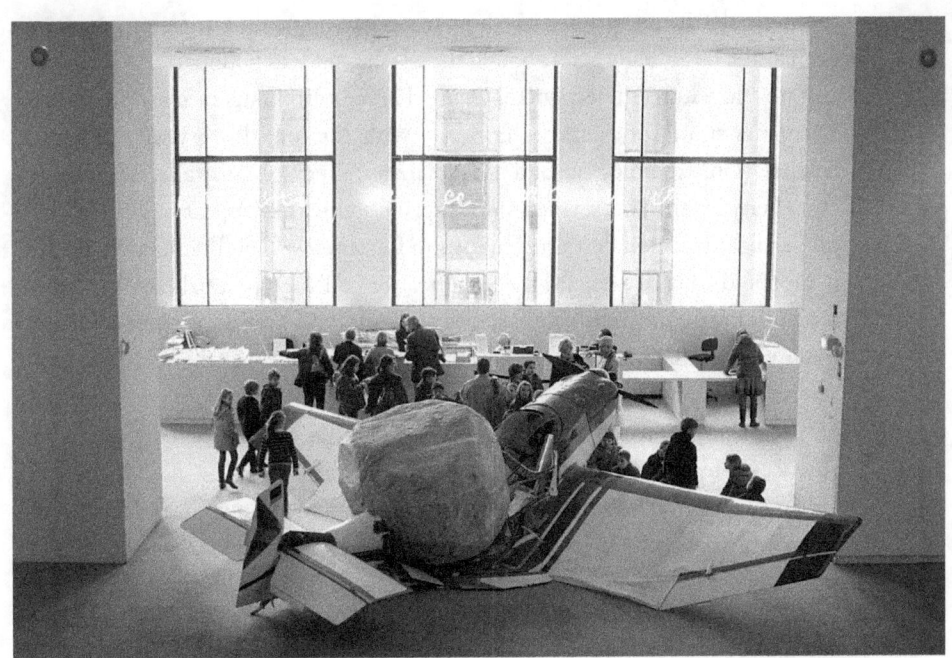

E.7 Jimmie Durham, *Encore tranquillité*, 2008. Airplane, stone, chains, 150 × 860 × 860 cm. Installation view, foyer of the Museum of Modern Art, Paris. Collection of the National Gallery of Canada. Photo by Jessica L. Horton.

targeted in motion, empty, defunct? Here the boulder not only communicates liveliness, but also asks acknowledgment from visitors for intervening on behalf of nameless human lives in a scenario of neocolonial injustice.

Wayfinders

The most sustained reading of Durham's work with stone to date appears in several essays by German critic and curator Anselm Franke and a dissertation by art historian Richard William Hill exploring "the question of agency" across the whole of Durham's oeuvre.[20] Concerned primarily with what anthropological definitions of "animism" tell us about a dominant European modernity, Franke argued that works like *Encore tranquillité* possess "strong negativity." Durham is busy "accounting for the five hundred years of continuous disenfranchisement, the experience of having one's culture 'rendered negative' with all due consequences exterior and interior, from genocide to the destruction of cultural memory."[21] Like Durham's earlier bones and automobile detritus, the stones in Franke's account turn the force of negation against the "seemingly stable boundaries—the modern boundaries—between culture and nature, subject and object."[22] I agree with Franke's assessment that Durham's stonework engages critically with the long history of European colonization, extending beyond the Americas to include Australia, Africa, and elsewhere. Furthermore, when stones spring to life they appear to disobey the modern constitution described by Bruno Latour, to which Franke's argument is indebted. But to relegate the significance of lively materials solely to the disruption of European categories is to begin and end on covered ground. Such an account furthermore perpetuates valorization of the artist as subversive outsider, doomed to hold up a mirror to Europe from the nowhere of displacement. It misses Durham's invitation to relate, reorient, and form alliances—to rebuild the ground, one rock at a time.

Toward recovering the affirmative power of mineral matter, I want to acknowledge the scope of indigenous materialisms that resonate with Durham's stonework. My brief account is allied with that of Hill, who bridged Durham's "anti-architecture" with consideration of "a Cherokee receptiveness to the liveliness and sociability of one's 'physical' environment" as an alternative intellectual foundation.[23] I emphasize the unacknowledged cartographic dimensions of this practice by attending to stories across the Americas, in which rocks spring to life to protect humans against dangerous conditions of marginality. They appear at travelers' shrines, as vocal architecture, or as people temporarily stilled. They act as wayfinders, mnemonic aids, and sympathetic friends on long journeys. I have already discussed A. Irving Hallowell's account of Ojibwa understandings of stones as "other-than-human persons" whose lively potential could be latent or active, in chapter 5. Despite missionary incursions in the first half of the twentieth century, grammatically animate stones in various states of becoming remain integral to the organization of the world inhabited by the Saulteaux.[24] Lowell John Bean similarly wrote of power in indigenous California, "A rock that suddenly moves downhill may thereby demonstrate an ability 'to act,' and therefore reveal itself to be a power source. . . . Since a man is never absolutely certain whether or not anything is a power source until it is tested or reveals itself, he lives in a constantly perilous world fraught with danger."[25] More than tumbling threats, however, stones could also reveal themselves as kin. When writing the first dictionary of the Quechnajuisom language in Rome, Pablo Tac translated the verb *chocorris* as "to be like a mountain," explaining matter-of-factly that sometimes people return from the dead in the form of rocks (see chapter 2).[26] Echoing

Durham's account of vocal prison walls, Carolyn Dean theorized the sacred status of stones in the Andes during the fifteenth and sixteenth centuries as "potentially animate, transmutable, powerful, and sentient. However, if rocks to the Inka were the stuff of gods and culture heroes, they were also the stuff of houses, terrace walls, and llama corrals. Rocks were therefore simultaneously both normal and numinous."[27] Stephen Jett extensively mapped stones stacked at key points in Native trail networks from North to South America before and after European contact. He described heaps more than six feet high from Cherokee territory in the eastern United States, built prior to the Trail of Tears. There, indigenous travelers made offerings to ward off exhaustion and attacks from hostile strangers.[28] Inuit of the circumpolar region similarly construct venerated figures from found stones known as *inuksuit* (the singular *inuksuk* means something that "acts in the capacity of a human"), still utilized today as food caches and message centers for hunters navigating physical and spiritual landscapes.[29] Wayside rock piles are generically known by today's hikers as "cairns." But the Quechua word, *apatsixta*, translates as "burden depositor," referencing an understanding that a traveler's fatigue can be transmitted to stone and left behind.[30]

By invoking this array of indigenous-stone relations, it is not my intention to return Durham's work abroad to "frameworks of identity," a citizenship long ago renounced. His recent works effectively reroute the fullness of our attention from the identity of an "Indian," too readily signaled by the crafting of paint, feathers, and bones, to the power of material, latent in uncut rock found everywhere in the world. Durham's references to transmutable stones extend from Mexico to Japan in *Stone Heart* (2004), an artist's book in which discussions of obsidian prized by Aztecs mingle with reproductions of rock gardens in Kitakyushu.[31] Stones' wordless facility to "address the entire world," to incite a kick from Pori museum visitors emulating Chalma pilgrims or ground an airplane in Berlin slated for sale in Africa, comes close to making good on Durham's claim that the work of a Cherokee can be as "universal" as that of any other artist.[32] By reconnecting stories of mineral allies from across the Americas to the global contexts in which Durham's recent stonework speaks, I insist in turn upon the multiplicity of ideas and practices that precede and persist throughout the history of colonization. Stone sculptors join forces with the other indigenous references throughout this book to reconfigure an understanding of time, space, and material beyond the narrow construction of primitive beliefs, Europe's others, and marginalized persons and things assigned a negative role of disruption. They contribute to a corpus of intellectual and embodied resources cultivated in many interconnected "centers," long poised to answer the challenges of a shared modernity.

Stones additionally link the literal ground on which we stand to the conceptual means by which a wide array of humans dwell in and relate to the world. They are the indivisible, shared foundation of European categories of nature and culture and indigenous "animism," the strewn company of coyotes and the hewn blocks of prison walls. They bear witness to the rise and fall of oceans and nations. Scattered in the wake of Durham's travels through Chalma, Pori, Sydney, Berlin, and Kitakyushu, they form a crooked path linking humans and other-than-human persons across continents. I close with rocks as guides for mobile subjects that point beyond divisions and displacements. They simultaneously act as geographical cairns and transcultural wayfinders, nodes in a network of material and spiritual relations that collectively map an undivided earth. Stones mark many places to stand.

NOTES

Introduction

1. Durham and Fisher, "The Ground Has Been Covered," 101.

2. Most date the official beginning of AIM to 1968, the year that groups of activists formed the eponymous organization in Minneapolis and made a first, short-lived attempt to occupy Alcatraz Island in San Francisco Bay. Durham was director of the International Treaty Council from 1974 to 1979, when he resigned amid factionalism; by then the public era of AIM had waned. However, a version of the organization persists today: http://www.aimovement.org/.

3. The descriptor "settler colonial" is widespread in interdisciplinary Native studies, but rarely used in art history. On the marginalization of this concept, see Hoxie, "Retrieving the Red Continent."

4. I focus this study on Native artists hailing from the United States and Canada, where a discourse about indigenous art and politics under settler colonial conditions is closely shared. A thorough study of the specific impact of AIM beyond the borders of the United States has yet to be written, although Durham worked with groups engaged in decolonization struggles across the Americas and Africa. Houle, the one artist I discuss at length who lives within the boundaries of present-day Canada, attests to the profound impact of AIM on his political and artistic activity there. Houle in conversation with the author, Toronto, December 8, 2013.

5. See, for example, O'Brien et al., *Modern Art in Africa, Asia and Latin America*; Doyle and Winkiel, *Geomodernisms*; Mercer, *Cosmopolitan Modernisms*; Wollaeger, *The Oxford Handbook of Global Modernisms*; Wright, "Building Global Modernisms." Bill Anthes uses the phrase "alternative modernism" to describe Native American painting at midcentury in his book *Native Moderns*, xxi. In 2011 Ruth B. Phillips inaugurated a long-term project sponsored by the Clark Institute, "Multiple Modernisms: Twentieth-Century Artistic Modernisms in Global Perspective," including symposia and publications focusing on indigenous modernisms from Africa, North America, Australia, New Zealand, and the Pacific Islands: http://multiplemodernisms.org/. See also Phillips, "Aesthetic Primitivism Revisited."

6. Friedman, "Periodizing Modernism," 426. Historian of South Asian art Monica Juneja similarly writes that a rigorous approach to the global turn "demands more than

a simple extension of scholarship beyond regional frames. . . . It calls for explanatory paradigms that meaningfully address issues of multiple locations, palimpsestic temporalities, and processes of transcultural configurations." Juneja, "Global Art History and the 'Burden of Representation,'" 276.

7. This literature is large and growing. Foundational volumes addressing contemporary art and globalization include Fisher, *Global Visions*; Papastergiadis and Tsoutas, *Complex Entanglements*; Mosquera and Fisher, *Over Here*; Smith, Enwezor, and Condee, *Antinomies of Art and Culture*. See also Amor et al., "Liminalities." More sustained analyses appear in these recent single-authored works: Demos, *The Migrant Image*; Kwon, *One Place after Another*; and Pamela Lee, *Forgetting the Art World*. Critical accounts of the growth of mega-exhibitions appear in Filipovic, Hal, and Ovstebo, *The Biennial Reader*. Recent compilations addressing the larger question of "global art history" include Casid and D'Souza, *Art History in the Wake of the Global Turn*; Elkins, *Is Art History Global?* Since June 2014, key debates have also been highlighted by a rotating roster of scholars in the "Whither Art History?" column in *Art Bulletin*.

8. See Christov-Bakargiev, Martinez, and Berardi, *dOCUMENTA (13) Catalog 1/3*; de Zegher and McMaster, *The 18th Biennale of Sydney*. The latter built on the long inclusion of indigenous Aboriginal artists in previous iterations of the biennial, as well as a delegation of Canadian First Nations artists who participated in the Seventeenth Biennale of Sydney, *The Beauty of Distance: Songs of Survival in a Precarious Age*, in 2010. See Elliott, *17th Biennale of Sydney*.

9. Casid and D'Souza, *Art History in the Wake of the Global Turn*.

10. Prior to the discourse of global modernisms that primarily took off in the 2000s, the paradigmatic—and highly controversial—exhibition *Magiciens de la terre* at the Centre Pompidou in Paris in 1989 presented a superficially spatialized view of the globalization of contemporary art. Curator Jean-Hubert Martin was criticized for juxtaposing Australian Aboriginal house poles and Navajo sandpaintings with earthworks by British and American artists without thoroughly addressing the colonial histories and politics shaping such choices. See Buchloh, "The Whole Earth Show"; Fisher, "Fictional Histories"; Steeds et al., *Making Art Global (Part 2)*. Directors of the Eighteenth Biennale of Sydney and dOCUMENTA (13) made comparatively strong efforts to foreground political frames of reference, although historical depth—and audience attention span—was inevitably sacrificed inside these sprawling events. On the relationships between Aboriginal Australian and Native American artists that unfolded around the Eighteenth Biennale through the work of the U.S.-based media collective Postcommodity, see Watson, "'Centring the Indigenous.'" Watson's 2012 dissertation, "Diplomatic Aesthetics: Globalization and Contemporary Native Art," positions Native American artists, including Durham and Luna, within a global indigenous rights movement.

11. Terry Smith, "Introduction," 8–9. Similar claims to newness are made in Belting, *Art History after Modernism*. While my emphasis on continuity since 1492 highlights the profound impact of colonization on indigenous Americans, it need not preclude

recognition of dramatic geopolitical and/or technological changes that occur over time and are experienced differently around the world. See classic accounts in Appadurai, *Modernity at Large*; Benedict Anderson, *Imagined Communities*.

12. Demos, *The Migrant Image*, xiv–xv.

13. Mignolo argues that colonization entailed the deployment of Western philosophy to draft a "global design" that persists today. Mignolo, *Local Histories / Global Designs*, 17. See also Mignolo, *The Darker Side of the Renaissance*; Mignolo, *The Darker Side of Western Modernity*. James Clifford likewise anchors globalization in a longer trajectory of colonization in *Routes*; Paul Gilroy grants a similarly foundational status to the transatlantic slave trade in *The Black Atlantic*.

14. Vine Deloria, *God Is Red*, 62. Numerous exhibitions of contemporary Native American art have taken land or place as their central thematic. See, for example, Ash-Milby, *Off the Map*; McMaster, *Reservation X*; Nemiroff, Houle, and Townsend-Gault, *Land, Spirit, Power*.

15. For a history of AIM, see Smith and Warrior, *Like a Hurricane*. Other sources are cited in chapter 1.

16. Kwon, *One Place after Another*, 156. Several scholars have recently recognized that artists who participate in globalization simultaneously produce it, ranging from neocolonial self-exoticization that plays to market tastes, to the privileged itinerancy enjoyed by a subset of superstar "postidentity" artists and curators. See especially Demos, *The Migrant Image*; Pamela Lee, *Forgetting the Art World*. All three authors see possibilities for artists to engage critically with globalization, albeit without recourse to an "outside" position. Nicolas Bourriaud offers a more favorable account of the role of the itinerant artist as a needed cultural translator in Bourriaud, *The Radicant*.

17. Vine Deloria, *God Is Red*, 63. Gerald McMaster describes a similar colonial relation of time and space, "a one-way movement and progress, a colonization into the space of the Other," in "Towards an Aboriginal Art History," 84. I give an overview of contested notions of indigenous places with relevant citations in Horton, "Alone on the Snow, Alone on the Beach." The essay informed my thinking for this book but lacks the historical dimension on which this project is based.

18. Rickard, "Visualizing Sovereignty in the Time of Biometric Sensors," 469.

19. Huhndorf, *Mapping the Americas*, 11.

20. Alfred, *Wasáse*, 4–5. See also Alfred, *Peace, Power, Righteousness*.

21. Chadwick Allen, *Trans-Indigenous*; Forte, *Indigenous Cosmopolitans*; Huang et al., "Charting Transnational Native American Studies"; Huhndorf, *Mapping the Americas*; Kalbfleisch, "Bordering on Feminism"; Ostrowitz, *Interventions*; *Vision, Space, Desire*; Rickard, "The Emergence of Global Indigenous Art"; Warrior, "Native American Scholarship and the Transnational Turn."

22. Rickard, "Visualizing Sovereignty in the Time of Biometric Sensors," 470–71, 468. Rickard first articulated her notion of visual sovereignty in "Sovereignty." On "intellectual sovereignty," see Warrior, *Tribal Secrets*.

23. Rickard, "Visualizing Sovereignty in the Time of Biometric Sensors," 469.

24. Mithlo, "History Is Dangerous," 50.

25. "Survivance" is explained and used throughout Vizenor, *Manifest Manners*.

26. Philip J. Deloria, "Historiography," 21. For a thorough critique of the modern ordering of time and space in Western anthropology, see Fabian, *Time and the Other*. Relevant here is Shanna Ketchum's argument that "the arts of Native Americans [need] to be addressed on a continuum that does not adhere to Western philosophies of time and space" in "Native American Cosmopolitan Modernism(s)," 361. It is equally important to acknowledge that many indigenous-authored artworks and histories *do* subscribe to Western temporal and spatial premises.

27. Among works of art historical scholarship that urge tampering with time, I note especially Bal, *Quoting Caravaggio*; Boym, *The Future of Nostalgia*; Goldberg and Menon, "Queering History"; Harris, "Untimely Mediations"; Nagel, *Medieval Modern*. Nearly all of these authors note the influence of Walter Benjamin, especially *The Arcades Project* and "Theses on the Philosophy of History." While I name a range of allies throughout this book, I focus especially on lesser-known art and scholarship by and about Native North Americans.

28. Luna is quoted in Lee-Ann Martin, "Cross Over with Mr. Luna," 32. My account is informed by the theories of geographer Doreen Massey, whose phrase "a global sense of place" relies heavily on a historical dimension to restore dynamism to a late twentieth-century spatial imagination that she argues is fundamentally static. See Massey, *For Space*, 81–89.

29. Foster, "An Archival Impulse," 21.

30. Hirsch and Taylor, "The Archive in Transit."

31. Enwezor, *Archive Fever*, 18. Enwezor is referencing arguments from Foucault, *The Archaeology of Knowledge and the Discourse on Language*. Foucault notes that this promise can never be realized: "The archive cannot be described in its totality. . . . It emerges in fragments, regions, levels" (130). Enwezor borrowed the title of his major 2008 exhibition from Derrida, *Archive Fever* (1998). On imperialism and archives, see also Richards, *The Imperial Archive*; Stoler, *Along the Archival Grain*.

32. Taylor, *The Archive and the Repertoire*, 19.

33. Rebecca Schneider, "Archives," 102; Enwezor, *Archive Fever*, 21. While Taylor and Schneider see the "repertoire" of embodied performance as one answer to the objectifying power of the archive, both Enwezor and Foster describe artists who persist in tampering with the hard stuff. Enwezor sees two main possibilities for artistic intervention here: The first is primarily deconstructive, taking "aim at the structural and functional principles underlying the use of the archival document." The second is constructive, resulting in "the creation of another archival structure as a means of establishing an archeological relationship to history, evidence, information, and data that will give rise to its own interpretive categories." Enwezor, *Archive Fever*, 18. While all of these accounts are founded on Western assumptions of a firm line dividing subjects

and objects, performance studies approaches tend to be most closely allied with AIM-generation artistic practices, as I explore at length in chapter 2.

34. Paul Chaat Smith, "Luna Remembers," 33.

35. The Alcatraz Proclamation of 1969 is quoted and discussed in Ronan, "Native Empowerment, the New Museology, and the National Museum of the American Indian," 141.

36. Enwezor, *Archive Fever*, 20.

37. Throughout this book, I borrow A. Irving Hallowell's phrase, "other-than-human persons," used to describe Ojibwa conceptions of the latent or active powers of a wide variety of materials, in place of the binary distinction between humans and "nonhumans" currently popular in academic discourses. Hallowell's important essay, "Ojibwa Ontology, Behavior, and World View," is discussed at length in chapter 5.

38. See, for example, Bennett, *Vibrant Matter*; Coole and Frost, *New Materialisms*; Latour, *We Have Never Been Modern*. These and other sources are discussed in chapter 5.

39. For a concise summary of this problem, see Seth, *Europe's Indians*, 11.

40. Tawadros, "Preface," 9.

41. See Bhabha, *The Location of Culture*; Durham, "A Central Margin."

42. Seth, *Europe's Indians*. Additional studies of European attitudes toward Native Americans include Burns, "Innocence Abroad"; Wernitznig, *Europe's Indians*; Honour, *The New Golden Land*; Moffitt and Sebastián, *The European Invention of the American Indian*. Seth's argument is particularly rich because it interweaves accounts from India and the Americas to yield an expansive understanding of Europe as constituted through colonial relations over time.

43. Feest, *Indians and Europe*; Denzin, *Indians on Display*; Flint, *The Transatlantic Indian*; Foreman, *Indians Abroad*; Muller, "From Palace to Longhouse"; Weaver, *The Red Atlantic*; Vaughan, *Transatlantic Encounters*. Weaver's *The Red Atlantic* is the first book-length project centered wholly on indigenous perspectives of transatlantic travel. Denzin's experimental text takes the form of a theatrical script, interweaving contemporary Native artists' and writers' perspectives with subversive readings of nineteenth-century Anglo showmen and artists who used Native American images to their own ends, such as American painter Charles Bird King (1785–1862), George Catlin (1796–1872), "Buffalo" Bill Cody (1846–1917), and German author Karl May (1842–1912). Flint's *The Transatlantic Indian* argues for the centrality of the Indian—real and imagined—to British imperial identity from the American Revolution to the early decades of the twentieth century, including consideration of the perspectives of the Ojibwa and Iowa who traveled with Catlin, testimonies from performers who traveled with Buffalo Bill's Wild West Show at the turn of the twentieth century, and the experiences of Iroquois poet Pauline Johnson in London in the 1890s. Feest, in contrast, states that "'Indians and Europe' is dealing . . . specifically with European views of this relationship, with images that are part of the Old World's cultural heritage. In those instances in which Native American visitors seem to offer their opinions

on Europe and the Europeans ... there is reason to believe that they themselves or those who wrote or spoke for them, stood firmly in a European tradition" (2). He does not elaborate on the "reason to believe," but we may speculate that it is precisely the travelers' seemingly exceptional mobility that renders them, in this view, wholly European. Unmoored from indigenous places, where else could these subjects stand except "firmly in a European tradition"? I unravel this binary while focusing my narrative on indigenous agents, past and present.

44. Philip J. Deloria, *Indians in Unexpected Places*, 14.

45. I especially disagree with arts writers' use of exile to describe Durham's voluntary tenure in Europe, as I explain in chapter 1. It is worth noting that Durham has used the term to refer to his displacement from other Cherokee people *inside* the United States. Durham, "Jimmie Durham," 143.

46. Durham, "Belief in Europe," 291; Durham, *A Certain Lack of Coherence*, 249.

47. The phrase "provincializing Europe" is used by Indian postcolonial theorist Dipesh Chakrabarty, who argues that "places leave their imprints on thought in such a way as to call into question the idea of purely abstract categories." He especially urges scholarly reflexivity regarding the wide export of European historicism, which inflects the everyday habits of colonized subjects while paving over "local" conceptions of time and space. Chakrabarty, *Provincializing Europe*, xiii.

48. Durham is quoted in Paul Chaat Smith, "Delta One-Fifty," 34.

49. I draw this phrase from the major exhibition *The Decade Show: Frameworks of Identity in the 1980s*.

50. Said, "Reflections on Exile," 173.

51. Durham's title is in Cherokee. In an email to me on December 30, 2015, he noted that the title in the 1988 exhibition pamphlet contained a spelling error: "Ake" should be "Ale." I use the corrected title except when citing the pamphlet.

52. These terms, defined at length in chapter 2, are respectively borrowed from Taylor, *The Archive and the Repertoire*, and Latour, "'Thou Shalt Not Take the Lord's Name in Vain.'"

53. Anthes, "Contemporary Native Artists and International Biennale Culture," 115.

54. Here I draw on arguments in Foucault, *The Order of Things*, and Seth, *Europe's Indians*.

55. Terry Smith, "Introduction," 9.

One. "The Word for World"

The title quote is from Durham, *Mataoka Ake Attakulakula Anel Guledisgo Hnihi*, n.p.

1. Durham, "A Central Margin."

2. Patton, "The Agenda for the Eighties," 78.

3. Patton and many others involved in the show would likely agree with the viewpoint of prominent postcolonial theorist Homi K. Bhabha: "To interrogate 'identity'

rather than assert its inviolability represented the best version of minoritarian move." Bhabha, "Making Difference," 73. For critical studies addressing race and identity during this period, see English, *How to See a Work of Art in Total Darkness*, 27–70; González, *Subject to Display*; Cherise Smith, *Enacting Others*.

4. On subsequent attitudes toward art of the 1980s, see essays in *Artforum International*, 40th Anniversary Edition, parts I and II (2003); Molesworth, *This Will Have Been*. Postidentity phrases in the arts emerged in the early 2000s primarily to describe a new generation of black, Chicano, and Native artists producing work that aims to circumvent racial identity categories. For a concise summary of key artists, exhibitions, and debates and a fairly comprehensive bibliography, see Horton and Smith, "The Particulars of Postidentity." As we discussed in this introduction to a special section of *American Art*, "post-Indian" was popularized in the form of the traveling exhibition *Remix: New Modernities in a Post-Indian World*, cocurated by Gerald McMaster and Joe Baker at the National Museum of the American Indian and the Heard Museum in 2007. However, Gerald Vizenor first coined the term "postindian" at least as early as 1994 to signify Native peoples' rejection of colonial misnomers (the "simulations" I discuss later in this chapter), thereby clearing the way to reconnect to older forms of indigenous knowledge and collectivity, especially dynamic tribal storytelling practices. Vizenor's use of "postindian" is far closer in spirit to Durham's artistic trajectory than subsequent iterations, which will be clear by the end of this chapter. Vizenor, *Manifest Manners*; Vizenor and Lee, *Postindian Conversations*. One short essay we commissioned, Mark Watson's "Jimmie Durham's Building a Nation," contains an excellent discussion of Durham's 2005 installation, *Building a Nation*, in terms of its relevance to recent discourses of postidentity, postnationalism, and multiple modernities.

5. Durham, email to the author, April 24, 2012. Durham claimed that curators "dreamed up" identity to anesthetize the work of nonwhite artists whose ascendency challenged white norms and privileges in "Silly Crimes of the Academicians," an unpublished essay he circulated among friends in response to the exhibition *Don't You Know Who I Am? Art after Identity Politics* at M HKA in Antwerp in 2014. Durham, email to the author, July 19, 2014.

6. "Interview: Dirk Snauwaert in Conversation with Jimmie Durham," 9.

7. As this book goes to press, I am writing an essay for Durham's first solo exhibition in the United States in over two decades. See Horton, "Jimmie Durham's Stones and Bones." Curated by Anne Ellegood, the comprehensive retrospective *Jimmie Durham: At the Center of the World* opens at the Hammer Museum in January 2017, then travels to the Walker Art Center and the Whitney Museum of American Art.

8. Massey, *For Space*, 9. Massey took an integrated approach to theorizing space and time, with particular sensitivity to feminist and indigenous concerns. Her account resonates strongly with articulations of spatial thinking discussed by Durham, Vine Deloria Jr., and others discussed later in this chapter, as well as recent indigenous theorizations of transnationalism and cosmopolitanism by Philip J. Deloria, Maximilian C.

Forte, Shari M. Huhndorf, Jolene Rickard, Robert Warrior, and others mentioned in the introduction.

9. Durham and Fisher, "The Ground Has Been Covered."

10. In the 1960s, Italian film director Sergio Leone made "spaghetti westerns," featuring American cowboys and Mexicans more often than Indians, in Italy and Spain.

11. Said, "Reflections on Exile," 173.

12. Kaplan, *Questions of Travel*, 28.

13. Kaplan, *Questions of Travel*, 38, 45. This primitivist fantasy belongs to what Renato Rosaldo terms "imperialist nostalgia," whereby "the agents of colonialism long for the very forms of life they intentionally altered or destroyed." Rosaldo, "Imperialist Nostalgia," 107–8. Abigail Solomon-Godeau similarly critiqued the colonial motivations for French painter Paul Gauguin in Tahiti in her seminal essay "Going Native," discussed in chapter 4. Ruth B. Phillips argued that European artists in exile in North America were key to the development of primitivism in relation to Native American art in the early twentieth century. Phillips, "The Turn of the Primitive."

14. I thank A. Joan Saab for pointing out the Joe Hill connection, confirmed by Durham in conversation with the author, Rome, Italy, October 2011. See Foner, *The Case of Joe Hill*.

15. Rouch and Morin, *Chronique d'un été*. I draw this comparison without ascribing intentionality to the artist; Durham told me he was not aware of the resemblance between café scenes when he made *La poursuite du bonheur*. Durham in conversation with the author, Rome, Italy, October 2011.

16. Demos, *The Migrant Image*, 15. See also Kwon, *One Place after Another*, 156.

17. The Trail of Tears earned its name from the removal of the Choctaw Nation in 1831, but is most often used to describe the relocation of the Cherokee a few years later. Today the Cherokee Nation in Oklahoma hosts an excellent online resource including a timeline of the Trail of Tears, relevant government documents, and discussion of the aftermath of relocation: http://www.cherokee.org/AboutTheNation /History/TrailofTears/ABriefHistoryoftheTrailofTears.aspx.

18. Lippard, "Jimmie Durham," 64–65; Bossé and Garimorth, "Interview with Jimmie Durham," 14.

19. Durham, *Columbus Day*, 5.

20. Camnitzer, "Jimmie Durham," 8–9.

21. Durham, *Columbus Day*, 5.

22. Durham, *Columbus Day*, 5.

23. Quoted in Camnitzer, "Jimmie Durham," 9.

24. Camnitzer, "Jimmie Durham," 8; Bossé and Garimorth, "Interview with Jimmie Durham," 14.

25. See Josephy, Nagel, and Johnson, *Red Power*, for speeches and other primary documents by AIM leaders.

26. According to Vine Deloria, Indians had lost nearly 90 million acres through

land sales by 1934, many of them fraudulent. Vine Deloria, *Custer Died for Your Sins*, 53. The General Allotment Act is available at Indian Affairs: Laws and Treaties, Vol. 1, Laws: http://digital.library.okstate.edu/kappler/vol1/html_files/ses0033.html.

27. For more on this devastating period in American Indian policy, see Adams, *Education for Extinction*; Hoxie, *A Final Promise*. The BIA used blood quantum to determine who qualified for private land plots during the General Allotment Act and continues to issue a Certificate of Degree of Indian Blood. Today federally recognized tribal nations have independent criteria for determining membership (often including proof of ancestral enrollment and/or blood quantum), following a series of twentieth-century court cases establishing this precedent, especially the 1975 Indian Self-Determination Act and Education Assistance Act. Villazor, "Blood Quantum Land Laws and the Race versus Political Identity Dilemma," 108–9. On the complexity of blood quantum and its effects, see also Garroutte, *Real Indians*; Sturm, "Blood Politics, Racial Classification, and Cherokee National Identity."

28. For background on Indian treaty termination and relocation at midcentury, see Vine Deloria, *Custer Died for Your Sins*, 60–82; Cobb, *Native Activism in Cold War America*.

29. Smith and Warrior, *Like a Hurricane*, vii. See also Baylor, "Media Framing of Movement Protest." For broader accounts of Native activism before, during, and after AIM, see Johnson, Nagel, and Champagne, *American Indian Activism*; Cobb and Fowler, *Beyond Red Power*; Cobb, *Native Activism in Cold War America*.

30. Activists issued a twenty-point position paper entitled "An Indian Manifesto: Restitution, Reparations, Restoration of Lands for a Reconstruction of an Indian Future in America," available on the AIM website: http://www.aimovement.org/ggc/trailofbrokentreaties.html. See also Vine Deloria, *Behind the Trial of Broken Treaties*.

31. Vine Deloria, *God Is Red*, 4–24. The AIM and the IITC persist under different leadership today: http://www.aimovement.org/.

32. Vine Deloria, *God Is Red*, 66–67. See also Vine Deloria, *Custer Died for Your Sins*.

33. Vine Deloria, *God Is Red*, 63.

34. Vine Deloria, *God Is Red*, 10.

35. Durham, "American Indian Culture," in *A Certain Lack of Coherence*, 13–14. The original version was circulated as a study paper for the Native American Support Committee of AIM.

36. Durham, "American Indian Culture," 17, 15. For variations on this theme, see LaDuke, *All Our Relations*; Waters, *American Indian Thought*; Wildcat, *Red Alert!*

37. Durham, "American Indian Culture," 14. Deloria approached Durham's view when he stated that "revelation was seen as a continuous process of adjustment to the natural surroundings and not as a specific message valid for all times and places." Vine Deloria, *God Is Red*, 67.

38. Durham made a nearly identical argument about Native American art in 1986, writing, "Constant change—adaptability, the inclusion of new ways and new

material—is a tradition that our artists have particularly celebrated and have used to move and strengthen our societies. . . . Every object, every material brought in from Europe was taken and transformed with great energy." Durham, "Ni' Go Tlunh A Doh Ka," in *A Certain Lack of Coherence*, 108. See also Massey, *For Space*, 9.

39. Durham and Fisher, "The Ground Has Been Covered."

40. Durham, *A Certain Lack of Coherence*, vii.

41. Durham, "United Nations Conference on Indians" (January 1978), in *A Certain Lack of Coherence*, 27.

42. See "Declaration of Continuing Independence by the First International Indian Treaty Council at Standing Rock Indian Country, June 1974," reproduced on the International Indian Treaty Council website: http://www.iitc.org/about-iitc/the -declaration-of-continuing-independence-june-1974/.

43. Rickard, "Visualizing Sovereignty in the Time of Biometric Sensors," 469. Rickard summarized ideas laid out in Lyons, Mohawk, and Barreiro, "Spiritualism: The Highest Form of Political Consciousness," one of three papers given by Haude-nosaunee leaders before the UN in 1977.

44. Durham later surmised that although AIM efforts in Geneva garnered support from Cuba, Syria, and other countries beyond Europe, "no one had even come close to achieving UN action or resolution on a matter inside the US." Durham, "An Open Letter on Recent Developments in the American Indian Movement / International Indian Treaty Council," in *A Certain Lack of Coherence*, 47. One hundred forty-three member countries voted in favor of the declaration in 2007; the United States, Canada, New Zealand, and Australia abstained, although each later reversed its position under pressure from the international community. The declaration is available on the UN website: www.un.org/esa/socdev/unpfii/documents/DRIPS_en.pdf.

45. Huhndorf, *Mapping the Americas*, 11. See Alfred, *Wasáse*; Alfred, *Peace, Power, Righteousness*; Rickard, "Visualizing Sovereignty in the Time of Biometric Sensors," 465–86; Warrior, *Tribal Secrets*.

46. A recently uncovered video archive could make a considerable contribution to scholarship in this area. In the 1970s, Andrea Tonacci, an Italian filmmaker living in Brazil, traveled across the Americas recording interviews with indigenous leaders. Durham, together with Alves and art historian Richard William Hill, debuted the unseen video archive, titled *Indigenous Activism in the Americas: Andrea Tonacci's Film Archive*, at the Berlin Documentary Forum at Haus der Kulturen der Welt in Berlin on May 30, 2014.

47. Durham, "American Indian Culture," 15.

48. Durham, "An Open Letter on Recent Developments in the American Indian Movement / International Indian Treaty Council," 48.

49. "Red Power" is often used as a synonym for AIM. Deloria noted as early as 1969 that urban Indians were the center of activism and warned of the impending danger of

factionalism. Vine Deloria, *Custer Died for Your Sins*, 196–221. The importance of Deloria's prediction is discussed in Smith and Warrior, *Like a Hurricane*, 125.

50. Vizenor, *The People Named the Chippewa*, 130.

51. Jack Foley, "Interview with Gerald Vizenor," 310. See also Baudrillard, *Simulacra and Simulation*; Vizenor, *Manifest Manners*, 8–9.

52. Robert A. Lee, *Loosening the Seams*, 64. See also Baylor, "Media Framing of Movement Protest."

53. Durham discussed this issue with me, indicating his support for the indigenous feminist activist group, Women of All Red Nations, established in 1974 alongside the IITC. Durham in conversation with the author, Rome, Italy, October 2011. See also Huhndorf, *Mapping the Americas*; Andrea Smith, "Native American Feminism, Sovereignty, and Social Change," 117–19; Mihesuah, *Indigenous American Women*, 115–42. Disillusionment with the sexism of AIM-era nationalisms provided a key motivation for sisters Lisa Mayo, Gloria Miguel, and Muriel Miguel to form the indigenous-feminist Spiderwoman Theater in New York City in 1975. While their male peers staged dramas for the newspapers, they performed the painful intersection of patriarchy and colonialism with raucous humor. Katherine Young Evans, "'Our Lives Will Be Different Now.'"

54. Vizenor, *Manifest Manners*, 19.

55. Scholder, *Scholder/Indians*, 46. Kristine K. Ronan gave a brilliant reading of the relationship between AIM activism and Scholder's "Indian pop politics" in her dissertation, "Buffalo Dancer: The Biography of an Image."

56. Scholder publicly refused to be aligned with the activists, stating in 1971, "I don't dig Red Power and I don't identify with protest Indian art." Quoted in "Young Indians 'Dig' Fritz Scholder's Art," *Arizona Republic*, March 8, 1971. I discuss *Massacre at Wounded Knee* and other paintings by Scholder in Horton, "Painter, Traveler, Diplomat." Scholder avoided claiming a Native identity despite his one-quarter Luiseño heritage, was publicly ambivalent about the success of his Indian series, and stopped painting Native American portraits around 1980, just as Durham, Luna, and other artists in this book were developing their practices. See Paul Chaat Smith, "Monster Love," 25–35.

57. Durham and Fisher, "The Ground Has Been Covered," 101.

58. Durham wrote of his predecessors in 1990, "In the 1970s many American Indian artists rebelled against the decorative and nostalgic art demanded of us and began producing works reflecting the militancy of the times. But . . . it is a rarified and deliberately marginal sect of the art world that seeks comfort in [Indian] art. The Indian artists who were made into mini stars within that corner were R. C. Gorman and Fritz Scholder, who could perform squarely within the required frame but with little stylistic changes." Durham, "A Central Margin," 167. Similarly, in 1995 he stated, "I could have become a Fritz Scholder . . . who paints pictures of Indians. . . . I could see how silly that was, it was so obvious." "Interview: Dirk Snauwaert in Conversation with Jimmie Durham," 13.

59. For more on Heap of Birds's sign work, see Anthes, *Edgar Heap of Birds*; Anthes, "Ethics in a World of Strangers"; Lippard, "Signs of Unrest"; Morris, "Reading between the Lines"; Rushing, "In Our Language."

60. Durham, *Columbus Day*, 23.

61. The Museum of the American Indian was established by George Gustav Heye in 1916 to house his extensive collections of indigenous objects from the Americas. See Force, *Politics and the Museum of the American Indian*; Kidwell, "Every Last Dishcloth"; McMullen, "Reinventing George Heye." On the origins of Native American collections in ethnographic missions of the nineteenth and early twentieth centuries, see Berlo, *The Early Years of Native American Art History*.

62. González, *Subject to Display*, 2.

63. González, *Subject to Display*, 13.

64. This feature is discussed in Shiff, "The Necessity of Jimmie Durham's Jokes," 75–76.

65. Massey, *For Space*; Soja, *Postmodern Geographies*; Soja, "The Socio-Spatial Dialectic." Similar critiques issued from the discipline of anthropology appear in Low and Lawrence-Zúñiga, *The Anthropology of Space and Place*. The "spatial turn" was prompted in part by Henri Lefebvre's seminal 1974 text, *The Production of Space*, in which he addressed the social production of (primarily urban) space according to a dialectics of theory, practice, and imagination.

66. Ferguson et al., *Out There: Marginalization and Contemporary Cultures* (1990), a volume of essays that accompanied *The Decade Show* and addressed the exclusion of various groups from "dominant" cultures around the globe, is a case in point. See also hooks, "Choosing the Margin as a Space of Radical Openness"; Fraser, "An Artist's Statement." Darby English used the phrase "black representational space" in a similar manner in *How to See a Work of Art in Total Darkness* (27–70). Period conceptions of insiders and outsiders also referenced concrete divisions of wealth and race in urban spaces—for example, in Kobena Mercer's characterization of an "enclave of bohemian outsiders" on the Lower East Side of New York in Mercer, "Where the Streets Have No Name," 137. In *The Lure of the Local* (1998), Lucy R. Lippard answered the trend toward a dematerialized spatial imaginary by advocating for human connectedness to particular places understood as "intersections of nature, culture, history, and ideology" (7). However, she inadvertently romanticized the local as a retreat from the global forces of capitalism, as Kwon critiqued in *One Place after Another* (157–59).

67. Massey, *For Space*, 20–21. See also Massey, *Space, Place, and Gender*.

68. González, *Subject to Display*, 54; Deleuze and Guattari, *A Thousand Plateaus*. Although González cited Deleuze and Guattari, her use of these terms is equally indebted to anthropology, where deterritorialization has come to mean "a general weakening of the ties between culture and place, to the dislodging of cultural subjects and objects from particular or fixed locations in space and time." Inda and Rosaldo, *The Anthropology of Globalization*, 14. On installation as an inherently spatialized practice, see also Reiss, *From Margin to Center*; Bishop, *Installation Art*.

69. González, *Subject to Display*, 10. See especially Appadurai, *The Social Life of Things*; Brown, *Things*.

70. González, *Subject to Display*, 37.

71. *No Beads—No Trinkets* is the title of an exhibition that Heap of Birds curated in Geneva in 1984. Abbott, *I Stand in the Center of the Good*, 29–30.

72. This fragment from Durham's bulletin has been widely quoted and is usually attributed to its reproduction in Lippard, "Jimmie Durham," 66.

73. *Badger* is reproduced in Mulvey, Snauwaert, and Durant, *Jimmie Durham*, 99.

74. Durham, "Attending to the Words and the Bones," 48; Durham in conversation with the author, Rome, Italy, October 2011. A longer discussion and reproductions of this work appear in Horton, "Jimmie Durham's Stones and Bones," 82.

75. "Interview: Dirk Snauwaert in Conversation with Jimmie Durham," 17.

76. Excerpted in Kuoni, *Energy Plan for the Western Man*, 141. See also Blume, "Joseph Beuys' 'I Like America and America Likes Me.'"

77. Luna intended that his performance be both a parody and an homage, asking, "But isn't [Hollywood] a part of our reality?" Luna, "Sun and Moon Blues," 152.

78. Lippard, "Jimmie Durham," 55.

79. Shiff, "The Necessity of Jimmie Durham's Jokes," 79.

80. Shiff, "The Necessity of Jimmie Durham's Jokes," 80.

81. For a concise summary of the extensive anthropological literature on tricksters and a comparison with their role in poststructuralist discourse from a literary perspective, see Doueihi, "Trickster."

82. Spivak, "Can the Subaltern Speak?" Other seminal works of postcolonial theory widely read in the late twentieth century include Bhabha, *The Location of Culture*; Clifford, *The Predicament of Culture*; Said, *Orientalism*. Frantz Fanon's *Black Skin, White Masks*, cited by Durham in art and writing during the 1980s, was first translated into English in 1968.

83. Fisher, *Vampire in the Text*, 216.

84. Turney, "Ceci n'est pas Jimmie Durham," 431.

85. Lippard, "Jimmie Durham," 55, 63–68. See also Rushing, "Jimmie Durham."

86. In a related argument, Rasheed Araeen stated that by the late twentieth century, exile had "become a fundamental pillar of postcolonial cultural theory, and Said is often quoted to justify facile art practices on the basis of exile." Araeen's criticism is directed less at Said than at those who appropriate him. Araeen, "A New Beginning," 337. On the ubiquity of irony, Smith wrote, "It was the eighties. Irony and I had achieved a détente of sorts. He was pretty busy, flying around the country for important clients, but he would call up a couple of times a year and invite me over to his suite at the Plaza." Paul Chaat Smith, *Everything You Know about Indians Is Wrong*, 147.

87. McMaster, *Edward Poitras*, 38.

88. Ryan identifies "a sensibility, a spirit at work and at play in the practice of many . . . artists, grounded in a fundamentally comic world view and embodied in the

traditional Native American trickster. . . . Transcending geographical boundaries and tribal distinctions, it is most often characterized by frequent teasing, outrageous punning, constant wordplay, surprising association, extreme subtlety, layered and serious reference, and considerable compassion." Ryan, *The Trickster Shift*, xii. See also Ryan, "Postmodern Parody."

89. Ryan, "Postmodern Parody," 265. For more on *Coyote*, which Poitras repurposed for various artistic projects such as the Canadian Pavilion of the Venice Biennale in 1995, see McMaster, *Edward Poitras*, 92. Durham wrote about Poitras's bones as "our Grandfather Coyote" in an essay about Poitras's 1991 installation, *Marginal Recession*, at Dunlop Art Gallery in Regina, Canada. Durham, "Free Tickets," in *A Certain Lack of Coherence*, 207.

90. For Durham's assessment of this approach, see "A Central Margin," 167.

91. Durham, "A Central Margin," 167; Durham, "Savage Attacks on White Women as Usual," 19; Durham, "Ni' Go Tlunh A Doh Ka," in *A Certain Lack of Coherence*, 107–19.

92. WalkingStick, quoted in Patricia Malarcher, "The Meanings of 'Duality' in Art," *New York Times*, December 22, 1985, NJ16; WalkingStick, quoted in *What Follows*, a video documenting her residency in the Department of Fine Art, University of Colorado, Boulder, 1992, 38:00; Luna, email to the author, May 23, 2015.

93. Houle, "The Spiritual Legacy of the Ancient Ones," 45. See chapter 5 for further discussion of this essay.

94. Luna, "Everybody Wants to Be an Indian," presentation for the Eightieth Annual College Art Association Conference, Chicago, Illinois, February 12–15, 1992, archived on audiocassette, collection of the artist; Durland, "'Call Me in '93.'"

95. Luna, "I've Always Wanted to Be an American Indian."

96. McMaster, "Indigena," 66.

97. Quick-to-See Smith, *The Submuloc Show*, 3. Quick-to-See Smith was instrumental in consolidating a network of Native artists beginning in the late 1970s.

98. Durham, quoted in Quick-to-See Smith, *The Submuloc Show*, 9.

99. WalkingStick, quoted in Quick-to-See Smith, *The Submuloc Show*, 66.

100. For a discussion of this work, see Kastner, *Jaune Quick-to-See Smith*, 51–59.

101. L. Frank Baum, "Editorial," *Aberdeen Saturday Pioneer*, Aberdeen, South Dakota, December 20, 1890. Baum is quoted and *The Wizard Speaks, the Cavalry Listens* discussed in Valentino, "'Mistaken Identity,'" 70.

102. Durham related that allies at American Indian Contemporary Arts were willing to keep the show despite the potential legal ramifications, but decided in dialogue with the artist that it should go to the Luggage Store Gallery in order to protect their federal funding. Durham, email to the author, March 1, 2016.

103. For discussions, see Barker, "Indian™ U.S.A"; Grinde, "Who Is an American Indian?"; McMaster, "Borderzones." The Indian Arts and Crafts Act of 1990 is "a truth-in-advertising law that prohibits misrepresentation in marketing of Indian arts

and crafts products within the United States. It is illegal to offer or display for sale, or sell any art or craft product in a manner that falsely suggests it is Indian produced, an Indian product, or the product of a particular Indian or Indian Tribe or Indian arts and crafts organization, resident within the United States. For a first time violation of the Act, an individual can face civil or criminal penalties up to a $250,000 fine or a 5-year prison term, or both. If a business violates the Act, it can face civil penalties or can be prosecuted and fined up to $1,000,000. . . . Under the Act, an Indian is defined as a member of any federally or State recognized Indian Tribe, or an individual certified as an Indian artisan by an Indian Tribe." Quoted in U.S. Department of the Interior Indian Arts and Crafts Board, "The Indian Arts and Crafts Act of 1990": http://www .doi.gov/iacb/act.html.

104. A public airing of Durham's Cherokee identity took place in an exchange between Bradley and Ward Churchill, a former AIM activist and supporter of Durham's work who was likewise targeted as a "Wannabee." See Churchill, "Nobody's Pet Poodle." Bradley responded to Churchill's published essay in a circular, "The Columbus Syndrome and Ward Churchill Chief of the Wannabees, a Tribe of the Master Race," 1992, Heard Museum Artists Resource Collection, Jimmie Durham file. Shortly after, in response to an admiring article about Durham's work by Lippard in *Art in America* in 1993, Nancy Marie Mitchell (now Mithlo), a Chiricahua Apache scholar who has curated nine exhibitions of Native American art at the Venice Biennale since 1999 (see chapter 2), warned readers, "He knows your language, which boxes you need to check, which names to drop, and what injustices to cry." Durham responded to her attack with another ironic statement: "I am not Cherokee. I am not an American Indian. This is in concurrence with recent US legislation, because I am not enrolled on any reservation or in any American Indian community." Lippard replied, "I continue to admire Durham's failure to fit either Indian or mainstream norms. . . . Given his statement here, it looks as though his disillusion with communal infighting is now complete." Lippard, "Jimmie Durham"; Jimmie Durham, Lucy R. Lippard, and Nancy Marie Mitchell, "Letters," *Art in America* 81, no. 7 (July 1993): 23.

105. See, for example, Justice, "'Go Away Water!'"; Rifkin, *When Did Indians Become Straight*, both discussed in chapter 4.

106. WalkingStick, "Democracy, Inc.," 120–21. Durham discussed the General Allotment Act, the IACA, and their significance for Cherokee history in Papastergiadis and Turney, *On Becoming Authentic*, 31–37.

107. Jimmie Durham, open letter circulated in 1991, quoted in Shiff, "The Necessity of Jimmie Durham's Jokes," 75–76. For additional discussion, see Hill, "After Authenticity."

108. Papastergiadis and Turney, *On Becoming Authentic*, 31.

109. Quoted in Lippard, "Little Red Lies," 22.

110. "Interview: Dirk Snauwaert in Conversation with Jimmie Durham," 26. Note that Durham selectively reintroduced bones more than a decade later in works such as

Mulholland Drive (2007), composed of a decorated horse skull mounted on plywood and PVC pipe.

111. Anthes, "Contemporary Native Artists and International Biennial Culture," 124; Paul Chaat Smith, "Luna Remembers," 27. See also Lippard, "Little Red Lies," 22.

112. Said, "Reflections on Exile," 173.

113. Durham and Fisher, "The Ground Has Been Covered," 101.

114. In 1988, Durham also created a body of work addressing English oppression of the Irish during a residency at Orchard Gallery in Derry, Northern Ireland. The work hints at another vector of Durham's practice abroad, distinct from the historical preoccupations of *Mataoka Ale Attakulakula Anel Guledisgo Hnihi*, which explores comparative frameworks for anticolonial solidarities beyond specific national, racial, or cultural affiliations. Durham, . . . *Very Much Like the Wild Irish*. I discussed this tendency in Durham's recent work in "'Study It Lightly.'" After his relocation from Mexico in 1994, Durham called his new home "Eurasia": "I live on the continent of Eurasia and I am always trying to find the division between Europe and Asia," in Durham, *Ucelli/ Birds*, 94.

115. Durham, *Mataoka Ake Attakulakula Anel Guledisgo Hnihi*, n.p.

116. See Paula Gunn Allen, *Pocahontas*. On the long life of the "Indian princess" stereotype, including its subversion by contemporary Native American female artists, see Mithlo, *Our Indian Princess*.

117. Durham, *A Certain Lack of Coherence*, 221. In the pamphlet accompanying the exhibition, Durham explained his theory that Rolfe's story of Pocahontas and Smith "was taken whole-cloth from a book by Richard Hakluyt, published in London in 1603. Hakluyt's book, however, told the story with a heroic crusader captain and a beautiful Arab princess as the two characters." Hakluyt later moved to Virginia, where Rolfe may have encountered his "script." Durham, *Mataoka Ake Attakulakula Anel Guledisgo Hnihi*, n.p.

118. Sardar, "Walt Disney and the Double Victimization of Pocahontas," 193. Sardar referenced Mason, *Deconstructing America*.

119. Pueblo scholar Paula Gunn Allen answered simulations in the archive of Pocahontas by attempting to re-create "the entire life system: that community of living things, geography, climate, spirit people, and supernaturals" that surrounded her. In a review of Allen's book, Michelle LeMaster pointed out inaccuracies in Allen's account and argued that it should be understood as "an illuminating exercise in modern pan-Indian spirituality." Paula Gunn Allen, *Pocahontas*, 2; LeMaster, "Pocahontas," 779. See also Townsend, *Pocahontas and the Powhatan Dilemma*.

120. Durham, *Mataoka Ake Attakulakula Anel Guledisgo Hnihi*.

121. Tobacco was a profitable colonial commodity by the time Pocahontas traveled to England in 1616. The Jamestown colonists appropriated as much land as they could for the new plantations. Vaughan, *Transatlantic Encounters*, 90. See also Sessions, *The Shipcarvers' Art*.

122. Fisher, "In Search of the 'Inauthentic,'" 47.

123. Lippard, "Jimmie Durham," 68. Myths about Malinche serve a similar role in Mexican nationalism to those concerning Pocahontas in the United States. Anna Lanyon foregrounded this problem in *Malinche's Conquest*. See also Karttunen, *Between Worlds*; Townsend, *Malintzin's Choices*.

124. Mike Gabriel and Eric Goldberg, dirs., *Pocahontas* (Walt Disney, 1995).

125. Durham, *Mataoka Ake Attakulakula Anel Guledisgo Hnihi*. The painting is in the collection of the Smithsonian National Portrait Gallery in Washington, DC. For a discussion of the "whitening" of Pocahontas in this and other portraits, see Ickes, "The Sartorial and the Skin."

126. Vaughan, *Transatlantic Encounters*, 146–47.

127. De Certeau, *The Writing of History*, 216.

128. Jimmie Durham, "A Few Words Exchanged at Charleston," audio play, component of *Mataoka Ake Attakulakula Anel Guledisgo Hnihi*, 1988, 12:47 min., Matt's Gallery Archive. I thank director Robin Klassnik and the staff at Matt's Gallery for sharing an MP3 of the rediscovered cassette with me.

129. According to historian Jack D. Forbes, "From 1670 onward the English of South Carolina engaged regularly in the American slave trade, sending natives in the tens of thousands to the West Indies and other markets. . . . They were a major source of income for the British." Forbes, *Africans and Native Americans*, 56.

130. Durham was joined by friends from New York, Jay Johnson as 1st Cherokee and Robbie McCauley as 2nd Cherokee. Durham, email to the author, December 19, 2013.

131. Durham, *Mataoka Ake Attakulakula Anel Guledisgo Hnihi*, n.p.

132. Fabian, *Time and the Other*. On the complexity and variety of Native American approaches to history, see Philip J. Deloria, "Historiography"; Nabokov, *A Forest of Time*.

133. Durham, "Statement Presented to the U.S. House of Representatives' Merchant Marine and Fisheries Committee Hearings on the Re-Authorization of the Endangered Species Act / June 20, 1978," in Durham, *Columbus Day*, 70.

134. Durham, "Jimmie Durham," 145.

135. In a brief account of this work, Monika Siebert wrote evocatively, "Durham's indices return material presence to Indian ghosts, insisting on crowding out the immaterial ways of representing indigeneity." Siebert, *Indians Playing Indian*, 154. Mark Watson discussed the installation in his dissertation, "Diplomatic Aesthetics," to set up a longer discussion of Durham's 2005 installation, *Building a Nation* (86–92).

136. Durham, *Mataoka Ake Attakulakula Anel Guledisgo Hnihi*, n.p.

137. Kelly, "Notable Persons in Cherokee History," 10.

138. In 1900, anthropologist James Mooney translated the word "rattlesnake" from the eastern Cherokee dialect as "he has a bell." Ellison, *James Mooney's History, Myths, and Sacred Formulas of the Cherokees*, 295.

139. Durham, *Between the Furniture and the Building (Between a Rock and a Hard Place)*, 21.

140. The notion that words and material could be joined together runs against prevailing poststructural understandings of language as a system of signs apart from the world and subject to continual deferral. These issues are taken up in relation to art history in a seminal essay by Bal and Bryson, "Semiotics in Art History." See also the classic text of deconstruction: Derrida, "Différance."

141. Appleford, "Jimmie Durham and the Carpentry of Ambivalence," 93.

142. Durham, *Columbus Day*, 8.

143. Ellison, *James Mooney's History, Myths, and Sacred Formulas of the Cherokees*, 297–98.

144. Durham, *Mataoka Ake Attakulakula Anel Guledisgo Hnihi*, n.p.

Two. *"Now That We Are Christians"*

The title quote is from Tac, "Indian Life and Customs at Mission San Luis Rey," 101.

1. Tac, "Indian Life and Customs at Mission San Luis Rey," 88.

2. They attended San Fernando de México in Mexico City. In the late 1600s, Franciscan friars—who operated more missions in the Spanish-occupied Americas than any other religious order except the Jesuits—began to build a string of such missionary colleges abroad, supported by Rome and modeled after European antecedents. They aimed to train friars to reignite faith among Christians and convert indigenous peoples using their own languages. Weber, *Bárbaros*, 116–17.

3. I borrow this shorthand from Latour, "'Thou Shalt Not Take the Lord's Name in Vain,'" 219. See also Latour, *Rejoicing*. For extensive commentary on Latour's ideas about modernity, see chapter 5.

4. Luna is Payómkawichum, a band of the Luiseño distinct from Tac's Quechnajuisom people. However, Luna notes that they may be related through his great-great-grandmother. Conversation with the author, La Jolla Indian Reservation, July 5, 2015.

5. Luna, "Fasten Your Seat Belts, Prepare for Landing," 42.

6. Taylor, *The Archive and the Repertoire*, 59–60. For other citations and discussion of the "archival impulse" in contemporary art, see the introduction.

7. "Fondazione Querini Stampalia," www.querinistampalia.it. For details on Smith's installation, which took inspiration from the Querini Stampalia family collection, see Bittencourt and Katz, *Kiki Smith*.

8. Luna ordered his own designs, including gypsum flowers growing in his backyard, transformed into tapestries by a company in Belgium. Luna in conversation with the author, telephone, December 19, 2013.

9. Jorge Arevalo mixed the soundtrack specially for *Emendatio*. Jane Blocker suggests that the song "humorously [invokes] the stereotypical reference to the white man as a 'pale face.'" Blocker, "Ambivalent Entertainments," 66.

10. Luna, "Fasten Your Seat Belts, Prepare for Landing," 41.

11. Taylor, *The Archive and the Repertoire*, 19.

12. Taylor, *The Archive and the Repertoire*, 19–20.

13. Haas, "The Life and Writing of Luiseño Scholar Pablo Tac, 1820–1841," 9.

14. Taylor, *The Archive and the Repertoire*, 33–34.

15. As background to this theme, see Svetlana Boym's account of the transformation of nostalgia from a treatable disease to an incurable condition of modernity in *The Future of Nostalgia*. See also Rosaldo, "Imperialist Nostalgia."

16. Rebecca Schneider, "Archives," 102; Derrida, *Archive Fever*.

17. Nora, "Between Memory and History," 7.

18. Rebecca Schneider, "Archives," 102.

19. See Cohodas, *Basket Weavers for the California Curio Trade*; Hutchinson, *The Indian Craze*.

20. Haas, "The Life and Writing of Luiseño Scholar Pablo Tac, 1820–1841," 20.

21. Duhaut-Cilly, *A Voyage to California, the Sandwich Islands, and around the World in the Years 1826–1829*, 119.

22. Haas, "The Life and Writing of Luiseño Scholar Pablo Tac, 1820–1841," 3.

23. Haas, "The Life and Writing of Luiseño Scholar Pablo Tac, 1820–1841," 21–22; Stoler, *Along the Archival Grain*. Stoler's notion of "reading along the archival grain," although primarily concerned with the construction and limits of European colonial knowledge, leaves room for colonized subjects to insert their voices into official archives.

24. Rebecca Schneider, "Archives," 104; Haas, "The Life and Writing of Luiseño Scholar Pablo Tac, 1820–1841," 34.

25. Haas writes, "Textiles were among the most common imports to the missions, and textile factories and workrooms existed at each, creating cloth and clothing from the wool of each mission's many sheep." Haas, "'Raise Your Sword and I Will Eat You,'" 102.

26. Tac, "Indian Life and Customs at Mission San Luis Rey," 103.

27. Haas, "'Raise Your Sword and I Will Eat You,'" 101.

28. Tac, "Indian Life and Customs at Mission San Luis Rey," 102–3.

29. Blocker, "Ambivalent Entertainments," 67. See chapter 1 for a discussion of Gerald Vizenor's use of "simulations."

30. Luna in conversation with the author, La Jolla Indian Reservation, July 5, 2015.

31. Paul Chaat Smith, "Luna Remembers," 31. See chapter 1 for extensive discussion of AIM and relevant literature.

32. Luna told me that at one such conference, he saw a movie that "changed my whole focus in art." *The Exiles* (1961), by non-Native director Kent MacKenzie, represented a day in the lives of Native Americans who moved from reservations to Bunker Hill in Los Angeles as a result of the assimilationist U.S. Indian Relocation Act of 1956. Luna said, "This isn't Tonto. . . . These are things I grew up with at the bars. . . .

These are my uncles. . . . This is real to me." Luna in conversation with the author, La Jolla Indian Reservation, August 12, 2013, and July 5, 2015.

33. Luna, "Sun and Moon Blues," 149.

34. See also Blocker's discussion of *Artifact Piece* and other performances by Luna in "Failures of Self-Seeing."

35. Blocker, "Ambivalent Entertainments," 54. See also Phelan, *Unmarked*.

36. Rebecca Schneider, "Archives," 11.

37. Blocker, "Ambivalent Entertainments," 55.

38. Jones, "Live Art in Art History," 154.

39. González, *Subject to Display*, 31–33.

40. González, *Subject to Display*, 35–36. See chapter 1 for further discussion of González's scholarship. Kerri Sakamoto makes a similar argument, stating that Luna's artworks "cross the ground from self-made object to subject." Sakamoto, "Transgressions," 1.

41. Jones, "'The Artist Is Present,'" 18. See also Jones, "Introduction"; Lambert-Beatty, *Being Watched*; Lepecki, "The Body as Archive."

42. Lowe and Smith, *James Luna*, 12.

43. Louis Young, *The Decade Show*. Lord performed at the NMAI and the Museum of the North in Fairbanks, Alaska. Laura M. Evans, "The Artifact Piece and Artifact Piece, Revisited." Documentation can be seen on Lord's website: http://ericalord.com/home.html. Rebecca Belmore performed *Artifact 671B* (1988), a work indebted to *Artifact Piece*, in which she sat immobile on a blanket in a vitrine outside Thunder Bay Art Gallery in Vancouver, bearing an acquisition number drawn from the Liquor Control Board of Ontario's code for cheap red wine, a Shell Oil logo, and a Canadian flag upside-down on her back. She was protesting the Canadian government, which had given Shell support to drill on Lubicon Cree lands, as well as an exhibition of First Nations art that Shell sponsored at Calgary's Glenbow Museum in conjunction with the 1988 Winter Olympics. For a discussion of this and other performances, see *Rebecca Belmore*; Bradley and Rickard, *Rebecca Belmore*.

44. Blocker, "Ambivalent Entertainments," 56–57. Blocker's basic observation—that bodies, too, are subject to the logic of the archive and global processes of commodification—aligns with recent interest in "thing theory," especially evident in the work of anthropologist Arjun Appadurai and literary scholar Bill Brown. Appadurai argued that both people and objects live "social lives," during which they may cycle in and out of seemingly stable ontological categories of subject and object. This shared sociability in turn reveals those categories to be culturally constructed and unstable. To better account for everyday entanglements between people and objects, Brown preferred the more elusive and mutable term *thing*, which "really names less an object than a particular subject-object relation." He urged that we should be asking "not whether things are but what work they perform . . . not about things themselves but about the subject-object relation in particular temporal and spatial contexts." Brown's challenge becomes

all the more pressing under translation, if we consider—as I do whenever possible throughout this book—the ways in which indigenous languages and worldviews distribute agency among humans and other-than-human entities. Appadurai, *The Social Life of Things*; Brown, *Things*, 4, 7.

45. Luna, *James Luna*, n.p.

46. Luna in conversation with the author, La Jolla Indian Reservation, August 12, 2013.

47. Blocker, "Ambivalent Entertainments," 72.

48. Luna's *End of the Trail* is discussed in Blocker, "Failures of Self-Seeing," 21–22. James Earle Fraser's sculpture of a Native American slumped on the back of a stumbling horse, still holding his spear, was erected for the Panama-Pacific International Exposition in 1915. Fraser reiterated a canonical stereotype of the "disappearing Indian" that many contemporary Native artists have been determined to deconstruct. It is the defeated counterpart of the popular image of a cowboy riding into the sunset—upright—in the final scene of a Hollywood western. Fritz Scholder responded to this imagery in a lithographed silhouette, *Indian Cliché* (1978). Kent Monkman (Cree) recreates Jean-Léon Gérôme's *Pygmalion and Galatea* (c. 1890) in *Icon for a New Empire* (2007), featuring a Fraser-like sculpture brought to life by the kiss of an artist dressed like a colonial fur trader. See Joseph R. Wolin, "Kent Monkman's Two-Spirited Images Shake Up the Museum of the American Indian," *Time Out New York*, June 11, 2008, http://www.timeout.com/newyork/attractions/native-tongue.

49. Blocker, "Ambivalent Entertainments," 67. Blocker borrows a notion of the "mestizo mind" from Serge Gruzinski to argue that the artist draws on the "ambivalence inherent in composite worlds" to reject "categorical purity, any intellectual appeal to authenticity" (63–64). Finally, "to the degree that ambivalence involves the anxiety of conflicted desire, it is also an intellectual tool, one that makes a joke of being two things at once" (70). See Gruzinski, *The Mestizo Mind*. A similar argument about Luna's humorous response to the long-standing allegorical role of the "Indian" in the white imagination appears in Townsend-Gault, "Rebecca Belmore and James Luna on Location in Venice."

50. Blocker, "Ambivalent Entertainments," 67.

51. Rebecca Belmore achieves an analogous effect in *Fountain* in the nearby Canadian Pavilion of the Venice Biennale in 2005, when she projected a performance video on a sheet of falling water, as I have discussed at length in a previous essay. Horton, "Alone on the Snow, Alone on the Beach," 15.

52. Blocker, "Ambivalent Entertainments," 67.

53. James, *Picturesque Pala*. Both San Antonio de Pala and San Luis Rey missions have undergone significant renovations over the decades and no longer appear as they did when Tac lived there. See notes 24 and 27 in Tac, "Indian Life and Customs at Mission San Luis Rey," 95–96.

54. Hackel, *Children of Coyote, Missionaries of Saint Francis*, 163.

55. The equal-armed cross likewise appears in works by Kay WalkingStick and Robert Houle discussed in chapters 4 and 5, respectively.

56. Kroeber, "Basketry Designs of the Mission Indians," 12.

57. Tac, "Indian Life and Customs at Mission San Luis Rey," 104–6; Luna in conversation with the author, telephone, December 19, 2013.

58. George Cyprian Alston, "Chapel," *Catholic Encyclopedia*, vol. 3 (New York: Robert Appleton Company, 1908), http://www.newadvent.org/cathen/03574b.htm.

59. Weber, "Arts and Architecture, Force and Fear," 3.

60. Sylvest, *Motifs of Franciscan Mission Theory in Sixteenth Century New Spain Province of the Holy Gospel*, 44, 102–6.

61. Silverman, "Purgatory," 323.

62. Bargellini, "Art at the Missions of Northern New Spain," 68–69, 88. On the challenges faced by the Franciscans, see Curiel and Hackel, "Franciscan Missionaries in Late Colonial Sonora."

63. The story, drawn from Francisco Palóu's biography of Serra, is recounted in Holway, *The Art of the Old World in New Spain and the Mission Days of Alta California*, 146.

64. Nabokov and Easton, *Native American Architecture*, 314. See also Kroeber, *Handbook of the Indians of California*, 661–65.

65. Bean, "California Indian Shamanism and Folk Curing," 54–83.

66. Silverman, "Purgatory," 323. Silverman borrows the notion of "middle ground" from Richard White, *The Middle Ground*.

67. Hackel, *Children of Coyote, Missionaries of Saint Francis*, 168. A reproduction of the painting appears on p. 169.

68. Hackel, *Children of Coyote, Missionaries of Saint Francis*, 15–20; Kroeber, *Indian Myths of South Central California*, 199–201. In a performance called *Fire, Movement, Water, and Voices* at the Herron School of Art and Design, Indiana University Purdue in 2007, Luna played the roles of turtle, eagle, coyote, and diabetic "Uncle Jimmy," invoking connections to founding indigenous figures and stories in the midst of present challenges. Lee-Ann Martin, "Cross Over with Mr. Luna," 31–32.

69. Benjamin, "Theses on the Philosophy of History," 257, 262.

70. Latour, "'Thou Shalt Not Take the Lord's Name in Vain,'" 219.

71. Latour, "'Thou Shalt Not Take the Lord's Name in Vain,'" 232.

72. Latour, "'Thou Shalt Not Take the Lord's Name in Vain,'" 219. Benjamin, "Theses on the Philosophy of History," 259. Highly relevant here is Vine Deloria Jr.'s description of the conflict between temporal and spatial thinking, discussed already in the introduction and chapter 1. Vine Deloria, *God Is Red*.

73. Benjamin, "Theses on the Philosophy of History," 263.

74. Latour, "'Thou Shalt Not Take the Lord's Name in Vain,'" 218–19, 232; Latour, *Rejoicing*. Latour includes agnostics and atheists in his ethical gathering.

75. They are actually plain white feathers painted to look like eagle feathers. Luna

did not take advantage of U.S. government-issued eagle transport permits, which override prohibitions detailed in the U.S. Bald and Golden Eagle Protection Act to allow tribally enrolled Native Americans to travel outside the country with legally obtained feathers. See "Traveling Overseas with Eagle Items: Guidelines for U.S. Native Americans," http://www.fws.gov/le/travel-over-seas-with-eagle-items.html.

76. Nagel, "Art Out of Time," 234.

77. Nagel's examples range from Bauhaus architecture, to Robert Smithson's non-sites, to installations by Ilya Kabakov and Felix González-Torres. Perhaps the best-known example is Mark Rothko's commission of a suite of color field paintings for an interfaith chapel in Houston, Texas. See Barnes, *The Rothko Chapel*; Menil, *The Rothko Chapel*; Nodelman, *The Rothko Chapel Paintings*.

78. Luna in conversation with the author, telephone, December 19, 2013.

79. For discussions of the significant role of basketry in the Anglo "curio trade" spurred by the transcontinental rail travel in the nineteenth century, see Cohodas, "Louisa Keyser and the Cohns"; Cohodas, *Basket Weavers for the California Curio Trade*; Hutchinson, *The Indian Craze*. On related developments in New Mexico, especially Santa Fe, see Batkin, *The Native American Curio Trade in New Mexico*; Bernstein, *Santa Fe Indian Market*. For a theorization of the complex cultural meanings that adhere in Native arts sold as "souvenirs," see Phillips, *Trading Identities*.

80. Hedges, *Fibers and Forms*, 6–9.

81. I thank contemporary Kumeyaay basket weaver Eva Salazar for sharing her extensive knowledge of process with me in 2007, when I curated the exhibition *Weaving Connections*, at the California Center for the Arts in Escondido.

82. Timbrook, *Chumash Ethnobotany*, 12.

83. Potentially relevant here is Isleta Pueblo scholar Ted Jojola's theorization of the countless "migration spirals" appearing in baskets, pottery, and petroglyphs throughout the American Southwest. According to Jojola's "transformative model," spirals embody the cyclical migrations made by Native communities in pursuit of "experiential knowledge" in intimate relation to ecosystems of North America. After completing a journey in each of the four sacred directions, the clans return to their particular "origin or centerplace"—a geographically stable point on earth that has special spiritual significance for the group in question. In contrast to a closed circle, signaling closure or completion, Jojola asks us to imagine the two-dimensional spiral expanding into a dynamic three-dimensional helix—a move that parallels the activity of weaving a coiled basket. On returning to the centerplace, "the clan has not simply completed a cycle, but in the process of its experiential journey, its collective mind has been elevated or transformed to a higher ideological level of consciousness. . . . With movement comes not only enlightenment, but a force that ultimately results in adaptation and change in the community." Jojola, "Notes on Identity, Time, Space, and Place," 89–93.

84. Timbrook, "Native American Arts in the Spanish Missions," 327–30. See also Timbrook, "Six Chumash Presentation Baskets," 51–53.

85. Chumash women wielded political and spiritual power in their villages, both before and after European contact. Gamble, *The Chumash World at European Contact*, 216. However, it is uncertain whether Sitmelelene held such a position in the eyes of her community at the mission.

86. Miller, *Chumash*, 119.

87. For more on world fairs, see Greenhalgh, *Ephemeral Vistas*; Harvey, *Hybrids of Modernity*; Rydell and Gwinn, *Fair Representations*; Rydell, *World of Fairs*.

88. The number of countries hosting national pavilions expanded significantly in the 1930s and throughout the Cold War. The Arsenale, a guest-curated large-scale exhibition of the work of international artists, was added in 1980, echoing the format of most contemporary art biennales today. For general background on the history of the biennial, see Alloway, *The Venice Biennale*; Anthes, "Contemporary Native Artists and International Biennial Culture."

89. See, for example, Anthes, "Contemporary Native Artists and International Biennial Culture," 115; Rickard, "The Emergence of Global Indigenous Art," 56.

90. The text appeared in an artist's book that included drawings of the proposed work made with the help of Durham's friend, Mexican artist Abraham Cruzvillegas. Durham, *A Road Book*, 203, 37–38. In fact, Anne Ellegood of the Hirshhorn Museum (who is now at the University of California, Los Angeles, Hammer Museum), with Smith of the NMAI, pursued a bid to sponsor Durham and Sam Durant for the 2007 U.S. Pavilion, but a variety of "restrictions" convinced Durham to pull out before submitting. Anne Ellegood, email to the author, July 14, 2015. Durham's work has been included in the Arsenale group exhibition five times since 1993. The Solomon R. Guggenheim Foundation has owned the pavilion since 1980 and works with the U.S. Department of State to manage the exhibitions. Curators in the United States may submit proposals every two years, which are reviewed by the National Endowment for the Arts Federal Advisory Committee on International Exhibitions. The winning bid is forwarded to the Bureau of Educational and Cultural Affairs for final approval. "La Biennale di Venezia U.S. Pavilion": http://joanjonasvenice2015.com/la-biennale-di-venezia/. For more on the history of the U.S. Pavilion, see chapter 3 and Rylands, *Flying the Flag for Art*.

91. Vetrocq, "Venice Biennale," 115.

92. Anthes, "Contemporary Native Artists and International Biennial Culture," 116.

93. Mithlo, "Give, Give, Giving," 86. See also Mithlo, "Reappropriating Redskins"; Mithlo, "'We Have All Been Colonized.'"

94. Scholars have extensively explored the complex politics and history of this institution elsewhere. See Berlo and Jonaitis, "'Indian Country' on Washington's Mall"; Lonetree and Cobb-Greetham, *The National Museum of the American Indian*; Phillips, "Disrupting Past Paradigms"; Rickard, "Visualizing Sovereignty in the Time of Biometric Sensors"; Ronan, "Native Empowerment, the New Museology, and the National Museum of the American Indian"; Sleeper-Smith, *Contesting Knowledge*.

95. West, "Foreword," 10. For more on the events of 2005, see Bradley and Rickard,

Rebecca Belmore; Hill, "Built on Running Water"; Horton, "Alone on the Snow, Alone on the Beach"; Lee-Ann Martin, "The Waters of Venice"; Townsend-Gault, "Rebecca Belmore and James Luna on Location in Venice."

96. Fisher, *Global Visions*, xiii. Curators had already directly engaged this problem in mega-exhibitions with varying degrees of success in 1989, notably in *Magiciens de la Terre* at the Centre Pompidou and the Third Havana Biennial. See Steeds et al., *Making Art Global (Part 2)*; Weiss et al., *Making Art Global (Part 1)*.

97. Rickard, "The Local and the Global," 64–65.

98. McMaster, "Introduction," 20.

99. Mithlo, "Give, Give, Giving," 89.

100. Paul Chaat Smith, "Delta One-Fifty," 38.

101. See the artists' websites: www.jamesluna.com; www.rebeccabelmore.com; heapofbirds.ou.edu. One exception to the silence about Durham's work appears in the final pages of Anthes, "Contemporary Native Artists and International Biennial Culture," 22–25. Despite Durham's participation in the Arsenale in 2005, he was conspicuously absent from *Vision, Space, Desire*, reminding us that exclusion occurs on all sides.

102. See Demos, *The Migrant Image*; Kwon, *One Place after Another*; Pamela Lee, *Forgetting the Art World*.

103. Anthes, "Contemporary Native Artists and International Biennial Culture," 109. On nomadism, Anthes quotes Kwon, *One Place after Another*, 156.

104. Anthes, "Contemporary Native Artists and International Biennial Culture," 111.

105. Durham and Fisher, "The Ground Has Been Covered," 101.

106. For more on the installation and the broader context of Heap of Birds's work abroad, see Anthes, *Edgar Heap of Birds*, esp. 150–61; Anthes, "Ethics in a World of Strangers"; Ash-Milby and Lowe, *Most Serene Republics*. During a 1998 residency in Giverny, France, Arthur Amiotte retraced the journeys of his own ancestor, Luther Standing Bear, who traveled with Buffalo Bill Cody across Europe, in a series of collage works. See Berlo and Amiotte, *Arthur Amiotte*. Like Tac and the Ojibwa leader Maungwudaus (see chapter 5) before him, Standing Bear wrote an account of his people that included his travels in Europe, reproduced in Standing Bear, Brininstool, and Ellis, *My People the Sioux*. For more on Buffalo Bill in Europe, see Burns, "Innocence Abroad"; Griffin, *Four Years in Europe with Buffalo Bill*; Jonnes, *Eiffel's Tower*; Rydell and Kroes, *Buffalo Bill in Bologna*.

107. Anthes, *Edgar Heap of Birds*, 28. I discuss Heap of Birds's important work only briefly due to its thorough treatment in Anthes's book.

Three. "They Sent Me Way Out"

The title quote is from Seymour, *When the Rainbow Touches Down*, 245–46. An earlier version of this chapter was published as "A Cloudburst in Venice: Fred Kabotie and the US Pavilion of 1932," *American Art* 29, no. 1 (Spring 2015). Republished with permission of the publisher. I am grateful to the University of Chicago Press for granting me permission to reproduce this material here.

1. Rylands, *Flying the Flag for Art*, 56.

2. Brock, *George Bellows*, 142, 281–82.

3. The Taos Society of Artists was formally established in 1915 in the northern New Mexico community of Taos by Ernest Blumenschein, Joseph Henry Sharp, Bert Phillips, E. Irving Couse, Oscar E. Berninghaus, and W. Herbert Dunton, although Blumenschein and Phillips first visited in 1898. Robert R. White, *The Taos Society of Artists*, 1–5.

4. Hassrick and Cunningham, *In Contemporary Rhythm*, 190. Blumenschein's complex relationship to Pueblo cultures is explored in Scott, "Unwrapping Ernest L. Blumenschein's 'The Gift.'" See also Eldredge, Schimmel, and Truettner, *Art in New Mexico, 1900–1945*; Scott, *Strange Mixture*.

5. The model for the male figure was likely Jim Mirabal, a Native man from Taos Pueblo who appeared frequently in Ufer's work. Their relationship is explored in Ott, "Reform in Redface."

6. See chapter 2 for history and relevant citations regarding the Venice Biennale.

7. See, for example, Rickard, "The Emergence of Global Indigenous Art," 56; Anthes, "Contemporary Native Artists and International Biennial Culture," 115.

8. *XVIII Esposizione Biennale Internazionale d'Arte*, 287–88. The exceptions are two potters from San Ildefonso, Maria Martinez and Tonita Roybal, whose work was also claimed as an American modernism alongside that of the painters. For more on these artists, see Marriott, *María, the Potter of San Ildefonso*; Wade, "Straddling the Cultural Fence."

9. "My Idea of American Art," radio address by Dr. Christian Brinton, New York, December 1931, College Art Association. Amelia Elizabeth White Files, School for Advanced Research, Santa Fe, NM (hereafter EAW SAR), AC18.337.

10. Wimmer and Schiller, "Methodological Nationalism, the Social Sciences, and the Study of Migration"; Amelina et al., *Beyond Methodological Nationalism*.

11. An exception in the literature on early Pueblo painting is Janet Catherine Berlo's two-part essay exploring the publication of a series of limited-edition portfolios of prints of Native American paintings at an art publishing house in Nice, France, beginning in 1929. Berlo, "The Szwedzicki Portfolios."

12. Foundational texts are Broder, *Hopi Painting*; Brody, *Indian Painters and White Patrons*; Brody, *Pueblo Indian Painting*; Tanner, *Southwest Indian Painting*. For histories that include discussions of Dunn and the Studio School, see Bernstein and Rushing, *Modern by Tradition*; Dunn, *American Indian Painting of the Southwest and Plains Areas*; McGeough, *Through Their Eyes*. There was a parallel painting movement begun by five Kiowa artists known as the "Kiowa Five"—Monroe Tsatoke, Stephen Mopope, Spencer Asah, James Auchiah, and Jack Hokeah—in Oklahoma in the 1910s, resulting in formal arts training for Native students under Oscar B. Jacobson at the University of Oklahoma. See Ellison and Libhart, *Contemporary Southern Plains Indian Painting*. We

discussed other national and international developments related to Pueblo painting in 1932 in Horton and Berlo, "Pueblo Painting in 1932."

13. Quoted in Oxendine, "23 Contemporary Indian Artists," 58. For a description of subsequent debates about modernism and early Native painting as "Bambi art," see the preface to Anthes, *Native Moderns*, xi–xxvii. See also Gritton, *The Institute of American Indian Arts*.

14. I was able to locate *Mountain Sheep Dance* and *Snake Dance* but not *Hopi Rain God* because so little information was provided in the biennial catalogue.

15. For a history of the school, see Hyer, *One House, One Voice, One Heart*.

16. Trafzer, Keller, and Sisquoc, *Boarding School Blues*; David Wallace Adams, "Schooling the Hopi." In the first chapter of his autobiography, titled "Exile at Six," Kabotie recounted memories of the traumatic split between factions of Hopi in 1906 in response to government incursions. While some Hopi were willing to work with the government, Kabotie's family belonged to a faction that "wanted to be left alone to live in the old Hopi way, and did not want their children in school." Kabotie's family was temporarily uprooted from Shungopavi, and several of Kabotie's uncles were sent to Carlisle Indian School in Pennsylvania. Kabotie and Belknap, *Fred Kabotie, Hopi Indian Artist*, 1. Peter M. Whiteley gave an in-depth account of the split and its profound effects on Hopi society in *Deliberate Acts*.

17. McCoy, "Hopi Artist Fred Kabotie, 1900–1986," 42. J. J. Brody noted that Kabotie first visited in 1922. Brody, *Pueblo Indian Painting*, 90.

18. Kabotie and Belknap, *Fred Kabotie, Hopi Indian Artist*, 18.

19. "Indian Cannot Be Kept as He Was 100 Years Ago, Says Official; Progress Vital," *Santa Fe New Mexican*, May 11, 1916.

20. As Michel Foucault elaborated, modern institutions such as the military, prison, and school followed a disciplinary regime aimed at producing "docile bodies" suited to industrial labor. Crucial to this procedure was the ordered mapping of bodies in space and time. Foucault, *Discipline and Punish*, 144–51. For critiques of the modern organization of time, discussed throughout this book, see Vine Deloria, *God Is Red*; Fabian, *Time and the Other*; Latour, *We Have Never Been Modern*.

21. Lonergan and others who submitted reports to the Bureau of Indian Affairs in Washington, DC, later compiled into the notorious "Secret Dance File," are quoted in Jacobs, *Engendered Encounters*, 109. The files are held at the National Anthropological Archives, MS 7070, Smithsonian Institution, Washington, DC.

22. Jacobs, *Engendered Encounters*, 111.

23. This history is recounted in depth along with summaries of the students' biographies in Brody, *Pueblo Indian Painting*, 71–149. For a parallel account of antimodernism in New Mexico, see Flannery Burke, *From Greenwich Village to Taos*. Kabotie discussed his relationship with Velino Herrera and Awa Tsireh in Kabotie, "Odyssey of Three Native American Artists," 31–37. For more on Tonita Peña, see Gray, *Tonita Peña*; Jantzer-White, "Tonita Peña (Quah Ah), Pueblo Painter."

24. Penney and Roberts, "America's Pueblo Artists," 23, 36.

25. Quoted in Seymour, *When the Rainbow Touches Down*, 245–46.

26. In the catalogue that accompanied a major exhibition at the Wheelwright Museum in 2009, McGeough gathered interviews with early painters' families and friends to bolster her claim for their work as "visual documents of the artists' worldviews and cultural values, and as expressions of both individual and collective responses to a rapidly changing world." McGeough, *Through Their Eyes*, 10–11. Scott similarly argued that "artists were engaged in a two-way dialogue with colonial settlers, one conditioned by each participant's political needs and cultural and epistemological values." Scott, "Awa Tsireh and the Art of Subtle Resistance," 599. Welton positioned Kabotie at the start of the "Santa Fe style" and argued for respecting the multistoried dimensions of this history in her 2014 dissertation, "Fred Kabotie, Elizabeth Willis DeHuff, and the Genesis of the Santa Fe Style."

27. Conversation with Ed Kabotie, November 27, 2013. Kabotie's son, Michael, and grandson, Ed, both pursued careers as professional artists. For more on the relationship between generations, see Welton and Pearlstone, "Recontextualizing the Art of Fred and Michael Kabotie."

28. Appadurai, *The Social Life of Things*.

29. Penney and Roberts, "America's Pueblo Artists," 25. The authors actually refer to the paintings as "autoethnographic," following Mary Louise Pratt, *Imperial Eyes*.

30. Rushing, "Pictures of Katsina Tithu," 25; Brody, *Pueblo Indian Painting*, 4.

31. Most readings of the paintings, including those I just cited, fall somewhere between these poles.

32. Kabotie and Belknap, *Fred Kabotie, Hopi Indian Artist*, 28. There are numerous factual errors in Kabotie's autobiography, an oral account that was recorded and edited by Kabotie's friend, Bill Belknap. I nonetheless consider the book a reflection of what Kabotie chose to communicate about his life, a sentiment shared by his family. Conversation with Ed Kabotie, October 13, 2013. Note that I use the currently favored spellings, *Katsina* and *Katsinam* (plural). Since the word is a phonetic translation of Hopi language, spellings from quoted sources vary.

33. Seymour, *When the Rainbow Touches Down*, 246, 222.

34. Secakuku, "Katsinam," 112. Secakuku explained that Ma'saw, creator and ruler of the earth, gave the Hopis the mesas and charged them with the responsibility to maintain the harmony of the world through "bountiful harvests and the replenishment of sacred springs," in Secakuku, *Following the Sun and the Moon*, 2. While I have chosen to rely primarily on Hopi sources regarding the meaning of ceremonies, non-Hopi have published extensively on this topic—for example, in Loftin, *Religion and Hopi Life*; Schaafsma, *Kachinas in the Pueblo World*.

35. Sekaquaptewa, "Hopi Indian Ceremonies," 38.

36. A kiva is a circular subterranean structure used for ceremonies.

37. Knowledgeable Hopis can unlock meanings in these paintings that I cannot access.

I learned this firsthand when I shared reproductions of Fred Kabotie's works from the collections of the National Museum of the American Indian over breakfast at the Hopi Cultural Center with Ed Kabotie on October 13, 2013. Several Hopi families stopped by to offer spontaneous commentary on the images (though not about esoteric themes).

38. Sekaquaptewa, "Hopi Indian Ceremonies," 36; Secakuku, *Following the Sun and the Moon*, 88.

39. Brody, *Pueblo Indian Painting*, 96.

40. Quoted in Seymour, *When the Rainbow Touches Down*, 241.

41. Hopi artist Charles Loloma discussed the composition of songs drawn from sounds in the natural world in Seymour, *When the Rainbow Touches Down*.

42. See Udall, *John Marin in New Mexico*.

43. Strand, "American Water Colors at the Brooklyn Museum," 152.

44. Seymour DeKoven, "John Marin, Whitman of American Painting," *Magazine of the Art World, Chicago Evening Post*, June 1, 1926, 5. See also Tedeschi, "John Marin's Loaded Brush." The relationship between music, color, and form and a related crossover of sensory effects known as synaesthesia are common themes in transatlantic modernism. See, for example, Brougher and Mattis, *Visual Music*; Udall and Weekly, *Sensory Crossovers*.

45. Cohn, *Wash and Gouache*, 11.

46. Kabotie and Belknap, *Fred Kabotie, Hopi Indian Artist*, 28.

47. Bender and Marrinan, *The Culture of Diagram*, 23.

48. There is no equivalent to Western musical notation in Hopi. In fact, Hopi songs have stumped ethnomusicologists by refusing to conform to Western notation standards. List, *Stability and Variation in Hopi Song*, 21.

49. Kabotie and Belknap, *Fred Kabotie, Hopi Indian Artist*, 32, 39–40; Seymour, *When the Rainbow Touches Down*, 241.

50. Dahl, "The Rise and Fall of Literacy in Classical Music," 68.

51. Kabotie and Belknap, *Fred Kabotie, Hopi Indian Artist*, 247.

52. Bender and Marrinan, *The Culture of Diagram*, 23.

53. Secakuku, *Following the Sun and the Moon*, 2. John Loftin quoted Shungopavi elders during a collective speech to the commissioner of Indian affairs in 1951: "Our land, our religion, and our life are one." Loftin, *Religion and Hopi Life*, xxii.

54. Schaafsma, "Pueblo Painting and Place," 7.

55. Peter M. Whiteley explained, "Hopi navoti (traditional power/knowledge) adheres to particular social persons . . . and is fundamentally untransactable. Western commodifications of Hopi culture detach knowledge from its sentient agents and put it into (relatively) free circulation." Whiteley, *Rethinking Hopi Ethnography*, 3. Likewise, Cynthia Chavez Lamar wrote in a dissertation on the subject, "Pueblo people have beliefs that scholarship conveying esoteric information harbors a certain supernatural power which . . . can be unleashed if it is not handled by the proper practitioners." Chavez, "Negotiated Representations," 31.

56. Scholars often trace the emergence of "nonceremonial" painting to anthropologist Jesse Walter Fewkes's commission of Katsina drawings during his fieldwork at Hopi in 1900, first published in Fewkes, "Hopi Katcinas Drawn by Native Artists." While Kabotie and Polelonema painted in Santa Fe, Hopi artisans were also selling *Katsina tithu* (commonly referred to as Katsina dolls) to tourists and collectors. On the commodification and appropriation of Katsinam, see Pearlstone, *Katsina*; Kastner, "Changing Perspectives on Cultural Patrimony," 99–109. For a comprehensive account of changing religious life at Hopi in the twentieth century, see Clemmer, *Roads in the Sky*. Protocols are subject to ongoing debate and negotiation within and beyond the community, given the large numbers of Hopi who make a living as painters and carvers. The Hopi Cultural Preservation Office was established in 1989, circulating guidelines in response to the long history incursions by Anglos eager to access secret knowledge. See "Protocol for Research, Publication, and Recordings: Motion, Visual, Sound, Multimedia and other Mechanical Devices": http://www8.nau.edu/hcpo-p /ResProto.pdf. I requested review of the materials included in this chapter on multiple occasions, receiving only one reply through the Museum of Indian Arts and Culture, asking me not to publish *Young Men's Spring Ceremony*.

57. While this chapter deals exclusively with Kabotie's Santa Fe period, it is notable that after his return to Hopi in 1930, Kabotie forwent a diagrammatic mode altogether, painting illusionistic scenes of dances and reproducing symbolic forms from pottery and kiva murals. In 1933, the Fred Harvey Company commissioned Kabotie to paint a mural of the Hopi Snake Legend inside the Watchtower, a building designed by Mary Colter on the south rim of the Grand Canyon. Kabotie was also hired to paint reproductions of three-hundred-year-old murals from the Puebloan archaeological site of Awatovi for the exhibition *Indian Art of the United States* at the Museum of Modern Art in 1941. In 1949, Kabotie published a book in which he reproduced and interpreted ancient Mimbres pottery designs with support from a Guggenheim Fellowship. See Douglas and d'Harnoncourt, *Indian Art of the United States*; Kabotie, *Designs from the Ancient Mimbreños*; Welton, "The Watchtower Murals."

58. In an award-winning article about Awa Tsireh's work, Scott argued that protocols protecting esoteric information led Pueblo painters to omit elements present even in the public portion of dances, or alter symbols to redirect viewers away from sensitive material. Scott, "Awa Tsireh and the Art of Subtle Resistance." While all of the early artists shared some of the pressures outlined in Scott's valuable case study, the protocols of each Pueblo differ from one another and change over time, as do artists' relationships to their communities. In an interview in 1975, Kabotie noted that while Velino Herrera was condemned by members of Zia Pueblo for painting Katsinam, "never did I once paint anything secret and never was I ostracized by my pueblo." Quoted in Highwater, *Song from the Earth*, 142.

59. Secakuku, *Following the Sun and the Moon*, 36. My own experience of Kabotie's

paintings is impacted by attending numerous dances at the Rio Grande Pueblos, although I have only seen Tewa dances performed at Hopi.

60. Kabotie discussed the components of the dance and its significance in Seymour, *When the Rainbow Touches Down*, 260–61.

61. Roediger, *Ceremonial Costumes of the Pueblo Indians*, 219–20.

62. The effect is far more pronounced in *Young Men's Spring Ceremony* than in *Hopi Butterfly Dance*.

63. McCoy, "Hopi Artist Fred Kabotie, 1900–1986," 42.

64. Gilbert, *Education beyond the Mesas*, xxxi.

65. Gilbert, *Education beyond the Mesas*, xxx. Gilbert borrowed the phrase "turned the power" from Trafzer, Keller, and Sisquoc, *Boarding School Blues*.

66. Bourke, *The Snake-Dance of the Moquis of Arizona*, 163.

67. Fewkes, *Hopi Snake Ceremonies*, 986.

68. D. H. Lawrence, "Just Back from the Snake-Dance—Tired Out," *Laughing Horse*, no. 11 (1924): 4. See also Udall, "The Irresistible Other"; Dilworth, *Imagining Indians in the Southwest*.

69. Warburg, *Images from the Region of the Pueblo Indians of North America*. Warburg never actually witnessed a snake dance, although he lectured about it extensively. See Freedberg, "Pathos a Oraibi." On the fraught legacy of Warburg among contemporary Hopi, see Farago, "Epilogue."

70. Dilworth, *Imagining Indians in the Southwest*, 61.

71. Seymour, *When the Rainbow Touches Down*, 222. Of flute and snake dances held on alternative years, Secakuku wrote, "The purpose of these ceremonies is to bring the last summer rains to insure the maturity of corn and other crops before harvest, and to prepare the fields for the next planting season." Secakuku, *Following the Sun and the Moon*, 96.

72. Kabotie managed the Fred Harvey Company gift shop in the Grand Canyon in 1926. McCoy, "Hopi Artist Fred Kabotie, 1900–1986," 42.

73. Quoted in Highwater, *Song from the Earth*, 143.

74. Hewett, "Native American Artists."

75. Rushing, *Native American Art and the New York Avant-Garde*, 15. See also Sloan, "The Indian Dance from an Artist's Point of View."

76. Hartley, "Red Man Ceremonials," 7. See also Hartley, "The Scientific Esthetic of the Red Man I" and "The Scientific Esthetic of the Red Man II." For similar arguments, see Douglas, "Indian Art and American Art"; Douglas, "Indian Art as a Basis for American Art"; La Farge, "An Art That Is Really American"; Millington, "American Indian Water Colors." Allied accounts in the press surrounding the touring *Exposition of Indian Tribal Arts* in 1931 are archived in EAW SAR AC18 337 and John Sloan Collections, Organizational Records, Exposition of Indian Tribal Arts (hereafter JSC EITA).

77. Penney and Roberts, "America's Pueblo Artists," 32–33.

78. For more on American modernism, Pueblo dance bans, and related indigenous activism, see Scott, *Strange Mixture*; Wenger, *We Have a Religion*. On the broader search for a distinctly American art during these same years, see Corn, *The Great American Thing*.

79. Strand, "American Water Colors at the Brooklyn Museum," 151.

80. Troyen, "A War Waged on Paper," xiv. Troyen made the point that period constructions of O'Keeffe and Marin as untutored "primitives" belie the fact that they were both extremely well educated. Troyen, "A War Waged on Paper," xlv.

81. Rushing, *Native American Art and the New York Avant-Garde*, 99.

82. Sloan and La Farge, *Introduction to American Indian Art*, 1, 7.

83. "My Idea of American Art," radio address by Dr. Christian Brinton, New York, December 1931, The College Art Association, EAW SAR AC18.337. A thorough, critical discussion of the Exposition and other developments in Native American art in New York in the 1930s appears in Rushing, *Native American Art and the New York Avant-Garde*, 97–120.

84. Clark, *Leaves from an Artist's Memory*, 119. Clark conceived and ran the Grand Central Art Galleries as a cooperative system in which promising young American artists could sell work without losing enormous cuts to middlemen. Clarke, "The Grand Central Art Gallery, New York," *Art and Archaeology Magazine* 15, no. 6 (June 1923): 279. The pavilion was designed by New York–based architects Delano & Aldrich in 1929, the same year as the New York Museum of Modern Art and the Whitney Museum of American Art. Rylands, *Flying the Flag for Art*, 55.

85. Extensive correspondence between White and Sloan regarding the Seville and Venice exhibitions is archived at EAW SAR AC18.056, box 3, Exposition of Indian Tribal Arts folder.

86. Berlo, "The Szwedzicki Portfolios."

87. *Art News* 30, no. 36 (June 4, 1932): 12.

88. Antonio Maraini, letter to Walter L. Clark, December 13, 1931, Historical Archives of Contemporary Art (hereafter "ASAC"), Venice, Italy, ASAC 15. Maraini refers to Paul Manship, but I am uncertain about "Stern." It is possible that I have misread Maraini's handwriting.

89. Erwin S. Barrie, letter to Antonio Maraini, December 24, 1931, ASAC 15. Clark's own letters make it clear that he had not yet begun planning at this time. Clark, letter to Antonio Maraini, December 18, 1931, ASAC 15.

90. Barrie, letter to Antonio Maraini, January 25, 1931, ASAC 15. Barrie does not mention that pragmatic as much as aesthetic concerns likely influenced the decision. Discussions of financial constraints faced during the Great Depression pervade letters between organizers in the United States but are noticeably absent from the transatlantic correspondences. The Native-authored works were valued at rates far lower than the primarily oil canvases chosen for the other rooms, and watercolor paper was

light and easy to ship. This was especially important given evidence that the Galleries had not yet secured generous underwriting of the exhibition costs by George Pratt (Grand Central Trustee and benefactor of the Metropolitan Museum of Art) when the decision to exhibit Indian art was announced in January. Letters between Martin Birnbaum and Antonio Maraini, March 6–18, 1932, ASAC 15; Report of the Finance Committee of the Exposition of Indian Tribal Arts, February 13, 1931, JSC EITA, box 41.

91. *XVIII Esposizione Biennale Internazionale d'Arte*, 280.

92. *XVIII Esposizione Biennale Internazionale d'Arte*, 281. Robert Henri was a leader of the Ashcan School, a group of realist painters known for their work in poor neighborhoods of New York City in the early twentieth century. Sloan also belonged to this group.

93. A selection of textiles, pottery, and paintings from New Mexico filled the fireplace and covered the mantels and walls of the ambassador's bedroom of the U.S. Consular building at the Ibero-American Exposition, foreshadowing the appearance of Indian art as modernist home décor in *Indian Art of the United States* in 1941. EAW SAR AC18–346. On this domestic trend, see Douglas and d'Harnoncourt, *Indian Art of the United States*; Hutchinson, *The Indian Craze*; Helen Johnson Keyes, "Tribal Arts for American Homes," *Christian Science Monitor*, January 16, 1932; Rushing, "Marketing the Affinity of the Primitive and the Modern."

94. Sloan and La Farge, *Introduction to American Indian Art*, 7; Hartley, "Red Man Ceremonials," 7.

95. Walter L. Clark, letter to Antonio Maraini, June 2, 1932, ASAC 15.

96. Martin Birnbaum, letter to Yoi Maraini, June 13, 1932, ASAC 15.

97. Birnbaum's account of silence in the press is exaggerated. In a blurb in the *New York Times*, he is quoted as declaring that the indigenous gallery was "the most popular exhibition of the entire display of all the nations." He may have prompted a reporter for *Art News* to rave, "Not only was this feature an outstanding success in our own national representation, but the Indian room was acclaimed as the most popular exhibition among all the rich and varied displays there assembled." "Italy Honors W. L. Clark," *New York Times*, May 25, 1932, 49; "Indian Art," *Art News* 30, no. 36 (1932): 12.

98. Francesco Monotti, "Americans in Venice," *New York Times*, August 28, 1932, XX8.

99. Cecchi, "Disegni Indiani," 566.

100. Cecchi, "Disegni Indiani," 566.

101. Cecchi, "Disegni Indiani," 573. By "some universities" Cecchi probably meant the University of Oklahoma and the newly opened Studio School of the Santa Fe Indian School. A lengthier discussion of Cecchi's essay appears in Horton and Berlo, "Pueblo Painting in 1932."

102. For a description of the events leading to Grand Central Art Galleries' withdrawal from the Biennale in 1936, see Rylands, *Flying the Flag for Art*, 63–69. Although Cecchi signed the antifascist Manifesto in Italy in 1925, by the early 1930s

he had adopted a more conservative attitude toward both art and politics, looking to Mussolini's government to preserve Italy's classical heritage in the face of encroaching modernity. Burdett, *Journeys through Fascism*, 14–15. See also Alloway, *The Venice Biennale, 1895–1968*, 116–17. On the spread of fascism in Europe in the 1930s, see Large, *Between Two Fires*.

103. Kabotie, *Designs from the Ancient Mimbreños*, 36.

104. Secakuku, *Following the Sun and the Moon*, 35–36.

105. John Sloan, letter to Charles H. Rhoads, Commissioner of Indian Affairs, Department of the Interior, July 23, 1932; letters between Amelia Elizabeth White and Dolly Sloan, October 3–November 14, 1932, EAW SAR AC18.056.1.

106. Erwin S. Barrie, letter to Romolo Bazzioni, Administrative Director of the Venice Biennale, April 24, 1934, ASAC 15.

107. Terry Smith, "Introduction," 8–9, 13. See also Terry Smith, *What Is Contemporary Art?*

Four. "Dance Is the One Activity"

The title quote is from WalkingStick in conversation with the author, December 19, 2013, Queens, NY.

1. WalkingStick in conversation with the author, December 15, 2014, Easton, PA; email to the author, December 8, 2015. The relationship between WalkingStick's Catholic faith and her artistic experiences abroad is explored in Seppi, "The Artist in Italy." Seppi's essay appears in a significant catalogue accompanying a retrospective of WalkingStick's work at the National Museum of the American Indian in 2015; along with that book, Seppi's 2005 dissertation offers the most comprehensive and in-depth treatment of WalkingStick's life and work to date. See Ash-Milby and Penney, *Kay WalkingStick*; Roberts (now Seppi), "Beyond the Body."

2. Eloise Quiñones Keber discussed the complex issue of establishing a date and provenance for Codex Vaticanus A in *Codex Telleriano-Remensis*, 129–30.

3. Keber, *Codex Telleriano-Remensis*, 165–66; Keber, "Collecting Cultures," 238. Keber included translations of numerous Christianized annotations in "Collecting Cultures," 237–38.

4. Nicholson, *Topiltzin Quetzalcoatl*, 65.

5. Keber, *Codex Telleriano-Remensis*, 110; Keber, "Collecting Cultures," 236.

6. Mignolo, *The Darker Side of the Renaissance*.

7. WalkingStick, email to the author, December 8, 2015.

8. I draw this connection without ascribing intention to the artist. In an email to me on December 8, 2015, WalkingStick was clear that her experiences in Italy were about artistic, not scholarly, engagement.

9. Seth, *Europe's Indians*, 19–59.

10. Solomon-Godeau, "Going Native," 120.

11. WalkingStick in conversation with the author, December 19, 2013, Queens, NY. WalkingStick earned a BFA from Arcadia University (formerly Beaver College) in Pennsylvania in 1959 and an MFA at the Pratt Institute in Brooklyn in 1975, and taught at Cornell University from 1995 to 2005.

12. Jardin, *Worldly Goods*, 9. For early collecting practices in Europe, see Impey and MacGregor, *The Origins of Museums*; Farago, *Reframing the Renaissance*.

13. Kay WalkingStick, email to the author, December 10, 2015. The black devil is from a painting by Maestro dell'Avicenna, *Paradiso e Inferno* (c. 1435), in the Pinacoteca Nazionale di Bologna.

14. WalkingStick in conversation with the author, December 19, 2013, Queens, NY.

15. Solomon-Godeau, "Going Native," 120.

16. Foucault, *The Order of Things*, 19.

17. Foucault, *The Order of Things*, 21.

18. Foucault, *The Order of Things*, 21–23.

19. Foucault, *The Order of Things*, 39.

20. Foucault, *The Order of Things*, 30.

21. Bambach, *Drawing and Painting in the Italian Renaissance Workshop*, 81.

22. Bambach, *Drawing and Painting in the Italian Renaissance Workshop*, 83.

23. Quoted in the Codex Urbinas (fol. 39 verso), reproduced in Kemp, *Leonardo on Painting*, 193.

24. Seth, *Europe's Indians*, 57. On the complex and overlapping temporalities of Renaissance art, see Nagel and Wood, *Anachronic Renaissance*. Seth's analysis runs against the grain of established accounts of the conquest such as Todorov, *The Conquest of America*, which takes as its subject "the discovery self makes of the other" (3).

25. Seth, *Europe's Indians*, 14.

26. Seth, *Europe's Indians*, 56–57.

27. Nicholson, *Topiltzin Quetzalcoatl*, 70.

28. Pohl and Lyons, *The Aztec Pantheon and the Art of Empire*, 17. Scholars today consider the Florentine Codex to be the most complete source of information about Aztec culture.

29. Pohl and Lyons, *The Aztec Pantheon and the Art of Empire*, 35–36.

30. Keber, "The Use of Native Pictorial Sources and What Was Made of Them in Deity Images of the Florentine Codex," paper presented at the conference *Visual and Textual Dialogues in Colonial Mexico and Europe: The Florentine Codex*, University of California, Los Angeles, April 17–18, 2015; Keber, *Codex Telleriano-Remensis*, 111.

31. Pohl and Lyons, *The Aztec Pantheon and the Art of Empire*, 1.

32. Gruzinski, *The Mestizo Mind*, 36–37.

33. Magaloni-Kerpel, "Painting a New Era," 126. She discussed book 12, a rare and extensive interpretation of the conquest written by Aztecs who lived through it. For a translation of the Nahuatl text, see Lockhart, *We People Here*, 27–36.

34. Magaloni-Kerpel, "Painting a New Era," 128.

35. Keber, *Codex Telleriano-Remensis*, 177.

36. Peterson, "Synthesis and Survival," 20.

37. Pohl and Lyons, *The Aztec Pantheon and the Art of Empire*, 76–77.

38. Russo, *The Untranslatable Image*, 12–13.

39. Foucault, *The Order of Things*, 30.

40. Foucault, *The Order of Things*, 47–49; Seth, *Europe's Indians*, 61–63.

41. Seth, *Europe's Indians*, 175.

42. Benjamin, "On the Mimetic Faculty," 160–61.

43. Benjamin, "On the Mimetic Faculty," 161. On his first encounter with the people of Tierra del Fuego in 1832, Charles Darwin wrote in his diary that they possessed a unique "power of mimicry . . . a consequence of the more practiced habits of perception and keener senses, common to all men in a savage state, as compared with those long civilized." Darwin, *Journal of Researches*, 206. For an analysis of this passage, see Taussig, *Mimesis and Alterity*, 70–81.

44. Franklin and McKinnon, "Introduction," 6.

45. Superintendent of Pueblo Day Schools P. T. Lonergan reporting on Pueblo dances to the federal government in 1915, quoted in Jacobs, *Engendered Encounters*, 109; Rifkin, *When Did Indians Become Straight?*, 6. See also Scott, *Strange Mixture*.

46. Justice, "'Go Away Water!,'" 151.

47. Hartley, "Red Man Ceremonials," 7.

48. Benjamin, "On the Mimetic Faculty," 161; Rosaldo, "Imperialist Nostalgia."

49. For a review of relevant anthropological and interdisciplinary literature on kinship, see Rifkin, *When Did Indians Become Straight?*, 3–43. See also the important compilation by Franklin and McKinnon, *Relative Values*. On poststructuralist theories of human-animal kinship, see Oliver, *Animal Lessons*.

50. Of the variable meanings of the symbol, WalkingStick wrote, "The cross symbolizes the four sacred directions, and has that meaning to me because it directly addresses the earth and its spirit, but if it is seen as a Christian cross or a plus sign or the astrological sign for Gaia, that's fine, too. All of these meanings are appropriate." WalkingStick, "Seeking the Spiritual," 185. Further discussion of the cross appears in chapters 2 and 5.

51. Hartley, "Red Man Ceremonials," 7.

52. WalkingStick had her first solo exhibition in New York at Cannabis Gallery in 1969 while teaching art in a variety of part-time positions. See Ash-Milby, "A Life," 31.

53. Kay WalkingStick, "On the Decade Show," unpublished lecture, c. 1990, 2. Heard Museum Artists Resource Collection, Kay WalkingStick file (hereafter HMARC KW), Box 1.

54. WalkingStick said, "The Cherokee never had tepees—they lived in permanent dwellings—but the tepee is kind of a symbol of Indianness to a white world." Quoted in Abbott, *I Stand in the Center of the Good*, 272. She recalled that a professor at Pratt responded that it was "too ethnic": "By that time, it was more or less OK to

be a woman, but still not OK to be other than white." WalkingStick, "On the Decade Show," 2.

55. WalkingStick, quoted in Archuleta, "Kay WalkingStick," 18.

56. WalkingStick, quoted in *What Follows*, documentary video of an artist's residency in the Department of Fine Art, University of Colorado, Boulder, 1992, 38:00. WalkingStick relates that Quick-to-See Smith first contacted her around 1978 in WalkingStick, "On the Decade Show," 3. Refer to chapter 1 for further discussion of period exhibition contexts for Native Americans.

57. For discussions of Hartley's and Gottlieb's relationship to Native American art, respectively, see Rushing, *Native American Art and the New York Avant-Garde*, 55–58, 161–68.

58. Thomas W. Leavitt, "Foreword," in Cotter, *Kay WalkingStick Paintings*, 3. For a critique of WalkingStick's reception, see Valentino, "'Mistaken Identity.'"

59. WalkingStick, "Seeking the Spiritual," 185. When she began the *Chief Joseph* series, WalkingStick cited various examples of "fabric draped or stretched over or around formal straight, structural lines," including clotheslines, tepees, and bridges, as the inspiration for what was ultimately intended to be a synthetic, nonspecific form. WalkingStick, "A Photographic Record of an Exhibition of Paintings with a Corollary Statement by Kay WalkingStick," MFA thesis, Pratt Institute, 1975, 3. Heard Museum Archive, Kay WalkingStick Collection (hereafter HMA KWC), RC165:536.

60. The MoMA show coincided with the publication of David Schneider's *A Critique of the Study of Kinship*, credited as the first major study to expose the Eurocentric racial determinism lurking in kinship discourse. Schneider argued that "the study of kinship derives directly and practically unaltered from the ethnoepistemology of European culture." David Schneider, *A Critique of the Study of Kinship*, 175.

61. Rubin, "Modernist Primitivism," 2.

62. Foster, "The 'Primitive' Unconscious of Modern Art," 45–46.

63. Solomon-Godeau, "Going Native," 120.

64. The classic study of artistic primitivism is Robert Goldwater's 1966 *Primitivism in Modern Art*. For other historical accounts, see Flam and Deutch, *Primitivism and Twentieth Century Art*. Additional critiques of primitivism in the wake of the 1984 show include Errington, *The Death of Authentic Primitive Art*; Hiller, *The Myth of Primitivism*; Krauss, "Preying on 'Primitivism'"; Price, *Primitive Art in Civilized Places*; Sweeney, *From Fetish to Subject*. Accounts that address the occluded agencies of Native Americans include Anthes, *Native Moderns*; Hutchinson, *The Indian Craze*; Phillips, "The Turn of the Primitive"; Rushing, *Native American Art and the New York Avant-Garde*.

65. R. C. Gorman, quoted in Oxendine, "23 Contemporary Indian Artists," 58; Anthes, *Native Moderns*, xi–xxvii; Gritton, *The Institute of American Indian Arts*.

66. WalkingStick, "Native American Art in the Postmodern Era," 15.

67. WalkingStick, quoted in Abbott, *I Stand in the Center of the Good*, 278.

68. Statement by WalkingStick, June 27, 1985, HMARC KW, Box 1.

69. Schaafsma, "Pueblo Painting and Place," 7. See also Jojola, "Notes on Identity, Time, Space, and Place."

70. See Ash-Milby and Penney, *Kay WalkingStick*, especially essays by Penney and Seppi. WalkingStick corroborated these views, speaking of the two different kinds of memory embodied in the diptychs: one short-term, like a snapshot, the other belonging to the earth that "reaches back into history to the beginning of time, but also stretches forward to the unknown future." Quoted in Abbott, *I Stand in the Center of the Good*, 27. In a letter to Lucy Lippard in 1985 she wrote, "Now, the diptych form is interesting to me because I am biracial. Two sides singing in concert, each very different from the other yet united as a whole." Quoted in Lippard, *Mixed Blessings*, 186.

71. Vezolles, "Personal Journeys," 56; Robert Yoskowitz, "Kay WalkingStick," *Arts Magazine* 54, no. 10 (June 1980): 12. See also Penney, *Native American Art Masterpieces*, 112.

72. WalkingStick credited a semester she spent as a visiting artist at Fort Lewis College in Durango, Colorado, in 1984 with prompting her interest in landscape painting. WalkingStick, email to Thomas Howe, May 27, 1999, HMA KWC, RC165:2412.

73. WalkingStick, email to Thomas Howe, May 27, 1999, HMA KWC, RC165:2412. In 1984, WalkingStick requested to visit Georgia O'Keeffe in New Mexico using a grant she received from the National Endowment for the Arts; she was politely refused. WalkingStick, letter to Juan Hamilton, January 30, 1984, and response from Judy Lopez, February 7, 1984, HMA KWC, RC165:1198–99. On O'Keeffe's relationship to Pueblo art, see Lynes and Kastner, *Georgia O'Keeffe in New Mexico.*

74. Phillips, "Aesthetic Primitivism Revisited," 10.

75. Flatley, "Like," 75–76.

76. WalkingStick, "Democracy, Inc.," 20.

77. WalkingStick, "Democracy, Inc.," 21. See chapter 1 for additional sources and commentary on the relationship between laws.

78. Justice, "'Go Away Water!,'" 150.

79. WalkingStick, quoted in *What Follows.*

80. WalkingStick, quoted in Patricia Malarcher, "The Meanings of 'Duality' in Art," *New York Times*, December 22, 1985, NJ16; WalkingStick, quoted in *What Follows.*

81. Hill, "After Authenticity," 107.

82. Justice, "'Go Away Water!,'" 150–51.

83. See, for example, LaDuke, *All Our Relations*. Plains Cree curator Gerald McMaster and Netherlandish curator Catherine de Zegher, artistic codirectors of the Eighteenth Biennale of Sydney in 2012, conceived of a global exhibition titled *all our relations*, which I discussed briefly in the introduction. The phrase was selected by the curators not only for its ecological import, but as a means of conceptualizing kinship and solidarity among diversely situated artists from around the world. A different model emerged in *Sakahàn: International Indigenous Art* at the National Gallery of

Canada in Ottawa in 2013, the first mega-exhibition dedicated entirely to indigenous artists, loosely and inconsistently defined as those living in ongoing colonial situations in Australia, New Zealand, Canada, India, Japan, and elsewhere. The exhibition raised questions about the definition of "indigenous" and whether a global exhibition based exclusively on such an identity perpetuates a colonial binary of selves and others in reverse (and if so, to what ends). In an illuminating review, Richard William Hill proposed that we might "think of 'Indigenous' as a theme rather than the identity of the participants, and open it up further to potential non-Indigenous allies whom we would like to bring into the conversation." Hill, "Sakahàn," 42. The shift from blood relations to creative kin I see occurring in WalkingStick's work bears out such a possibility. See de Zegher and McMaster, *The 18th Biennale of Sydney*; Hill, Hopkins, and LaLonde, *Sakahàn*.

84. Feminist scholar Kelly Oliver similarly wrote, "How do we become kin if not through descent? . . . Perhaps . . . both our sameness and our differences are ultimately undecidable, even though we are forced to decide everyday as a matter of practical relationship and ethical obligation." Oliver, *Animal Lessons*, 224.

85. See Nemiroff, Houle, and Townsend-Gault, *Land, Spirit, Power*; Phil Young, *For the Seventh Generation*; Quick-to-See Smith, *The Submuloc Show*. WalkingStick wrote to Joe Federson, who helped to curate *The Submuloc Show / Columbus Wohs*, "I do not usually make such politically loaded art . . . but for this it seemed right." WalkingStick, letter to Joe Federson, March 1, 1991, HMA KWC, RC165–2330.

86. *Where Are the Generations?* was exhibited in *Land, Spirit, Power: First Nations at the National Gallery of Canada*, discussed in chapter 1. Describing *Tears* (1991), a related sculpture that included a funereal bundle and a repoussé panel bearing the same inscription (exhibited in *The Submuloc Show / Columbus Wohs*), WalkingStick stated that white children learn copper repoussé in summer camp, the "'Indian crafts' part of US education . . . [that] takes the place of actually learning about First Nation Peoples (I like the Canadian term)." She noted that the numbers address Native populations north of the Rio Grande and are widely debated. The artist was beginning to learn Cherokee at the time she made these works (*Land, Spirit, Power: First Nations at the National Gallery of Canada*). A written form of the Cherokee language was developed by the man known as Sequoyah between 1809 and 1821. An account of this history is available on the Cherokee Nation website, "Sequoyah and the Cherokee Syllabary": http://www.cherokee.org/AboutTheNation/History/Facts/SequoyahandtheCherokee Syllabary.aspx; see also Bender, *Signs of Cherokee Culture*.

87. Kay WalkingStick, *Terra Corpo*, 1996. Watercolor sketchbook in the collection of the artist.

88. Seppi, "The Artist in Italy," 128.

89. WalkingStick, "A Roman Holiday: A Journey of Visual Discovery," notes for a lecture presented at *Creativity: A Symposium*, Cornell University, April 18, 1997, 2, HMA KWC, RC165(2)310. The name Kokopelli is a rough phonetic translation of a Hopi

Katsina associated with human and vegetal fertility, often confused with the distinctive hunchback flute player found throughout the Four Corners region of the Southwest since about AD 800. Malotki, *Kokopelli*, 6–9.

90. Larson, *Greek Nymphs*, 91–98.

91. The notion of "Mitochondrial Eve" has fascinated the artist since the early 1980s. See WalkingStick's *Genesis / Violent Garden* (1981), in the permanent collection of the Met, one of several early works that references these theories. WalkingStick in conversation with the author, December 15, 2014, Easton, PA. See also Seppi's discussion of Eve in "The Artist in Italy," 130, and Willoughby, *Evolution of Modern Humans in Africa*.

92. Donatello's David is at the Museo Nazionale del Bargello.

93. Penney, "Afterword," 167.

94. WalkingStick noted that seeing Spero's figures prompted her to "get around my tendency to draw with a romantic line." WalkingStick, "A Roman Holiday," 3. For more on the 1996 exhibition of twenty-two panels at Studio Stefania Miscetti in Rome, see Spero, *The Black and the Red III*. Flatley described a similar production of "likeness precisely as distinct from sameness" in Andy Warhol's silkscreen prints of celebrities in Flatley, "Like," 78.

95. Oliver, *Animal Lessons*, 224.

96. WalkingStick in conversation with the author, December 19, 2013, Queens, NY.

97. WalkingStick, "Seeking the Spiritual," 187.

98. WalkingStick, "Seeking the Spiritual."

99. Gell, *Art and Agency*, 80–81, 86.

100. Euripides, "Bacchae," in *The Tragedies of Euripides*, lines 705–10.

101. Nietzsche, *The Birth of Tragedy*. On the influence of Nietzsche on American modernism and primitivism, see Rushing, *Native American Art and the New York Avant-Garde*, 127–28.

102. Matisse was likely inspired by witnessing a Catalonian folk dance and a Parisian version of a Provençal farandole. The Russian dance company Ballets Russes also debuted in Paris in May 1909. Flam, *Matisse*, 24–25. Matisse's debt to African sculpture is explored in Flam, "Matisse and the Fauves."

103. Rickard, "Visualizing Sovereignty in the Time of Biometric Sensors," 469.

104. *The Journal of Christopher Columbus*, 194, 196. Columbus's letter to the Spanish court of February 15, 1493, was widely reproduced throughout Europe in the following months, including a Latin edition in Rome. See L. A. Vigneras, "Foreword," in Columbus, *The Journal of Christopher Columbus*, xxi.

105. Elisabetta Povoledo, "Early Images of American Indians Found in a Vatican Fresco," *New York Times ArtsBeat*, May 6, 2013, http://artsbeat.blogs.nytimes.com/2013/05/06/early-images-of-american-indians-found-in-a-vatican-fresco/?_r=0. I thank Arnold Nesselrath, who supervised the restoration, for his email communications beginning on December 16, 2016. See Nesselrath, "Blickwinkel / Points of View," 73; Nesselrath, "Le code secret d'Alexandre VI."

106. I thank Alexander Nagel for talking about the painting with me by telephone on April 24, 2015. Nagel discussed Europeans' shifting geographical orientation after 1492, concluding that the emergence of "a truly old world to the east and the truly new world to the west, gave a new position to Europe, truly in the middle," in *Some Discoveries of 1492*, 34. None of this was remotely settled when the Pinturicchio workshop completed *The Resurrection* in 1494, which helps to explain the uncertainty registered in the placement of horse-flanked figures presumed to be from Asia.

107. Parks, "On the Meaning of Pinturicchio's 'Sala dei Santi,'" 294; Riess, "Raphael's Stanze and Pinturicchio's Borgia Apartments," 62.

108. Parks, "On the Meaning of Pinturicchio's 'Sala dei Santi,'" 304.

109. "The Bull Inter Caetera (Alexander VI), May 4, 1493."

110. Columbus, *The Journal of Christopher Columbus*, 200.

111. Mignolo, *The Darker Side of the Renaissance*.

112. Anne Dunlop interpreted Pinturicchio's characteristic juxtaposition of ancient motifs and biblical narratives elsewhere in terms of "pagan antiquity overcome by Christian goodness." Dunlop, "Pinturicchio and the Pilgrims," 284.

Five. "They Advanced to the Portraits"

The title quote is from Catlin, *Catlin's Notes*, 1:107. An earlier version of this chapter was published as "Ojibwa *Tableaux Vivants*: George Catlin, Robert Houle, and Transcultural Materialism," *Art History* 39, no. 1 (February 2016). Republished with permission of the publisher. I am grateful to the Association of Art Historians for granting me permission to reproduce this material here.

1. The Saulteaux are a branch of the Ojibwa First Nations who migrated into the western plains of present-day Canada from the Great Lakes region in the late eighteenth century under pressure from colonial settlement, epidemic disease, and the fur trade. The name means "people of the falls" in French, referring to the concentration of indigenous peoples French colonizers first encountered in the area of the trading post Sault Ste. Marie. Many living today in northwestern Ontario and southern Manitoba call themselves Anishinabeg, meaning "first peoples." Peers, *The Ojibwa of Western Canada*, ix–xviii. The party of Ojibwa performers who traveled with Catlin in Europe were Mississauga from the headwaters of the Grand River in south-central Ontario and not directly related to Houle.

2. Houle, "A Transatlantic Return Home through the Magic of Art," 52.

3. Walter Benjamin coined this enduring phrase as the title of a 1935 essay, "Paris, Capital of the Nineteenth Century."

4. Houle commissioned the architecture of *Paris/Ojibwa* from the Centaur Theatre scenery shop in Montreal upon his return. Although *Paris/Ojibwa* traveled to exhibition venues in the United States and Canada, my discussion focuses on its debut at the Canadian Cultural Center in 2010. Houle includes an animated video he

commissioned from Parisian artist Hervé Dagois, titled *uhnemekéka* (2010), depicting a twentieth-century Ojibwa healing dance. In *uhnemekéka*, animated dancers perform the "jingle dance" in a loop from Toronto to Paris to Morocco and back to Toronto, much like the live dancers who perform the same dance in intertribal powwows. See Delanoë, "Making the Past Dance," 29. The catalogue published by the Art Gallery of Peterborough contains additional background on collaborative components of the exhibition, including a detailed account by Barry Ace of four dances he performed on the opening day, April 13, 2010, including in front of the Louvre and on the stage of *Paris/Ojibwa*. A friend of Houle's, Ace described himself as "a contemporary Southern Straight powwow dancer" who felt "an overwhelming sense of affinity with [the Ojibwa] dancers." See Barry Ace, "A Reparative Act," 34.

5. Truettner, *The Natural Man Observed*, 9. Contemporary Cree artist Kent Monkman mocked and appropriated Catlin's legacy, primarily through the escapades of his alter ego, Miss Chief Eagle Testickle, a sequined and feather-bedecked artist-anthropologist who undertakes an exhaustive taxonomy of the European male. On Monkman's artistic response to Catlin's painting, *Dance to the Berdache*, see Horton, "Of Mimicry and Drag." Monkman is one of the many characters who commented on Catlin's legacy in Norman K. Denzin's experimental text, *Indians on Display*, 75–113.

6. Tweedie, "The Suspended Spectacle of History," 396.

7. See, for example, Bennett, *Vibrant Matter*; Brown, *Things*; Coole and Frost, *New Materialisms*.

8. Latour, *We Have Never Been Modern*. I thank Richard William Hill for generously sharing with me in the spring of 2012 his 2010 dissertation, which takes up Latour's ideas in relation to the art of Jimmie Durham in a manner allied with my own. Hill, "The Question of Agency in the Art and Writing of Jimmie Durham." In our email conversations that spring I was highly critical of Latour's Eurocentrism, reflected in "Beyond the Mirror: Indigenous Ecologies and 'New Materialisms' in Contemporary Art," an essay I coauthored around that time with Janet Catherine Berlo for a special issue of *Third Text* devoted to contemporary art and the politics of ecology. I have since somewhat softened my views on Latour, resulting in part from conversations with Hill, as well as feedback from two anonymous reviewers of my *Art History* submission. Here I would additionally like to note a correction to "Beyond the Mirror." While we thank Hill in the acknowledgments, in our documentation we erroneously omitted his important dissertation, an oversight that was brought to my attention after publication.

9. "Transcultural" derives from "transculturation," coined in Spanish in 1940 by Cuban anthropologist Fernando Ortiz, now in wide usage. I use it to refer to a process of convergence, translation, and transformation, especially in the context of the colonization of the Americas, whereby elements from previously separate cultures merge to form new objects, practices, and ideas. Ortiz, *Cuban Counterpoint*, 97–98.

10. Bibiana Obler and Benjamin Tilghman, "CFP: Objects, Objectives, Objections,"

College Art Association 102nd Annual Conference, February 12–15, 2014, in *H-ArtHist*, March 27, 2013, http://arthist.net/archive/4940.

11. Coole and Frost, *New Materialisms*, 37.

12. Obler and Tilghman, "CFP."

13. Rickard, "Visualizing Sovereignty in the Time of Biometric Sensors," 469. Anthropological engagements with Native American materialisms that have been influential beyond the discipline include Callicott and Nelson, *American Indian Environmental Ethics*; Hallowell, *Contributions to Ojibwe Studies*; Ingold, *The Perception of the Environment*; Surrallés and Hierro, *The Land Within*. For Native American authors writing about the environment, see Vine Deloria, *God Is Red*; Waters, *American Indian Thought*; Wildcat, *Red Alert!*

14. Latour, *We Have Never Been Modern*, 9.

15. Latour, *We Have Never Been Modern*, 55–67.

16. Masters, "Reading the Book of Nature, Inscribing the Savage Mind," 64. For related arguments, see John, "Benevolent Imperialism"; Truettner, *The Natural Man Observed*.

17. The catalogue is published in Catlin, *Catlin's Notes*, 1:248.

18. For a historical analysis of the events in Washington, see Haverstock, *The Indian Gallery*, 156–92; Heyman, "George Catlin and the Smithsonian."

19. Catlin claimed he sailed with 600 paintings, while scholar Christopher Mulvey recorded 310 portraits and 197 scenes of Indian life. Catlin, *Catlin's Notes*, 1:1–2; Mulvey, "George Catlin in Europe," 64.

20. Quoted in Mulvey, "George Catlin in Europe," 66.

21. Rosaldo, "Imperialist Nostalgia," 107–8. For more on British sentiments toward Native Americans, see Honour, *The New Golden Land*; Stephanie Pratt, *American Indians in British Art*; Vaughan, *Transatlantic Encounters*.

22. Catlin, *Catlin's Notes*, 1:94.

23. Catlin included two distinct evening programs in his travelogue. Catlin, *Catlin's Notes*, 1:94–97.

24. Catlin, *Catlin's Notes*, 1:94–95. An uncritical account of Catlin's deployment of tableaux vivants, beginning when Catlin's wife, Clara, dressed up as an "Indian squaw," appears in Eisler, *The Red Man's Bones*, 276–89.

25. Tweedie argues that an important function of tableaux vivants is to "reinforce through repetition an already prevalent conception of a particular cultural heritage," lending the impression that the mimicked originals "'belong' to their audience and performers." Tweedie, "The Suspended Spectacle of History," 387. For a related analysis of "playing Indian" and its relationship to nationalism in the United States, see Philip J. Deloria, *Playing Indian*.

26. Catlin, *Catlin's Notes*, 1:95.

27. Catlin, *Catlin's Notes*, 1:96.

28. Mulvey argued that Catlin's images helped to create Europe's "most typical idea

of what the North American Indian looked like." Mulvey, "George Catlin in Europe," 89. This claim should be balanced with recognition that Native Americans frequently crossed the Atlantic.

29. Mulvey, "George Catlin in Europe," 91.

30. Catlin, *Catlin's Notes*, 2:224. He published a book about Mandan ceremony and customs in London in 1867: see Catlin, *O-kee-pa*. Elizabeth A. Fenn recounted the history of the Mandan and the survival of "three hundred at most" following the smallpox epidemic of 1837–38 in Fenn, *Encounters at the Heart of the World*, xiv. See also Hight, "'Doomed to Perish.'"

31. Tweedie argued that although a given tableau vivant was, by definition, enslaved to an archetype, it could also "exploit its difference to construct a hybrid between art and commentary." Tweedie, "The Suspended Spectacle of History," 387. Film scholar Scott Durham went further, borrowing the notion of the "originally virtual" from Gilles Deleuze to describe the logic of tableaux vivants. Scott Durham, *Phantom Communities*, 80. See Deleuze, *Difference and Repetition*.

32. Truettner, *The Natural Man Observed*, 41.

33. Latour, *We Have Never Been Modern*, 37.

34. Latour, *We Have Never Been Modern*, 41.

35. Catlin, *Catlin's Notes*, 1:95.

36. Reproduced in Catlin, *Catlin's Notes*, 2:211.

37. Britain governed colonies in Ojibwa territory in present-day southern Ontario and Quebec until the federation of Canada in 1867. On this difficult period for the Ojibwa, see Donald B. Smith, *Sacred Feathers*.

38. Catlin, *Catlin's Notes*, 1:102.

39. Haverstock, *The Indian Gallery*, 175.

40. Quoted in Haverstock, *The Indian Gallery*, 175.

41. Catlin, *Catlin's Notes*, 2:224.

42. Catlin, *Catlin's Notes*, 2:304.

43. Catlin, *Catlin's Notes*, 2:280.

44. For two different versions of this terrible period, see Catlin, *Catlin's Notes*, 2:295–301; Maungwudaus, *An Account of the Chippewa Indians*, 7–9.

45. American collector Joseph Harrison rescued Catlin's Indian Gallery from dispersal. He paid Catlin's creditors in London, purchased the collection, and stored it in Philadelphia. His widow eventually donated the collection to the U.S. government in 1979, and it finally went on view at the newly opened United States National Museum from 1883 to 1890. See Heyman, "George Catlin and the Smithsonian."

46. Catlin, *Catlin's Notes*, 2:301.

47. *The Natchez* is the only known oil painting of Native American subjects completed by Delacroix. It imagines a scene from François-René de Chateaubriand's popular 1801 novel, *Atala*, in which the "last" Natchez couple on the banks of the Mississippi watch their baby die because the mother is unable to produce milk. The paint-

ing (Metropolitan Museum of Art 1989.328) is reproduced in Houle, "A Transatlantic Return Home through the Magic of Art," 53. See also Moffitt, "Native American 'Sauvage' as Pictured by French Romantic Artists and Writers."

48. Nochlin, "The Imaginary Orient," 123. Nochlin referred specifically to Delacroix's *Death of Sardanapalus*. While Catlin was perpetuating mythologies of the American West, Delacroix, Girardet, and others helped to produce and circulate the visual culture of French empire in Africa and Southeast Asia. See also Said, *Orientalism*. Houle previously wrote critically about *The Natchez* for perpetuating "enduring romantic images" of "the noble savage." Houle, "The Spiritual Legacy of the Ancient Ones," 60.

49. Greenberg, for one, declared, "Delacroix marked one of the great turning-points in the history of Western painting. . . . After him . . . all turns and goes toward a new future." Greenberg, *The Collected Essays and Criticism*, 1:243 (first published in 1944). French historian Nelcya Delanoë recounted sharing her essay about the French response to the Ojibwa in Paris with Houle prior to the creation of *Paris/Ojibwa*, which inspired him to come to Paris to see Delacroix's sketches and other collections in person. See Delanoë, "Making the Past Dance," 27; Delanoë, "Dernière recontre."

50. Houle, "The Spiritual Legacy of the Ancient Ones," 72, 70. See also Nemiroff, "Modernism, Nationalism, and Beyond," for an account of Canadian institutions' engagement with modernist primitivism.

51. Cheetham's understanding of infection draws on Kazimir Malevich's theory of Suprematism, which also directly influenced Houle. Cheetham, "The Transformative Abstraction of Robert Houle," 27. See also Cheetham, *The Rhetoric of Purity*; Greenberg, *The Collected Essays and Criticism*, vols. 1 and 4; Malevich, *The Non-Objective World*.

52. Rushing, "Troubling Abstraction," 27. For more on parfleche, see Spier, *Plains Indian Parfleche Designs*; Torrence, *The American Indian Parfleche*.

53. Rushing, "Troubling Abstraction," 32.

54. Cheetham, "The Transformative Abstraction of Robert Houle," 45. For more on Newman's relationship to Native art, including discussions of an important exhibition, *Northwest Coast Indian Painting*, that he organized for Betty Parsons Gallery in New York in 1946, see Anthes, *Native Moderns*, 59–88; Rushing, *Native American Art and the New York Avant-Garde*, 126–37; Rushing, "The Impact of Nietzsche and Northwest Coast Indian Art on Barnett Newman's Idea of Redemption in the Abstract Sublime."

55. Houle in conversation with the author, Toronto, December 12, 2013. Hearings on this subject through Canada's Truth and Reconciliation Commission (TRC) were completed in 2015. The final report is available on the TRC website: http://www.trc.ca /websites/trcinstitution. For a series of works based on Houle's abuse at the residential school at Sandy Bay First Nation Reserve, see Houle, *Robert Houle: enuhmo andúhuaun (the road home)*.

56. Bell, "Conversation with Robert Houle," 13, 19. Today Houle describes himself as a "non-practising Catholic." Houle, email to the author, January 29, 2015.

57. That same year, Houle participated in the Salzburg International Summer Academy for drawing and painting, granting him a firsthand introduction to European art history.

58. This radio conversation between U.S.- and Canada-based activists gives a concise picture of the spread of AIM in Canada: "American Indian Movement Shakes Up Canada," *Our Native Land* (radio program), Canadian Broadcast Corporation, June 8, 1974, http://www.cbc.ca/archives/discover/programs/o/our-native-land-1/american-indian-movement-shakes-up-canada.html.

59. Houle in conversation with the author, Toronto, December 12, 2013.

60. On the name changes, see "Museum of Civilization to Become History," *Huffington Post*, December 15, 2012, http://www.huffingtonpost.ca/2012/10/15/museum-of-civilization-history_n_1968622.html.

61. Houle in conversation with Hargittay, "The Struggle against Cultural Apartheid," 58.

62. Phillips, *Patterns of Power*, 27. See my discussions of the equal-armed cross in chapters 2 and 4.

63. Houle, "The Spiritual Legacy of the Ancient Ones," 53.

64. Houle, "The Spiritual Legacy of the Ancient Ones," 70.

65. The titles are translated in McIntosh, "Traveling Light," 16.

66. Phillips, *Patterns of Power*, 25.

67. Phillips, *Patterns of Power*, 27.

68. Phillips, *Patterns of Power*, 26. Houle similarly explains, "The point of putting things together is to create a paradigm to create some type of power." Bell, "Conversation with Robert Houle," 15.

69. Hallowell, "Ojibwa Ontology, Behavior, and World View," 20–22.

70. Hallowell, "Ojibwa Ontology, Behavior, and World View," 33–34.

71. Phillips, *Patterns of Power*, 26.

72. Latour, *We Have Never Been Modern*, 55.

73. Donald B. Smith, *Mississauga Portraits*, 126–63.

74. For example, Hallowell notes the influence of Christianity in Ojibwa understandings of success in the afterlife as a reflection of proper behavior during one's lifetime, but notes that his informants remained skeptical about a concept of hell. Hallowell, *Contributions to Ojibwe Studies*, 414.

75. Writings on the sublime by European philosophers Edmund Burke in 1757 and Immanuel Kant in 1790 spurred the development of romanticism on both sides of the Atlantic. See Burke, *A Philosophical Enquiry into the Origins of the Sublime and Beautiful*, 49–200; Kant, *Kant's Critique of Judgment*, 101–30. On the relationship between Friedrich's paintings and the sublime, see Prager, "Kant in Casper David Friedrich's Frames"; Michael Fried interpreted the effects of identification with Friedrich's rear figures at length in "Orientation in Painting: Caspar David Friedrich," public lecture, George Washington University Department of Fine Arts and Art History, November

11, 2013. A U.S. variant of the romantic landscape tradition was developed by Hudson River School painters in the nineteenth century, sometimes featuring encampments of Indians or buffalo hunts integrated with the vast landscape, as in the canvases of Albert Bierstadt (1830–1902). See Ferber and Miller, "Albert Bierstadt, Landscape Aesthetics, and the Meanings of the West in the Civil War Era"; Wilton and Barringer, *American Sublime*; Wolf, *Romantic Re-Vision*.

76. Ojibwa stories relate that the first people came down from the star world through a hole in the sky. See accounts by contemporary spiritual leaders recorded in Conway, "The Conjurer's Lodge."

77. Hallowell, *Contributions to Ojibwe Studies*, 406.

78. Hallowell, *Contributions to Ojibwe Studies*, 415–17.

79. Houle discussed the sacred importance of tobacco and its role in his work in Bell, "Conversation with Robert Houle," 15–16.

80. Vennum, *The Ojibwa Dance Drum*, 33; see also Southcott, *The Sound of the Drum*.

81. The Kicking Woman Singers perform traditional Blackfoot music at intertribal powwows. The people who belong to the Blackfoot Confederacy of Northern Montana and Alberta are related to Ojibwa/Anishinaabe peoples.

82. Houle, "The Spiritual Legacy of the Ancient Ones," 62; Houle and Madill, *Robert Houle*, 6–8.

83. Houle stated, "The ancestors and the manitous will hear the entry song." Houle, "A Transatlantic Return Home through the Magic of Art," 44.

84. Houle, "A Transatlantic Return Home through the Magic of Art," 52.

85. Horse Capture and Vitart, *Robes of Splendor*, 61. Horse Capture described the same robe that inspired Houle on p. 110.

86. For analyses of this installation, see Berlo and Jonaitis, "'Indian Country' on Washington's Mall," 23; Rickard, "Visualizing Sovereignty in the Time of Biometric Sensors," 465–68.

87. Peers, *The Ojibwa of Western Canada*, 18–19, 141–42. See also Fenn, *Pox Americana*.

88. Warren, the son of an Ojibwa woman and a French fur trader, did not believe these accounts and gave an alternative version of the notorious smallpox outbreak of 1780–83. Warren and Schenck, *History of the Ojibway People*, 228–33. For a careful and comprehensive consideration of the historical evidence for germ warfare, see Fenn, "Biological Warfare in Eighteenth-Century North America." Fenn made the case that regardless of whether specific accounts in which colonial officials intentionally spread smallpox to Native communities can be verified, the ideology and "codes of war" to back such maneuvers were soundly in place, making it likely that germ warfare did, in fact, occur with some frequency (1580). A key article that set off these debates is Knollenberg, "General Amherst and Germ Warfare." Mayor explored the discursive resonance of these and other circulating accounts of smallpox-infested blankets in

"The Nessus Shirt in the New World." See also Amherst and Webster, *The Journal of Jeffery Amherst*.

89. Pontiac's Confederacy was a collective of allied Native American groups from the region of the Great Lakes and present-day Illinois and Ohio led by the Odawa chief Pontiac, who challenged British policies following the French defeat in the French and Indian Wars. Among the many publications outlining this decade of formative colonial struggle between the French, British, and Native American powers, see Fred Anderson, *Crucible of War*; Borneman, *The French and Indian War*; Calloway, *The Scratch of a Pen*; Nester, *"Haughty Conquerors."*

90. Cheetham observed that the canvases of *Palisade* echo the green and white vertical bands of a wampum belt—a diplomatic contract between nations—allegedly used by Pontiac in his dealings with the British military. Cheetham, "The Transformative Abstraction of Robert Houle," 45–47. See also Bell, *Robert Houle's Palisade*.

91. Houle, "A Transatlantic Return Home through the Magic of Art," 50.

92. See Kastner, *Jaune Quick-to-See Smith*, plate 31k.

93. Kate Flint argued that the Iowa and Ojibwa used their travels as an opportunity "that the British should recognize how the host country was implicated in the causes of the Indian poverty that underlay their reasons for crossing the Atlantic to raise money, including the introduction of smallpox, venereal disease, and the sale of 'fire-water.'" Flint, *The Transatlantic Indian*, 79. Native responses are also discussed in Mulvey, "Among the Sag-a-noshes."

94. Slight, *Indian Researches*, 43.

95. Houle in conversation with the author, Toronto, December 12, 2013; Donald B. Smith, *Sacred Feathers*, 187–88. For a detailed account of the life of Maungwudaus, see Donald B. Smith, *Mississauga Portraits*, 126–63.

96. Maungwudaus, *An Account of the Chippewa Indians*, 11.

97. Some of Latour's most convincing illustrations of quasi-objects appear in his studies of nineteenth-century laboratories and the development of microbiology. For example, in an analysis of French scientist Louis Pasteur's famous 1857 essay on lactic acid yeast, Latour wrote, "The reader [of Pasteur's text] lives in a world where a ferment is as lively as a specific life form." Latour, "Pasteur on Lactic Acid Yeast," 133. For more on the invention of the microscope and its associated culture of objectivity, see Wilson, *The Invisible World*; Daston and Galison, *Objectivity*.

98. The first transatlantic steamship service began in 1838. *Steamships: Wester's Timeline History, 1762–2007* (San Diego, 2007), n.p. It is not clear what type of service Maungwudaus and the other Ojibwa used to travel to London in 1843, although we know that they returned aboard the *Yorktown*, a conventional sailing ship, in 1848. Maungwudaus, *An Account of the Chippewa Indians*, 9.

99. See McLuhan and Hill, *Norval Morrisseau and the Emergence of the Image Makers*.

100. Houle in conversation with the author, Toronto, December 12, 2013.

101. For a description of Morrisseau's relationship to the Ojibwa Midewiwin Society scrolls when he was growing up in the 1930s and 1940s, see Blundell and Phillips, "If It's Not Shamanic, Is It Sham?," 119. See also Morrisseau, *Legends of My People*. For discussions of the role of sacred birchbark scrolls in the Ojibwa religious order of the *Midéwiwin*, see Dewdney, *The Sacred Scrolls of the Southern Ojibway*; Landes, *Ojibwa Religion and the Midéwiwin*; Whiteford, "Mystic and Decorative Art of the Anishinabe (Chippewa/Ojibwa)," 81.

102. The Norval Morrisseau estate did not respond to my request to reproduce this work. It is in the collections of the National Museum of the American Indian and can be viewed on the NMAI website: http://www.nmai.si.edu/searchcollections/item .aspx?irn=280248&culid=952.

103. Blundell and Phillips, "If It's Not Shamanic, Is It Sham?," 120.

104. "Norval Morrisseau Retrospective a First for National Gallery of Canada," National Gallery of Canada press release, February 1, 2006, http://www.gallery.ca/en /about/379.php. See also Jean Martin, *Magiciens de La Terre*; Steeds et al., *Making Art Global (Part 2)*; Stevens, *A Picasso from the North Country*.

105. Hallowell, *Contributions to Ojibwe Studies*, 135.

106. Houle, "The Spiritual Legacy of the Ancient Ones," 44.

107. Franke, *Animism*; Folie and Franke, *Animism*. We take up the work of Franke and Latour in relation to contemporary Native American art in Horton and Berlo, "Beyond the Mirror."

108. Franke, "Much Trouble in the Transportation of Souls," 11.

109. Franke, "Much Trouble in the Transportation of Souls."

110. Hill, "The Dangers of Petrification"; Viveiros de Castro, "Exchanging Perspectives." Hill does not discuss indigenous worldviews in relation to Durham's work in his short catalogue essay.

111. Quoted in Damien McElroy, "Sale of Native American Masks Approved by Court," *Telegraph*, April 12, 2013, http://www.telegraph.co.uk/news/worldnews /northamerica/usa/9990169/Sale-of-Native-American-masks-approved-by-court .html. See also Dominique Godreche, "Hopi Katsinam Auction in Paris: A Conversation with the Auctioneer," *Indian Country Today Media Network*, April 9, 2013, http:// indiancountrytodaymedianetwork.com/2013/04/09/hopi-katsinam-auction-paris -conversation-auctioneer-148705. For a succinct summary and analysis of the case, see Ronald McCoy, "Controversial Katsinam Auction in Paris," *American Indian Art Magazine* 29, no. 4 (Autumn 2013): 29, 92–93. The Hopi tribal government, with support from the U.S. State Department, numerous American museum directors, celebrities such as Robert Redford, and the international indigenous advocacy group Survival International, protested the sale, claiming that the materials (which were dated to the late nineteenth and early twentieth centuries) were stolen from the reservation in the 1930s and 1940s. They were unable to assemble evidence in support of this claim. Although the Hopi were granted a hearing at a Paris court on April 11, the judge ruled to

permit the auction, as no national or international law currently exists to enforce re-patriation of sacred materials from France. The logic of objectification wedded to the power of transnational capital ruled the day. The United States' own Native American Graves and Repatriation Act (NAGPRA, 1990) was impotent in this context, as was the nonbinding United Nations Declaration on the Rights of Indigenous Peoples (2007), mentioned in chapter 1. See especially Article 11: "1. Indigenous peoples have the right to practise and revitalize their cultural traditions and customs. This includes the right to maintain, protect and develop the past, present and future manifestations of their cultures, such as archaeological and historical sites, artefacts, designs, ceremonies, tech-nologies and visual and performing arts and literature. 2. States shall provide redress through effective mechanisms, which may include restitution, developed in conjunc-tion with indigenous peoples, with respect to their cultural, intellectual, religious and spiritual property taken without their free, prior and informed consent or in violation of their laws, traditions and customs." See the United Nations Permanent Forum on Indigenous Issues website for the full text: http://social.un.org/index/Indigenous Peoples/DeclarationontheRightsofIndigenousPeoples.aspx. For a description of NAGPRA, see the official website: http://www.nps.gov/nagpra/.

112. Franke, "Much Trouble in the Transportation of Souls," 11.

113. Vizenor, *Shrouds of White Earth*, 142. On the history and controversy surround-ing the Musée du quai Branly, see Price, *Paris Primitive*.

114. Vizenor, *Shrouds of White Earth*, 140.

115. Franke and Latour, "Angels without Wings," 86.

116. Catlin, *Catlin's Notes*, 1:107.

Epilogue

1. Ford automobiles were first produced in Australia in 1925, after Henry Ford granted manufacturing rights to the British Empire. See Stephen, *The Empire of Prog-ress*, 150.

2. Taussig, "Jimmie Durham," 84; Stephen Gibbs, "One Car a Stone's Throw from Becoming Art," *Sydney Morning Herald*, May 27, 2004, sec. Entertainment/Arts, http://www.smh.com.au/articles/2004/05/26/1085461823825.html.

3. Papastergiadis, "A Thousand Beautiful Things," 50. While in Sydney during the 2012 Biennale, I visited the work at its current resting place in the center of a traffic circle on Hickson Road and Pottinger Street on Walsh Bay, near the Opera House.

4. Demos, *The Migrant Image*, xiv–xv.

5. Latour, *We Have Never Been Modern*.

6. Demos, *The Exiles of Marcel Duchamp*, 62.

7. Quoted in "Interview: Dirk Snauwaert in Conversation with Jimmie Durham," 28.

8. Demos, *The Exiles of Marcel Duchamp*, 84.

9. Durham, "Middle," in *Columbus Day*, 30.

10. Durham, "Tarascan Guitars," in *Columbus Day*, 48. I discuss this poem at greater length in Horton, "Jimmie Durham's Stones and Bones," 83.

11. Durham, *Columbus Day*, 7.

12. Durham, *Columbus Day*, 85.

13. Durham, "They Forgot That Their Prison Is Made of Stone, and Stone Is Our Ally," in *Columbus Day*, 86.

14. Foucault, *Discipline and Punish*.

15. In the wall text Durham locates Chalma in "the southern part of North America," rather than the modern nation of Mexico.

16. Durham, *Between the Furniture and the Building*, 99, 103.

17. Elsewhere Durham has marked at least eleven such centers with staffs, ranging from Winnipeg, Canada, to Yakutia, Siberia. See discussions in Hill, "The Question of Agency in the Art and Writing of Jimmie Durham," 169–76; Hill and Koski, "The Centre of the World Is Several Places"; Papastergiadis and Turney, *On Becoming Authentic*, 29–31.

18. Durham, "1000 Words," 189.

19. At this point the boulder was replaced by a fiberglass replica.

20. Hill, "The Question of Agency in the Art and Writing of Jimmie Durham."

21. Franke, "Untying the Modern Knot," 32. See also Franke, "Autonomy and Mirrors."

22. Franke, "Untying the Modern Knot," 32.

23. Hill, "The Malice and Benevolence of Inanimate Objects," 77. Hill continued, "Durham animates stone against its metaphorical stability in architecture . . . by literally or imaginatively putting it into motion as an agent" (78). The essay is based on chapter 4, "The Malice of Inanimate Objects: Anti-Architecture and the Freedom and Mobility of Stones," in Hill, "The Question of Agency in the Art and Writing of Jimmie Durham," 177–225.

24. Hallowell, "Ojibwa Ontology, Behavior, and World View."

25. Bean, "Power and Its Application in Native California," 23.

26. Quoted in Haas, "'Raise Your Sword and I Will Eat You,'" 94.

27. Dean, *A Culture of Stone*, 5.

28. Jett, "Cairn and Brush Travel Shrines in the United States Northeast and Southeast"; Jett, "Cairn Trail Shrines in Middle and South America," 8.

29. Hallendy, *Inuksuit*, 22.

30. Jett, "Cairn Trail Shrines in Middle and South America," 5.

31. Durham, *Stone Heart*. For other cultural references to animate stone beyond the Americas, see Dean, *A Culture of Stone*, 6.

32. Durham and Fisher, "The Ground Has Been Covered," 101; Camnitzer, "Jimmie Durham," 8.

BIBLIOGRAPHY

Abbott, Lawrence, ed. *I Stand in the Center of the Good: Interviews with Contemporary Native American Artists.* Lincoln: University of Nebraska Press, 1994.

Ace, Barry. "A Reparative Act." In *Robert Houle's Paris/Ojibwa*, edited by Paul Gardner, 34–43. Peterborough, ON: Art Gallery of Peterborough, 2011.

Adams, David Wallace. *Education for Extinction: American Indians and the Boarding School Experience, 1875–1928.* Lawrence: University Press of Kansas, 1995.

———. "Schooling the Hopi: Federal Indian Policy Writ Small, 1887–1917." In *American Vistas, 1887 to the Present,* edited by Leonard Dinnerstein and Kenneth T. Jackson, 27–44. New York: Oxford University Press, 1995.

Alfred, Taiaiake. *Peace, Power, Righteousness: An Indigenous Manifesto.* Oxford: Oxford University Press, 1999.

———. *Wasáse: Indigenous Pathways of Action and Freedom.* Toronto: University of Toronto Press Higher Education, 2005.

Allen, Chadwick. *Trans-Indigenous: Methodologies for Global Native Literary Studies.* Minneapolis: University of Minnesota Press, 2012.

Allen, Paula Gunn. *Pocahontas: Medicine Woman, Spy, Entrepreneur, Diplomat.* New York: HarperCollins, 2003.

Alloway, Lawrence. *The Venice Biennale, 1895–1968: From Salon to Goldfish Bowl.* Greenwich, CT: New York Graphic Society, 1968.

Amelina, Anna, Devrimsel D. Nergiz, Thomas Faist, and Nina Glick Schiller, eds. *Beyond Methodological Nationalism: Research Methodologies for Cross-Border Studies.* New York: Routledge, 2012.

Amherst, Jeffery, and John Clarence Webster. *The Journal of Jeffery Amherst: Recording the Military Career of General Amherst in America from 1758 to 1763.* Chicago: University of Chicago Press, 1931.

Amor, Mónica, Okwui Enwezor, Gao Minglu, Oscar Ho, Kobena Mercer, and Irit Rogoff. "Liminalities: Discussions on the Global and the Local." *Art Journal* 57, no. 4 (Winter 1998): 29–49.

Anderson, Benedict. *Imagined Communities: Reflections on the Origin and Spread of Nationalism.* Rev. ed. London: Verso, 1991.

Anderson, Fred. *Crucible of War: The Seven Years' War and the Fate of Empire in British North America, 1754–1766.* New York: Alfred A. Knopf, 2000.

Anthes, Bill. "Contemporary Native Artists and International Biennial Culture." *Visual Anthropology Review* 25, no. 2 (2009): 109–27.

———. *Edgar Heap of Birds*. Durham, NC: Duke University Press, 2015.

———. "Ethics in a World of Strangers: Edgar Heap of Birds at Home and Abroad." *Art Journal* 71, no. 3 (Fall 2012): 58–77.

———. *Native Moderns: American Indian Painting, 1940–1960*. Durham, NC: Duke University Press, 2006.

Appadurai, Arjun. *Modernity at Large: Cultural Dimensions of Globalization*. Minneapolis: University of Minnesota Press, 1996.

———, ed. *The Social Life of Things*. Cambridge: Cambridge University Press, 2003.

Appleford, Rob. "Jimmie Durham and the Carpentry of Ambivalence." *Social Text* 28, no. 4 (Winter 2010): 91–111.

Araeen, Rasheed. "A New Beginning: Beyond Postcolonial Cultural Theory and Identity Politics." In *The Third Text Reader on Art, Culture, and Theory*, edited by Rasheed Araeen, Sean Cubitt, and Ziauddin Sardar, 333–45. London: Continuum, 2002.

Archuleta, Margaret. "Kay WalkingStick." In *Path Breakers: The Eiteljorg Fellowship for Native American Fine Art, 2003*, 13–31. Indianapolis: Eiteljorg Museum, 2003.

Artforum International, 40th anniversary ed., *The 1980s: Parts I and II* (March–April 2003).

Ash-Milby, Kathleen. "A Life." In *Kay WalkingStick: An American Artist*, edited by Kathleen Ash-Milby and David W. Penney, 25–41. Washington, DC: Smithsonian National Museum of the American Indian, 2015.

———. *Off the Map: Landscape in the Native Imagination*. Washington, DC: Smithsonian National Museum of the American Indian, 2007.

Ash-Milby, Kathleen, and Truman T. Lowe. *Most Serene Republics: Edgar Heap of Birds*. Washington, DC: Smithsonian National Museum of the American Indian, 2007.

Ash-Milby, Kathleen, and David W. Penney, eds. *Kay WalkingStick: An American Artist*. Washington, DC: Smithsonian National Museum of the American Indian, 2015.

Bal, Mieke. *Quoting Caravaggio: Contemporary Art, Preposterous History*. Chicago: University of Chicago Press, 1999.

Bal, Mieke, and Norman Bryson. "Semiotics in Art History." *Art Bulletin* 73, no. 2 (1991): 174–208.

Bambach, Carmen C. *Drawing and Painting in the Italian Renaissance Workshop: Theory and Practice, 1300–1600*. Cambridge: Cambridge University Press, 1999.

Bargellini, Clara. "Art at the Missions of Northern New Spain." In *The Arts of the Missions of Northern New Spain, 1600–1821*, edited by Clara Bargellini, 54–93. Mexico City: Antiguo Colegio de San Ildefonso, 2009.

Barker, Joanne. "Indian™ U.S.A." *Wicazo Sa Review* 18, no. 1 (Spring 2003): 25–79.

Barnes, Susan J. *The Rothko Chapel: An Act of Faith*. Houston: Menil Foundation, 1989.

Barolsky, Paul. "Domenichino's 'Diana' and the Art of Seeing." *Source: Notes in the History of Art* 14, no. 1 (Fall 1994): 18–20.

Batkin, Jonathan. *The Native American Curio Trade in New Mexico.* Santa Fe, NM: Wheelwright Museum of the American Indian, 2008.

Baudrillard, Jean. *Simulacra and Simulation.* Translated by Sheila Faria Glaser. Ann Arbor: University of Michigan Press, 1994.

Baylor, Tim. "Media Framing of Movement Protest: The Case of American Indian Protest." *Social Science Journal* 33, no. 3 (1996): 241–55.

Bean, Lowell John. "California Indian Shamanism and Folk Curing." In *California Indian Shamanism,* edited by John Lowell Bean, 53–66. Banning, CA: Ballena Press, 1992.

———. "Power and Its Application in Native California." In *California Indian Shamanism,* edited by John Lowell Bean, 21–32. Banning, CA: Ballena Press, 1992.

Bell, Michael. "Conversation with Robert Houle." In *Kanata: Robert Houle's Histories,* edited by Michael Bell, 13–23. Ottawa: Carleton University Art Gallery, 1993.

———. *Robert Houle's Palisade.* Ottawa: Carleton University Art Gallery, 2001.

Belting, Hans. *Art History after Modernism.* Translated by Caroline Saltzwedel, Mitch Cohen, and Kenneth Northcott. Chicago: University of Chicago Press, 2003.

Bender, John, and Michael Marrinan. *The Culture of Diagram.* Palo Alto, CA: Stanford University Press, 2010.

Bender, Margaret. *Signs of Cherokee Culture: Sequoyah's Syllabary in Eastern Cherokee Life.* Chapel Hill: University of North Carolina Press, 2002.

Benjamin, Walter. *The Arcades Project.* Edited by Rolf Tiedemann. Translated by Howard Eiland and Kevin McLaughlin. Cambridge, MA: Belknap Press, 2002.

———. "On the Mimetic Faculty." In *One-Way Street and Other Writings,* trans. Edmund Jephcott and Kingsley Shorter, 160–63. Thetford, Norfolk: Lowe & Brydone, 1979.

———. "Paris, Capital of the Nineteenth Century." In *Reflections: Essays, Aphorisms, Autobiographical Writings,* edited by Peter Demetz, 146–62. New York: Schocken, 1986.

———. "Theses on the Philosophy of History." In *Illuminations: Essays and Reflections,* edited by Hannah Arendt, translated by Harry Zohn, 253–64. 1940; New York: Schocken, 2007.

Bennett, Jane. *Vibrant Matter: A Political Ecology of Things.* Durham, NC: Duke University Press, 2010.

Berlo, Janet Catherine, ed. *The Early Years of Native American Art History: The Politics of Scholarship and Collecting.* Vancouver: University of British Columbia Press, 1992.

———. "The Szwedzicki Portfolios: Native American Fine Art and American Visual Culture, 1917–1952." Parts 1 and 2, *American Indian Art Magazine* 34, nos. 2–3 (Spring–Summer 2009): 36–45, 58–67.

Berlo, Janet Catherine, and Arthur Amiotte. *Arthur Amiotte: Collages, 1988–2006*. Santa Fe, NM: Wheelwright Museum of the American Indian, 2006.

Berlo, Janet Catherine, and Aldona Jonaitis. "'Indian Country' on Washington's Mall: The National Museum of the American Indian: A Review Essay." *Museum Anthropology* 28, no. 2 (2005): 17–30.

Bernstein, Bruce. *Santa Fe Indian Market: A History of Native Arts and the Marketplace*. Albuquerque: Museum of New Mexico Press, 2012.

Bernstein, Bruce, and W. Jackson Rushing. *Modern by Tradition: American Indian Painting in the Studio Style*. Albuquerque: Museum of New Mexico Press, 1995.

Bhabha, Homi K. *The Location of Culture*. New York: Routledge, 2004.

———. "Making Difference: Homi K. Bhabha on the Legacy of the Culture Wars." *Artforum International* 40th Anniversary, *The 1980s: Part 2* (April 2013): 73–76, 234–37.

Bishop, Claire. *Installation Art: A Critical History*. New York: Routledge, 2005.

Bittencourt, Vivien, and Vincent Katz. *Kiki Smith: The Venice Story*. Milan: Charta, 2006.

Blocker, Jane. "Ambivalent Entertainments: James Luna, Performance, and the Archive." *Grey Room*, no. 37 (Fall 2009): 52–77.

———. "Failures of Self-Seeing: James Luna Remembers Dino." *PAJ: A Journal of Performance and Art* 23, no. 1 (January 2001): 18–32.

Blume, Eugen. "Joseph Beuys' 'I Like America and America Likes Me.'" In *I Like America: Fictions of the Wild West*, edited by Pamela Kort and Max Hollein, 358–70. London: Prestel, 2006.

Blundell, Valda, and Ruth B. Phillips. "If It's Not Shamanic, Is It Sham? An Examination of Media Responses to Woodland School Art." *Anthropologica*, n.s., 25, no. 1 (1983): 117–32.

Borneman, Walter R. *The French and Indian War: Deciding the Fate of North America*. New York: HarperCollins, 2006.

Bossé, Laurence, and Julia Garimorth. "Interview with Jimmie Durham." In *Jimmie Durham: Rejected Stones*, 13–16. Paris: Musée d'Art Moderne de la Ville de Paris/ ARC, 2009.

Bourke, John Gregory. *The Snake-Dance of the Moquis of Arizona*. 1884; Chicago: Rio Grande Press, 1962.

Bourriaud, Nicolas. *The Radicant*. Berlin: Lukas & Sternberg, 2009.

Boym, Svetlana. *The Future of Nostalgia*. New York: Basic Books, 2001.

Bradley, Jessica, and Jolene Rickard. *Rebecca Belmore: Fountain*. Vancouver: Morris and Helen Belkin Art Gallery, 2005.

Brock, Charles, ed. *George Bellows*. Washington, DC: National Gallery of Art, 2012.

Broder, Patricia. *Hopi Painting: The World of the Hopis*. New York: Dutton, 1978.

Brody, J. J. *Indian Painters and White Patrons*. Albuquerque: University of New Mexico Press, 1971.

———. *Pueblo Indian Painting: Tradition and Modernism in New Mexico, 1900–1930.* Santa Fe, NM: School of American Research Press, 1997.

Brougher, Kerry, and Olivia Mattis. *Visual Music: Synaesthesia in Art and Music since 1900.* London: Thames & Hudson, 2005.

Brown, Bill, ed. *Things.* Chicago: University of Chicago Press, 2004.

Buchloh, Benjamin H. D. "The Whole Earth Show: An Interview with Jean Hubert Martin." *Art in America* (May 1989): 150–58, 211, 213.

"The Bull Inter Caetera (Alexander VI), May 4, 1493." In *European Treaties bearing on the History of the United States and Its Dependencies to 1648,* edited by Frances Gardiner Davenport, 75–78. Washington, DC: Carnegie Institution of Washington, 1917.

Burdett, Charles. *Journeys through Fascism: Italian Travel Writing between the Wars.* New York: Berghahn, 2007.

Burke, Edmund. *A Philosophical Enquiry into the Origins of the Sublime and Beautiful: And Other Pre-Revolutionary Writings.* London: Penguin, 1999.

Burke, Flannery. *From Greenwich Village to Taos: Primitivism and Place at Mabel Dodge Luhan's.* Lawrence: University Press of Kansas, 2008.

Burns, Emily. "Innocence Abroad: The Construction and Marketing of an American Artistic Identity in Paris, 1880–1910." PhD diss., Washington University, St. Louis, 2012.

Callicott, J. Baird, and Michael P. Nelson. *American Indian Environmental Ethics: An Ojibwa Case Study.* Upper Saddle River, NJ: Pearson, 2004.

Calloway, Colin G. *The Scratch of a Pen: 1763 and the Transformation of North America.* Oxford: Oxford University Press, 2006.

Camnitzer, Luis. "Jimmie Durham: Dancing Serious Dances." In *Jimmie Durham: The Bishop's Moose and the Pinkerton Men,* edited by Jeanette Ingberman, 6–10. New York: Exit Art, 1989.

Carrasco, Davíd. *Quetzalcoatl and the Irony of Empire: Myths and Prophecies in the Aztec Tradition.* 1982; Boulder: University Press of Colorado, 2000.

Casid, Jill H., and Aruna D'Souza. *Art History in the Wake of the Global Turn.* New Haven, CT: Yale University Press, 2014.

Catlin, George. *Catlin's Notes of Eight Years' Travels and Residence in Europe with His North American Indian Collection: With Anecdotes and Incidents of the Travels and Adventures of Three Different Parties of American Indians Whom He Introduced to the Courts of England, France, and Belgium.* Vols. 1 and 2. London: The Author, 1848.

———. *O-kee-pa, a Religious Ceremony, and Other Customs of the Mandans.* London: Truebner and Company, 1867.

Cecchi, Emilio. "Disegni Indiani." *Dedalo (Milano-Roma)* 12 (1932): 563–73.

Chakrabarty, Dipesh. *Provincializing Europe: Postcolonial Thought and Historical Difference.* Princeton, NJ: Princeton University Press, 2000.

Chavez, Cynthia L. "Negotiated Representations: Pueblo Artists and Culture." PhD diss., University of New Mexico, 2001.

Cheetham, Mark A. *The Rhetoric of Purity: Essentialist Theory and the Advent of Abstract Painting*. Cambridge, MA: Harvard University Press, 1994.

———. "The Transformative Abstraction of Robert Houle." In *Troubling Abstraction: Robert Houle*, edited by Carol Podedworny, 41–55. Hamilton, ON: McMaster Museum of Art, 2007.

Christov-Bakargiev, Carolyn, Chús Martinez, and Franco Berardi. *dOCUMENTA (13) Catalog 1/3: The Book of Books*. Ostfildern-Ruit: Hatje Cantz Verlag, 2012.

Churchill, Ward. "Nobody's Pet Poodle: Jimmie Durham: An Artist for North America" (1991). In *Indians Are Us? Culture and Genocide in Native North America*, 89–113. Monroe, ME: Common Courage, 1994.

Clark, Walter L. *Leaves from an Artist's Memory*. New York: Hadden Craftsmen, 1937.

Clemmer, Richard O. *Roads in the Sky: The Hopi Indians in a Century of Change*. Boulder, CO: Westview, 1995.

Clifford, James. *The Predicament of Culture: Twentieth-Century Ethnography, Literature, and Art*. Cambridge, MA: Harvard University Press, 1988.

———. *Routes: Travel and Translation in the Late Twentieth Century*. Cambridge, MA: Harvard University Press, 1997.

Cobb, Daniel M. *Native Activism in Cold War America: The Struggle for Sovereignty*. Lawrence: University Press of Kansas, 2008.

Cobb, Daniel M., and Loretta Fowler, eds. *Beyond Red Power: American Indian Politics and Activism since 1900*. Santa Fe, NM: School for Advanced Research Press, 2007.

Cohn, Marjorie B. *Wash and Gouache: A Study of the Development of the Materials of Watercolor*. Cambridge, MA: Fogg Art Museum, 1977.

Cohodas, Marvin. *Basket Weavers for the California Curio Trade: Elizabeth and Louise Hickox*. Tucson: University of Arizona Press, 1997.

———. "Louisa Keyser and the Cohns: Mythmaking and Basket Making in the American West." In *The Early Years of Native American Art History: The Politics of Scholarship and Collecting*, edited by Janet Catherine Berlo, 88–133. Vancouver: University of British Columbia Press, 1992.

Columbus, Christopher. *The Journal of Christopher Columbus*. Translated by Cecil Jane. London: Anthony Blond & the Orion Press, 1960.

Conway, Thor. "The Conjurer's Lodge: Celestial Narratives from Algonkian Shamans." In *Earth and Sky: Visions of the Cosmos in Native American Folklore*, edited by Ray A. Williamson and Claire R. Farrer, 236–59. Albuquerque: University of New Mexico Press, 1992.

Coole, Diana, and Samantha Frost, eds. *New Materialisms: Ontology, Agency, and Politics*. Durham, NC: Duke University Press, 2010.

Corn, Wanda. *The Great American Thing: Modern Art and National Identity, 1915–1935*. Berkeley: University of California Press, 2001.

Cotter, Holland. *Kay WalkingStick Paintings, 1974–1990*. Long Island, NY: Hillwood Art Museum, 1991.

Curiel, José Refugio de la Torre, and Steven W. Hackel. "Franciscan Missionaries in Late Colonial Sonora: Five Decades of Change and Conflict." In *Alta California: Peoples in Motion, Identities in Formation,* edited by Steven W. Hackel, 47–75. Berkeley: University of California Press, 2010.

Dahl, Per. "The Rise and Fall of Literacy in Classical Music: An Essay on Musical Notation." *Fontes Artis Musicae* 56, no. 1 (January 2009): 66–76.

Darwin, Charles. *Journal of Researches into the Natural History and Geology of the Countries Visited during the Voyage of H.M.S. Beagle Round the World, under the Command of Capt. Fitz Roy, R.N.* New York: D. Appleton and Company, 1896.

Daston, Lorraine J., and Peter Galison. *Objectivity.* New York: Zone Books, 2007.

Dean, Carolyn. *A Culture of Stone: Inka Perspectives on Rock.* Durham, NC: Duke University Press, 2010.

de Certeau, Michel. *The Practice of Everyday Life.* Berkeley: University of California Press, 2011.

———. *The Writing of History.* New York: Columbia University Press, 1988.

Delanoë, Nelcya. "Dernière recontre, ou comment Baudelaire, George Sand et Delacroix s'épirent des Indiens du peintre Catlin." In *Destins croisés: Cinq siècles de recontres avec les Amérindiens,* 263–81. Paris: UNESCO, Bibliothèque Albin Michel, 1992.

———. "Making the Past Dance." In *Robert Houle's Paris/Ojibwa,* edited by Paul Gardner, 24–29. Peterborough, ON: Art Gallery of Peterborough, 2011.

Deleuze, Gilles. *Difference and Repetition.* Translated by Paul Patton. New York: Columbia University Press, 1995.

Deleuze, Gilles, and Félix Guattari. *A Thousand Plateaus: Capitalism and Schizophrenia.* Translated by Brian Massumi. Minneapolis: University of Minnesota Press, 1987.

Deloria, Philip J. "Historiography." In *A Companion to American Indian History,* edited by Philip J. Deloria and Neal Salisbury, 6–24. London: Blackwell, 2007.

———. *Indians in Unexpected Places.* Lawrence: University Press of Kansas, 2004.

———. *Playing Indian.* New Haven, CT: Yale University Press, 1999.

Deloria, Vine, Jr. *Behind the Trail of Broken Treaties: An Indian Declaration of Independence.* 1974; Austin: University of Texas Press, 1985.

———. *Custer Died for Your Sins: An Indian Manifesto.* 1969; Norman: University of Oklahoma Press, 1988.

———. *God Is Red: A Native View of Religion.* 1972; Golden, CO: Fulcrum, 2003.

Demos, T. J. *The Exiles of Marcel Duchamp.* Cambridge, MA: MIT Press, 2007.

———. *The Migrant Image: The Art and Politics of Documentary during Global Crisis.* Durham, NC: Duke University Press, 2013.

Denzin, Norman K. *Indians on Display: Global Commodification of Native America in Performance, Art, and Museums.* Walnut Creek, CA: Left Coast, 2013.

Denzin, Norman K., Yvonna S. Lincoln, and Linda Tuhiwai Smith, eds. *Handbook of Indigenous Methodologies.* Los Angeles: Sage, 2008.

Derrida, Jacques. *Archive Fever: A Freudian Impression.* Translated by Eric Prenowitz. Chicago: University of Chicago Press, 1998.

———. "Différance." In *Margins of Philosophy*, translated by Alan Bass, 3–27. Chicago: University of Chicago Press, 1982.

Dewdney, Selwyn H. *The Sacred Scrolls of the Southern Ojibway.* Toronto: University of Toronto Press, 1975.

de Zegher, Catherine, and Gerald McMaster. *The 18th Biennale of Sydney: All Our Relations.* Woolloomooloo, NSW: Biennale of Sydney, 2012.

Dilworth, Leah. *Imagining Indians in the Southwest: Persistent Visions of a Primitive Past.* Washington, DC: Smithsonian Institution Scholarly Press, 1997.

Doueihi, Anne. "Trickster: On Inhabiting the Space between Discourse and Story." *Soundings: An Interdisciplinary Journal* 67, no. 3 (1984): 283–311.

Douglas, Frederic H. "Indian Art and American Art." *Western Artist* 1, no. 8 (1935): 3.

———. "Indian Art as a Basis for American Art." *American Library Association* 29, no. 9 (1935): 575–78.

Douglas, Frederic H., and Rene d'Harnoncourt. *Indian Art of the United States.* New York: Museum of Modern Art, 1941.

Doyle, Laura, and Laura Winkiel, eds. *Geomodernisms: Race, Modernism, Modernity.* Bloomington: Indiana University Press, 2005.

Duhaut-Cilly, Auguste. *A Voyage to California, the Sandwich Islands, and around the World in the Years 1826–1829.* Edited by August Frugé and Neal Harlow. Berkeley: University of California Press, 1999.

Dunlop, Anne. "Pinturicchio and the Pilgrims: Devotion and the Past at Santa Maria Del Popolo." *Papers of the British School at Rome*, no. 71 (2003): 259–85.

Dunn, Dorothy. *American Indian Painting of the Southwest and Plains Areas.* Albuquerque: University of New Mexico Press, 1968.

Durham, Jimmie. "1000 Words." *Artforum International* 47, no. 5 (January 2009): 189.

———. "American Indian Culture: Traditionalism and Spiritualism in a Revolutionary Struggle." Study paper, 1974.

———. "Attending to the Words and the Bones: An Interview with Jean Fisher." *Art and Design* 10, no. 7–8 (1995): 47–56.

———. "Belief in Europe." In *Unpacking Europe: Towards a Critical Reading*, edited by Salah Hassan and Iftikhar Dadi, 290–93. Rotterdam: NAi, 2002.

———. *Between the Furniture and the Building (Between a Rock and a Hard Place).* Munich, Berlin, Cologne: Kunstverein München; Berliner Künstlerprogramm DAAD; König, 1998.

———. "A Central Margin." In *The Decade Show: Frameworks of Identity in the 1980s*, edited by Louis Young, 162–79. New York: New Museum of Contemporary Art, 1990.

———. *A Certain Lack of Coherence: Writings on Art and Cultural Politics.* Edited by Jean Fisher. London: Kala, 1993.

————. *Columbus Day: Poems, Drawings and Stories about American Indian Life and Death in the Nineteen-Seventies.* Minneapolis: West End, 1983.

————. "Jimmie Durham." In *Land, Spirit, Power: First Nations Art at the National Gallery of Canada,* edited by Diana Nemiroff, Robert Houle, and Charlotte Townsend-Gault, 143–46. Ottawa: National Gallery of Canada, 1992.

————. *Mataoka Ake Attakulakula Anel Guledisgo Hnihi: Pocahontas and the Little Carpenter in London.* London: Matt's Gallery, 1988.

————. *A Road Book.* London: Koenig Books, 2011.

————. "Savage Attacks on White Women as Usual." In *We the People,* edited by Jimmie Durham and Jean Fisher, 14–19. New York: Artists Space, 1987.

————. *Stone Heart.* Kitakyushu, Japan: Center for Contemporary Art, CCA Kitakyushu, 2001.

————. *Ucelli/Birds.* Rome: Zerynthia, 1997.

————. *. . . Very Much Like the Wild Irish: Notes on a Process Which Has No End in Sight.* Derry, Northern Ireland: Orchard Gallery, 1988.

Durham, Jimmie, and Jean Fisher. "The Ground Has Been Covered." *Artforum International* 26, no. 10 (Summer 1988): 99–105.

Durham, Scott. *Phantom Communities: The Simulacrum and the Limits of Postmodernism.* Palo Alto, CA: Stanford University Press, 1998.

Durland, Steven. "'Call Me in '93': An Interview with James Luna." *High Performance* 56 (Winter 1991): 34–39.

Eisler, Benita. *The Red Man's Bones: George Catlin, Artist and Showman.* New York: W. W. Norton, 2013.

Eldredge, Charles C., Julie Schimmel, and William H. Truettner. *Art in New Mexico, 1900–1945: Paths to Taos and Santa Fe.* Washington, DC: National Museum of American Art, Smithsonian Institution, and Abbeville Press, 1986.

Elkins, James. *Is Art History Global?* London: Routledge, 2006.

Elkins, James, and David Morgan, *Re-Enchantment.* New York: Routledge, 2007.

Elliott, David. *17th Biennale of Sydney: The Beauty of Distance: Songs of Survival in a Precarious Age.* Woolloomooloo, NSW: Biennale of Sydney, 2010.

Ellison, George, ed. *James Mooney's History, Myths, and Sacred Formulas of the Cherokees.* Asheville, NC: Bright Mountain Books, 1992.

Ellison, Rosemary, and Myles Libhart. *Contemporary Southern Plains Indian Painting.* Anadarko: Oklahoma Indian Arts and Crafts Board, 1972.

English, Darby. *How to See a Work of Art in Total Darkness.* Cambridge, MA: MIT Press, 2007.

Enwezor, Okwui. *Archive Fever: Uses of the Document in Contemporary Art.* Göttingen: Steidl, 2008.

Errington, Shelly. *The Death of Authentic Primitive Art and Other Tales of Progress.* Berkeley: University of California Press, 1998.

Euripides. *The Tragedies of Euripides.* Translated by T. A. Buckley. London: Henry G. Bohn, 1850.

Evans, Katherine Young. "'Our Lives Will Be Different Now': The Indigenous Feminist Performances of Spiderwoman Theater." In *Indigenous Women and Feminism: Politics, Activism, Culture*, edited by Cheryl Suzack, Shari M. Huhndorf, Jeanne Perreault, and Jean Barman, 258–77. Vancouver: University of British Columbia Press, 2010.

Evans, Laura M. "The Artifact Piece and Artifact Piece, Revisited." In *Action and Agency: Advancing the Dialogue on Native Performance Art*, edited by Nancy J. Blomberg, 63–88. Denver: Denver Art Museum, 2010.

Fabian, Johannes. *Time and the Other: How Anthropology Makes Its Object.* New York: Columbia University Press, 2002.

Fanon, Frantz. *Black Skin, White Masks.* 1952; New York: Grove, 1994.

Farago, Claire. "Epilogue: Re(f)using Art: Aby Warburg and the Ethics of Scholarship." In *Transforming Images: New Mexican Santos in-between Worlds*, edited by Claire Farago and Donna Pierce, 259–73. University Park: Penn State University Press, 2006.

———, ed. *Reframing the Renaissance: Visual Culture in Europe and Latin America, 1450–1650.* New Haven, CT: Yale University Press, 1995.

Feest, Christian F., ed. *Indians and Europe: An Interdisciplinary Collection of Essays.* Lincoln: University of Nebraska Press, 1999.

Fenn, Elizabeth A. "Biological Warfare in Eighteenth-Century North America: Beyond Jeffery Amherst." *Journal of American History* 86, no. 4 (March 1, 2000): 1552–80.

———. *Encounters at the Heart of the World: A History of the Mandan People.* New York: Hill and Wang, 2014.

———. *Pox Americana: The Great Smallpox Epidemic of 1775–82.* New York: Hill and Wang, 2001.

Ferber, Linda S., and Angela Miller. "Albert Bierstadt, Landscape Aesthetics, and the Meanings of the West in the Civil War Era." *Art Institute of Chicago Museum Studies* 27, no. 1 (January 2001): 40–102.

Ferguson, Russell, Martha Gever, Trinh T. Minh-ha, and Cornel West, eds. *Out There: Marginalization and Contemporary Cultures.* Cambridge, MA: MIT Press, 1990.

Fewkes, Jesse Walter. "Hopi Katcinas Drawn by Native Artists." In *Twenty-First Annual Report of the Bureau of American Ethnology*, 3–126. Washington, DC: Government Printing Office, 1903.

———. *Hopi Snake Ceremonies: An Eyewitness Account.* 1894–98; Albuquerque: Avanyu, 1986.

Filipovic, Elena, Marieke Van Hal, and Solveig Øvstebo, eds. *The Biennial Reader.* Stuttgart: Hatje Cantz, 2010.

Fisher, Jean. "Fictional Histories: Magiciens de la Terre." *Artforum International* 28 (September 1989): 158–62.

————, ed. *Global Visions: Towards a New Internationalism in the Visual Arts*. London: Kala Press; Institute of International Visual Arts, 1994.

————. "In Search of the 'Inauthentic': Disturbing Signs in Contemporary Native American Art." In "Recent Native American Art," edited by W. Jackson Rushing and Kay WalkingStick, special issue, *Art Journal* 51, no. 3 (Fall 1992): 44–50.

————. *Vampire in the Text: Narratives of Contemporary Art*. London: Institute of International Visual Arts, 2003.

Flam, Jack D. "Matisse and the Fauves." In *"Primitivism" in 20th Century Art: Affinity of the Tribal and the Modern*, edited by William Rubin, 211–40. New York: Museum of Modern Art, 1984.

————. *Matisse: The Dance*. Washington, DC: National Gallery of Art, 1993.

Flam, Jack D., and Miriam Deutch, eds. *Primitivism and Twentieth Century Art: A Documentary History*. Berkeley: University of California Press, 2003.

Flatley, Jonathan. "Like: Collecting and Collectivity." *October* 132 (Spring 2010): 71–98.

Flint, Kate. *The Transatlantic Indian, 1776–1930*. Princeton, NJ: Princeton University Press, 2009.

Foley, Jack. "Interview with Gerald Vizenor." *Mythosphere* 1, no. 3 (1999): 304–17.

Folie, Sabine, and Anselm Franke, eds. *Animism: Modernity through the Looking Glass*. Cologne: Walther König, 2012.

Foner, Philip Sheldon. *The Case of Joe Hill*. New York: International Publishers, 1965.

Forbes, Jack D. *Africans and Native Americans: The Language of Race and the Evolution of Red-Black Peoples*. Chicago: University of Illinois Press, 1993.

Force, Roland W. *Politics and the Museum of the American Indian: The Heye and the Mighty*. Honolulu: Mechas, 1999.

Foreman, Carolyn Thomas. *Indians Abroad, 1493–1938*. Norman: University of Oklahoma Press, 1943.

Forte, Maximilian C., ed. *Indigenous Cosmopolitans: Transnational and Transcultural Indigeneity in the Twenty-First Century*. New York: Peter Lang, 2009.

Foster, Hal. "An Archival Impulse." *October*, no. 110 (October 2004): 3–22.

————. "The 'Primitive' Unconscious of Modern Art." *October*, no. 34 (Autumn 1985): 45–70.

Foucault, Michel. *The Archaeology of Knowledge and the Discourse on Language*. Translated by Rupert Swyer. 1971; New York: Vintage, 1982.

————. *Discipline and Punish: The Birth of the Prison*. New York: Knopf Doubleday, 1977.

————. *The Order of Things: An Archaeology of the Human Sciences*. 1966; New York: Routledge, 2002.

Franke, Anselm. "Across the Rationalist Veil." *e-flux journal*, no. 8 (September 2009): http://www.e-flux.com/journal/view/79.

————, ed. *Animism Volume I*. Antwerp: Sternberg Press / Extra City, 2010.

————. "Autonomy and Mirrors." In *Jimmie Durham: Essence*. Zurich: de Pury & Luxembourg, 2007.

————. "Much Trouble in the Transportation of Souls, or: The Sudden Disorganization of Boundaries." In *Animism Volume I*, edited by Anselm Franke, 11–53. Antwerp: Sternberg Press / Extra City, 2010.

————. "Untying the Modern Knot." In *Jimmie Durham: Rejected Stones*, 30–35. Paris: Musée d'Art Moderne de la Ville de Paris/ARC, 2009.

Franke, Anselm, and Bruno Latour. "Angels without Wings." In *Animism Volume I*, edited by Anselm Franke, 86–96. Antwerp: Sternberg Press / Extra City, 2010.

Franklin, Sarah, and Susan McKinnon. "Introduction." In *Relative Values: Reconfiguring Kinship Studies*, edited by Sarah Franklin and Susan McKinnon, 1–28. Durham, NC: Duke University Press, 2001.

————, eds. *Relative Values: Reconfiguring Kinship Studies*. Durham, NC: Duke University Press, 2001.

Fraser, Andrea. "An Artist's Statement" (1994). In *Institutional Critique: An Anthology of Artists' Writings*, edited by Alexander Alberro and Blake Stimson, 318–29. Cambridge, MA: MIT Press, 2009.

Freedberg, David. "Pathos a Oraibi: Ciò che Warburg non vide." In *Lo Sguardo di Giano, Aby Warburg fra tempo e memoria*, edited by Claudia Cieri Via and Pietro Montani, 569–611. Turin: Nino Aragno, 2004.

Friedman, Susan Stanford. "Periodizing Modernism: Postcolonial Modernities and the Space/Time Borders of Modernist Studies." *Modernism/Modernity* 13, no. 3 (September 2006): 425–43.

Gamble, Lynn H. *The Chumash World at European Contact: Power, Trade, and Feasting among Complex Hunter-Gatherers*. Berkeley: University of California Press, 2008.

Garroutte, Eva. *Real Indians: Identity and the Survival of Native America*. Berkeley: University of California Press, 2003.

Gell, Alfred. *Art and Agency: An Anthropological Theory*. Oxford: Oxford University Press, 1998.

Gilbert, Matthew Sakiestewa. *Education beyond the Mesas: Hopi Students at Sherman Institute, 1902–1929*. Lincoln: University of Nebraska Press, 2010.

Gilroy, Paul. *The Black Atlantic: Modernity and Double-Consciousness*. Cambridge, MA: Harvard University Press, 1993.

Goldberg, Jonathan, and Madhavi Menon. "Queering History." *PMLA* 120, no. 5 (October 2005): 1608–17.

Goldwater, Robert. *Primitivism in Modern Art*. 1966; Cambridge, MA: Belknap Press, 1986.

González, Jennifer A. *Subject to Display: Reframing Race in Contemporary Installation Art*. Cambridge, MA: MIT Press, 2008.

Gray, Samuel L. *Tonita Peña: Quah Ah, 1893–1949*. Albuquerque: Avanyu, 1990.

Greenberg, Clement. *The Collected Essays and Criticism*, vol. 1: *Perceptions and Judgments, 1939–1944*. Edited by John O'Brian. Chicago: University of Chicago Press, 1986.

————. *The Collected Essays and Criticism*, vol. 4: *Modernism with a Vengeance, 1957–1969*. Edited by John O'Brian. Chicago: University of Chicago Press, 1993.

Greenhalgh, Paul. *Ephemeral Vistas: The Expositions Universelles, Great Exhibitions, and World's Fairs, 1851–1939*. Manchester, UK: Manchester University Press, 1988.

Griffin, Charles Eldridge. *Four Years in Europe with Buffalo Bill*. Edited by Chris Dixon. Lincoln: University of Nebraska Press, 2010.

Grinde, Donald A., Jr. "Who Is an American Indian?" *Indigenous Thoughts* 1 (June 1991): 24A.

Gritton, Joy L. *The Institute of American Indian Arts: Modernism and U.S. Indian Policy*. Albuquerque: University of New Mexico Press, 2000.

Gruzinski, Serge. *The Mestizo Mind: The Intellectual Dynamics of Colonization and Globalization*. Translated by Deke Dusinberre. New York: Routledge, 2002.

Gurney, George, and Therese Thau Heyman, eds. *George Catlin and His Indian Gallery*. Washington, DC: Smithsonian American Art Museum, 2002.

Haas, Lisbeth. "The Life and Writing of Luiseño Scholar Pablo Tac, 1820–1841." In Lisbeth Haas, James Luna, and Pablo Tac, *Pablo Tac, Indigenous Scholar*, 3–40. Berkeley: University of California Press, 2011.

————. "'Raise Your Sword and I Will Eat You': Luiseño Scholar Pablo Tac, ca. 1841." In *Alta California: Peoples in Motion, Identities in Formation, 1769–1850*, edited by Steven W. Hackel, 79–110. Berkeley: University of California Press, 2010.

Hackel, Steven W. *Children of Coyote, Missionaries of Saint Francis: Indian-Spanish Relations in Colonial California, 1769–1850*. Chapel Hill: University of North Carolina Press, 2005.

Hallendy, Norman. *Inuksuit: Silent Messengers of the Arctic*. Vancouver: Douglas & McIntyre, 2000.

Hallowell, A. Irving. *Contributions to Ojibwe Studies: Essays, 1934–1972*. Critical Studies in the History of Anthropology. Lincoln: University of Nebraska Press, 2010.

————. "Ojibwa Ontology, Behavior, and World View." In *Culture in History: Essays in Honor of Paul Radin*, 19–52. New York: Columbia University Press, 1960.

Harris, Jonathan Gil. "Untimely Mediations." *Early Modern Culture: An Electronic Seminar*, no. 6 (2007): http://emc.eserver.org/1–6/harris.html.

Hartley, Marsden. "Red Man Ceremonials: An American Plea for American Esthetics." *Art and Archaeology* 9, no. 1 (January 1920): 7–14.

————. "The Scientific Esthetic of the Red Man I." *Art and Archaeology* 13, no. 3 (1922): 113–19.

————. "The Scientific Esthetic of the Red Man II." *Art and Archaeology* 14, no. 3 (1922): 137–40.

Harvey, Penelope. *Hybrids of Modernity: Anthropology, the Nation State and the Universal Exhibition*. New York: Routledge, 1996.

Hassan, Salah, and Iftikhar Dadi, eds. *Unpacking Europe*. Rotterdam: NAi, 2002.

Hassrick, Peter H., and Elizabeth J. Cunningham. *In Contemporary Rhythm: The Art of Ernest L. Blumenschein*. Norman: University of Oklahoma Press, 2008.

Haverstock, Mary Sayre. *The Indian Gallery: The Story of George Catlin*. New York: Four Winds, 1973.

Hedges, Ken. *Fibers and Forms: Native American Basketry of the West*. San Diego: San Diego Museum of Man, 1997.

Hewett, Edgar L. "Native American Artists." *Art and Archaeology* 13, no. 3 (March 1922): 103–12.

Heyman, Therese Thau. "George Catlin and the Smithsonian." In *George Catlin and His Indian Gallery*, edited by George Gurney and Therese Thau Heyman, 249–71. Washington, DC: Smithsonian American Art Museum, 2002.

Hight, Kathryn S. "'Doomed to Perish': George Catlin's Depictions of the Mandan." *Art Journal* 49, no. 2 (Summer 1990): 119–24.

Highwater, Jamake. *Song from the Earth: American Indian Painting*. Boston: New York Graphic Society, 1976.

Hill, Greg A., Candice Hopkins, and Christine LaLonde. *Sakahàn: International Indigenous Art*. Ottawa: National Gallery of Canada, 2013.

Hill, Richard William. "After Authenticity: A Postmortem on the Racialized Indian Body." In *Hide: Skin as Material and Metaphor*, edited by Kathleen Ash-Milby, 97–107. Washington, DC: Smithsonian National Museum of the American Indian, 2010.

———. "Built on Running Water: Rebecca Belmore's *Fountain*." *Ruse* 29, no. 1 (2006): 49–51.

———. "The Dangers of Petrification, or 'The Work of Art and the Ages of Mineral Reproduction.'" *Animism Volume I*, edited by Anselme Franke, 134–37. Antwerp: Sternberg Press / Extra City, 2010.

———. "The Malice and Benevolence of Inanimate Objects: Jimmie Durham's Anti-Architecture." In Jimmie Durham, *A Matter of Life and Death and Singing*, 75–83. Antwerp: MUHKA, 2012.

———. "The Question of Agency in the Art and Writing of Jimmie Durham." PhD diss., Middlesex University, 2010.

———. "Sakahàn: International Indigenous Art." *Fuse Magazine* 36, no. 4 (November 2013): 40–42.

Hill, Richard William, and Beverly Koski. "The Centre of the World Is Several Places, Parts I and II." *FUSE Magazine* 21, nos. 3 and 4 (1998): 24–33, 46–53.

Hiller, Susan, ed. *The Myth of Primitivism: Perspectives on Art*. London: Routledge, 1991.

Hirsch, Marianne, and Diana Taylor. "The Archive in Transit." *E-misférica* 9, nos. 1 and 2 (Summer 2012). On the Subject of Archives, edited by Marianne Hirsch and Diana Taylor: http://hemisphericinstitute.org/hemi/en/e-misferica-91.

Holway, Mary Gordon. *The Art of the Old World in New Spain and the Mission Days of Alta California*. San Francisco: A. M. Robertson, 1922.

Honour, Hugh. *The New Golden Land: European Images of America from the Discoveries to the Present Time*. New York: Pantheon, 1975.

hooks, bell. "Choosing the Margin as a Space of Radical Openness." In *Yearnings: Race, Gender, and Cultural Politics*, 203–9. Cambridge, MA: South End, 1999.

Horse Capture, George P., and Anne Vitart. *Robes of Splendor: Native American Painted Buffalo Hides*. New York: New Press, 1993.

Horton, Jessica L. "Alone on the Snow, Alone on the Beach: 'A Global Sense of Place' in *Atanarjuat* and *Fountain*." *Journal of Transnational American Studies* 4, no. 1 (2012): 1–25.

———. "Jimmie Durham's Stones and Bones." In *Jimmie Durham: At the Center of the World*, edited by Anne Ellegood, 78–85. Los Angeles: Hammer Museum, 2011.

———. "Of Mimicry and Drag: Homi Bhabha and Kent Monkman." In *Theorizing Visual Studies: Writing through the Discipline*, edited by James Elkins, Kristi McGuire, Maureen Burns, Alicia Chester, and Joel Kuennen, 169–91. New York: Routledge, 2013.

———. "Painter, Traveler, Diplomat." In *Super Indian: Fritz Scholder*, edited by John P. Lukavic, 41–53. New York: Prestel.

———. "'Study It Lightly.'" *Parkett*, no. 92 (June 2013): 48–58.

Horton, Jessica L., and Janet Catherine Berlo. "Beyond the Mirror: Indigenous Ecologies and 'New Materialisms' in Contemporary Art." *Third Text*, no. 120 (2013).

———. "Pueblo Painting in 1932: Folding Narratives of Native Art into American Art History." In *A Companion to American Art History*, edited by Jennifer Greenhill, John Davis, and Jason LaFountain, 264–80. London: Blackwell, 2015.

Horton, Jessica L., and Cherise Smith. "The Particulars of Postidentity." *American Art* 28, no. 1 (Spring 2014): 2–8.

Houle, Robert. *Robert Houle: enuhmo andúhuaun (the road home)*. Winnipeg: University of Manitoba School of Art Gallery, 2012.

———. "The Spiritual Legacy of the Ancient Ones." In *Land, Spirit, Power: First Nations at the National Gallery of Canada*, edited by Diana Nemiroff, Robert Houle, and Charlotte Townsend-Gault, 43–74. Ottawa: National Gallery of Canada, 1992.

———. "A Transatlantic Return Home through the Magic of Art." In *Robert Houle's Paris/Ojibwa*, edited by Paul Gardner, 44–56. Peterborough, ON: Art Gallery of Peterborough, 2011.

Houle, Robert, in conversation with Clara Hargittay. "The Struggle against Cultural Apartheid." *Muse* 6, no. 3 (Autumn 1988): 58–60.

Houle, Robert, and Shirley Madill. *Robert Houle: Sovereignty over Subjectivity*. Winnipeg: Winnipeg Art Gallery, 1999.

Hoxie, Frederick E. *A Final Promise: The Campaign to Assimilate the Indians, 1880–1920*. Lincoln: University of Nebraska Press, 2001.

———. "Retrieving the Red Continent: Settler Colonialism and the History of

American Indians in the U.S." *Ethnic and Racial Studies* 31 (September 2008): 1153–67.

Huang, Hsinya, Philip J. Deloria, Laurie M. Furlan, and John Gambler. "Charting Transnational Native American Studies." *Journal of Transnational American Studies* 4, no. 1 (2012): 1–15.

Huhndorf, Shari M. *Mapping the Americas: The Transnational Politics of Contemporary Native Culture.* Ithaca, NY: Cornell University Press, 2009.

Hutchinson, Elizabeth. *The Indian Craze: Primitivism, Modernism, and Trans-culturation in American Art, 1890–1915.* Durham, NC: Duke University Press, 2009.

Hyer, Sally. *One House, One Voice, One Heart: Native American Education at the Santa Fe Indian School.* Albuquerque: Museum of New Mexico Press, 1990.

Ickes, Charlotte. "The Sartorial and the Skin: Portraits of Pocahontas and Allegories of English Empire." *American Art* 29, no. 1 (Spring 2015): 82–105.

Impey, Oliver, and Arthur MacGregor, eds. *The Origins of Museums: The Cabinet of Curiosities in Sixteenth- and Seventeenth-Century Europe.* Oxford: Clarendon, 1985.

Inda, Jonathan Xavier, and Renato Rosaldo. *The Anthropology of Globalization.* Oxford: Blackwell, 2008.

Ingberman, Jeanette, ed. *Jimmie Durham: The Bishop's Moose and the Pinkerton Men.* New York: Exit Art, 1989.

Ingold, Tim. *The Perception of the Environment: Essays on Livelihood, Dwelling and Skill.* London: Routledge, 2011.

"Interview: Dirk Snauwaert in Conversation with Jimmie Durham." In *Jimmie Durham*, edited by Laura Mulvey, Dirk Snauwaert, and Mark Alice Durant, 6–29. London: Phaidon, 1995.

Jacobs, Margaret. *Engendered Encounters: Feminism and Pueblo Cultures, 1879–1934.* Lincoln: University of Nebraska Press, 1999.

James, George Wharton. *Picturesque Pala: The Story of the Mission Chapel of San Antonio de Padua, Connected with Mission San Luis Rey.* Fairfield, CA: James Stevenson, 2002.

Jantzer-White, Marilee. "Tonita Peña (Quah Ah), Pueblo Painter: Asserting Identity through Continuity and Change." *American Indian Quarterly* 18, no. 3 (Summer 1994): 369–82.

Jardin, Lisa. *Worldly Goods: A New History of the Renaissance.* New York: Doubleday, 1996.

Jett, Stephen C. "Cairn and Brush Travel Shrines in the United States Northeast and Southeast." *Northeast Anthropology* 48 (1994): 61–67.

———. "Cairn Trail Shrines in Middle and South America." *Yearbook/Conference of Latin Americanist Geographers* 20 (1994): 1–8.

Jimmie Durham: Rejected Stones. Paris: Musée d'Art Moderne de la Ville de Paris/ARC, 2009.

John, Gareth E. "Benevolent Imperialism: George Catlin and the Practice of

Jeffersonian Geography." *Journal of Historical Geography* 30, no. 4 (October 2004): 597–617.

Johnson, Troy, Joane Nagel, and Duane Champagne, eds. *American Indian Activism: Alcatraz to the Longest Walk.* Urbana: University of Illinois Press, 1997.

Jojola, Ted. "Notes on Identity, Time, Space, and Place." In *American Indian Thought: Philosophical Essays,* edited by Anne Waters, 87–96. Malden, MA: Blackwell, 2004.

Jones, Amelia. "'The Artist Is Present': Artistic Re-Enactments and the Impossibility of Presence." *TDR: The Drama Review* 55, no. 1 (Spring 2011): 16–45.

———. "Introduction." In "Forum: Performance, Live or Dead," special issue, *Art Journal* 70, no. 3 (Fall 2011): 33–38.

———. "Live Art in Art History: A Paradox?" In *The Cambridge Companion to Performance Studies,* edited by Tracy C. Davis, 151–65. Cambridge: Cambridge University Press, 2008.

Jonnes, Jill. *Eiffel's Tower: And the World's Fair Where Buffalo Bill Beguiled Paris, the Artists Quarreled, and Thomas Edison Became a Count.* New York: Penguin, 2010.

Josephy, Alvin M., Jr., Joane Nagel, and Troy R. Johnson, eds. *Red Power: The American Indians' Fight for Freedom.* 2nd ed. Lincoln: University of Nebraska Press, 1999.

Juneja, Monica. "Global Art History and the 'Burden of Representation.'" In *Global Studies: Mapping Contemporary Art and Culture,* edited by Hans Belting, Jakob Birken, and Andrea Buddensieg, 274–97. Stuttgart: Hatje Cantz, 2011.

Justice, Daniel Heath. "'Go Away Water!': Kinship Criticism and the Decolonization Imperative." In *Reasoning Together: The Native Critics Collective,* edited by Craig S. Womack, Daniel Heath Justice, and Christopher B. Teuton, 147–68. Norman: University of Oklahoma Press, 2008.

Kabotie, Fred. *Designs from the Ancient Mimbreños: With a Hopi Interpretation.* 1949; Flagstaff, AZ: Northland, 1982.

———. "Odyssey of Three Native American Artists: Bicycling to Jemez Springs in 1922." *El Palacio* 88, no. 7 (1988): 31–37.

Kabotie, Fred, and Bill Belknap. *Fred Kabotie, Hopi Indian Artist: An Autobiography Told with Bill Belknap.* Flagstaff: Museum of Northern Arizona, 1977.

Kalbfleisch, Elizabeth. "Bordering on Feminism: Home and Transnational Sites in Recent Visual Culture and Native Women's Art." PhD diss., University of Rochester, 2009.

Kant, Immanuel. *Kant's Critique of Judgment.* 2nd ed. Translated by J. H. Bernard. London: Macmillan and Co., 1914.

Kaplan, Caren. *Questions of Travel: Postmodern Discourses of Displacement.* Durham, NC: Duke University Press, 1996.

Karttunen, Frances. *Between Worlds: Interpreters, Guides, and Survivors.* Newark, NJ: Rutgers University Press, 1996.

Kastner, Carolyn. "Changing Perspectives on Cultural Patrimony: Katsina Tithu." In *Georgia O'Keeffe in New Mexico: Architecture, Katsinam, and the Land,* edited by

Barbara Buhler Lynes and Carolyn Kastner, 99–110. Santa Fe: Museum of New Mexico Press, 2012.

———. *Jaune Quick-to-See Smith: An American Modernist*. Albuquerque: University of New Mexico Press, 2013.

Keber, Eloise Quiñones. *Codex Telleriano-Remensis: Ritual, Divination, and History in a Pictorial Aztec Manuscript*. Austin: University of Texas Press, 1995.

———. "Collecting Cultures: A Mexican Manuscript in the Vatican Library." In *Reframing the Renaissance: Visual Culture in Europe and Latin America, 1450–1650*, edited by Claire Farago, 229–42. New Haven, CT: Yale University Press, 1995.

Kelly, James C. "Notable Persons in Cherokee History: Attakullakulla." *Journal of Cherokee Studies* 3, no. 1 (Winter 1978): 2–34.

Kemp, Martin, ed. *Leonardo on Painting*. Translated by Martin Kemp and Margaret Walker. New Haven, CT: Yale University Press, 1989.

Kester, Grant. *The One and the Many: Contemporary Collaborative Art in a Global Context*. Durham, NC: Duke University Press, 2011.

Ketchum, Shanna. "Native American Cosmopolitan Modernism(s): A Re-Articulation of Presence through Time and Space." *Third Text* 19, no. 4 (2005): 357–64.

Kidwell, Clara Sue. "Every Last Dishcloth: The Prodigious Collecting of George Gustav Heye." In *Collecting Native America*, edited by Shepard Krech III and Barbara A. Hail, 232–58. Washington, DC: Smithsonian Institution Press, 1999.

Knollenberg, Bernhard. "General Amherst and Germ Warfare." *Mississippi Valley Historical Review* 41, no. 3 (1954): 489–94.

Krauss, Rosalind E. "Preying on 'Primitivism.'" *Art and Text*, no. 17 (April 1985): 58–62.

Kroeber, Alfred L. "Basketry Designs of the Mission Indians." *American Museum of Natural History Guide Leaflet*, no. 55 (July 1922).

———. *Handbook of the Indians of California*. 1925; New York: Dover, 1976.

———. *Indian Myths of South Central California*. Vol. 4, no. 4. Berkeley: University of California Publications, American Archaeology and Ethnology, 1907.

Kuoni, Caren. *Energy Plan for the Western Man: Joseph Beuys in America*. New York: Four Walls Eight Windows, 1990.

Kwon, Miwon. *One Place after Another: Site-Specific Art and Locational Identity*. Cambridge, MA: MIT Press, 2004.

LaDuke, Winona. *All Our Relations: Native Struggles for Land and Life*. Cambridge, MA: South End Press, 1999.

La Farge, Oliver. "An Art That Is Really American." *Washington Post*, April 26, 1931, 2, 15.

Lambert-Beatty, Carrie. *Being Watched: Yvonne Rainer and the 1960s*. Cambridge, MA: MIT Press, 2008.

Landes, Ruth. *Ojibwa Religion and the Midéwiwin*. Madison: University of Wisconsin Press, 1968.

Lanyon, Anna. *Malinche's Conquest*. St. Leonards, Australia: Allen & Unwin Academic, 2000.

Large, David Clay. *Between Two Fires: Europe's Path in the 1930s.* New York: W. W. Norton, 1991.

Larson, Jennifer. *Greek Nymphs: Myth, Cult, Lore.* Oxford: Oxford University Press, 2001.

Latour, Bruno. "Pasteur on Lactic Acid Yeast: A Partial Semiotic Analysis." In *Configurations* 1, no. 1 (1993): 129–46.

———. *Rejoicing: Or the Torments of Religious Speech.* Cambridge: Polity, 2013.

———. "'Thou Shalt Not Take the Lord's Name in Vain'—Being a Sort of Sermon on the Hesitations of Religious Speech." *Res,* no. 39 (Spring 2001): 215–34.

———. *We Have Never Been Modern.* Translated by Catherine Porter. Cambridge, MA: Harvard University Press, 1993.

Lee, A. Robert, ed. *Loosening the Seams: Interpretations of Gerald Vizenor.* Bowling Green, OH: Bowling Green State University Popular Press, 2000.

Lee, Pamela M. *Forgetting the Art World.* Cambridge, MA: MIT Press, 2012.

Lefebvre, Henri. *The Production of Space.* Translated by Donald Nicholson-Smith. 1974; Oxford: Wiley-Blackwell, 1992.

LeMaster, Michelle. "Pocahontas: (De)Constructing an American Myth." *William and Mary Quarterly* 62, no. 4 (2005): 774–81.

Lepecki, André. "The Body as Archive: Will to Re-Enact and the Afterlives of Dances." *Dance Research Journal* 42, no. 2 (2010): 28–48.

Lippard, Lucy R. "Jimmie Durham: Postmodernist 'Savage.'" *Art in America* 81, no. 2 (February 1993): 55, 63–68.

———. "Little Red Lies." In *Jimmie Durham: The Bishop's Moose and the Pinkerton Men,* edited by Jeanette Ingberman, 22–29. New York: Exit Art, 1989.

———. *The Lure of the Local: Senses of Place in a Multicentered Society.* New York: New Press, 1998.

———. *Mixed Blessings: New Art in a Multicultural America.* New York: New Press, 1990.

———. "Signs of Unrest." In *Most Serene Republics: Edgar Heap of Birds,* edited by Kathleen Ash-Milby and Truman T. Lowe, 17–33. Washington, DC: Smithsonian National Museum of the American Indian, 2007.

List, George. *Stability and Variation in Hopi Song.* Philadelphia: American Philosophical Society, 1993.

Lockhart, James, ed. and trans. *We People Here: Nahuatl Accounts of the Conquest of Mexico, Vol. 1.* Eugene, OR: Wipf & Stock, 1993.

Loftin, John D. *Religion and Hopi Life.* 2nd ed. Indianapolis: Indiana University Press, 2003.

Lonetree, Amy, and Amanda J. Cobb-Greetham, eds. *The National Museum of the American Indian: Critical Conversations.* Lincoln: University of Nebraska Press, 2008.

Low, Setha, and Denise Lawrence-Zúñiga, eds. *The Anthropology of Space and Place: Locating Culture.* Malden, MA: Blackwell, 2003.

Lowe, Truman, and Paul Chaat Smith, eds. *James Luna: Emendatio.* Washington, DC: Smithsonian National Museum of the American Indian, 2005.

Luna, James. "Fasten Your Seat Belts, Prepare for Landing: The Travels of Payom-kowishum Art Warriors." In Lisbeth Haas, James Luna, and Pablo Tac, *Pablo Tac, Indigenous Scholar*, 41–45. Berkeley: University of California Press, 2011.

———. "I've Always Wanted to Be an American Indian." In "Recent Native American Art," edited by W. Jackson Rushing and Kay WalkingStick, special issue, *Art Journal* 51, no. 3 (Fall 1992): 18–27.

———. *James Luna*. San Diego: Centro Cultural de la Raza, 1985.

———. *The Sacred Colors*. Sacramento, CA: Galeria Posada, 1992.

———. "Sun and Moon Blues." In *Obsession, Compulsion, Collection: On Objects, Display, Culture and Interpretation*, edited by Anthony Kiendl, 146–53. Banff, Alberta: Banff Centre Press, 2004.

Lynes, Barbara Buhler, and Carolyn Kastner, eds. *Georgia O'Keeffe in New Mexico: Architecture, Katsinam, and the Land*. Santa Fe: Museum of New Mexico Press, 2012.

Lyons, Chief Oren, John Mohawk, and José Barreiro. "Spiritualism: The Highest Form of Political Consciousness: The Haudenosaunee Message to the Western World" (1977). In *A Basic Call to Consciousness*, 85–91. Summertown, TN: Book Publishing Company, 2005.

Magaloni-Kerpel, Diana. "Painting a New Era: Conquest, Prophecy, and the World to Come." In *Invasion and Transformation: Interdisciplinary Perspectives on the Conquest of Mexico*, edited by Rebecca P. Brienen and Margaret A. Jackson, 125–49. Boulder: University Press of Colorado, 2008.

Malevich, Kasimir. *The Non-Objective World: The Manifesto of Suprematism*. New York: Dover, 2003.

Malotki, Ekkehart. *Kokopelli: The Making of an Icon*. Lincoln: University of Nebraska Press, 2000.

Marriott, Alice. *María, the Potter of San Ildefonso*. Norman: University of Oklahoma Press, 1948.

Martin, Jean. *Magiciens de la Terre*. Paris: Editions du Centre Pompidou, 1989.

Martin, Lee-Ann. "Cross Over with Mr. Luna." In *Diversity and Dialogue: The Eiteljorg Fellowship for Native American Fine Art*, 25–32. Indianapolis: Eiteljorg Museum of American Indians and Western Art, 2007.

———. "The Waters of Venice: Rebecca Belmore at the 51st Biennale." *Canadian Art* 22, no. 2 (2005): 48–53.

Mason, Peter. *Deconstructing America: Representations of the Other*. London: Routledge, 1990.

Massey, Doreen. *For Space*. London: Sage, 2005.

———. *Space, Place, and Gender*. Minneapolis: University of Minnesota Press, 1994.

Masters, Joshua J. "Reading the Book of Nature, Inscribing the Savage Mind: George Catlin and the Textualization of the American West." *American Studies* 46, no. 2 (Summer 2005): 63–89.

Maungwudaus. *An Account of the Chippewa Indians: Who Have Been Travelling among*

the Whites, in the United States, England, Ireland, Scotland, France and Belgium, with
    Very Interesting Incidents in Relation to the General Characteristics of the English, Irish,
    Scotch, French, and Americans, with Regard to Their Hospitality, Peculiarities, Etc.
    Boston: The Author, 1848.

Mayor, Adrienne. "The Nessus Shirt in the New World: Smallpox Blankets in History
    and Legend." Journal of American Folklore 108, no. 427 (1995): 54–77.

McCoy, Ronald. "Hopi Artist Fred Kabotie, 1900–1986." American Indian Art
    Magazine (Autumn 1990): 40–49.

McGeough, Michelle. Through Their Eyes: Indian Painting in Santa Fe, 1918–1945.
    Santa Fe: Wheelwright Museum of the American Indian, 2009.

McIntosh, David. "Traveling Light: Paris/Ojibwa." In Robert Houle's Paris/Ojibwa,
    edited by Paul Gardner, 14–19. Peterborough, ON: Art Gallery of Peterborough,
    2011.

McLuhan, Elizabeth, and Tom Hill. Norval Morrisseau and the Emergence of the Image
    Makers. Toronto: Art Gallery of Ontario, 1984.

McMaster, Gerald. "Borderzones: The 'Injun-uity' of Aesthetic Tricks." Cultural
    Studies 9, no. 1 (January 1995): 74–90.

———. Edward Poitras: Canada Xlvi Biennale di Venezia. Seattle: University of
    Washington Press, 1995.

———. "Indigena: A Native Curator's Perspective." In "Recent Native American Art,"
    edited by W. Jackson Rushing and Kay WalkingStick, special issue, Art Journal 51,
    no. 3 (Fall 1992): 66–73.

———. "Introduction: New Art / New Contexts." In Vision, Space, Desire: Global
    Perspectives and Cultural Hybridity, 15–29. Washington, DC: Smithsonian
    Institution National Museum of the American Indian, 2006.

———, ed. Reservation X: The Power of Place. Seattle: University of Washington Press,
    1998.

———. "Towards an Aboriginal Art History." In Native American Art in the Twentieth
    Century: Makers, Meanings, Histories, edited by W. Jackson Rushing, 81–96. New
    York: Routledge, 1999.

McMaster, Gerald, and Joe Baker. Remix: New Modernities in a Post-Indian World.
    Washington, DC: Smithsonian National Museum of the American Indian, 2007.

McMullen, Ann. "Reinventing George Heye: Nationalizing the Museum of the
    American Indian and Its Collection." In Contesting Knowledge: Museums and
    Indigenous Perspectives, edited by Susan Sleeper-Smith, 65–105. Nebraska:
    University of Nebraska Press, 2009.

Menil, Dominique de. The Rothko Chapel: Writings on Art and the Threshold of the
    Divine. Houston: Rothko Chapel, 2010.

Mercer, Kobena, ed. Cosmopolitan Modernisms. Cambridge, MA: MIT Press, 2005.

———, ed. Exiles, Diasporas and Strangers. Cambridge, MA: MIT Press, 2008.

———. "Where the Streets Have No Name." In This Will Have Been: Art, Love and

Politics in the 1980s, edited by Helen Molesworth, 235–47. New Haven, CT: Yale University Press, 2012.

Mignolo, Walter D. *The Darker Side of the Renaissance: Literacy, Territoriality, and Colonization*. Ann Arbor: University of Michigan Press, 2003.

———. *The Darker Side of Western Modernity: Global Futures, Decolonial Options*. Durham, NC: Duke University Press, 2011.

———. *Local Histories / Global Designs: Coloniality, Subaltern Knowledges, and Border Thinking*. Princeton, NJ: Princeton University Press, 2000.

Mihesuah, Devon Abbott. *Indigenous American Women: Decolonization, Empowerment, Activism*. Lincoln: University of Nebraska Press, 2003.

Miller, Bruce W. *Chumash: A Picture of Their World*. Los Osos, CA: Sand River, 1988.

Millington, C. Norris. "American Indian Water Colors." *Magazine of American Art* 25, no. 2 (1932): 83–92.

Mithlo, Nancy M. "Give, Give, Giving: Cultural Translations." In *Vision, Space, Desire: Global Perspectives and Cultural Hybridity*, 85–97. Washington, DC: Smithsonian Institution National Museum of the American Indian, 2006.

———. "History Is Dangerous." *Museum Anthropology* 19, no. 2 (1995): 50–57.

———. *Our Indian Princess: Subverting the Stereotype*. Santa Fe, NM: School for Advanced Research Press, 2009.

———. "Reappropriating Redskins: Pellerossasogna (Red Skin Dream): Shelley Niro at the 50th La Biennale di Venezia." *Visual Anthropology Review* 20, no. 2 (2005): 22–35.

———. "'We Have All Been Colonized': Subordination and Resistance on a Global Arts Stage." *Visual Anthropology* 17, no. 3 (2004): 229–45.

Moffitt, John F. "Native American 'Sauvage' as Pictured by French Romantic Artists and Writers." *Gazette des Beaux-Arts* 134, no. 1568 (September 1999): 120–26.

Moffitt, John F., and Santiago Sebastián. *The European Invention of the American Indian*. Albuquerque: University of New Mexico Press, 1996.

Molesworth, Helen, ed. *This Will Have Been: Art, Love and Politics in the 1980s*. New Haven, CT: Yale University Press, 2012.

Morgan, David, and Sally M. Promey. *The Visual Culture of American Religions*. Berkeley: University of California Press, 2000.

Morris, Kate. "Reading between the Lines: Text and Image in Contemporary Native American Art." *American Indian Art Magazine* 34, no. 2 (Spring 2009): 52–59.

Morrisseau, Norval. *Legends of My People: The Great Ojibway*. Edited by Selwyn Dewdney. Toronto: Ryerson, 1965.

Mosquera, Gerardo, and Jean Fisher, eds. *Over Here: International Perspectives on Art and Culture*. Cambridge, MA: MIT Press, 2004.

Muller, Kevin R. "From Palace to Longhouse: Portraits of the Four Indian Kings in a Transatlantic Context." *American Art* 22, no. 3 (Fall 2008): 26–49.

Mulvey, Christopher. "Among the Sag-a-noshes: Ojibwa and Iowa Indians with

George Catlin in Europe, 1843–1848." In *Indians and Europe: An Interdisciplinary Collection of Essays*, edited by Christian F. Feest, 253–76. Lincoln: University of Nebraska Press, 1999.

———. "George Catlin in Europe." In *George Catlin and His Indian Gallery*, edited by George Gurney and Therese Thau Heyman, 63–91. Washington, DC: Smithsonian American Art Museum, 2002.

Mulvey, Laura, Dirk Snauwaert, and Mark Alice Durant, eds. *Jimmie Durham*. London: Phaidon, 1995.

Nabokov, Peter. *A Forest of Time: American Indian Ways of History*. Cambridge: Cambridge University Press, 2002.

Nabokov, Peter, and Robert Easton. *Native American Architecture*. Oxford: Oxford University Press, 1990.

Nagel, Alexander. "Art Out of Time." *Artforum International* (October 2012): 233–39.

———. *Medieval Modern: Art Out of Time*. New York: Thames & Hudson, 2012.

———. *Some Discoveries of 1492: Eastern Antiquities and Renaissance Europe*. Groningen, Germany: The Gerson Lectures Foundation, 2013.

Nagel, Alexander, and Christopher S. Wood. *Anachronic Renaissance*. New York: Zone Books, 2010.

Nemiroff, Diana. "Modernism, Nationalism, and Beyond: A Critical History of Exhibitions of First Nations Art." In *Land, Spirit, Power: First Nations at the National Gallery of Canada*, edited by Diana Nemiroff, Robert Houle, and Charlotte Townsend-Gault, 16–41. Ottawa: National Gallery of Canada, 1992.

Nemiroff, Diana, Robert Houle, and Charlotte Townsend-Gault, eds. *Land, Spirit, Power: First Nations at the National Gallery of Canada*. Ottawa: National Gallery of Canada, 1992.

Nesselrath, Arnold. "Blickwinkel / Points of View." In *Tehcumseh, Keokuk, Black Hawk: Indianerbildnisse in Zeiten von Verträgen und Vertreibung / Portrayals of Native Americans in Times of Treaties and Removals*, German and English edition, edited by Iris Adenheiser and Strid Nielsen, 65–79. Dresden: Arnoldsche Art Publishers, 2013.

———. "Le code secret d'Alexandre VI." *Le Figaro*, hors-série "Le temps des Borgia" (September 2014): 70–77.

Nester, William Raymond. *"Haughty Conquerors": Amherst and the Great Indian Uprising of 1763*. Westport, CT: Praeger, 2000.

Nicholson, H. B. *Topiltzin Quetzalcoatl: The Once and Future Lord of the Toltecs*. Boulder: University Press of Colorado, 2001.

Nietzsche, Friedrich Wilhelm. *The Birth of Tragedy*. 1872; Oxford: Oxford University Press, 2000.

Nochlin, Linda. "The Imaginary Orient." *Art in America* (May 1983): 119–31, 186–91.

Nodelman, Sheldon. *The Rothko Chapel Paintings: Origins, Structure, Meaning*. Austin: University of Texas Press, 1997.

Nora, Pierre. "Between Memory and History: Les Lieux de Mémoire." In "Memory and Counter-Memory," special issue, *Representations*, no. 26 (Spring 1989): 7–24.

O'Brien, Elaine, Everlyn Nicodemus, Melissa Chiu, Benjamin Genocchio, Mary K. Coffey, and Roberto Tejada, eds. *Modern Art in Africa, Asia and Latin America: An Introduction to Global Modernisms.* London: Wiley-Blackwell, 2012.

Oliver, Kelly. *Animal Lessons: How They Teach Us to Be Human.* New York: Columbia University Press, 2009.

Ortiz, Fernando. *Cuban Counterpoint: Tobacco and Sugar.* Translated by Harriet de Onís. 1940; Durham, NC: Duke University Press, 1995.

Ostrowitz, Judith. *Interventions: Native American Art for Far-Flung Territories.* Seattle: University of Washington Press, 2009.

Ott, John. "Reform in Redface: The Taos Society of Artists Plays Indian." *American Art* 23, no. 2 (Summer 2009): 80–107.

Oxendine, Lloyd, E. "23 Contemporary Indian Artists." *Art in America* 60, no. 4 (August 1972): 58–69.

Papastergiadis, Nikos. "A Thousand Beautiful Things: An Interview with Jimmie Durham." In *Criticism + Engagement + Thought: 2004 Biennale of Sydney,* 43–50. Woolloomooloo, NSW: Biennale of Sydney, 2004.

Papastergiadis, Nikos, and Nicholas Tsoutas. *Complex Entanglements: Art, Globalisation and Cultural Difference.* London: Rivers Oram, 2003.

Papastergiadis, Nikos, and Laura Turney. *On Becoming Authentic: Interview with Jimmie Durham.* Prickly Pear Pamphlet No. 10. Cambridge, UK: Prickly Pear, 1996.

Parks, N. Randolph. "On the Meaning of Pinturicchio's 'Sala dei Santi.'" *Art History* 2, no. 3 (1979): 291–317.

Patton, Sharon F. "The Agenda for the Eighties: Socially Conscious Art." In *The Decade Show: Frameworks of Identity in the 1980s,* edited by Louis Young, 77–91. New York: New Museum of Contemporary Art, 1990.

Pearlstone, Zena, ed. *Katsina: Commodified and Appropriated Images of Hopi Supernaturals.* Los Angeles: UCLA Fowler Museum of Cultural History, 2001.

Peers, Laura. *The Ojibwa of Western Canada, 1780–1870.* St. Paul: Minnesota Historical Society Press, 1994.

Penney, David W. "Afterword: Kay WalkingStick: An American Artist." In *Kay WalkingStick: An American Artist,* edited by Kathleen Ash-Milby and David W. Penney, 165–67. Washington, DC: Smithsonian National Museum of the American Indian, 2015.

———. *Native American Art Masterpieces.* Fairfield, CT: Hugh Lauter Levin Associates, 1996.

Penney, David W., and Lisa A. Roberts. "America's Pueblo Artists: Encounters on the Borderlands." In *Native American Art in the Twentieth Century: Makers, Meanings, Histories,* edited by W. Jackson Rushing, 21–38. London: Routledge, 1999.

Peterson, Jeanette Favrot. "Synthesis and Survival: The Native Presence in Sixteenth-

Century Murals of New Spain." In *Native Artists and Patrons in Colonial Latin America*, edited by Emily Umberger and Tom Cummins, 14–35. Phoenix: Arizona State University, 1995.

Phelan, Peggy. *Unmarked: The Politics of Performance*. London: Routledge, 1993.

Phillips, Ruth B. "Aesthetic Primitivism Revisited: The Global Diaspora of 'Primitive Art' and the Rise of Indigenous Modernisms." *Journal of Art Historiography*, no. 12 (June 2015): 1–25.

———. "Disrupting Past Paradigms: The National Museum of the American Indian and the First Peoples Hall at the Canadian Museum of Civilization." *Public Historian* 28, no. 2 (Spring 2006): 75–80.

———. *Patterns of Power: The Jasper Grant Collection and Great Lakes Indian Art of the Early Nineteenth Century*. Kleinburg, ON: McMichael Canadian Collection, 1984.

———. *Trading Identities: The Souvenir in Native North American Art from the Northeast, 1700–1900*. Seattle: University of Washington Press, 1998.

———. "The Turn of the Primitive: Modernism, the Stranger, and the Indigenous Artist in Settler Art Histories." In *Exiles, Diasporas, and Strangers*, edited by Kobena Mercer, 46–71. Cambridge, MA: MIT Press, 2008.

Pohl, John M. D., and Claire L. Lyons. *The Aztec Pantheon and the Art of Empire*. Los Angeles: J. Paul Getty Museum, 2010.

Prager, Brad. "Kant in Casper David Friedrich's Frames." *Art History* 25, no. 1 (February 2002): 68–86.

Pratt, Mary Louise. *Imperial Eyes: Travel Writing and Transculturation*. New York: Routledge, 1995.

Pratt, Stephanie. *American Indians in British Art, 1700–1840*. Norman: University of Oklahoma Press, 2005.

Price, Sally. *Paris Primitive: Jacques Chirac's Museum on the Quai Branly*. Chicago: University of Chicago Press, 2007.

———. *Primitive Art in Civilized Places*. Chicago: University of Chicago Press, 1989.

Promey, Sally M. "The 'Return' of Religion in the Scholarship of American Art." *Art Bulletin* 85, no. 3 (September 2003): 581–603.

Quick-to-See Smith, Jaune. *The Submuloc Show / Columbus Wohs: A Visual Commentary on the Columbus Quincentennial from the Perspective of America's First People*. Phoenix: Atlatl, 1992.

Rebecca Belmore: The Named and the Unnamed. Vancouver: University of British Columbia, 2003.

Reiss, Julie H. *From Margin to Center: The Spaces of Installation Art*. Cambridge, MA: MIT Press, 2001.

Richards, Thomas. *The Imperial Archive: Knowledge and the Fantasy of Empire*. New York: Verso, 1993.

Rickard, Jolene. "The Emergence of Global Indigenous Art." In *Sakahàn: International Indigenous Art*, 53–60. Ottawa: National Gallery of Canada, 2013.

———. "The Local and the Global." In *Vision, Space, Desire: Global Perspectives and Cultural Hybridity*, 59–68. Washington, DC: Smithsonian Institution National Museum of the American Indian, 2006.

———. "Sovereignty: A Line in the Sand." In *Strong Hearts: Native American Visions and Voices*, 51–59. New York: Aperture, 1995.

———. "Visualizing Sovereignty in the Time of Biometric Sensors." *South Atlantic Quarterly* 110, no. 2 (Spring 2011): 465–86.

Riess, Jonathan B. "Raphael's Stanze and Pinturicchio's Borgia Apartments." *Notes in the History of Art* 3, no. 4 (Summer 1984): 57–67.

Rifkin, Mark. *When Did Indians Become Straight? Kinship, the History of Sexuality, and Native Sovereignty.* Oxford: Oxford University Press, 2011.

Roberts, Lisa A. "Beyond the Body: Metaphysics and Materiality in the Art of Kay WalkingStick." In *Kay WalkingStick*, n.p. Miami: Kendal Campus Art Gallery, 1999.

Roediger, Virginia. *Ceremonial Costumes of the Pueblo Indians: Their Evolution, Fabrication, and Significance in the Prayer Drama.* Berkeley: University of California Press, 1961.

Ronan, Kristine. "Buffalo Dancer: The Biography of an Image." PhD diss., University of Michigan, 2016.

———. "Native Empowerment, the New Museology, and the National Museum of the American Indian." *Museum and Society* 12, no. 1 (July 2014): 132–47.

Rosaldo, Renato. "Imperialist Nostalgia." *Representations*, no. 26 (April 1, 1989): 107–22.

Rouch, Jean, and Edgar Morin. *Chronique d'un été (Chronicle of a Summer).* Paris: Interspectacles, 1961.

Rubin, William. "Modernist Primitivism: An Introduction." In *"Primitivism" in 20th Century Art: Affinity of the Tribal and the Modern*, vol. 1, edited by William Rubin, 1–79. New York: Museum of Modern Art, 1984.

Rushing, W. Jackson. "The Impact of Nietzsche and Northwest Coast Indian Art on Barnett Newman's Idea of Redemption in the Abstract Sublime." *Art Journal* 47, no. 3 (1988): 187.

———. "In Our Language: The Art of Hachivi Edgar Heap of Birds." *Third Text* 19, no. 4 (2005): 365–84.

———. "Jimmie Durham: Trickster as Intervention." *Artspace* 16 (January–April 1992): 62–65.

———. "Marketing the Affinity of the Primitive and the Modern: René d'Harnoncourt and 'Indian Art of the United States.'" In *The Early Years of Native American Art History: The Politics of Scholarship and Collecting*, edited by Janet Catherine Berlo, 191–236. Vancouver: University of British Columbia Press, 1992.

———. *Native American Art and the New York Avant-Garde: A History of Cultural Primitivism.* Austin: University of Texas Press, 1995.

———, ed. *Native American Art in the Twentieth Century: Makers, Meanings, Histories.* New York: Routledge, 1999.

———. "Pictures of Katsina Tithu: Georgia O'Keeffe and Southwest Modernism."

In *Georgia O'Keeffe in New Mexico: Architecture, Katsinam, and the Land*, edited by Barbara Buhler Lynes and Carolyn Kastner, 19–40. Santa Fe: Museum of New Mexico Press, 2012.

———. "Troubling Abstraction: Robert Houle's Indigenous Modernism." In *Troubling Abstraction: Robert Houle*, edited by Carol Podedworny, 19–39. Hamilton, ON: McMaster Museum of Art, 2007.

Russo, Alessandra. *The Untranslatable Image: A Mestizo History of the Arts in New Spain, 1500–1600*. Austin: University of Texas Press, 2014.

Ryan, Allan J. "Postmodern Parody: A Political Strategy in Contemporary Canadian Native Art." In "Recent Native American Art," edited by W. Jackson Rushing and Kay WalkingStick, special issue, *Art Journal* 51, no. 3 (Fall 1992): 59–63.

———. *The Trickster Shift: Humour and Irony in Contemporary Native Art*. Seattle: University of Washington Press, 1999.

Rydell, Robert W. *World of Fairs: The Century-of-Progress Expositions*. Chicago: University of Chicago Press, 1993.

Rydell, Robert W., and Nancy E. Gwinn, eds. *Fair Representations: World's Fairs and the Modern World*. European Contributions to American Studies, vol. 27. Amsterdam: VU University Press, 1994.

Rydell, Robert W., and Rob Kroes. *Buffalo Bill in Bologna: The Americanization of the World, 1869–1922*. Chicago: University of Chicago Press, 2012.

Rylands, Philip. *Flying the Flag for Art: The United States and the Venice Biennale 1895–1991*. Richmond, VA: Wyldbore and Wolferstan, 1993.

Said, Edward W. *Orientalism*. New York: Vintage, 1979.

———. "Reflections on Exile." In *Reflections on Exile and Other Essays*, 173–86. Cambridge, MA: Harvard University Press, 2000.

Sakamoto, Kerri. "Transgressions: Stereotype, Authenticity, and the M-Word." In *James Luna: Indian Legends*, 1–22. Banff, Alberta: Walter Phillips Gallery, 1993.

Sardar, Ziauddin. "Walt Disney and the Double Victimization of Pocahontas." In *The Third Text Reader on Art, Culture, and Theory*, edited by Rasheed Araeen, Sean Cubitt, and Ziauddin Sardar, 193–203. London: Continuum, 2002.

Schaafsma, Polly. *Kachinas in the Pueblo World*. Albuquerque: University of New Mexico Press, 1994.

———. "Pueblo Painting and Place: An Introduction." *Plateau: The Land and People of the Colorado Plateau* 2, no. 2 (Fall/Winter 2005): 6–13.

Schneider, David Murray. *A Critique of the Study of Kinship*. Ann Arbor: University of Michigan Press, 1984.

Schneider, Rebecca. "Archives: Performance Remains." *Performance Research* 6, no. 2 (Summer 2001): 100–107.

Scholder, Fritz. *Scholder/Indians*. Flagstaff, AZ: Northland, 1972.

Scott, Sascha T. "Awa Tsireh and the Art of Subtle Resistance." *Art Bulletin* 95, no. 4 (December 2013): 597–622.

———. *A Strange Mixture: The Art and Politics of Painting Pueblo Indians*. Norman: University of Oklahoma Press, 2015.

———. "Unwrapping Ernest L. Blumenschein's 'The Gift.'" *American Art* 25, no. 3 (Fall 2011): 20–47.

Secakuku, Alph H. *Following the Sun and the Moon: Hopi Kachina Tradition*. Flagstaff, AZ: Northland and the Heard Museum, 1995.

———. "Katsinam: The Katsina Dolls in Pueblo Culture and as Depicted by Georgia O'Keeffe." In *Georgia O'Keeffe in New Mexico: Architecture, Katsinam, and the Land*, edited by Barbara Buhler Lynes and Carolyn Kastner, 111–17. Santa Fe: Museum of New Mexico Press, 2012.

Sekaquaptewa, Emory. "Hopi Indian Ceremonies." In *Seeing with a Native Eye: Essays on Native American Religion*, edited by Walter Holden Capps, 35–43. New York: Harper and Row, 1976.

Seppi, Lisa Roberts. "The Artist in Italy: Desire, the Body, and the Divine." In *Kay WalkingStick: An American Artist*, edited by Kathleen Ash-Milby and David W. Penney, 127–43. Washington, DC: Smithsonian National Museum of the American Indian, 2015.

———. "Metaphysics and Materiality: Landscape Painting and the Art of Kay WalkingStick." PhD diss., University of Illinois at Urbana Champaign, 2005.

Sessions, Ralph. *The Shipcarvers' Art: Figureheads and Cigar-Store Indians in Nineteenth-Century America*. Princeton, NJ: Princeton University Press, 2005.

Seth, Vanita. *Europe's Indians: Producing Racial Difference, 1500–1900*. Durham, NC: Duke University Press, 2010.

Seymour, Tryntje Van Ness. *When the Rainbow Touches Down: The Artists and Stories behind the Apache, Navajo, Rio Grande Pueblo, and Hopi Paintings in the William and Leslie Van Ness Denman Collection*. Seattle: University of Washington Press, 1988.

Shiff, Richard. "The Necessity of Jimmie Durham's Jokes." In "Recent Native American Art," edited by W. Jackson Rushing and Kay WalkingStick, special issue, *Art Journal* 51, no. 3 (Fall 1992): 74–80.

Siebert, Monika. *Indians Playing Indian: Multiculturalism and Contemporary Indigenous Art in North America*. Tuscaloosa: University of Alabama Press, 2015.

Silverman, David J. "Purgatory: Interpreting Christian Missions and North American Indians." In *Converging Worlds: Communities and Cultures in Colonial America*, edited by Louise A. Breen, 321–43. New York: Routledge, 2011.

Sims, Lowery Stokes, ed. *Fritz Scholder: Indian / Not Indian*. Washington, DC: Smithsonian National Museum of the American Indian, 2006.

Sleeper-Smith, Susan, ed. *Contesting Knowledge: Museums and Indigenous Perspectives*. Lincoln: University of Nebraska Press, 2009.

Slight, Benjamin. *Indian Researches; or, Facts concerning the North American Indians; Including Notices of Their Present State of Improvement, in Their Social, Civil and*

Religious Condition, with Hints for Their Future Advancement. Montreal: Printed for the Author by J. E. L. Miller, 1844.

Sloan, John. "The Indian Dance from an Artist's Point of View: An Answer to an Attack upon These Ceremonies of the Southwest as Immoral and Degrading." *Arts and Decoration* (January 1932): 17–18, 56.

Sloan, John, and Oliver La Farge. *Introduction to American Indian Art*, vols. 1 and 2. New York: Exposition of Indian Tribal Arts, 1931.

Smith, Andrea. "Native American Feminism, Sovereignty, and Social Change." *Feminist Studies* 31, no. 1 (Spring 2005): 116–32.

Smith, Cherise. *Enacting Others: Politics of Identity in Eleanor Antin, Nikki S. Lee, Adrian Piper, and Anna Deavere Smith.* Durham, NC: Duke University Press, 2011.

Smith, Donald B. *Mississauga Portraits: Ojibwe Voice from Nineteenth-Century Canada.* Toronto: University of Toronto Press, 2013.

———. *Sacred Feathers: The Reverend Peter Jones (Kahkewaquonaby) and the Mississauga Indians.* Lincoln: University of Nebraska Press, 1987.

Smith, Linda Tuhiwai. *Decolonizing Methodologies: Research and Indigenous Peoples.* London: Zed, 1999.

Smith, Paul Chaat. "Delta One-Fifty." In *Vision, Space, Desire: Global Perspectives and Cultural Hybridity*, 31–40. Washington, DC: Smithsonian National Museum of the American Indian, 2006.

———. *Everything You Know about Indians Is Wrong.* Minneapolis: University of Minnesota Press, 2009.

———. "Luna Remembers." In *James Luna: Emendatio*, edited by Truman T. Lowe and Paul Chaat Smith, 25–48. Washington, DC: Smithsonian National Museum of the American Indian, 2005.

———. "Monster Love." In *Fritz Scholder: Indian / Not Indian*, edited by Lowery Stokes Sims, 25–36. Washington, DC: Smithsonian National Museum of the American Indian, 2008.

Smith, Paul Chaat, and Robert Allen Warrior. *Like a Hurricane: The Indian Movement from Alcatraz to Wounded Knee.* New York: New Press, 1997.

Smith, Terry. "Introduction: The Contemporary Question." In *Antinomies of Art and Culture: Modernity, Postmodernity, Contemporaneity*, edited by Terry Smith, Okwui Enwezor, and Nancy Condee, 1–19. Durham, NC: Duke University Press, 2008.

———. *What Is Contemporary Art?* Chicago: University of Chicago Press, 2009.

Smith, Terry, Okwin Enwezor, and Nancy Condee, eds. *Antinomies of Art and Culture: Modernity, Postmodernity, Contemporaneity.* Durham, NC: Duke University Press, 2008.

Soja, Edward W. *Postmodern Geographies: The Reassertion of Space in Critical Social Theory.* London: Verso, 1990.

———. "The Socio-Spatial Dialectic." *Annals of the Association of American Geographers* 70, no. 2 (June 1980): 207–25.

Solomon-Godeau, Abigail. "Going Native: Paul Gauguin and the Invention of Primitivist Modernism." *Art in America*, no. 77 (July 1989): 118–29.

Southcott, Beth. *The Sound of the Drum: The Sacred Art of the Anishnabec*. Erin, ON: Boston Mills, 1984.

Spero, Nancy. *The Black and the Red III*. Rome: Studio Stafania Miscetti, 1996.

Spier, Leslie. *Plains Indian Parfleche Designs*. Seattle: University of Washington Press, 1931.

Spivak, Gayatri Chakravorty. "Can the Subaltern Speak?" In *Marxism and the Interpretation of Culture*, edited by Cary Nelson and Lawrence Grossberg, 271–315. Chicago: University of Illinois Press, 1988.

Standing Bear, Luther, Earl Alonzo Brininstool, and Richard N. Ellis. *My People the Sioux*. 1928; Lincoln: University of Nebraska Press, 2006.

Steeds, Lucy, and other authors. *Making Art Global (Part 2): Magiciens de la Terre 1989*. London: Afterall Books, 2013.

Stephen, Daniel. *The Empire of Progress: West Africans, Indians, and Britons at the British Empire Exhibition, 1924–1925*. New York: Palgrave Macmillan, 2013.

Stevens, James R. *A Picasso from the North Country: The Wild Journey of Canadian Artist, Norval Morrisseau*. Thunder Bay, ON: Lake Superior Art Gallery, 2011.

Stoler, Ann Laura. *Along the Archival Grain: Epistemic Anxieties and Colonial Common Sense*. Princeton, NJ: Princeton University Press, 2010.

Strand, Paul. "American Water Colors at the Brooklyn Museum." *The Arts* 2, no. 3 (December 1921): 148–52.

Sturm, Circe. "Blood Politics, Racial Classification, and Cherokee National Identity: The Trials and Tribulations of the Cherokee Freedmen." *American Indian Quarterly* 22, nos. 1–2 (Winter–Spring 1998): 230–58.

Surrallés, Alexandre, and Pedro Garcia Hierro, eds. *The Land Within: Indigenous Territory and the Perception of the Environment*. Copenhagen: International Work Group for Indigenous Affairs, 2005.

Sweeney, Carole. *From Fetish to Subject: Race, Modernism, and Primitivism, 1919–1935*. Westport, CT: Praeger, 2004.

Sylvest, Edwin Edward. *Motifs of Franciscan Mission Theory in Sixteenth Century New Spain Province of the Holy Gospel*. Academy of American Franciscan History, vol. 11. Washington, DC: Academy of American Franciscan History, 1975.

Tac, Pablo. "Indian Life and Customs at Mission San Luis Rey." Translated by Minna Hewes and Gordon Hewes. *The Americas* 9, no. 1 (July 1952): 87–106.

Tanner, Clara Lee. *Southwest Indian Painting: A Changing Art*. Tucson: University of Arizona Press, 1973.

Taussig, Michael. "Jimmie Durham." In *On Reason and Emotion: 14th Biennale of Sydney 2004*, edited by Isabel Carlos, 82–84. Woolloomooloo: Biennale of Sydney, 2004.

———. *Mimesis and Alterity: A Particular History of the Senses.* New York: Routledge, 1993.

Tawadros, Gilane. "Preface: Modern Europeans." In *Unpacking Europe: Towards a Critical Reading,* edited by Salah Hassan and Iftikhar Dadi, 8–11. Rotterdam: NAi, 2001.

Taylor, Diana. *The Archive and the Repertoire: Performing Cultural Memory in the Americas.* Durham, NC: Duke University Press, 2003.

Tedeschi, Martha. "John Marin's Loaded Brush: Orchestrating the Modern American Watercolor." In *John Marin's Watercolors: A Medium for Modernism,* edited by Martha Tedeschi, 21–39. Chicago: Art Institute of Chicago, 2011.

Timbrook, Jan. *Chumash Ethnobotany: Plant Knowledge among the Chumash People of Southern California.* Santa Barbara, CA: Santa Barbara Museum of Natural History, 2007.

———. "Native American Arts in the Spanish Missions: Chumash Basketry." In *The Arts of the Missions of Northern New Spain, 1600–1821,* edited by Clara Bargellini, 327–32. Mexico City: Antiguo Colegio de San Ildefonso, 2009.

———. "Six Chumash Presentation Baskets." *American Indian Art Magazine* 39, no. 3 (Summer 2014): 50–57.

Todorov, Tzvetan. *The Conquest of America: The Question of the Other.* 1982; Norman: University of Oklahoma Press, 1999.

Torrence, Gaylord. *The American Indian Parfleche: A Tradition of Abstract Painting.* Seattle: University of Washington Press, 1994.

Townsend, Camilla. *Malintzin's Choices: An Indian Woman in the Conquest of Mexico.* Albuquerque: University of New Mexico Press, 2006.

———. *Pocahontas and the Powhatan Dilemma.* New York: Hill and Wang, 2005.

Townsend-Gault, Charlotte. "Rebecca Belmore and James Luna on Location in Venice: The Allegorical Indian Redux." *Art History* 29, no. 4 (2006): 721–55.

Trafzer, Clifford E., Jean A. Keller, and Lorene Sisquoc, eds. *Boarding School Blues: Revisiting American Indian Educational Experiences.* Lincoln: University of Nebraska Press, 2006.

Troyen, Carol. "A War Waged on Paper: Watercolor and Modern Art in America." In *Awash in Color: American Watercolors in the Museum of Fine Arts, Boston.* Boston: Bulfinch, 2000.

Truettner, William B. *The Natural Man Observed: A Study of Catlin's Indian Gallery.* Fort Worth, TX, and Washington, DC: Amon Carter Museum of Western Art and Smithsonian Institution Press, 1979.

Turney, Laura. "Ceci n'est pas Jimmie Durham." *Critique of Anthropology* 19, no. 4 (December 1999): 423–42.

Tweedie, James. "The Suspended Spectacle of History: Derek Jarman's *Caravaggio.*" *Screen* 44, no. 4 (Winter 2003): 379–403.

Udall, Sharyn Rohlfsen. "The Irresistible Other: Hopi Ritual Drama and Euro-American Audiences." *TDR* 36, no. 2 (Summer 1992): 23–43.

———. *John Marin in New Mexico*. Albuquerque: Albuquerque Museum, 1999.

Udall, Sharyn Rohlfsen, and Nancy Weekly. *Sensory Crossovers: Synesthesia in American Art*. Albuquerque: Albuquerque Museum, 2010.

Valentino, Erin. "'Mistaken Identity': Between Death and Pleasure in the Art of Kay WalkingStick." *Third Text* 8, no. 2 (1994): 61–73.

Vaughan, Alden T. *Transatlantic Encounters: American Indians in Britain, 1500–1776*. Cambridge: Cambridge University Press, 2006.

Vennum, Thomas. *The Ojibwa Dance Drum: Its History and Construction*. Washington, DC: Smithsonian Institution Press, 1982.

Vetrocq, Marcia E. "Venice Biennale: Be Careful What You Wish For." *Art in America* 93, no. 8 (September 2005): 109–19.

Vezolles, Christy A. "Personal Journeys: Kay WalkingStick's Paintings Reveal an Exploration of Land, History, and Spirit." *Western Art Collector*, no. 32 (April 2010): 56–61.

Villazor, Rose Cuison. "Blood Quantum Land Laws and the Race versus Political Identity Dilemma." *California Law Review* 96 (2008): 801–38.

Vision, Space, Desire: Global Perspectives and Cultural Hybridity. Washington, DC: Smithsonian National Museum of the American Indian, 2006.

Viveiros de Castro, Eduardo. "Exchanging Perspectives: The Transformation of Objects into Subjects in Amerindian Ontologies." In *Animism Volume I*, edited by Anselme Franke, 227–42. Antwerp: Sternberg Press / Extra City, 2010.

Vizenor, Gerald. *Manifest Manners: Postindian Warriors of Survivance*. Lincoln: University of Nebraska Press, 1999.

———. *The People Named the Chippewa: Narrative Histories*. Minneapolis: University of Minnesota Press, 1984.

———. *Shrouds of White Earth*. Albany: State University of New York Press, 2010.

Vizenor, Gerald, and A. Robert Lee. *Postindian Conversations*. Lincoln: University of Nebraska Press, 1999.

Wade, Edwin L. "Straddling the Cultural Fence: The Conflict for Ethnic Artists within Pueblo Societies." In *The Arts of the North American Indian: Native Traditions in Evolution*, edited by Edwin L. Wade, 243–54. New York: Hudson Hills, 1986.

WalkingStick, Kay. "Democracy, Inc.: Kay WalkingStick on Indian Law." *Artforum* 30, no. 3 (November 1991): 20–21.

———. "Native American Art in the Postmodern Era." In "Recent Native American Art," edited by W. Jackson Rushing and Kay WalkingStick, special issue, *Art Journal* 51, no. 3 (Fall 1992): 15–17.

———. "Seeking the Spiritual." In *Native American Art in the Twentieth Century: Makers, Meanings, Histories*, edited by W. Jackson Rushing, 184–88. New York: Routledge, 1999.

Warburg, Aby. *Images from the Region of the Pueblo Indians of North America*. Ithaca, NY: Cornell University Press, 1995.

Warren, William W., and Theresa Schenck. *History of the Ojibway People*. St. Paul: Minnesota Historical Society Press, 1999.

Warrior, Robert Allen. "Native American Scholarship and the Transnational Turn." *Cultural Studies Review* 15, no. 2 (September 2009): 119–30.

———. *Tribal Secrets: Recovering American Indian Literary Traditions*. Minneapolis: University of Minnesota Press, 1995.

Waters, Anne, ed. *American Indian Thought: Philosophical Essays*. Malden, MA: Blackwell, 2004.

Watson, Mark. "Centring the Indigenous: Postcommodity's Trans-Indigenous Relational Art." *Third Text* 29, no. 3 (2015): 141–54.

———. "Diplomatic Aesthetics: Globalization and Contemporary Native Art." PhD diss., Columbia University, 2012.

———. "Jimmie Durham's Building a Nation: Across Post-Indian, Post-American Modernities." *American Art* 28, no. 1 (Spring 2014): 16–24.

Weaver, Jace. *The Red Atlantic: American Indigenes and the Making of the Modern World, 1000–1927*. Chapel Hill: University of North Carolina Press, 2014.

Weber, David J. "Arts and Architecture, Force and Fear: The Struggle for Sacred Space." In *The Arts of the Missions of Northern New Spain, 1600–1821*, edited by Clara Bargellini, 3–23. Mexico City: Antiguo Colegio de San Ildefonso, 2009.

———. *Bárbaros: Spaniards and Their Savages in the Age of Enlightenment*. New Haven, CT: Yale University Press, 2005.

Weiss, Rachel, and other authors. *Making Art Global (Part 1): The Third Havana Biennial 1989*. London: Afterall Books, 2011.

Welton, Jessica W. "Fred Kabotie, Elizabeth Willis DeHuff, and the Genesis of the Santa Fe Style." PhD diss., Virginia Commonwealth University, 2014.

———. "The Watchtower Murals: 1930s Paintings by Fred Kabotie." *Plateau: The Land and People of the Colorado Plateau* 2, no. 2 (2005): 42–51.

Welton, Jessica W., and Zena Pearlstone. "Recontextualizing the Art of Fred and Michael Kabotie." *American Indian Art Magazine* 36, no. 2 (Spring 2011): 36–47.

Wenger, Tisa. *We Have a Religion: The 1920s Pueblo Indian Dance Controversy and American Religious Freedom*. Chapel Hill: University of North Carolina Press, 2009.

Wernitznig, Dagmar. *Europe's Indians, Indians in Europe*. Lanham, MD: University Press of America, 2007.

West, W. Richard, Jr. "Foreword: At the Table, in the Big Tent." In *Vision, Space, Desire: Global Perspectives and Cultural Hybridity*, 10–14. Washington, DC: Smithsonian Institution National Museum of the American Indian, 2006.

White, Richard. *The Middle Ground: Indians, Empires, and Republics in the Great Lakes Region, 1650–1815*. Cambridge: Cambridge University Press, 1991.

White, Robert R. *The Taos Society of Artists*. Albuquerque: University of New Mexico Press, 1998.

Whiteford, Andrew Hunter. "Mystic and Decorative Art of the Anishinabe (Chippewa/Ojibwa)." *Arctic Anthropology* 28, no. 1 (1991): 74–83.

Whiteley, Peter M. *Deliberate Acts: Changing Hopi Culture through the Oraibi Split.* Tucson: University of Arizona Press, 1988.

———. *Rethinking Hopi Ethnography.* Washington, DC: Smithsonian Institution Press, 1988.

Wildcat, Daniel R. *Red Alert! Saving the Planet with Indigenous Knowledge.* Golden, CO: Fulcrum Publishing, 2009.

Willoughby, Pamela R. *Evolution of Modern Humans in Africa: A Comprehensive Guide.* Lanham, MD: Altamira, 2007.

Wilson, Catherine. *The Invisible World: Early Modern Philosophy and the Invention of the Microscope.* Princeton, NJ: Princeton University Press, 1995.

Wilton, Andrew, and Tim Barringer. *American Sublime: Landscape Painting in the United States, 1820–1880.* Princeton, NJ: Princeton University Press, 2002.

Wimmer, Andreas, and Nina Glick Schiller. "Methodological Nationalism, the Social Sciences, and the Study of Migration: An Essay in Historical Epistemology." *International Migration Review* 37, no. 3 (2003): 576–610.

Wolf, Bryan J. *Romantic Re-Vision: Culture and Consciousness in Nineteenth-Century American Painting and Literature.* Chicago: University of Chicago Press, 1982.

Wollaeger, Mark, ed. *The Oxford Handbook of Global Modernisms.* Oxford: Oxford University Press, 2012.

Wright, Gwendolyn. "Building Global Modernisms." *Grey Room*, no. 7 (April 2002): 124–34.

XVIII Esposizione Biennale Internazionale d'Arte. Venice, Italy, 1932.

Young, Louis, ed. *The Decade Show: Frameworks of Identity in the 1980s.* New York: New Museum of Contemporary Art, 1990.

Young, Phil. *For the Seventh Generation: Native American Artists Counter the Quincentenary.* Columbus, NY: Golden Artist Colors Gallery, 1992.

INDEX

archive, 23, 33, 52, 94, 106, 127; archival impulse, 8, 12–13, 32; limitations of, 54–58; material and performative dimensions of, 9, 15, 33–34, 61–78, 88, 92–93, 155, 165, 170, 177, 182–83, 185; and repertoire, 13, 62–67, 72–74, 78, 88, 93

Arkansas, 21, 58

Artforum, 1, 48, 139

art history: and anthropology, 14, 38, 90, 102–3, 119, 134, 156, 165–70; and the exclusion of Native American art, 13, 39, 89, 97, 121, 127, 134, 136–37, 198n10; and settler colonialism, 197n3; undivided, 125, 128, 132, 138, 141–51. *See also* abstraction in art; modernisms

Artifact #671B (Belmore), 216n43

Artifact Piece (Luna), 35–38, 71–76, 170

Art in America, 89, 97, 211n104

Art Journal, special issue on "Recent Native American Art" (1992), 46

art market: contemporary, 3, 199n16; Indian, 35, 37–38, 48, 72, 86, 210n103

assimilation: Canadian policy of, 162, 168; cultural and religious, 12, 27, 62, 172; U.S. policy of, 22, 28, 97, 101–2, 134, 139, 145, 162. *See also* boarding schools; Bureau of Indian Affairs; General Allotment Act; missionization

Attakulakula, 2, 10, 18, 50–51, 57–59, 62, 69, 122

"Attakulakula" (Durham), 52, 57–59, 69. See also *Mataoka Ale Attakulakula Anel Guledisgo Hnihi* (Durham)

auction, 180–81

Australia, 3, 91, 184, 194; and Aboriginal artists, 198n10, 234n83

authenticity: critique of, 37, 49, 73, 102, 217n49; of performers in George Catlin's Indian Gallery, 159–62

Author Painting a Chief at the Base of the Rocky Mountains, The (Catlin), 159–60

Aztec: codices, 2, 14; Spanish conquest of, 131–32; use of obsidian, 195. *See also* Codex Vaticanus A; Florentine Codex

Bargellini, Clara, 82

Barrie, Edwin W., 117, 230n106. *See also* Grand Central Art Galleries

baskets: indigenous Californian, 9, 37, 65, 67, 69–80, 84, 86; in Pueblo ceremonies and paintings, 110–13, 121; by Juana Basilia Sitmelelene, 87–88. *See also* "Chapel for Pablo Tac" (Luna)

Baudrillard, Jean, 28

Baum, L. Frank, 47–48

Bellows, George, 94. *See also individual works*

Belmore, Rebecca, 89–91, 216n43

Benjamin, Walter, 83–84, 133, 200n27

Berlin, 192–93, 195–96

Beuys, Joseph, 40–41. *See also individual works*

Biennale of Sydney, 3, 13, 184–85, 234–35n83

biennial, 3, 5, 13, 21, 91, 221n96. *See also* Biennale of Sydney; *Sakahàn: International Indigenous Art*

Birnbaum, Martin, 117–21

Black. *See* civil rights; postidentity

blanket, 9, 40, 64, 67, 71, 75–76, 87, 216n43; Pendleton, 77; smallpox-infested, 46, 177

Blocker, Jane, 71–76, 214n9

blood quantum, and Native identity, 23, 92, 127, 144, 205n27. *See also* General Allotment Act

Blumenschein, Ernest Leonard, 94, 97, 118. *See also individual works*

boarding schools, and Indian education, 23, 112. *See also* assimilation; General Allotment Act; Santa Fe Indian School

bone: in archival theory, 8, 62, 64–65, 71–74; in Jimmie Durham's artwork, 12, 35, 38–43, 49, 54, 58, 185, 188, 194–95; and James Luna's artwork, 37, 67, 71

Bradley, David, 48

Britain. *See* London

Brown, Bill, 216–17n44

Buffalo Bill Cody's Wild West Show, 201n43, 221n106; in Edgar Heap of Birds's artwork, 2, 93

Bureau of Indian Affairs, and the American Indian Movement, 5, 9, 22–23. *See also* assimilation; General Allotment Act

cairn, 195. *See also* stone
California Mission Daze (Avalos, Luna, Small, and Weeks), 72–73
Canada, 135; and the American Indian Movement, 22, 26, 168–69; Canadian Cultural Center in Paris, 14, 152, 178–79; and contemporary indigenous artists, 3, 7, 11, 13, 33, 43, 45–46, 56, 90–92, 135, 216n43, 235n86; Robert Houle's life in, 168–69; Pavilion of the Venice Biennale, 43, 89–90, 96, 217n51; Truth and Reconciliation Commission, 241n55
Canadian Cultural Center in Paris, 14, 152, 178–79
Canadian Pavilion of the Venice Biennale, 43, 89–90, 96, 217n51
capitalism, 28, 38, 139. *See also* globalization
carpentry, Cherokee: in the work of Jimmie Durham, 12, 18, 50, 55–59. See also *Mataoka Ale Attakulakula Anel Guledisco Hnihi* (Durham)
Catlin, George: Indian Gallery of, 2, 14–15, 154–66, 170, 173, 178, 182–83, 201n43. *See also individual works*
Cecchi, Emilio, 119–20
center: and margins, 10, 17, 31, 35, 59, 90; modernity, indigenous people at, 1, 3, 12, 83, 91, 196; in Pueblo cosmology, 107, 219n83
Center of the World at Chalma, The (Durham), 189–91
Chalma, 189–91, 195–96. See also *Center of the World at Chalma, The* (Durham)
chapel: Catholic definition of, 79–81; in modern and contemporary art, 85
"Chapel for Pablo Tac" (Luna), 2, 12, 62–89, 92–93. See also *Emendatio* (Luna)
Chapel of the Sacred Colors (Luna), 72
Cheetham, Mark, 166–67, 177
Cherokee: carpentry, 12, 18, 50, 55–59;

diplomat Attakulakula, 2, 10, 18, 50–51, 57–59, 62, 69, 122; Jimmie Durham's heritage, 20–22, 48–49, 194–95; jeep, 89; language and culture, 55–56, 58–59, 62, 141; slavery, 54; Trail of Tears, 21, 23, 48, 195, 235n86; Treaty of Whitehall, 2, 52; trickster, 38; Kay WalkingStick's heritage, 48, 127, 135–36, 139
Cherokee Nation, 48, 135, 139
Cheyenne-Arapaho Nation, 186
Cheyenne language, 31, 93. See also *In Our Language* (Heap of Birds); *Most Serene Republics* (Heap of Birds)
Chief Joseph series (WalkingStick), 135–36
Christianity: in Robert Houle's artwork, 45, 168, 172–73; in James Luna's artwork, 13, 61–88; and Maungwudaus, 178; and Pocahontas, 50; and Kay WalkingStick's artwork, 123–32, 149–51. *See also* missionization
Chronique d'un été, 20–21
Chumash, 83–84, 87–88
Churchill, Ward, 211n104
cigar store Indian, 51
Cinq études d'Indiens (Delacroix), 9, 152–53, 166, 170, 183
civil rights, African American, 17, 33
Clark, Walter L., 115–19. *See also* Grand Central Art Galleries
Codex Vaticanus A, 123–26, 130–32
cognitive stickiness, 147
collage, 19, 27, 144, 177
College Art Association, 46, 115, 156
colonial exposition, 13, 88
colonization, of the Americas, 1–11, 17–18, 20, 32–33, 47, 50, 61, 67, 71, 91–93, 122, 132, 151, 157, 172, 179, 193–95. *See also* assimilation; decolonization; displacement; missionization
Columbus, Christopher, 45–47, 139, 141, 149–50. See also *Resurrection of Christ, The* (Pinturicchio)
Columbus Quincentennial, 5, 14, 18, 29, 44–48, 56, 139, 141, 149, 169, 235nn85–86

communism, 139; and the American Indian Movement, 25, 28

contemporaneity, 73, 119; in Terry Smith's scholarship, 4, 121–22

Cornell University, 10, 231n11; Art in Rome program, 128

Cortés, Hernán, 51, 131

Couse, E. Irving, 112–13, 222n3. *See also individual works*

cowboys, 19, 20; and Indians, 27, 75, 217n48. See also *La poursuite du bonheur* (Durham)

coyote, 133; in Jimmie Durham's artwork, 38, 40–43, 50, 59, 185, 189, 196; in indigenous Californian origin stories, 83. *See also* trickster

creative kinship, 13–14, 98, 106, 127, 135, 139–45, 148–51. *See also* kinship

crisis globalization, 4, 185–86. *See also* Demos, T. J.; globalization

cross: Christian, 27, 72, 79, 82, 87–88, 123, 169, 173; indigenous equal-armed, 63, 79–80, 86, 169, 171, 173; Barnet Newman's *Stations of the Cross*, 167

"Current Trends in Indian Land Ownership" (Durham), 33–35. See also *On Loan from the Museum of the American Indian* (Durham)

Curtis, Edward S., 28

Dagois, Hervé, 237–38n4. *See also individual works*

dance: bans on Pueblo, 13, 98, 101, 112, 114, 133; and Walter Benjamin's theory of mimicry, 133; and George Catlin's Indian Gallery, 158, 178; in Jimmie Durham's poetry, 189; in Robert Houle's artwork, 170, 173–75, 179; in Fred Kabotie's artwork, 2–3, 12, 93, 95–98, 101–15, 118, 120–21; in James Luna's artwork, 2, 12, 61–69, 75–76, 82; in Fritz Scholder's artwork, 29; in Kay WalkingStick's artwork, 12–13, 125, 127–28, 133–34, 137, 144–51. *See also* Katsina

Dance (I) (Matisse), 148

Dance of the Santo Domingo Indians (Marin), 105–7

"Dancer" (Houle), 14, 152, 166, 170–75, 179, 183

Dawes Act. *See* General Allotment Act

Decade Show: Frameworks of Identity in the 1980s, The, 12, 16–19, 43, 45, 49, 74, 195, 208n66, 232n53

Declaration of Independence, U.S., 19–20, 22

decolonization: in Africa, 20–22, 197n4, 209n82; in the Americas, 6, 22, 24, 26, 33, 140, 169. *See also* American Indian Movement

deconstruction: of archival logic, 8, 37, 54, 200n33; in postmodern theory, 9, 42, 58, 134, 214n140

DeHuff, Elizabeth, 101

DeHuff, John David, 101

Delacroix, Eugène, 9, 14, 152–53, 155, 166, 170, 183. *See also individual works*

Deloria, Philip J., 7, 11

Deloria, Vine, 5–6, 24–25, 33, 35, 140, 205n37. *See also individual works*

Demos, T. J., 4, 21, 91, 185, 186–88

Denzin, Norman K., 10, 238n5

Derrida, Jacques, 42, 65, 200n31, 214n140

deterritorialization, and reterritorialization, 36–37

diagram: in Jimmie Durham's artwork, 33; in Fred Kabotie's artwork, 13, 98, 102–11, 113, 121, 147

Dickens, Charles, 163

diplomacy: in Jimmie Durham's career, 50, 57–58; in Robert Houle's artwork, 177; and indigenous Californian baskets, 86–88. *See also* International Indian Treaty Council; treaty

disease: as an element of colonization, 9, 162, 193; of indigenous performers in Europe, 14, 155, 175, 178–79. *See also* smallpox

displacement: as a condition for Fred

Kabotie's paintings, 93, 98–112; of indigenous people due to colonization, 1, 5, 12–13, 18–21, 48–49, 54, 59–60, 92–93, 145, 188, 194; and institutional critique, 32–37; and trickster humor, 41–43, 58. *See also* exile; itinerancy; mobility

dOCUMENTA (13), 3

Duchamp, Marcel, 38, 186–88. *See also* readymade; *and individual works*

Dunn, Dorothy, 97

Durham, Jimmie, 1, 12, 121, 132; and the American Indian Movement, 21–31, 49, 140; artwork in Europe, 2, 4, 9–11, 15, 49–60, 62, 69, 91–92, 184–96; and identity politics, 16–18, 44–49, 139–40; and institutional critique, 8, 31–37, 71, 169–70, 180; and modernist exile, 19–21; and trickster humor, 38–44, 136; and the U.S. Pavilion of the Venice Biennale, 89–90. *See also individual works*

eagle, 63, 83, 86, 125, 131–33, 143, 189, 218n68, 238n5

ecology, 25, 140, 234n83. *See also* kinship; land; sovereignty; space

Egyptian Hall, 159, 163, 182

Eloheh, 56–59

Emendatio (Luna), 12–13, 29, 62–69, 74–93

Encore tranquillité (Durham), 208–9

End of the Trail (Fraser), 75

End of the Trail (Luna), 75

Enwezor, Okwui, 8

equal-armed cross, 63, 79–80, 86, 169, 171, 173

ethnography, salvage, 15, 112, 155–62, 182–83. *See also* anthropology

Eurocentrism, 6, 45; of art history, 3, 127, 133–34

Europe, 8, 15, 17, 22, 49, 97–98, 112–13, 119, 154, 165, 178, 186, 190, 192; archives based in, 9, 54, 61, 94–95, 155, 183; arts, languages, and cultures of, 6, 12–14, 24, 55–57, 64–66, 81, 85, 87, 108, 123, 128–32, 136–37, 142, 145, 148–49, 155, 161–62, 166, 171–72, 180–82, 188, 194, 196; as a center of modernity, 3, 10; and the colonization of the Americas, 1, 2, 4, 8, 10, 11, 19–21, 33, 46, 48, 50, 52, 88, 92–93, 125, 140, 157–58, 185; vs. United States, 114–16, 159

Eve, 142, 144–45

Eve Energy (WalkingStick), 144–45

exile: as a condition for indigenous artists, 11, 17, 22, 49, 59, 92, 106, 223n16; as a modernist trope, 19–21, 43, 186–88. *See also* displacement; itinerancy; mobility

Federal Bureau of Investigation, role of in the American Indian Movement, 25, 28

feminism: and the American Indian Movement, 29, 207n53; and contemporary art, 16, 63, 69; intersections with indigenous theory, 6, 26, 203n8; second wave, 134–35

fertility, 123, 127, 141–44

Fewkes, Jesse Walter, 112, 226n56

"Few Words Exchanged at Charleston, A" (Durham), 54, 213n128. See also *Mataoka Ale Attakulakula Anel Guledisgo Hnihi* (Durham)

Fire, Movement, Water, and Voices (Luna), 218n68

Fisher, Jean, 42, 45, 51, 90

Flatley, Jonathan, 139, 236n94

Flint, Kate, 10, 244n93

Florentine Codex, 130–31

Fonseca, Harry, 59–60. *See also individual works*

Foster, Hal, 8, 136

Foucault, Michel, 129, 139–41, 200n31, 202n54, 223n20

Fountain (Belmore), 89, 217n51

Fountain (Duchamp), 202–4. *See also* readymade

France. *See* Paris

Franke, Anselm, 179–82, 193–94

Fraser, James, 75. *See also individual works*

Fred Harvey Company, 112–13, 226n57

Friedman, Susan Stanford, 3

Gell, Alfred, 147

General Allotment Act, 23, 48, 98, 133, 139

Genesis/Violent Garden (WalkingStick), 236n91

Geneva: Jimmie Durham's art and diplomacy in, 21–22, 26, 38, 59; Edgar Heap of Birds in, 209n71

Gilbert, Matthew Sakiestewa, 112

Girardet, Karl, 166–67, 241n48

globalization: crisis, 4, 185; impact on contemporary art, 3–5, 49, 63, 91, 122; indigenous approaches to, 6–7. *See also* capitalism; contemporaneity; deterritorialization and reterritorialization

global modernisms. *See* modernisms

God Is Red (Vine Deloria), 5–6, 24–25, 33, 35, 140, 205n37

González, Jennifer, 32–33, 36–37, 73

Gorman, R. C., 97, 207n58

Gottlieb, Adolf, 136. *See also individual works*

Gramercy Park (Bellows), 94

Grand Central Art Galleries, 94, 115–17, 120. *See also* Clark, Walter L.

Greenberg, Clement, 156, 241n49

"Ground Has Been Covered, The" (Durham), 1–2, 12, 15, 18, 185, 196

Hackel, Steven, 839

Hallowell, Irving A., 171–75, 179, 194, 201n37. *See also* other-than-human person

Hammons, David, 16–17

Hartley, Marsden, 114, 119–20, 134–36, 138, 140–41, 148. *See also individual works*

"Healer" (Houle), 14, 152, 166, 170–75, 179, 183

Heap of Birds, Edgar, 1–2, 31, 37, 45, 89, 91–93. *See also individual works*

Herrera, Velino (Ma Pe Wi), 101, 107, 114, 226n58

He said I was always juxtaposing, but I thought he said just opposing. So to prove him wrong I agreed with him. Over the next few years we drifted apart (Durham), 186–88

"High-Tech Peace Pipe" (Luna), 72–73

Hill, Joe, 19–20

Hill, Richard William, 140, 180, 193–94, 234–35n83, 238n8

history: angel of, 83–84; and colonial archival logic, 8–9, 33, 37, 52–54, 65–66, 68, 72, 74, 155; creative retelling by AIM-generation artists, 2–4, 6–7, 11–12, 78, 80, 91–92, 137, 166, 188; critiques of European teleological approaches to, 6, 24–25, 72; as defined by violent colonization, 7, 47–48, 102, 177; as world in Jimmie Durham's artwork, 12, 18, 50, 54–60, 195–96. *See also* art history; temporality

Hopi Basket Ceremony (Kabotie), 110–11, 113

Hopi Butterfly Dance (Kabotie), 110–11, 113

Hopi Cultural Preservation Office, 110, 226n56

Hopi Tribe: and federal dance bans, 98–101; religion and ceremony, 2, 13, 97–98, 102–13, 145; sacred beings sold at auction in France, 180–81

Houle, Robert, 1, 2, 134, 139; artwork in Europe, 9, 14, 15, 92, 152–57, 165–66, 170–79, 183; curatorial work, 45–46, 168–70; and modernist abstraction, 44, 137, 166–67. *See also individual works*

Hovenweep #331 (WalkingStick), 137–39, 142

Huhndorf, Shari M., 6, 26, 29

humor, in art, 1, 8, 19, 32–44, 46, 51, 54, 71–76, 127, 138, 190, 207n53. *See also* trickster

identity: and the Indian Arts and Crafts Act of 1990, 48–49, 92, 133, 139–40, 149; politics of, 1, 12, 16–19, 26, 33, 43–44, 46, 195; U.S. national, 114–15. *See also* blood quantum; postidentity; *Decade Show: Frameworks of Identity in the 1980s, The*

I Like America and America Likes Me (Beuys), 40–41

imperialist nostalgia, 158, 204n13

Indian Arts and Crafts Act of 1990, 14, 18, 44–45, 48–49, 133, 139–40, 149

Indians of All Tribes, 23

London, 4, 11, 119, 122, 155, 186, 201n42; George Catlin's Indian Gallery in, 157–63, 165, 182–83; Jimmie Durham's artwork in, 1, 2, 9, 12, 18, 49–59, 62

Louis-Philippe assistant dans un salon des Tuileries à la danse d'Indiens hovas. 21 avril, 1845 (Girardet), 166–67

Louvre, 152–53, 165, 181

Luiseño: James Luna's heritage, 69; scholar Pablo Tac, 2, 9–10, 12, 61–70, 76, 80, 93, 122, 194–95; Fritz Scholder's heritage, 207n56

Luna, James, 1, 8, 44–45, 136, 139–40, 169, 185–86; artwork in Europe, 2, 9, 12–13, 62–69, 75–93, 98, 121, 134; and the Columbus Quincentennial, 46; early installations, 32, 72–74; identity politics and performance, 16, 35–37, 40, 69–72, 74, 132, 170. *See also individual works*

Magiciens de la terre, 179, 198n10, 221n96

Mah-to-toh-pa, 159–162

Máh-to-tóh-pa, Four Bears, Second Chief, in Full Dress (Catlin), 160–61

Mandan, 159–62, 182

Manhattan Festival of the Dead (Durham), 38

manitou, 170–75

Manitou, 175

Maraini, Antonio, 116–20

margins. *See* center

Marin, John, 105, 107, 113–14, 134. *See also individual works*

Martinez, Maria, 138, 222n8

massacre at Wounded Knee. *See* Wounded Knee

Massacre at Wounded Knee (Scholder), 29–31, 33, 46–47

Massey, Doreen, 18, 33–35, 200n28

Mataoka. *See* Pocahontas

Mataoka Ale Attakulakula Anel Guledisco Hnihi (Durham), 12, 18, 49–60, 62, 186

materiality. *See* animism; new materialisms; other-than-human person; performing props; quasi-object; transcultural materialism

Matisse, Henri, 148. *See also individual works*

Maungwudaus (George Henry), 2, 10, 164–66, 172, 177–78, 221n106

McGeough, Michelle, 102, 222n12

McMaster, Gerald, 43, 46, 89, 91, 198n8, 199n17, 203n4

Means, Russell, 24, 29, 189

mega-exhibitions. *See* biennial

memory, 24, 93, 97, 185, 194; and archival logic, 65–66; in Jimmie Durham's artwork, 56; and imperialist nostalgia, 136, 155, 158, 160; in Fred Kabotie's artwork, 13, 101–14; and simulations, 28; in Pablo Tac's writing, 61, 64; in Kay WalkingStick's work, 138, 142. *See also* history

mestizo, in James Luna's artwork and identity, 72, 75–76

methodological nationalism, 97

Mexico, 195; Chalma, 190–91; in the context of New Spain, 61, 68, 82, 87; Jimmie Durham's move to Cuernavaca, 17–18, 212n114; Spanish conquest of, 123–32

Mignolo, Walter, 4, 125, 150

missionization: of indigenous Californians, 2, 12, 37, 61–88, 92, 145; of Mesoamericans, 123–25, 130–31, 149–50, 190; of the Ojibwa, 172–73, 177–78, 194; of the Pueblo, 101, 107, 138; of the Sioux, 26–27

Mission San Antonio de Pala, 79

Mission San Buenaventura, 87–88

Mission San Luis Rey de Francia, 2, 61–69, 79–81

Mission Santa Inés, 83–84

Mithlo, Nancy Marie, 7, 89, 91, 211n104, 212n116

mobility: as a central feature of colonial modernity, 1, 4, 5, 21, 59, 92, 185; and modern transportation technologies, 15, 89, 184–85, 192–93; and trickster discourse in contemporary art, 41–43. *See also* displacement; exile; itinerancy

modernism, European and American, 3, 12, 13, 85, 105, 127, 134, 136–38, 165–66, 222n8, 225n44. *See also* abstraction; antimodernism; primitivism; *"Primitivism" in 20th Century Art: Affinity of the Tribal and the Modern*

modernisms, 3–5, 10–11, 88, 93, 122, 127, 137–38, 166, 200n26, 222n8

modernity: and the colonization of the Americas, 1–15, 18–21, 49, 62–63, 65, 83, 89, 92–93, 122, 130, 134–35, 155–57, 172, 185, 193, 196; as theorized by Bruno Latour, 179–81

Moki Snake Dance—Prayer for Rain (Couse), 112–13

Monkman, Kent, 238n5

Monster Indian (Scholder), 29

Morrisseau, Norval, 178–79. *See also individual works*

Most Serene Republics (Heap of Birds), 2, 92–93

Mountain Men (WalkingStick), 142–43, 148

Mr. Catlin at His Easel (Catlin), 159–61

multiple modernisms. *See* modernisms

Mulvey, Christopher, 159–60

Musée de l'Homme, 36

Musée du quai Branly, 176, 181–82

museum: as archive, 8; and critiques of indigenous representation, 32–38, 50–51, 59, 71–76, 170. *See also individual museums*

Museum of Modern Art, 39, 128, 134, 136, 226n57, 228n84. *See also "Primitivism" in 20th Century Art: Affinity of the Tribal and the Modern*

Museum of the American Indian, 32–35, 37. See also *On Loan from the Museum of the American Indian* (Durham)

music: and George Catlin's Indian Gallery, 158–59; in Jimmie Durham's artwork, 19, 54, 71, 189; in Robert Houle's artwork, 171, 174–75, 179; in Fred Kabotie's artwork, 3, 13, 98, 104–10, 120–22; in James Luna's

artwork, 36, 63–64, 71, 76, 78; in Gerald Vizenor's *Shrouds of White Earth*, 182; in Kay WalkingStick's artwork, 142

Nagel, Alexander, 85

Narcissus (WalkingStick), 143–44

Natchez, The (Delacroix), 166

nationalism: in American art, 89, 97–98, 114–21; British, 158–59; as a colonial force, 6–7, 13, 19, 27, 186, 239n25; indigenous, 5–6, 26, 29; methodological, 97

National Museum of the American Indian, 32, 62, 74, 77, 89–93, 176, 216n43, 230n1

New Age, spiritualism, 51, 71–73

Newman, Barnett, 166–67. *See also individual works*

new materialisms, 9, 15, 156–57, 179, 183, 238n8. *See also* transcultural materialism

New Mexico, 21, 48; in American art, 94–95; Pueblo nations of, 13, 43, 100–101, 105, 107–8, 110, 114–15, 119–20, 133, 219n79, 219n83. *See also* Santa Fe

New Spain, 12, 82, 86. *See also* missionization; Spanish conquest

"New World," 2, 11, 20, 24, 54–55, 66, 87, 127, 130, 131

New York City: art in the 1920s, 114–15, 118–19; art in the 1980s, 11, 16–17, 31, 38–39, 40, 45, 74, 128, 135, 137, 208n66

"Ni'Go Tlunh a Doh Ka" (We Are Always Turning Around on Purpose), 45

Niman Kachina Dance (Kabotie), 104–7

nonhuman, European category of, 9, 33, 155–57, 161–62, 172, 182, 201n37. *See also* other-than-human person; quasi-object; *We Have Never Been Modern* (Latour)

Not Joseph Beuys' Coyote (Durham), 40–43, 51, 59

Ojibwa: art, language, and culture, 170–79, 194; Robert Houle's heritage, 152, 168; performers in Europe, 2, 14–15, 152–65, 182–83; and smallpox, 177–78; Gerald Vizenor's heritage, 28

the Tribal and the Modern, 38–39, 136–37

progress, critique of, 5–6, 15, 24–25, 46, 83–85, 101, 130. *See also* temporality

Provincializing Europe (Chakrabarty), 11

Psychic Space (Morrisseau), 178

Pueblo: bans on ceremony, 13, 98, 101, 112, 114, 133; dances, 2–3, 12, 43, 93, 95–98, 101–15, 118, 120–21; nations, 13, 100–101, 105, 107–8, 110, 112–15, 119–20, 133, 219n79, 219n83; paintings, 95–98, 101–3, 108, 114–22; San Ildefonso, 101; Santo Domingo, 105–6; Taos, 94, 119, 222n5; Tesuque, 119; Zia, 101; Zuni, 110, 180. *See also* Hopi Tribe

quasi-object, 14, 155, 157, 162, 165, 172, 178–79, 182. See also *We Have Never Been Modern* (Latour)

Quechnajuisom, 12, 61–70, 76, 80, 92, 122, 194–95. *See also* Luiseño

Queen Victoria, 163

Quetzalcoatl, 123–25, 128, 130. *See also* Codex Vaticanus A

race: biological definitions of, 127, 130, 133, 140; segregation based on, 7, 9, 22, 35, 48, 202–203n3; visual dimensions of, 32–33, 72, 146. *See also* blood quantum; identity; kinship

Ram and Antelope (Tsireh), 107–8

readymade, 38, 186–89

Red Power. *See* American Indian Movement

Renaissance, art and culture, 2, 10, 125, 128–34, 136, 141–43, 148–51

"Renewal (A Performance for Pablo Tac)" (Luna), 2, 63, 74–76

reservation, Indian, 7–8, 23, 28, 33, 38, 46, 48, 69, 71, 75, 135, 186, 211n104. *See also* Cherokee Nation; Hopi Tribe; La Jolla Indian Reservation; Pine Ridge Indian Reservation; Sandy Bay First Nation Reserve

Resurrection of Christ, The (Pinturicchio), 149–51

reterritorialization, 36–37

Rickard, Jolene, 6–7, 26, 91, 103, 156

Rifkin, Mark, 133

Rome, 11; Jimmie Durham's artwork in, 19; Pablo Tac in, 2, 12, 61, 64, 91, 122, 194; Kay WalkingStick's artwork in, 2, 4, 10, 14, 91, 123–28, 132, 141–50

Rushing, W. Jackson, 46, 102

Russo, Alessandra, 132

sacred. *See* spirit

Sacred Colors (Luna), 72

Said, Edward, 19, 49, 209n82

Saint Raphael, Chumash painting of, 83–84

Sakahàn: International Indigenous Art, 234–35n83

Sand Cart, The (Bellows), 94

San Diego Museum of Man, 36, 71, 78

Sandy Bay (Houle), 173–74

Sandy Bay First Nation Reserve, 168

Santa Fe, 48, 72, 89, 97–106, 110–15, 219n79. *See also* New Mexico

Santa Fe Indian School, 97–101, 229n101. *See also* boarding schools; Studio School

Sardar, Ziauddin, 50

Saulteaux, 152, 168, 172–75, 179, 194. *See also* Ojibwa; Sandy Bay First Nation Reserve

Say-say-gon, 165

Schneider, Rebecca, 65, 67, 71, 200n33

Scholder, Fritz, 29–33, 46, 137, 217n48; Jimmie Durham's attitude toward, 207n58

Scott, Sascha, 102, 222n4, 226n58, 228n78

sculpture: American, 75, 115; Italian, 116, 142; in New Spain, 82; in the work of Jimmie Durham, 9, 15, 38, 51, 184, 186–88, 195; in the work of Kay WalkingStick, 137, 141, 235n86. *See also* readymade

Secakuku, Alph H., 103, 107–8, 120–21, 227n71

Sekaquaptewa, Emory, 103

self-determination. *See* decolonization; sovereignty

survivance, 23. *See also* Vizenor, Gerald

Sydney, 196; Biennale of, 13, 184–85, 235–36n83; Opera House, 13, 184

tableau vivant, 9, 14–15, 154–65, 179, 182–83

Tac, Pablo, 2, 9–10, 12, 61–70, 76, 80, 93, 122, 194–95. *See also* "Chapel for Pablo Tac" (Luna); "Renewal (A Performance for Pablo Tac)" (Luna)

Taos: Pueblo, 119; Society of Artists, 94, 112, 115, 118

Taylor, Diana, 8, 13, 62, 64–67, 71–72, 74, 78, 88, 92. *See also* archive

Tears (WalkingStick), 235n86

temporality: in Walter Benjamin's writing, 83–84, 220n26; colonial conflict over, 6, 8, 24–25, 35, 45, 64–65, 101, 122, 143, 157; of diagrams, 13, 98, 107, 120–21; of Hopi ceremony, 108; indigenous alternatives to progressive, 1, 3–7, 56–57, 59–60, 84–85, 92–93, 182, 186, 195; and modernist primitivism, 136, 183; in Ojibwa cosmology, 173, 179; in Renaissance cosmology, 129–33. *See also* history; progress

tepee, 135–36, 159, 233n59

Terra Corpo (WalkingStick), 141–43

time. *See* temporality

Tluhn Datsi (Durham), 38–39

tobacco: colonial cultivation of, 51; indigenous offerings of, 174–75

Trail of Broken Treaties, 23. *See also* American Indian Movement

Trail of Tears, 21, 23, 48, 195, 235n86

transcultural materialism, 14–15, 155–57, 182–83, 196

transnationalism: and activism, 20–21, 26; and the art world, 92; and indigenous nations, 6–7, 203n8. *See also* capitalism

travel. *See* displacement; exile; itinerancy; mobility

treaty: broken, 5, 22, 23, 26, 48; between indigenous nations and the U.S.

government, 22–23, 57, 91; Sioux Treaty of 1868, 24; Treaty of Whitehall, 2, 52. *See also* American Indian Movement; International Indian Treaty Council

trickster, 12, 18, 38–44, 50, 58, 188

Tsireh, Awa (Alfonso Roybal), 96, 101, 107–8, 114, 226n58. *See also individual works*

"Two Johns, The" (Durham), 51. See also *Mataoka Ale Attakulakula Anel Guledisgo Hnihi* (Durham)

Two Riders (Ufer), 94–95, 118

Two Women (Bellows), 94

"Types of Arrows" (Durham), 32. See also *On Loan from the Museum of the American Indian* (Durham)

Ufer, Walter, 94, 118. *See also individual works*

uhnemekéka (Dagois), 237–38n4

Uktena, 59. *See also* snake

undivided earth, 5, 13, 18, 57, 62, 81, 86–89, 93, 128, 148, 157, 172–73, 183, 196. *See also* ecology; Eloheh; history: as world in Jimmie Durham's artwork; space; spirit

United Nations, 26, 246n111. *See also* International Indian Treaty Council

United Nations Declaration on the Rights of Indigenous Peoples, 26, 246n111

U.S. Pavilion of the Venice Biennale, 3, 12–13, 89, 94–98, 106, 112, 115–21

Vatican, 123, 128, 130, 149–51

Venice, 4, 8, 11; Buffalo Bill Cody's Wild West Show in, 2; Jimmie Durham's artwork in, 89; Edgar Heap of Birds's artwork in, 2, 92–93; Fred Kabotie's paintings in, 3, 7–8, 11, 96, 115–22; James Luna's artwork in, 12–13, 29, 62–69, 75–93, 98, 121, 134; other contemporary Native North American artists in, 7, 43, 88–93, 211n104, 217n51; Kay WalkingStick's artwork in, 91

www.ingramcontent.com/pod-product-compliance
Lightning Source LLC
Chambersburg PA
CBHW072130170526
45158CB00004BA/1311